P9-AOK-336

DISCARDED
THE
UNIVERSITY OF WINNIPEG
PORTAGE & BALMORAL
WINNIPEG 2, MAN.

PR
2636
.B22
1967

English Elements in Jonson's Early Comedy

BY

CHARLES READ BASKERVILL

GORDIAN PRESS, INC.
NEW YORK
1967

Originally Published 1911
Reprinted by Gordian Press, Inc. 1967
Library of Congress Catalog Card Number 67-21711

Printed in U.S.A. by
EDWARDS BROTHERS, INC.
Ann Arbor, Michigan

PREFACE

Several years ago I conceived the theory that Jonson was a much more sympathetic student of English literature than has commonly been supposed. In studying the problem, however, I have become convinced that his indebtedness was less to specific works used as sources than to certain specific trends in English literature with which he was thoroughly in accord. The present study is an attempt to follow out that idea. In view of the multitudinous phases of Jonson's work, as of all Elizabethan literature, it has proved convenient, even necessary, to limit my field, and the period of early comedies seems to furnish the best basis for the study. Not only do these plays form a fairly isolated group in Jonson's work, a group significant in the development of his peculiar literary powers and of his characteristic type of comedy, but they belong to a decade in English literature so decided and revolutionary in its trends that Jonson's relation to contemporary letters can be more easily tested in them than at any other period of his work. The closing decade of the sixteenth century, with its varied tendencies, its literary revolution, its plasticity, and its nice balance between free criticism and easy creation, offered a chance for the development of individual force such as perhaps no other like period of the drama offered, and yet scarcely allowed any writer to escape the impress of the time.

Jonson's relation to the movements of English literature at the end of the sixteenth century is the primary problem of this study, though at the same time I have attempted to trace the trends in his work as far back as they are discernible. The general point seems fairly clear that Jonson actually studied English literature and used the work of predecessors according to the Renaissance formulæ for imitation somewhat as he imitated Latin literature but less closely of course. Assuredly he was observant of the trends and conventions in English literature and readily utilized its types so far as they were suitable for comedy. It is my hope that I have presented enough evidence to throw some light on the relation of Jonson to his fellows and on the significance of literary trends for his work.

The Publication Committee of the University of Texas, who have been kind enough to publish this volume as a *Bulletin* of the University, have already waited patiently a year beyond the time when the work was to have been ready for the press, and, keenly as I realize the shortcomings and imperfections of the study, it seems imperative to close it. Indeed, under the conditions of my work, it is scarcely profitable to pursue the subject further. I particularly regret that much material which promised to be of interest for Jonson has been inaccessible to me, especially a number of works not yet reprinted which are satirical in nature or deal with manners. Even in the case of a few writers like Lodge and Guilpin, I have been forced to quote from copies of the most interesting portions of their work made when the books were temporarily accessible to me. Moreover, in the literature at hand I have undoubtedly missed much that would add to the roundedness of this treatment; but the nature of the work, I feel, makes the omissions less significant than they would otherwise be, for without any hope of exhausting the subject, I have merely attempted to gather together sufficient material to illustrate the point of view. The possible influence, also, of classical and continental Renaissance literature upon the types and conventions of English literature which led to Jonson, I have tried to weigh fairly, but, as I have naturally not been able to study this phase of the subject closely, there must be many non-English parallels to Jonson's work with which I am unacquainted. In the main, however, even Jonson's classicism seems to me to be strongly colored by contemporary attitudes, though I am aware that such a claim is, in many cases, not readily susceptible of proof.

It has been difficult in handling the material to give due credit for all that has been borrowed. The volume is already so cumbered with references and notes that I have deliberately avoided a multitude of references for such ideas as are generally current now. In the matter, also, of parallels to Jonson's treatment, though I have attempted to give credit whenever I have been aware that the material has been pointed out by others, the discovery of parallels has seemed to me so much less significant than the massing and the interpretation of them that I candidly confess I have not made any exhaustive search to learn whether each parallel which I have used is to be credited to some previous student.

The fact that my material has been gathered from modern editions of Elizabethan works has led to many inconsistencies. In titles and quotations I have tried to follow the various editors, and the result, which seems unavoidable, has been that the Elizabethan and the modern form jostle each other on the same line. There is much inconsistency, also, in the method of citing the sources of material. In the case of works accessible in only one edition or those easily referred to by the number of the satires, epigrams, sonnets, etc., I have not always been careful to indicate the edition from which I quote. Such are the satires of Marston and Middleton edited by Bullen, and *Skialetheia* and the works of Davies edited by Grosart. But, when the reference is by volume and page, my practice has of course been to give the edition, especially with the first reference. For Jonson's works, unless it is otherwise stated, I have referred to the three volume Gifford-Cunningham edition; and, as reference to this edition by act and scene is often hardly explicit enough, I have adopted the plan of giving also the page of the volume in which the play under consideration occurs. References to the quartos of the early plays are by line to Professor Bang's reprints in Materialien zur Kunde des älteren Englischen Dramas.

In closing this study I wish to express my thanks to two persons to whom I am principally indebted. Prof. J. M. Manly has made a number of suggestions, which have proved of value to me; and my wife, Catharine Q. Baskervill, has not only borne a great part of the burden of copying, verifying, indexing, etc., but has also offered innumerable suggestions that have entered into the body of the work. Without her criticism the volume would have gone forth in a far cruder form.

C. R. BASKERVILL.

University of Texas.
March, 1911.

CONTENTS

CHAPTER I

JONSON'S LITERARY IDEALS

CHAPTER II

THE ENGLISH TEMPER OF JONSON'S WORK

CHAPTER III

A STUDY OF HUMOURS

CHAPTER IV

A TALE OF A TUB

CHAPTER V

THE CASE IS ALTERED

CHAPTER VI

EVERY MAN IN HIS HUMOUR

CHAPTER VII

EVERY MAN OUT OF HIS HUMOUR

CHAPTER VIII

CYNTHIA'S REVELS

CHAPTER IX

POETASTER

ENGLISH ELEMENTS IN JONSON'S EARLY COMEDY

CHAPTER I

JONSON'S LITERARY IDEALS

When Jonson's *Every Man in his Humour* and *Every Man out of his Humour* appeared upon the stage in 1598 and 1599, a new era in the Elizabethan drama opened. Chapman, Dekker, Marston, Middleton, and Webster joined with Jonson in producing pure comedy. Even Shakespeare's work was influenced by the new movement. This change in dramatic mode and ideals we are justified in associating with Jonson not only because his work was the strongest but because it was the most distinctive of the new school. His thoroughgoing reformation in the theme and the technique of the drama, his close approach to unity of mood and structure, give his plays the appearance of complete detachment from the hybrid forms of the drama that were struggling toward a more realistic comedy in which the study of manners should be more than a mere series of scenes in mystery, morality, chronicle, or romantic comedy.

The source of the inspiration and power which gave Jonson this commanding place in the reform of the drama has justly been sought in his knowledge and love of classic literature. His work is larded with phrases and sentences drawn from the classics; many details of his plots have been traced to classic sources; and, most important of all, his intimate acquaintance with classic modes of thought and expression has resulted in intellectual clarity and restraint as dominant characteristics of his work. But this has usually been interpreted to mean that Jonson owes everything to classicism, and it would not greatly overstate what has been a fairly common estimate of his place in the development of the Elizabethan drama to say that this classical training along with the originality of the man is responsible for the Jonsonian comedy. Such a view, of course, recognizes the fact that material for English comedy must be furnished largely by English life, but it rates the influence of English literature upon Jonson as decidedly weak.

Though this view of Jonson as deriving his inspiration, power, and literary material almost solely from the classics has been greatly modified in the last decade, we have not yet come to a full realization of his indebtedness to English literary men and English literary trends. It is only recently that Professor Spingarn's study of Renaissance criticism has shown how greatly the classical standards of literary excellence were modified in passing through the hands of various theorists,—modified by the very literature that the theorists were attempting to bring into conformity with classic ideals,—and how greatly indebted Jonson was for his critical standards to the men who preceded him in the Renaissance.[1] Recently, also, various English sources for Jonson's plays and masques have been suggested.[2] Undoubtedly many passages and incidents in his work are borrowed directly from English literature, and their value in understanding his development is great enough. But to my mind they are secondary in importance to the presence of a greater mass of conventional material showing the influence of English literary ideals and tendencies. In other words, there is something more English in Jonson's work than these isolated loans. It is accordingly the purpose of this study to indicate the value of English literature rather than English life in the development of Jonson's comedy, to point out wherever possible the actual English sources of his work, but especially to show how conventional in the literature at the end of the sixteenth century was much of his material. Such a study will, I believe, reveal an influence of English literature on Jonson not so obvious as that of Latin literature but perhaps more pervasive and universal.

The period chosen as the basis of this study covers the years 1597 to 1601. The plays which I have regarded as falling within the period are *A Tale of a Tub, The Case is Altered, Every Man in his Humour, Every Man out of his Humour, Cynthia's Revels,* and *Poetaster*. The choice scarcely calls for defence. These

[1]For Prof. Spingarn's views, cf. his *Literary Criticism in the Renaissance* and the introduction to *Critical Essays of the Seventeenth Century.* The very decided English tradition in criticism, which is of supreme importance for Jonson's early comedy, is discussed excellently in the introduction to Gregory Smith's *Elizabethan Critical Essays.*

[2]Cf. Hart, *Works of Ben Jonson;* the editions of *The Devil is an Ass* and *The Staple of News* in Yale Studies in English; two papers by me in *Modern Philology,* Vol. VI, pp. 109 ff. and 257 ff.; etc.

comedies represent the formative period in Jonson's career, the time during which he evolved and perfected his conception of the humour types. They stand, then, on the whole, not necessarily for what is most enjoyable or artistically greatest in Jonson's work, but for what is most distinctive. Even *A Tale of a Tub* and *The Case is Altered,* if I am right in regarding them as the earliest of Jonson's comedies, are extremely interesting as showing the influences to which he was susceptible at the opening of his career, when, before he had found his own field in satiric comedy dealing with the follies of the higher social classes, he was trying his hand, as Shakespeare had done earlier, in different types of comedy popular with Elizabethan audiences. What I hope to show is that in developing his characteristic type of play Jonson seized upon ideas and methods which had run through English literature almost unconsciously and yet with increasing strength, and that after his own fashion he brought them to consciousness and to the dignity of a type and formulated the laws of that type. Before proceeding to a minute study of these plays, however, or of the fashions and trends that molded Jonson's comedy in this early period, it seems to mé advisable to take up at some length Jonson's relation to his age, his attitude to contemporary literature, and his general method of work, for we have to do with plays which, though they have fewest direct English sources, yet show the most pervasive flavor of English literary treatment.

On the personal side, Jonson's broad experience of life, his dominant individuality, and his eagerness to give expression to self mark him as a typical man of the Renaissance. In early life he served as common bricklayer, common soldier, and possibly common strolling player. As a soldier we know that he displayed his aggressiveness, courage, and love of prominence. We know, too, from the tributes of Beaumont and various other literary men that at an early date Jonson's learning and spirit of dominance had made him a leader in the tavern gatherings of wits. Dekker in *Satiromastix* twits Jonson with his eagerness to be recognized as a literary dictator in tavern and playhouse, and with his willingness to fawn upon knights for favor. From a knowledge of Jonson's life and works we realize the measure of truth in these charges; but whatever excess of tact the tactless Jonson may have been guilty of, he actually did make his way into the most exclusive circles, come into contact with men of social and political prominence, and at the same time win a position of leadership in the world of letters. We are forced to recognize the strength amid all of his limitations to understand why the hostility of those whom he fought and scorned, the coarseness of his features and the ungainliness of his figure, the lifelong poverty and the probable social crudeness of the man, the envy, pride, arrogance, or even impudence that he could not always restrain, did not prevent his winning recognition and disciples among the most envied of England's scholars and noblemen. The bricklayer ultimately found himself an important figure at the court. Insatiable in his thirst for knowledge, independent in his literary and social standards, stubbornly insistent upon his own ideals, sternly rational in his judgment of life, direct and matter-of-fact in his gluttonous taste as in his ambition, undisturbed by qualms in his sensual enjoyment of wine and women, Jonson drove doggedly to the front, a master of life in all its phases, as were few other Elizabethans even.

I have stressed the nature of the man to show not only that he will pretty certainly lead in whatever he undertakes, as he clearly does lead in the classicism of the Elizabethan or Stuart period, but that he will never stand aloof from the literary movements of his day. Jonson was first of all a student of books, and however disdainful might be his attitude toward the average man of letters in his time, however much he might stress his mission as a teacher of classic art, he was in the closest touch with all contemporary literature. It was the life of the man to be in the midst of things. Let a type like the drama or the masque become popular, and he is almost certain to adopt it and exert all his powers to excel in it. In fact, the popularity of the classics among the cultured people of England in Elizabethan times largely explains Jonson and his connection with the classics, while his pride, his ambition, and his scorn of what is commonplace led him into an avowed independence of English authors. But as a practical playwright eager to appeal to the men of his time, as an intimate of the greatest living English writers, and as a critic who claimed conformity to local conditions as the prerogative of the poet and dramatist, Jonson was likely in every phase of his work to be responsive to the literary movements of his day. This is entirely consistent with his recognized position as leader in a new form of drama; it is even consistent with his desire to improve English literary art by an appeal to the art of the great classic masters, for such an appeal was but part of the Renaissance.

Jonson's rich knowledge of life undoubtedly at times served to furnish him with material, as in much of *Bartholomew Fair,* and his belief in the value of English life for the work of the literary man is clear from many utterances. In the prologue to *The Alchemist* he says:

> Our scene is London, 'cause we would make known,
> No country's mirth is better than our own:
> No clime breeds better matter for your whore,
> Bawd, squire, impostor, many persons more,
> Whose manners, now called humours, feed the stage.

This is not to be interpreted, however, I think, as involving the question of a realistic treatment of life based on direct observation. Such a thing was not a part of the Renaissance literary creed. In the second prologue to *The Silent Woman* Jonson gives this warning:

> Then in this play . . . .
> . . . .
> . . . think nothing true:
> Lest so you make the maker to judge you.
> For he knows, poet never credit gained
> By writing truths, but things, like truths, well feigned.

The principle is repeated in the court prologue to *The Staple of News.* In *Timber,* also, Jonson follows the old definition of a poet as one who "feigneth and formeth a fable, and writes things like the truth" (Schelling's edition, p. 73). The very definition indicates the absence of any ideal of realism; things like truth do not involve an exact imitation of life. Professor Spingarn has pointed out that this idea of the poet's function is as old as Plato and Aristotle, and was thoroughly fixed in the Renaissance (*Literary Criticism in the Renaissance,* pp. 4 and 18). Sidney saw a weakness in history in that it cannot present the consummate type of vice or virtue but must be realistic, and Jonson told Drummond that he "thought not Bartas a Poet, but a Verser, because he wrote not fiction."

What, then, is to be the source of the poet's material? The

four requisites of a poet that Jonson adopts in *Timber* are: *ingenium,* or "goodness of natural wit"; *exercitatio,* or practice; *imitatio,* by which Jonson means, not imitation of life, but of those writers who have shown an understanding of life; and lastly *lectio,* which he translates "exactness of study and multiplicity of reading." Finally, "art must be added to make all these perfect" (pp. 75-78). There can be little doubt, I think, that whether or not this discussion of the requisites of a poet is merely a translation of some undiscovered author, it represents Jonson's own views. The ideas were generally accepted.[1] It is noteworthy that after endowment and practice, or training, Jonson finds the requisites of a poet to be a vast knowledge of books and a free borrowing from them. The poet may seek material anywhere so long as he unifies it, thus making it his own by his art. This is the essence of originality for Jonson. Of imitation Jonson says: "The third requisite in our poet or maker is imitation, *imitatio,* to be able to convert the substance or riches of another poet to his own use. . . . Not to imitate servilely, as Horace saith, and catch at vices for virtue, but to draw forth out of the best and choicest flowers, with the bee, and turn all into honey, work it into one relish and savor."[2] Of course imitation for Jonson as well as for other Renaissance writers means a coming into harmony with the literary instinct, the refined taste, the mode of thought, and the

[1]Professor Spingarn has shown that much of what Jonson has to say of poets and poetry is borrowed from Buchler and Heinsius, and he suggests Buchler as the source of some details in the discussion of these requisites (*Modern Philology,* Vol. II, p. 452, n.). Miss Woodbridge points to Sidney, who would entrust the "highest-flying wit" of the poet to the guidance of "art, imitation, and exercise" (*Defense of Poesy,* ed. Cook, p. 46). The points correspond to Jonson's except that Sidney omits *lectio,* or study. Miss Woodbridge suggests that both writers are indebted to Longinus (*Studies in Jonson's Comedy,* pp. 9, 10). These requisites for the literary man, however, were known in English criticism before Sidney. Wilson in *The Arte of Rhetorique,* 1560, (ed. Mair, pp. 4, 5) in telling "By what meanes Eloquence is attained", stresses "a wit, and an aptnesse"; the store of knowledge derived from books; exercise, or practice, in addition to art; and finally imitation, which is defined much as Jonson defines it.

[2]Of the requisites which Jonson mentions, imitation was the most widely treated in literature. Ascham's discussion of imitation in *The Scholemaster* is the most important in English, and the references that Ascham makes to other treatises furnish an excellent bibliography of the subject. Cf. Smith's notes to Ascham's discussion, *Eliz. Critical Essays,* Vol. I. In Cicero's *De Oratore,* Bk. II, chaps. xxi-xxiii, the same points are made in regard to imitation that Jonson makes, and the requisites of success in literary work appear incidentally.

art generally of the master imitated. One sentence that I omitted from Jonson's discussion of imitation demands that the poet "make choice of one excellent man above the rest, and so . . follow him till he grow very he, or so like him as the copy may be mistaken for the principal." But, if the phraseology of the passage on imitation does not clearly imply borrowing, that of the one on reading does. Jonson says that it is necessary for the poet in studying any poem "so to master the matter and style, as to show he knows how to handle, place, or dispose of either with elegancy when need shall be." Here Jonson stresses material and the handling of it as much as he does art.[1]

Nevertheless, Jonson is careful to protest against a slavish adherence to the art of the masters. Of *Every Man out of his Humour* he says in the induction that " 'tis strange, and of a particular kind by itself, somewhat like *Vetus Comœdia*."[2] Then he proceeds to a defense of innovation in poetry. Classic laws of comedy as we now have them, he says, are the result of a growth and an accommodation, and the later comic writers who came after Aristophanes, himself a model, "altered the property of the persons, their names, and natures, and augmented it [comedy] with all liberty, according to the elegancy and disposition of those times wherein they wrote. I see not then, but we should enjoy the same licence, or free power to illustrate and heighten our invention, as they did; and not be tied to those strict and regular forms which the niceness of a few, who are nothing but form, would thrust upon us."[3] That this conception of Jonson's in regard to

[1]Ascham's exhaustive discussion of imitation scarcely considers the imitation of the master's art so much as the borrowing of material. Ascham gives six ways in which one can imitate an author, and all imply the borrowing of material. One sentence of his may well stand for what seems to be Jonson's method of borrowing from English literature: "*Imitatio* is *dissimilis materiei similis tractatio;* and, also, *similis materiei dissimilis tractatio*" (*The Scholemaster*, Book II; quoted from Smith, *Eliz. Crit. Essays*, Vol. I, p. 8). Often I shall have occasion to point out that Jonson either uses the style or art of a contemporary, varying the matter, or handles the same material with some new device or fresh expression.

[2]See pp. 212 f. *infra* for a possible meaning of *Vetus Comœdia* in this passage.

[3]In *Timber* Jonson frequently returns to this matter of independence in the poet. See Schelling's edition, pp. 7, 66, and 79, 80. These passages have been traced to Vives and Heinsius. Cf. Simpson, *Mod. Lang. Review*, Vol. II, pp. 209, 210, and Spingarn, *Mod. Phil.*, Vol. II, pp. 453, 454. In this case again, however, they must represent Jonson's own ideas. Indeed,

the conformity of poetry to the disposition of the time was not a passing one is clear from a remark to Drummond made twenty years later. Drummond's note reads:

> His censure of my verses was:
>
> That they were all good, especiallie my Epitaphe of the Prince, save that they smelled too much of the Schooles, and were not after the fancie of the tyme: for a child (sayes he) may writte after the fashion of the Greeks and Latine verses in running; yett that he wished, to please the King, that piece of Forth Feasting had been his owne.

Two things stand out in these expressions of Jonson's: first, his dependence upon the work of his predecessors in literature, and second, his insistence upon conformity in literature to "the fancie of the tyme." If Jonson's ideals are not inconsistent, then, we may expect to find, first, that though his knowledge of life will color all of his writings and his independence will make his treatment of themes fresh, he will look to other writers for his models and for the bulk of his material; and, second, that in spite of an exceedingly strong classical influence, his work will be English in spirit and tone, and will follow pretty closely the currents of English literature. It is easy to point out cases where Jonson derived plot motives or ideas and phrases bodily from classic literature, but the English elements are often elusive. Jonson had a different attitude to borrowing from the classics and from native sources. To translate a fine classic phrase aptly he regarded almost as original work, while he scorned to steal phrases from the *Arcadia.* The one enriched the language; the other did not. This large and obvious indebtedness to classical literature, along with the possibility that Jonson derived his comic material directly from observation of life, has so blinded scholars that they have failed to study minutely his relation to his contemporaries. To my mind, he not only goes to them for a large number of suggestions as to what will be practical or appealing on the stage, but he brings his great skill and constructive power to bear upon a mass of hints

the principle of free invention was one of the earliest critical conventions to be introduced into English literature. Wilson in his *Arte of Rhetorique* emphasizes the fact that all the principles of literary art are derived from the inventions of literary men and that "a wiseman . . . will not be bound to any precise rules . . . being master ouer arte," etc. (pp. 159, 160; cf. also p. 5). Wilson may have followed Quintilian, *Institutiones Oratoriae,* Bk. X, Chap. ii.

and treatments of types and situations scattered through contemporary literature, crude and unfinished as they often are, and makes of these an original product. The pages immediately following, far afield as they apparently carry one from the humour plays, are merely to furnish illustrations of this idea from Jonson's other works, and to prepare for the study of the comedy of humours as a native development.

The studiousness of Jonson is indicated by the variety of themes in his work. *Tamquam explorator,* his motto, suggests the constant intellectual curiosity of the man. His dramas alone show how large a number of fields he explored, for always the central theme is entirely fresh in Jonsonian comedy. Most frequently it is an expansion of a hint in an earlier play, but the new play has entered another region of the complex life of the London and England that Jonson knew. Even the typical classes and the typical vices that Jonson repeats are viewed nearly always from a fresh angle. Perhaps nothing shows the variety of Jonson's work better than the fact that the object of an intrigue is never the same in any two plays and only once or twice does he repeat an intriguer. In *A Tale of a Tub* we have Chanon Hugh manipulating plots to control the marriage of a rustic maid; in *Every Man in his Humour* the crafty servingman acting as intriguer through mere exuberance of roguery; in *Every Man out of his Humour* the envious Macilente giving reins to his mischievous malcontent; in *Cynthia's Revels* the noble Crites tilting against wrongs in the court; in *Poetaster* the maligned Horace defending the dignity of his art; in *Volpone* the avaricious old Fox and his parasite Mosca overreaching themselves. The "cotes of clowns" of *A Tale of a Tub,* the inn life of *The New Inn,* the pastoral life of *The Sad Shepherd,* the allegory of news and money in *The Staple of News* and of the compass in *The Magnetic Lady* need only be mentioned to set one thinking of the variety of fields that Jonson entered.

This constant entering of fresh fields is an indication of Jonson's work as a student rather than as an observer, for in nearly every case the general plan of the play can be traced to certain types or motives popular in contemporary literature. That is to say, the influences that guided Jonson in his choice of fields and themes were nearly always English. In the two tragedies and in some of the masques, classic material is used with only the slightest admixture of English material, and yet the relation of some of this most thoroughly classic work to themes of contemporary literature indicates one side of the influence of the age. Roman tragedy, especially in *Julius Caesar,* had made a great success when Jonson, leaving the field of native tragedy that he had chosen in *Page of Plymouth* and *Robert II, King of Scots,* gave England in *Sejanus* what he considered an appropriate treatment of a classic theme. Here Jonson has taken pains to show that practically every idea and expression is paralleled in Latin authors. Yet there was a special reason for this strict classicism following a period of humour comedies. The references to classic sources for *Sejanus* are partly proof, at a time of danger for Jonson, that he was not satirizing the court or any contemporary in his great portrait of Pride and Ambition, but chiefly, perhaps, triumphant evidence that he who had been misunderstood, maligned, and scoffed at while he was trying to reform abuses and was writing in the mode of his fellows, could enter higher realms of literary work, make himself master of the thought and expression of the masters, and, leaving the treatment of contemporary manners and the mode of contemporary playwrights, sing

high and aloof,
Safe from the wolf's black jaw, and the dull ass's hoof.

The two tragedies, of course, represent Jonson's most rigid classicism, but several of the masques approach them closely. *Penates* and *The Entertainment at Theobalds* (1607), though short, are excellent examples of the mythological masque purely classic in its figures. And yet no one can doubt that the prominence given to mythological figures in pageant and masque from the time of Henry VIII on determined the form of these earlier masques. Jonson soon outgrew the purer classic type. In *The Masque of Hymen* his own notes reveal his classicism, but Reason, the Humours, and the Affections, typical abstractions of Elizabethan didacticism, almost overshadow Hymen, the chief mythological figure. *The Masque of Queens* mingles classical and medieval lore. Doubtless *Macbeth* had rendered witches popular before Jonson's work appeared, and at the same time had shown how the mystic rites of the witches could be turned into fascinating dramatic and operatic scenes. Jonson in *The Masque of Queens* has utilized the wild night scenes, the dances, and the conjurations of *Macbeth,* treating them according to the authoritative details that had come down to the learned in the Latin poets and the medieval masters of magic art. Perhaps he had boasted of this fact. At any rate, by the request of Prince Henry he annotated his masque, giving authority for every rite and every characteristic of the witches. But, though Jonson's picture of the House of Fame and the queens enthroned upon it may be referred to Chaucer, and he has indicated his intention to reconcile "the practice of antiquity to the neoteric" (*Works,* Vol. III, p. 50), his debt to contemporary literature is still unduly obscured, perhaps, by his parade of classical sources. Anders (*Jahrbuch,* Vol. XXXVIII, pp. 240 f.) has pointed out some verbal parallels between *The Masque of Queens* and Scot's *Discovery of Witchcraft.* Above all, in spite of the large amount of borrowing from classic sources, one would never associate *The Masque of Queens* with classicism; it echoes too thoroughly what might be called the romantic attitude to witchcraft in Jonson's own day.

More decidedly English is *The Satyr.* Here Jonson has joined the Latin satyr with the English Mab, and has closed the masque with a speech modeled on the old play of *Nobody and Somebody*[1] and introducing a morris dance. The presence of the Satyr is

[1]Cf. Fleay, *Biog. Chron. Eng. Drama,* Vol. II, p. 1. Not only are the plays upon words similar, but in Jonson's masque as in *Nobody and Somebody,* the dress of Nobody is "a pair of breeches which were made to come up to his neck, with his arms out at his pockets." In Greene's *Quip for an Upstart Courtier* (*Works,* ed. Grosart, Vol. XI, pp. 220 ff.), Velvet-breeches and Cloth-breeches are headless and bodiless, having merely legs. The idea as inherited from the *Odyssey* is used in Harvey's *Pierces Supererogation* (*Works,* ed. Grosart, Vol. II, p. 211), where there is a play on Outis, Nobody, and Somebody. Jonson has the play upon Outis and Nobody in *The Fortunate Isles.* Nemo is a character of *The Three Ladies of London* and *The Three Lords and Three Ladies of London.* Marston's *Antonio and Mellida* is dedicated to "Nobody, bounteous Mecænas of poetry and Lord Protector of oppressed innocence," and Day's *Humour out of Breath* is dedicated to Signior Nobody. Dyer has a poem called "A Praise of Nothing." In Breton's *Wit of Wit* (1599) "Scholler and Souldier" opens with plays upon the word nothing, and in the same year Nashe in his *Lenten Stuffe* (*Works,* ed. McKerrow, Vol. III, p. 177) makes a satirical allusion to the writer who "comes foorth with something in prayse of nothing." Cf. Ward, *Hist. Eng. Dram. Lit.,* Vol. I, p. 436, and Vol. II, p. 597; and Simpson, *School of Shakspere,* Vol. I, p. 270. This is an excellent example of how the most conventional or commonplace idea may appeal to Jonson.

misleading,[1] for the masque is purely English in tone and material and contains the most delicate poetry dealing with English fairy lore. Indeed it is full of conventional fairy material, and such an expression as

> Faeries, pinch him black and blue,
> Now you have him, make him rue,[2]

is to be found a score of times in English writers. The fairies and the morris dance again represent a convention in the masque that reaches back to Tudor times or earlier, when the folk customs began to furnish material for the first English masques and pageants. The satyr, in the form of the wild man of the wood especially, is also at home in the masque.[3] It was the taste of the times that induced Jonson to mingle classic and folk lore. So for masque after masque parallels could be given showing how Jonson, often gathering from classic sources, still drifts in his treatment to what is characteristic of English life and literature; and some of his masques, *The Masque of Christmas,* for instance, are as thoroughly English as is *Bartholomew Fair.*

Jonson's characteristic method of working, of gathering like the bee, may be seen at its best in the comedies, and here we naturally

[1]He is called Pug, or Puck, in one place, and in folk-lore Puck's functions are confused with those of Mab.

[2]Cf. *Endimion,* IV, 3, and Bond, *Works of Lyly,* Vol. III, p. 514, note. In *The Alchemist* Dapper is severely pinched while the supposed fairies cry "Ti, ti." This is closest to the pinching of Falstaff in *The Merry Wives,* but a similar incident is mentioned in *John a Kent and John a Cumber.*

[3]In *The Princely Pleasures at Kenilworth Castle,* there appeared in one device "one clad like a Sauage man, all in Iuie" called Silvester, and later his son called Audax (*Poems of Gascoigne,* ed. Hazlitt, Vol. II, pp. 96, 109, 113). Another entertainment was planned, in which Sylvanus was to appear (*ibid.,* p. 124).In *The Entertainment at Cowdray,* 1591, "a wilde man cladde in Iuie" addressed the Queen (*Works of Lyly,* ed. Bond, Vol. I, p. 425). In *The Entertainment at Elvetham,* 1591, the costume of Sylvanus, who addressed the Queen, is carefully described as that of a satyr, while "his followers were all couered with Iuy-leaues" (*ibid.,* p. 444). *Speeches Delivered to her Majesty at Bisham,* 1592, opens with an address by "a wilde man," who speaks of "wee Satyres" (*ibid.,* p. 472). Notices of masques in Feuillerat's *Documents relating to the Office of the Revels in the Time of Queen Elizabeth* indicate that the wild man was an earlier favorite. At the Christmas festivities of 1573-4 there was a masque of foresters and hunters with torchbearers clothed in moss and ivy. These latter are apparently spoken of later as "wylde Men" and the masque as the "Mask of Wyldemen" (pp. 193, 199, 457). In July, 1574, there was some theatrical performance, perhaps a pastoral, in which "wylde mannes" appeared (pp. 227, 458). Cf. Brotanek, *Die engl. Maskenspiele,* p. 3, etc.

have the strongest English influence. Sometimes the basis is Latin, as in *The Case is Altered* and *Poetaster;* sometimes Italian furnishes much, as in *The Alchemist,* if Bruno's *Il Candelaio* is a source, or in *The Devil is an Ass,* where two stories of Boccaccio are utilized; and sometimes the elements are purely English, as in *Bartholomew Fair.* Often, however, Jonson's material for any single play is furnished by many literatures of different ages. But the whole in each case is Jonson's in organization, in tone, and in final effect. Gathering from any source, with a wonderfully accurate and minute knowledge of literature, Jonson fuses into a unit and gives fresh life to his borrowed material. This is scarcely less true of what has been borrowed from classic literature than of what has been borrowed from English. And, to my mind, this unity, this consistency, arises largely from the fact that the whole is English in spirit, as Jonson was English to the core.

As an illustration of the English element in Jonson's comedies, *Bartholomew Fair* is the obvious choice. Here there is of course no question of classic influence; the question is whether Jonson drew his picture entirely from English life or was influenced by English literary treatment. I have elsewhere shown that the old play of *Sir Thomas More* offers a probable source for much of Jonson's cutpurse material in *Bartholomew Fair* (*Modern Philology,* Vol. VI, pp. 109-127). There are a number of similarities that indicate a direct dependence of the one play on the other. It is noticeable, however, that Jonson's treatment of the motives common to both plays is nearer to folk-lore than is his source, and that *Bartholomew Fair* shows Jonson's knowledge of other treatments of similar scenes. In particular Greene's coney-catching pamphlets seem to have given Jonson some important situations and some details of characterization. An interesting parallel, also, is the likeness of Autolycus of *Winter's Tale* to Lanthorn Leatherhead. I myself have little doubt that Jonson got from Shakespeare the suggestion for the character on the stage, but my belief rests merely on the nearness of the two plays in time of production and on the greater similarity of Jonson's rogues to Autolycus than to any other rogues that I recall. Both Shakespeare and Jonson have a long line of predecessors, however. In *The Blind Beggar of Bednal Green,* we have the young simpleton Strowd, who like Cokes is robbed again and again, and always reappears, full of zest and naiveté. The rogues here, like Jonson's, change quickly from one calling to another, from purse-cutting to fortune-telling and finally to producing puppet-shows, returning always to meet a foolish victim with new tricks. The rogues of *Look About You* and *The Dutch Courtezan,* too, while not so conventional in their tricks, perhaps, have the same resourcefulness, buoyancy, and perpetual success that belong to the imaginative dealing with rogues in general. Indeed, outside of the fact that Jonson is primarily the student of books and that many parallels to his treatment of rogues can actually be found in literature, there is evidence of his dependence on literature rather than on observation in that the whole tone of his treatment is in accord with the romantic roguery of literature and folk-lore.

Even in the puppet-show, where Hero and Leander are connected with the ghost of Dionysius, Jonson may be following the line of least resistance, for Nashe in his *Lenten Stuffe* (*Works,* ed. McKerrow, Vol. III, pp. 194 ff.) has a burlesque treatment of Dionysius followed immediately by a burlesque of Hero and Leander. In the treatment of the lovers, both Nashe and Jonson begin with praise of Marlowe's *Hero and Leander,* and proceed to travesty the story, destroying all romance, vulgarizing Hero, and stressing her unchastity. Both men are doubtless mocking romance as it is fed to the populace, one utilizing the puppet-shows and the other the commercial town of Yarmouth, where all sentiment is subordinated to the glory of the herring. This connection between the two works seems all the more probable if Gifford is right in his conjecture (*Works of Jonson,* Vol. II, p. 197) that Jonson's puppet-show "had been exhibited at an early period as a simple burlesque," and on account of its popularity was later reworked and inserted in *Bartholomew Fair.* In favor of Gifford's theory is the fact that at the close of the sixteenth century the parody of classical stories, especially love stories, was a fad of literary men. It is seen in *Love's Labour's Lost, Midsummer Night's Dream, Histriomastix,* and the academic *Narcissus.* Again, the Damon and Pithias quarrel in Jonson's show, according to Gifford (*Works of Jonson,* Vol. II, p. 203), is a burlesque on the quarrel between the pages in the play of *Damon and Pithias.* In method, at least, the abuse and the pointless echoing and repetition are alike in the two cases. Such exercises, of which the knave song of *Twelfth Night* (II, 3) is typical, were evidently favorites with Elizabethan audiences.

The Devil is an Ass furnishes a better basis of study than *Bartholomew Fair,* for the devil offers no chance of confusing the actualities of life with the conventionalities of literature, and, except for an element of folk superstition, we may be pretty sure that Jonson's treatment is derived from books wherever we find it agreeing with books. Perhaps it is partly in consequence of this that for *The Devil is an Ass,* so far as the devil motive is concerned, more sources have been pointed out in English than for any other play perhaps, though Jonson was probably not influenced by English literature to a much greater extent here than in a number of his other comedies. Jonson himself, however, calls attention in *The Devil is an Ass* to several of the devil plays and to the work of Darrel. Mr. W. S. Johnson in his edition of *The Devil is an Ass* for the Yale Studies in English has been the latest to consider the sources of this play. He has gathered together the work of his predecessors, added some new details, and altogether given one of the best expositions we have had of how Jonson used his sources. Mr. Johnson makes it clear, for instance, that the most important treatments of the devil in story and play furnished elements for Jonson's Pug. The basis of *The Devil is an Ass* he takes to be the old prose history of Friar Rush, but he finds Jonson's play closer in some respects to Dekker's *If this be not a Good Play,* which is itself founded upon the Rush story. Moreover, after discussing the relation of *The Devil is an Ass* to *Belfagor,* the novella of Machiavelli, Mr. Johnson asserts that "on the whole we are not warranted in concluding with any certainty that Jonson knew the novella at all." In *Grim, Collier of Croyden,* however, which is built upon the Belfagor legend, Mr. Johnson finds a close parallel to *The Devil is an Ass,* and he concludes: "The English comedy seems, indeed, to account adequately for all traces of the Belfagor story to be found in Jonson's play." Here, then, we apparently find Jonson following the line of treatment in contemporary dramatists rather than in foreign or remoter English sources.

This somewhat extended list of examples is sufficient, I believe, to establish the fact that Jonson, if we make all allowance for his love of the classics, for his independent attitude to English writers, for his professed scorn of borrowing, and for his broad experience of life as a source of material, still kept in close touch with the movements of English literature, especially of the drama, and was ready to adopt any device that fitted his purpose so long as he could handle it freshly.

CHAPTER II

THE ENGLISH TEMPER OF JONSON'S WORK

Before an attempt is made to trace the development of Jonson's type of humour comedy out of general English tendencies, something further should be said of his relation to contemporary literature in its most general aspects. Inevitably much that is to be dealt with more specifically later will be anticipated. But for an understanding of the later treatment a statement is needed of Jonson's thorough accord with the spirit of what I shall call English didacticism.

The humour comedies belong to the general trend toward formal satire that marks the close of the sixteenth century. Jonson himself calls *Every Man out of his Humour, Cynthia's Revels,* and *Poetaster* "comical satires." In 1601, the year in which the last play of the group was produced, two references to Jonson's work appeared which pretty definitely indicate the relation of the humour comedies to the strong contemporary movement toward satire. In *The Whipping of the Satyre* by W. I., directed, according to Collier, principally against Marston, Jonson, and Breton,—who are not mentioned but are clearly indicated,—the section headed *In Epigrammatistam et Humoristam* has the following passage:

> It seemes your brother *Satyre,* and ye twayne,
> Plotted three wayes to put the Divell downe:
> One should outrayle him by invective vaine:
> One all to flout him like a country clowne;
> And one in action on a stage out-face,
> And play upon him to his great disgrace.
>
> You Humorist, if it be true I heare,
> An action thus against the Divell brought,
> Sending your humours to each Theater,
> To serve the writ that ye had gotten out.
> That Mad-cap yet superiour praise doth win,
> Who, out of hope, even casts his cap at sin.[1]

[1]Quoted from Collier's *Rarest Books,* Vol. IV, pp. 253 ff. by Alden in *The Rise of Formal Satire in England under Classical Influence,* Publ. Univ. Penn., Vol. VII, No. 2, pp. 163, 164. The summary of Collier's account of the book is also from Prof. Alden.

The second work referring to the new school of comedy is *No Whippinge, nor trippinge: but a kinde friendly Snippinge.* Here again we have the humour comedies classified along with epigrams and formal satires as a distinct phase of the new satiric movement:

> 'Tis strange to see the humors of these daies:
> How first the Satyre bites at imperfections:
> The Epigrammist in his quips displaies
> A wicked course in shadowes of corrections:
> The Humorist hee strictly makes collections
> Of loth'd behaviours both in youthe and age:
> And makes them plaie their parts upon a stage.[1]

The interest in satire at the close of the century marks a renewed classicism following upon a period of sonnet and romance writing. More, Erasmus, and others had opened the century with classic ideals in literature uppermost, and the influence of the Latin classics is the dominant feature in the advance of English literary art for the first two thirds of the century. Then the prose romances, romantic dramas, and love poetry, especially the sonnets, of the Italian period engaged the greatest literary masters from the seventies of the century to the early nineties. Following that, the most conscious literary movement was the one toward formal satire. Here the classic satirists and epigrammatists naturally exerted a strong influence. In the drama, too, there is found a renewed interest in the classics. The most important influence on Jonson's plays of the period was English satire itself; but *The Case is Altered* is drawn from Plautus; *Every Man in* is influenced by Plautine types; *Cynthia's Revels* borrows from Lucian and apparently from Aristotle; and *Poetaster* owes much to the satires of Horace.

On the surface, then, the new satiric trend readily connects itself with classicism. But the conditions that called for a school of satire are to be found in English life itself, especially in the decadence of Italian culture in England. The picture of English life presented by the satirists is, of course, overcolored by the prevailing fashion of malcontent and satirical posing, but there can be little doubt that the elegance of the Italian culture, which in the beginning had introduced a refining influence into English literature and manners, in the end brought its train of abuses. Sidney

[1]Also quoted from Alden, *loc. cit.*, pp. 164, 165. The work has been reprinted in Isham Reprints, No. 3.

and Spenser followed the courtly fashions of poetry,—of pastoralism and chivalry and courtly love,—but their temper was idealistic, and a spiritual worth pervaded even their fashionable poetry. The high critical ideals of the ardent theorists of the early Renaissance in Italy were sacred to these two, although Sidney especially seems often to have caught the passing fad rather than imparted the great lesson. Undoubtedly, also, there is a moral wholesomeness underlying the romantic art of Shakespeare, and, even when Jonson began his work, the fine spiritualizing power of the Renaissance had not passed altogether. But the effect of the Renaissance in England had been in the end to build up rapidly and artificially a system essentially un-English. We scarcely realize now how much the abstract theories of the Renaissance, through the literature that embodied them, worked their way into the life of the period. The language of *Euphues* and *Arcadia,* the outgrowth of the study of rhetoric, entered into speech; the manners described by the writers of the Italian school became the conscious manners of England. English manners had no doubt been somewhat crude even during the early sixteenth century, though for such as would heed, a simple body of instruction had existed. Now the age seems to have waked to a fervid cultivation of elegance in manners, and the Italian courtesy books furnished the pattern. Castiglione's *Courtier,* the most brilliant of them, was followed by many others—some of them less worthy. But sane and moral as were Castiglione's instructions and those of other early writers, abuse soon followed. Indeed, the passion for the refinement and elegance of Italian culture degenerated in almost all its phases into a worship of form far beyond the worship that had ever been inspired by the ethical and esthetic qualities, the ease, grace, delicacy, and idealism of that culture.

The follies of the fashionable had for years been jealously watched by the Puritan. Now the satirist and the dramatist both turned to the attack, men whose temper was that of the middle-class Englishman—Greene, Nashe, Lodge, Chapman, Hall, Donne, Marston, and Jonson. Of all these men none was more uncompromising in attitude than Jonson and at the same time so honest. Marston may be bitterer, but the dignity of sincerity is lacking in his work; affectation runs riot in his satire against affectation. But grim earnestness drives Jonson on. The disgust at the frivolities and excesses of Italianate letters and manners finds its fullest and sternest expression in Jonson's criticism and satire. Everything connected with the courtly ideal he attacks, upholding in opposition a moral wholesomeness and a literary restraint.

To the sturdier type of Englishmen, the conditions reflected in the work of these satirists, discount their satire how we may, must have been well-nigh unbearable. The life of the courtly was apparently largely given over to the ceremony of living. Court of love conventions, Platonic love, and chivalry were cultivated to add to the dignity and elaboration of formal manners. Some fantastic conceit entered into the most ordinary act of the pretentious gallant's life—into smoking, drinking, dressing, bowing, talking, walking, riding, duelling; and for large numbers of the new-rich doubtless the readiest way to social distinction lay through the affectation of the forms of gallantry. The cultivation of "singularity," so often mentioned by the satirists, rendered men oblivious to the absurdity of their manners, until conceit and affectation became ends in themselves. With the fashionable the pursuit of letters also degenerated into a fashion. By a fixed convention every courtier must not only be a lover but he must write poetry in honor of his mistress. It is not strange, then, that one of the commonest subjects of satire is the love poetry of the courtly with its immense volume, its petty themes, its forced passion, and its affected diction. The most complete picture of all these follies is of course to be found in *Cynthia's Revels.* The play is a gigantic satire against the whole fabric of courtly manners and ideals. It voices Jonson's scorn for the conventions and poetry of courtly love, for the games of gallants, for the duello, for fashions in dress, perfumes, etc.; it ridicules the courtier, the gallant, the traveler, the upstart, the shallow woman of wealth. Against the futile and absurd social ideals of the day, Jonson sets Crites, the man of sanity and roundedness, and Arete, the woman guided solely by virtue.

But not alone the decadence of Italian culture brought reaction. England's holiday spirit was passing. The buoyancy of the general temper, the hope and vision of individual accomplishment, waned. Melancholy and pessimism became fashionable. Sonnet sequences gave place to series of epigrams and satires. Despite the fact that the material of the satirical school was conventionalized as the new type of literature grew in popularity, we feel that in the satire at the end of the sixteenth century there is much truth to the feeling of England, a real echo of changing conditions. The change was more than a reaction in mood. Elizabeth was growing old, and political conditions were uncertain. Puritanism, which was becoming more and more insistent, brought greater acerbity to life. While the wealth of England was increasing throughout the century, the masses felt keenly the rise of prices, and the rich and the new-rich felt perhaps as keenly the clash of social readjustment. Nearly all of this is to be gathered from Jonson's satire. Such a study as that of the corn-hoarder Sordido indicates the attention paid to economic conditions. The numerous gulls and pretenders reveal the struggle attendant upon social readjustment. In the rather harsh and bitter satire of the end of the century with its reaction against the youthful hope and enthusiasm, the ideals and dreams, of Renaissance poetry there are thus embodied themes indicating that England had developed too fast for stability, that she had allowed the same zestful ferment in economic and civic affairs as in intellectual pursuits and was now being forced to take reckoning.

The revival of classical satire at the end of the century and the spirit of excess and disillusionment that called forth this satire are still not sufficient to explain Jonson's art, his temper, or his themes and literary material. This reaction against the glamor of the Renaissance culture was in fact largely a reassertion of the more normal English attitude of the century, marked by earnestness and morality. Steadily English life was tending toward certain moral and social ideals despite fads of the literary and the noble, the passing of a ruler, or the outcome of wars and political schemes. In morality or religion, the trend took the form of Puritanism. In social life, the trend was toward democracy. This spirit of democracy expressed itself in the clash of prentices and gentlemen, in the stern struggle between the London burgesses and the Crown over the suppression of the theatres, and finally in the Commonwealth.

It is to this deeper current of English sentiment that Jonson belongs. Into his work enters the whole mood of middle-class England. His intellectual and moral temper springs not from his classical training but from his stubborn English instinct and genius. Jonson's satire is not a matter of fashion; it is the compound result of all the forces that made conservative middle-class English sentiment, with the added force of a greater classical culture than the average man possessed even in Jonson's day. As a humanist, Jonson was bitterly opposed to Puritanism with its hostility to the fine arts. Yet the difference is largely a matter of point of view. The seriousness, the dogged intentness, the instincts and prejudices of the democratic Englishman colored the mental and moral attitude of Jonson as well as that of the Puritan, and made at once the strength and the limitation of both. Jonson and Puritanism are equally expressive of the English genius. Jonson was also in accord with the democratic spirit of the average Englishman. His democracy appears in his jealousy of the regard paid him by nobles and in his obstinate claim to equality with the best. It appears still more pervasively in his whole attitude to the idea of the courtly. To my mind *Cynthia's Revels* is the most illuminating of Jonson's plays as an expression of his own feeling. Presumably his satire is directed against the abuses of the system which he portrays, but through the play there runs a strong current of hostility to the whole idea underlying the system itself. It is noticeable that whereas Castiglione had presented the ideal type as the courtier whose nobility rests upon birth and wealth, Jonson's ideal, Crites, is poor, seemingly of humble birth, and scorns the graces of the court.[1]

This native and bourgeois instinct of Jonson's is apparent in his lack of sympathy with romantic and courtly literature. In

[1]For *The Courtier* itself Jonson seems to have had at a later period at any rate high regard. In *Timber* (ed. Schelling, p. 71) he classes it with Cicero's *De Oratore* as a valuable source of illustrative material, and he assuredly borrows from it for *Every Man Out*. At the end of the sixteenth century, however, Castiglione's name was employed by the satirists to designate an obnoxious type of gallant. Marston uses the name Castilio for the type in both of his collections of satires and in *Antonio and Mellida;* and Guilpin in *Skialetheia* uses Castilio as well as Balthazer for satire on court types. Cf. pp. 195 f. *infra* for these passages of Marston and Guilpin. The kinship of Puntarvolo with Marston's and especially with Guilpin's Castilio type, and the fierce satire in *Cynthia's Revels* on courtly ideals raise the question whether Jonson's favorable opinion of *The Courtier* did not come at a later period when he himself had close relations with the court and was one of the courtly. Perhaps, however, like Ascham, in spite of his hostility to Italian manners Jonson recognized in *The Courtier* a high moral influence and a noble idealism. Nevertheless, Jonson's ideal type for the court, Crites, differs from the ideal courtier of Castiglione in almost all details, in spite of the fact that both were probably influenced by Aristotle's conception of the "high-minded man."

The Case is Altered he essayed to follow the prevailing fashion and even utilized some romantic conventions in addition to those borrowed from Plautus. But the true romantic heroine Rachel is handled charily and apparently with lack of ease and spirit, while a number of the other characters fit well the satiric tone of the play, being little more than studies in clownage or in humours. Jonson evidently could not abandon himself to the world of romance. This might be said to indicate a limitation of his genius rather than of his sympathies, but he really seems to have shared the bourgeois distaste for the literature of mere enjoyment. The love poetry of the day was especially distasteful to him. "Songs and sonnets" he constantly employs as a term of contempt. A part of his attitude may, of course, be traced to classicism. His appreciation of the best ideals of classicism would probably account sufficiently for his fierce satire on Euphuism, Arcadianism, and all the forms of affected and extravagant diction in the Italianate school of writers which sprang out of a perverted classicism. In this he but follows the most English of the fine classicists produced at the height of the Latin phase of the Renaissance in England—Cheke, Ascham, Wilson, and others.[1] Jonson's admiration for classic art would also account for such criticism on the courtly literature as is based on lack of consistency or on crudeness of workmanship. But his early lack of sympathy with the whole spirit of romancing could hardly be attributed to the influence of a literature that included among its writers Virgil, a master of the finest spirit of romancing, and Seneca, who contributed largely to English romantic tragedy, men most highly honored by Jonson. Much that I have said, however, as to Jonson's attitude to this lighter body of literature applies more especially to the plays of the period we are studying. Contact with the courtly in the years following *Cynthia's Revels* may have softened his asperity to some extent. In his own later work there is certainly much courtly

[1]Professor Raleigh has stated admirably the hostility of this early group to excessive Latinity and other forms of word-mongery, and at the same time to the Italianate influence. Cf. his introduction to Hoby's translation of *The Courtier*, pp. xi ff. Devotion to classic learning inspired these men, but the greatest force is their sturdy English reformation temper. An interesting instance of the accord of these men with Jonson lies in the fact that Ascham and Cheke (*Scholemaster*, ed. Arber, p. 155) as well as Jonson (dedication to *Volpone*) insist on the moral life of the writer as a source of power in literary work.

compliment, and Jonson is often guilty of the sins he attacks most fiercely in *Cynthia's Revels.* Moreover, some lyrics and *The Sad Shepherd* at the close of his career disarm the criticism that his muse lacked grace and delicacy, that his work was not artistic is the highest sense of the word. Much of Herrick's perfection is due to Jonson's lessoning. And yet, when this is said, we readily recognize the opposition of Jonson's work to all that Shakespeare's stands for.

But the dominance of Shakespeare in the whole age and the connection of the greatest names of the period with the Italian influence brought by the Renaissance should not cause us to forget that the close of the sixteenth century and the opening of the seventeenth were as profoundly affected by a serious mood as by the mood represented in romantic and folk literature. The blither spirit of the courtier with his Italianate romance or love poetry and of the common man with his medieval ballad or tale produced the supreme literature of England. But Jonson and his fellows represent just as great a constituency. In other words, Jonson, for all his classicism, carries on much of the literary art that had been fairly consistent in tone and purpose during the century and that represented the democratic masses of England. Didactic is the word that most aptly describes the general temper of this literature. Much of the spirit and a great bulk of the thought and material of the didactic writers seems to me to be jointly an inheritance from the Middle Ages and an outgrowth, determined largely by the Reformation, of sixteenth century English life. The product in England was a great mass of serious literature, thoroughly English in spirit although affected from time to time by other literatures. It is here that we must look for the most important elements of Jonsonian comedy.

First, the effect of this more genuinely English literature in modifying Jonson's classicism may be mentioned, though an attempt to indicate the amount of adaptation that must take place in any such transfer from literature to literature would be futile. Indeed, a considerable amount of modification would be taken for granted. But certain forces, not accidental, affected first the intensity of the moral purpose underlying his work and second the temper and spirit of his satire.

The didacticism of much of Latin literature takes a Christian and Anglican turn in Jonson's classicism. The dictum of Horace that literature must be profitable was hardly so narrowly interpreted by him as by Jonson, nor was it so binding. In adapting classic ideals, the early theorists of the Renaissance, partly, no doubt, under the influence of medieval Christianity with its hostility to the purely artistic, had laid a strong stress upon the moral function of poetry. It was chiefly by emphasizing this moral function that the early critics like Sidney had defended the dignity and moral worth of their art against the attacks of the Puritans, and the principles of Sidney and of the school of critics who were called upon to defend the newly arising imaginative literature, Jonson adopted as his own with *Every Man in.* But the deeper seriousness that entered into the expression of critical tenets for Jonson makes itself felt practically as a vital force in his literary work. The overserious tone and the unimaginative art of a vast body of medieval literature, in which stories are made *exempla* and men and women mere moral abstractions, continued and manifested itself in Elizabethan literature, even in the case of many writers who were classic in spirit and belonged heartily to the Renaissance. Sidney himself uses the didactic nature of this older body of English literature as a defense of the art of "poesie" in England. But whereas to Sidney, whose genius was more inspired, the principles of *The Defense of Poesy* were merely for general guidance, Jonson accepts them as actual working rules. The spirit of Jonson's literary work is thus expressive not only of classicism but of certain aspects of his own character and, even more, of the forces in English literature that made for an exaggerated moral seriousness.

The spirit of Jonson's satiric treatment was perhaps another heritage from classicism which came to him partly through the medium of his contemporaries and was colored by his own English intenseness. It is often stated that Juvenal, as most in accord with the English temper, was the Latin satirist to whom the English school of satire was most indebted. Juvenal clearly exerted a strong influence on Jonson's portraiture of Asper. But in sustained intensity and acerbity the satiric literature of the sixteenth century doubtless passes the bounds set by even the bitterest of the classic satirists. This is the result partly of the English temper, and partly, no doubt, of the satiric license exhibited in the bitter personal quarrels of the century, in Skelton's attacks on Wolsey, in the Martin-Marprelate controversy, and in the Nashe-Harvey quarrel. Jonson was scarcely so unrestrained as Hall or Marston or a number of his fellows, but the reader will look in vain for any trace of urbanity in his satire.

This influence of native English literature upon borrowed classicism is naturally in large part an influence upon modes of handling character. For the satirist inevitably turned to English types and individuals, and already native literature had developed characteristic attitudes, groupings, and methods of analysis, from which men did not readily free themselves. Jonson's primary concern in his humour plays is with the treatment not of incident but of character, and with the mirroring of life in his characters. Consequently, he is very susceptible to native influence, and many of his typical figures, much of his method of characterization, indeed much of his art in general, reflects native English and even medieval character treatment.

First of all, the whole humour conception owes a great deal to that body of medieval English literature which I have spoken of as contributing to English didacticism in the sixteenth century. Under the Renaissance rule of decorum, which demanded consistency in the treatment of character, some tendencies of classical literature would naturally lead to abstractions rather than flesh-and-blood men and women. The Theophrastan character sketch with its choice of a single adjective that gave the unifying idea was one, and such analyses extended into satire and other forms of literature. Many characters of Latin comedy, also, especially the boaster, illustrate one quality. The idea of decorum was evidently formulated for and from such cases. But the use of allegory had made the abstraction the most prominent feature of medieval literature, and, before the conception of humours became prevalent, the closer approach of these abstractions of allegory, and especially of the morality, to real life had been leading directly toward a treatment of character that was substantially the same thing as Jonson's treatment of humours. This greater verisimilitude sprang of course from a keen desire for artistic excellence in the delineation of character,—a desire awakened perhaps by the Renaissance,—but, in the coming of humanism and the resulting interest in the analysis of individuals from life, men did not altogether lose touch with medieval art, or revolt from the moral symbolism to which they were accustomed in its character treatment, or cast away all of its results in thought, its influence on the attitude to men and women. The point of view survived in the new humour types, and an abstract idea or principle, sometimes a social class, is represented by most of Jonson's characters. Macilente is almost a pure abstraction, a portrayal of Envy in much of the characterization. So Carlo Buffone is a representation of Detraction and Derision combined. Both characters show a similarity to the older medieval treatment of the abstractions which would indicate the influence of medieval art in Jonson's characteristic work. Moreover, outside of the fact that the sixteenth century mind was habituated to the characters of allegory and readily passed to the humour point of view, the attention paid to the didactic function of literature through the century called for a type of symbolism which down to Jonson's own time encouraged the allegorical method in character treatment and stressed the single trait, the dominant motive, the mastering inclination. Thus not only the humour types of Jonson, with their forerunners in the drama of Lyly and in prose fiction, but also the character sketch and the satire of the last quarter of the sixteenth century never lose the impress of the art of allegory. In spite of the elements of classical literature that are fused with the older English elements, we are conscious of the apparently inevitable English drift toward the moral and the allegorical.[1]

The combination of this allegorical point of view with the classical view of character treatment is easily accounted for. In fact the serious classicist like Sidney or Jonson was more prone to stress the analysis of character, the obvious trait, and the technique of treatment than a free-lance like Shakespeare, who merely catches the new spirit without being checked by reverence for precept. There is much in the abstractions of classical literature, in the principles of its philosophy, in the exaggerated but consistent follies of its comedy, and in its ratiocinative attitude to literary standards to suggest kinship with the ideals of allegory. Thus the medieval conception of character treatment gathered tenaciously around itself all those tendencies of classic literature that accorded with its own tendencies; or, at any rate, it was able to impose itself

[1]An attempt is made in the chapter below, "A Study of Humours," to trace with more detail this development of the treatment of character.

upon many writers who were thoroughly under the influence of classic models. For example, one of the strongest classic influences of the period toward a treatment of character in which one trait is dominant came from the Aristotelian and pseudo-Aristotelian virtues and vices, which were easily associated with the Christian virtues and vices. The lists of virtues as given by Plato and Aristotle had early been absorbed into the medieval point of view, as in Skelton's *Magnificence,* or had formed the basis of a truer Renaissance treatment, as in Elyot's *Governour.* Groups of virtues or vices could scarcely pass into English literature without being influenced by the typical groups of abstractions—such as the Seven Deadly Sins and the Four Daughters of God—that were handed down from medieval writers. Jonson in *Cynthia's Revels* has seemingly used the excesses of Aristotle's *Nichomachean Ethics* as equivalent to his humours, but to my mind there is to be detected here a stronger influence of Aristotle as already adapted in certain morality plays, Skelton's *Magnificence* first of all.

A different phase of this intermixture of the classical and the medieval is interestingly illustrated in Lodge's *Wits Miserie,* a work of some importance for Jonson. Here Lodge has grouped his devils as sons of the Seven Deadly Sins. The particular types portrayed, however, and the succinct analyses of them seem obviously influenced by the character sketches of Theophrastus, as well as by those common in the sixteenth century, such as the sketches of *The Ship of Fools, the Fraternitye of Vacabondes, Cocke Lorelles bote, The Arte of Flatterie,* etc. Indeed, it is probable, I think, that these medieval character sketches had their effect upon the classical sketch which played so prominent a part in the formal satire of Jonson's period. The typical epigram at the end of the century was oftenest a mere character sketch, though occasionally there was a sharp turn at the close. The satires of the period were also most frequently a mere series of these sketches. Thus the poetic character sketch exemplified in *The Ship of Fools, The Hye Way to the Spyttel Hous,* and many similar works, and even in Chaucer's *Prologue.* with their satirical purpose and their characteristic grouping, probably obtained a hold upon the people which would account in no small degree for the popularity of the type of epigram and satire just mentioned.

I have already spoken of the influence of medieval allegory in determining Jonson's character treatment in the humour plays. Jonson's work, indeed, shows a conscious bent toward the symbolic which connects him more readily with the medieval than with the classical. Not only are many of his characters abstractions, but his plays are often really allegorical—that is, their action is symbolical. Some of this allegory might have been suggested by classical literature, though even here there seems to me an evident influence of the sixteenth century morality. The allegory of money in *Cynthia's Revels* and *The Staple of News* may readily be traced to Aristophanes, as Gifford has traced it; but English allegories of money are so numerous, some of them, like that of *Piers the Plowman,* are so brilliant, and many are so close to Jonson in time, that we can easily understand how a man of Jonson's English bent would be attracted to the theme. Other allegorical treatments show more truly his kinship with Renaissance didacticism or with the surviving morality. Such a treatment is that of the compass in *The Magnetic Lady,* which has some kinship with the pedagogical allegories of the new learning. In *Eastward Hoe,* again, Jonson, Chapman, and Marston, the masters of satiric comedy, seem to have been influenced to some extent by one of the most typical didactic themes of the Renaissance, that of the Prodigal Son. Of all the moral allegories this is probably most distinctly a part of humanism and of the Reformation, for it enabled many writers, like Gascoigne in his *Glass of Government,* to treat the ideal in education and character, setting it in contrast with the imperfection of the prodigal. Still with Gascoigne and other dramatists the art and attitude in treating the subject is medieval. In *Cynthia's Revels* Jonson has made satiric use of another type of symbolism, which is somewhat akin to the allegory. Here the mythological play is combined with devices of the court of love. The poetry of the court of love utilized mythological and allegorical characters as well as characters from life, and exhibited the same type of fancy that is to be seen in the mythological play of Lyly, which succeeded the allegorical play. While the great bulk of this literature belongs, of course, to chivalric and courtly love, many writers had used the machinery for satire, notably Jean de Meun in very early days.

But, aside from the possible blending of classical and medieval influences, there are some aspects of Jonson's work that give it a flavor peculiarly medieval. There is still evident in his humour comedies, for instance, the influence of such works as *The Ship of Fools* and *A Quartern of Knaves* in determining the point of view for character treatment. The kinship lies chiefly in the method of treatment, in the presentation of fools, rogues, etc., in groups or companies, to be disposed of wholesale at the end, as it were. The typical endings for the humour plays seem to me to show the combined effect of the morality and *The Ship of Fools* conception. In the early humour comedies especially, all the characters receive proper punishment in connection with their overthrow; but the final solution is not so much a reform as a banishment in shame that is visited on all. The vices at the end of the moralities are thus driven out of the scenes, and a not dissimilar conception exists in the ship load of fools setting out on a journey. At any rate, Marston in *The Fawne* adds to Jonson's method of exposing and shaming folly at the end, the device of sentencing the humour types to the Ship of Fools.

But it is the general spirit with which Jonson handles his characters that most distinctly reflects the medieval attitude and art. In what may be his first experiment in comedy, *A Tale of a Tub,* we find him dealing with clownish characters, and the higher and the lower social types are characterized alike with broad farce and burlesque. The point of view and the art in this method of characterization are typical of much of the English drama at the end of the sixteenth century in its treatment of native types, as I attempt to show later, and these figures naturally disappear in Jonson's work, for the time at least, as the conception of humours takes full hold on him. But the spirit in which the humour types, and more especially the gulls, are treated connects them with the medieval fool of the Ship of Fools type, though the gulls present a more effective approach than the fools since as a class they are more definite and individual. In such early studies, also, as Brainworm and Shift there are traces of the picturesque medieval rogue, in spite of Brainworm's classic affiliations. More typically medieval is the coarseness with which Jonson's women are drawn. Classic writers are prone to satirize women lashingly, but Jonson's satire is different. His women show a coarseness, a vulgarity, a grossness, which is inherited from the fabliaux and from medieval realism in general, at a time when the crude form of living developed the coarsest types of men and women. Skelton's *Elynour Rummyng* is an extreme picture of the type, and the poem is the best example of the art of treatment. The attitude filtered through popular thought and lived on in humble life, appearing constantly in jest-books and folk-tales. This folk attitude to women as witches, shrews, and alewives, as coarse, vulgar, and sensual, reveals itself continually in Jonson's work, and indicates his social inheritance and sympathies. Ursula of *Bartholomew Fair* is Jonson's grossest picture, but the witch of *The Sad Shepherd* and Tib of *Every Man in his Humour* are also folk types, while the nurse and the midwife of *The Magnetic Lady,* probably more indebted to literature, are treated with even more of the brutal realism of the folk feeling. It is not alone the humbler figures, however, that are stripped of all feminine charm and grace. Moria, one of the leading court ladies of *Cynthia's Revels,* Lady Politick Would-be of *Volpone*, the Ladies Collegiates of *The Silent Woman,* Lady Tailbush and Lady Eitherside of *The Devil is an Ass* are all represented as sensual, coarse, and strident. In spite of their social leadership Jonson manages to impart to them an atmosphere of moral and physical foulness. *The New Inn,* again, shows his characteristic tendency. Lady Frampul, the mother of one of his most attractive heroines, is presented throughout the play in the disguise of "a poor chare-woman in the Inn, with one eye." The unnecessary addition of a physical deformity even where there is no satire in the treatment seems to me characteristic of Jonson. There are exceptions, of course, for he does give us some heroines in all good faith, but it is noticeable that his women of the most virtuous type are shallow or at best not strongly characterized. The romantic figure of Rachel in *The Case is Altered* furnishes an example. Except in *The Sad Shepherd* Jonson scarcely shows a trace of the idealizing touch that belongs to the treatment of women in romance, a touch that the Renaissance made vital.

In matters pertaining more directly to literary technique, also, Jonson is a product of the English didactic school. The spirit of the bourgeois English has already been spoken of as bringing the English satirists nearer to Juvenal than to the more urbane Horace. This was a natural result of what appears immediately to the most superficial reader in the English satirical school—its employment of direct rebuke and preaching, its bluntness and downrightness.

In other words, English satire of the sixteenth century was didactic rather than literary. In this respect Jonson felt pretty fully the influence of the age, for the serious message, the polemics of reform, the direct and angry rebuke of evil, and the uncompromising bluntness that belong to him as a middle-class Englishman spoil any lightness and play, any subtle mockery and laughing irony that we might expect from a genuine literary attitude to the objects of satire. Invective and arraignment are dominant in Jonson's work as in the age.

The failure to use the more subtle instruments of literary satire is partly due to the slow development of English literary style, but this lack of development itself is largely a result of English directness. Certainly the limitations of Jonson, trained classicist as he was and a follower of the best models, must be traced in no small part to his temper. A study of the classics would naturally lead a man of his type toward what is most readily perceived through the intellect and most readily analyzed. The fine simplicity, the artlessness of the supreme art, the imaginative spontaneity and grace in the portrayal of life, in short, the finest esthetic values of classic literature, seem to have escaped him as often as they did the classicists of the Restoration and Queen Anne periods, while the rhetoric and mechanics of Latin literature were readily caught by both. This estimate is perhaps not altogether fair to Jonson in view of the classic excellence of his best work in the lyric, in the epigram, in the masque, and in the drama. And yet I believe that he was influenced more by the externals than by the spirit of the best classic literature.

The reasons for this, outside of the limitations of Jonson's own nature, are probably twofold. First, classic art was interpreted by Renaissance criticism in terms of set academic rules, which necessarily dealt with externals and tended to make literature formal. Second, there was a still stronger influence of medievalism toward directness, formalism, and an intellectual art. The kinship of the two influences readily made them meet. This mechanical aspect of literary style in the sixteenth century and the quick recognition of the obvious rather than the feeling for the subtle are indicated in satire even by some divergences from the direct rebuke, for in most cases it is the form, the method, the particular device for indirect satire that has attracted attention. The fundamental irony in a device like the Ship of Fools laid hold upon the period, as the numerous imitations of the title and mode of treatment suggest. Erasmus, especially, taught the age its finest lessons in irony. One of his most famous bits of irony is his *Encomium Moriae*. Again in "The False Knight" of his *Colloquies* advice is given to the knight to cultivate just what is most foolish and disgusting in life. This last bit of irony Jonson borrows completely in *Every Man out of his Humour*. This type of satire became, of course, most famous through *Grobianus*. Another popular form of irony—and possibly a more subtle one—lay in the use of the testament, or will, on the principle of "like will to like."[1] The best indication of Jonson's attitude to such formal devices for satire is derived from the fact that he read to Drummond "a Satyre, telling there was no abuses to writte a satyre of, and [in] which he repeateth all the abuses in England and the World." That Jonson should have taken such interest in the irony of denial, a simple bit of form, as to emplcy it in what must have been a long poem, and to show such evident pride in the work as late as 1619 is indicative enough of his attitude to literary style and art.

Jonson's connection with the native English tradition and the influence of English didactic literature upon him will be traced in more detail in the following chapters. It is hoped that here I have been able, without any real perversion of the many-sided Jonson, to indicate the fundamental inclination of the man toward an intense Anglicism, and the result of this on his type of drama, his handling of characters, and his literary art in general.

[1]Cf. Routh, *Cambridge Hist. Eng. Lit.*, Vol. III, pp. 95-97.

CHAPTER III

A STUDY OF HUMOURS

Jonson's celebrated definition of humour has fixed the meaning of the word for us in connection with the comedy of manners. As Jonson defines the term, it is fairly inclusive and may represent almost any decided moral inclination or mental attitude. Beginning with the broadest definition of the term in the physical sense, he proceeds to the figurative meaning of the word (*Every Man out,* Induction, p. 67):

> Whatsoe'er hath fluxure and humidity,
> As wanting power to contain itself,
> Is humour. So in every human body,
> The choler, melancholy, phlegm, and blood,
> By reason that they flow continually
> In some one part, and are not continent,
> Receive the name of humours. Now thus far
> It may, by metaphor, apply itself
> Unto the general disposition:
> As when some one peculiar quality
> Doth so possess a man, that it doth draw
> All his effects, his spirits, and his powers,
> In their confluctions, all to run one way,
> This may be truly said to be a humour.

This derived meaning covers the pride and ambition of a Sejanus, the lust for conquest of a Tamburlaine, the thirst for sensuous and forbidden knowledge of a Faust, the idolatry of gold in a Volpone or a Barabas, as well as the sensuous luxuriousness of an Epicure Mammon, the envy of a Macilente, the pride of a Fastidious Brisk, the impatience of a Downright, or the jealousy of a Kitely. The words "as wanting power to contain itself" imply the essential defect in the character of one possessed of a humour, and other passages emphasize the abnormality of the humorist in the Jonsonian sense. Throughout the humour plays Jonson sets the balanced man as an ideal in contrast with the humorist. This contrast is voiced in *Every Man in* (II, 1, p. 16) when Kitely says of Wellbred:

> My brother Wellbred, sir, I know not how,
> Of late is much declined in what he was,
> And greatly altered in his disposition.
> When he came first to lodge here in my house,
> Ne'er trust me if I were not proud of him:
> Methought he bare himself in such a fashion,
> So full of man, and sweetness in his carriage,
> And what was chief, it shewed not borrowed in him,
> But all he did became him as his own,
> And seemed as perfect, proper, and possest,
> As breath with life, or colour with the blood.
> But now his course is so irregular,
> So loose, affected, and deprived of grace,
> . . . .
> He makes my house here common as a mart,
> A theatre, a public receptacle
> For giddy humour, and diseased riot.

In *Cynthia's Revels,* again, Mercury, in characterizing Crites, calls him "a creature of a most perfect and divine temper: one in whom the humours and elements are peaceably met, without emulation of precedency" (II, 1, p. 161). Then follows a long list of his excellences which contrast with the vices and follies of Jonson's humorists.

In his study of the so-called humour types, then, Jonson presents the man whose moral and emotional nature lacks sanity, whose mental attitude exalts follies. Thus the fundamental conception of humour with Jonson is of something temperamental, something more or less permanent in character bent. This is what I shall call the Jonsonian use of the word humour. But Jonson has almost spoiled some of his plays by the effort to emphasize in a more or less abstract way the mental and moral make-up of his characters; for in a drama of action much of the satire against evil ideas and evil ideals must take the form of satire against actions, social pursuits, dress, and so forth. In this definition Jonson excludes the use of humour to cover any such thing as a fad in dress, and in the mouth of Sogliardo he satirizes the use constantly, as Shakespeare does in *The Merry Wives of Windsor.* But it is the gallant's affectation of a humour through a fad in dress, etc. that Jonson objects to and satirizes in Sogliardo's spur as the "only humour," or Brisk's "stirring humours" [of vaulting]. Indeed, the use of the word to cover any fad or whimsicality had itself become a humour that called for rebuke from the satirist. Jonson does not seem entirely to have rejected this use of the word until he came to *Every Man out,* and the large number of meanings that the term covers at the end of the century nearly all appear in Jonson's work. Humour is first of all used to express a trait of the inner man, but that trait itself is often symbolized by outward peculiarities and fashions that in their turn naturally come to have the name humour applied to them. In other words, both the inner and the outer manifestations of the disposition may be signified by the term.

A passage which Jonson added to the folio edition of *Cynthia's Revels* is very interesting in this connection (IV, 1, pp. 173, 174):

> I would prove all manner of suitors, of all humours, and of all complexions, and never have any two of a sort. I would see how love, by the power of his object, could work inwardly alike, in a choleric man and a sanguine, in a melancholic and a phlegmatic, in a fool and a wise man, in a clown and a courtier, in a valiant man and a coward; and how he could vary outward, by letting this gallant express himself in dumb gaze; another with sighing and rubbing his fingers; a third, with play-ends and pitiful verses; a fourth with stabbing himself, and drinking healths, or writing languishing letters in his blood; a fifth, in coloured ribands and good clothes; with this lord to smile, and that lord to court, and the t'other lord to dote, and one lord to hang himself. And, then, I to have a book made of all this, which I would call the *Book of Humours,* etc.

This passage, pointing backward to the origin of the word, exemplifies Jonson's idea of the relation of humours to the physical man,[1] and at the same time shows how very general may be the inward disposition indicated by the word humour and how varied and specific may be the particular customs or fads that make manifest a character tendency. It is obvious from this passage, also, that the use of the term humour for an outward manifestation of a tendency will readily result in the extension of the term to the whim, fancy, or momentary inclination of whimsical and unstable characters, in other words, to just such a use of the term as Jonson satirizes.

It is evident, then, that Jonson's program of humour study will be a varied one. It includes the treatment of Envy, Wrath, Drunkenness, Avarice—indeed some phase of all the Seven Deadly Sins

[1]It should be noticed, too, that Jonson here uses complexions as practically synonymous with humours.

except perhaps Sloth. It deals with folly a
manners and dress as indicative of characte
vices, the follies, the manias, the fads and fa
indicative of mental or moral weakness are s
is the term that Jonson uses to cover them a

Until recently the idea has been rather
most characteristic use of the word humour
at any rate, and that the comedy of humo
from the brain of Jonson in *Every Man in.*
out, however, it is practically certain tha
Mirth preceded *Every Man in.* And yet it wou
of the mark to give this one play of Chapman the credit for Jonson's whole bent in the comedy of manners. The dominance of the idea of humours in Jonson's work is rather to be explained by the prevalence of the idea in the didactic literature belonging to the last twenty years of the sixteenth century, a body of literature that exercised a very strong influence on his whole conception of the function of comedy. Specifically, outside of *An Humorous Day's Mirth,* the influences that determined the use of the humour idea for Jonson were those of Lyly, Greene, Nashe, and Lodge, especially in their more serious prose. Here the word humour occurs with several meanings, as in Jonson, but the most characteristic meaning is the figurative one of Jonson's definition. Here, too, the characterization is of the sort typical with Jonson; one phase of a character, a vice or folly or fad, is stressed till it becomes dominant. These humours are studied in stories, as in Greene's numerous treatments of jealousy; in dramas, as in Lyly's *Woman in the Moon;* and in character sketches, as in Lodge's *Wits Miserie* and Nashe's *Pierce Penilesse.* It is especially in the character sketches of Nashe that the word humour is applied to an abnormal tendency. The character sketch of Jonson's type, however, is developed to its greatest perfection in Lodge's *Wits Miserie.* Moreover, just as the character sketch is an accompaniment of the study of humours in this group of prose writers, the crystallization of Jonson's idea of humours comes along with his highest development of the character sketch; that is, both reach their zenith in *Every Man out* and *Cynthia's Revels.*

But in order to understand the use of the word humour in the Elizabethan age, it may not be out of place, before discussing in greater detail these immediate predecessors of Jonson, to take up briefly the origin of the use of humour to represent what is temperamental and characteristic, and to suggest the general causes that led to the prominence of the humour conception in the literature of the end of the sixteenth century. I am not prepared to give any exhaustive study of the broadening use of the word, especially before the middle of the century, but the development of the Jonsonian use along with the shift from the study of abstract vices and follies to the study of human types near akin to them seems to me pretty definitely marked.

In the fourteenth century humour is common enough in England as applied to the supposed fluid constituents of man's body. The conception of humours on the physical side led in medical science and in popular literature to an association of certain dispositions and mental or nervous conditions with the preponderance of certain humours. We can readily see that humour to represent the mood or mental state supposedly caused by the preponderance of some physical humour is an easy extension of the use of the word as words expand in language. This use of humour in the transferred sense doubtless came in early, much earlier than I have been able to trace it. The earliest assured instance of it that is cited by the *New English Dictionary* is for the year 1525[1] from Thoms's *Anecdotes of Early English History* (Camden Soc., p. 11), and is given under the definition, "temporary state of mind or feeling; mood, temper." The passage reads: "Hacklewitt and another . . . in a madde humour . . . coyted him downe to the bottome of the stayres." About 1565, we find illustrated the still more transferred meaning, "a particular disposition, inclination, or liking, *esp.* one having no apparent ground or reason; mere

[1]The first example cited by *N. E. D.* as figurative dates from about 1475, but it is probably not figurative after all, as Professor Manly pointed out to me. The passage, which is quoted under the meaning "mental disposition," is from *Quia Amore Langueo*, Part II, a poem in *Political, Religious, and Love Poems* (E. E. T. S., XV). As given in the 1903 edition of the E. E. T. S. volume, the passage reads in Lambeth MS. 853, ll. 53-55, as follows:

¶In my loue was neu*er*e desaite,
Alle my*n* humour*s* y haue opened hir to,
Th*er*e my bodi hath maad hir hertis baite.

The Cambridge Univ. MS. Hh. 4.12 has substituted *membres* for *humours*. The general sense of the passage and the substitution of *membres* make it pretty clear that the word is used in the physical sense.

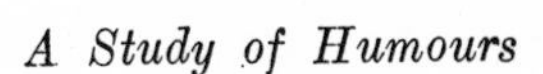
THE UNIVERSITY OF WINNIPEG
DISCARDED
WINNIPEG 2. MAN.

fancy, whim, caprice, freak, vagary." The example which the *New English Dictionary* cites is from Calfhill's *Answer to J. Martiall's Treatise of the Cross,* 1565, (Parker Soc., p. 94): "They neded no more for hallowing of a Church, but a sermon, and prayers, in which peraduenture (that I may feede your humor)[1] they made the signe of a crosse with their finger." These and other meanings[2] that developed later the *New English Dictionary* distinguishes from the strict Jonsonian use, which it defines as "mood natural to one's temperament; habitual frame of mind." In my own notes, which begin about the middle of the sixteenth century, it has not always seemed practical to make these distinctions, for the uses of the word humour to indicate a fairly permanent or distinctive quality all contribute to Jonson's conception. The first work in which I have found humour used freely in its derived sense dates from 1567; by 1580 the use of the word had become fairly widespread; and by 1592 humour seems to be the term most often chosen by the writers who deal with the follies of the time to indicate the inclination or moral weakness that leads to evil. The use of the word, indeed, increases in proportion to the attention that is paid to the study of manners.

Popular as the word humour was throughout two and a half centuries to represent a physical state invariably associated with a corresponding tendency of mind, it is surprising that the use of the word to represent the appropriate mental state itself developed as slowly as it did. In fact, as I have said, this use does not seem to have taken any very firm hold until well into the sixteenth century, or nearly two centuries after the physical conception of humour is revealed in Chaucer as a part of the thought of the age. The cause is probably two-fold. In the first place, as is often pointed out, the social class dominates over the individual in this

[1]This expression had already become stereotyped. The phrase is used often in Fenton's *Tragicall Discourses,* 1567, and it occurs frequently in later writers, at times in the works of writers who do not use humour in any other combination. Jonson in *Ev. M. in* (III, 2, p. 31), after speaking of humour as bred by affectation and fed by folly, makes Cash add: "Oh ay, humour is nothing if it be not fed: didst thou never hear that? it's a common phrase, *feed my humour.*"

[2]The *N. E. D.* gives, no doubt through a misprint, the date 1566 instead of 1656 for Cox's *Acteon and Diana . . . followed by the several conceited humours of Bumpkin,* etc., a work whose title is used as the first illustration of humours in the plural to mean "moods or fancies exhibited in action," etc.

early literature dealing with real life. Chaucer's character sketches analyze men, through the specific details of manners, on the basis of social class and trade, and do not generalize according to the inner nature of the man. Allegory, to be sure, was popular, but it dealt with abstract virtues and vices rather than with human types. It is clear, then, that the physical conception will not prevail in allegory; nor, in the treatment of actual men from the social point of view of class, will the vices and follies be those of temperament but of class. Naturally with the coming of the Renaissance, especially with the study of Aristotle and Plato, the emphasis was shifted to quality in the individual. In the second place, to go a little further in the same process, so long as the whole individual was the unit, so to speak, there were other words more suitable to the conception than humour. One humour predominated and determined the inclination of the man, but one humour could not be separated from the rest, and temperament was a compound result. Two words, especially, complexion and temperament, were suited for this conception of the combination and regulation of the humours and elements. These words are common in Chaucer to represent the characteristic tendencies in a man's nature. Temperament we still retain with its indication of one's general nature. Complexion is frequent in Shakespeare to suggest disposition and mood, and Jonson also uses the word, as in the passage from *Cynthia's Revels* quoted above in connection with humour. But, when the individual is subjected to dissection, and the typical qualities become more prominent in the characterization of the moralities and the satiric literature of the Renaissance, there results the stressing not of the combination of qualities but of the single dominant quality associated with the preponderance of one humour in the composition of the body.

This association of the new conception of humour with a new conception of character treatment, that which combines the study of a type and the study of an abstract folly or vice, is not at all new of course. Courthope, in his *History of English Poetry,* stresses the connection between the morality and the Jonsonian comedy. Another statement of this connection is found in Gayley's *Plays of our Forefathers.* According to Professor Gayley, the characters in the moralities, though called by abstract names, are often from life, and each character has a motive of action to distinguish it from the rest. "This kind of play is, therefore, the forerunner of Ben Jonson's comedy of humours" (p. 298). Again, Professor Gayley says that Haphazard of *Appius and Virginia* is "a Vice of the old type; but he is, also, the representative . . . of the caprice of the individual and the irony of fortune. He is the Vice, efficient for evil, but in process of evolution into the Inclinations or Humours of a somewhat later period of dramatic history: conceptions not immoral but unmoral, artistic impersonations of comic extravagance, where Every Man is in his Vice and every Vice is but a Humour"[1] (pp. 303 f. Cf. also p. 314). What we really see, then, in this new development in the treatment of types is the bringing of vices and follies home to men and women by the greater nearness to actual life, by the concreteness and individualization that the abstractions take on. It is this side of medieval literature that influenced Jonson most strongly in his conception of comedy and of the types appropriate to it.[2]

The new conception of character treatment, then, as I have indicated above, calls for a constant study of the nature of men and women. Analysis of character with the fixing upon some dominant mental or moral trait is found in Greene, Nashe, Lodge, Lyly, Spenser, and Marlowe. Along with the philosophical study of man went the physical, and the two were not dissociated; but, as the qualities of character were associated with the physical qualities of man, the physiological side plays, I believe, a greater part than the psychological in the thought of the age with regard to mankind. In fact, during the latter half of the sixteenth

[1]Inclination, almost synonymous with Humour, as Prof. Gayley recognizes, is the Vice of *Trial for Treasure.* Compare "Inclination the Vise" of *Sir Thomas More.* See p. 306 of Prof. Gayley's book for the spirit of comedy in *Trial for Treasure.*

[2]It is very interesting to find Wager in the prologue to *The Longer thou Liuest, the more Foole thou art,* just as literature is fastening most firmly on individual vices and follies, forestalling, much in Jonson's spirit, any charge of attack on individuals:

> By him we shall declare the vnthriftie abuse
> Of such as had leuer to Folly and Idlenes fall,
> Then to herken to Sapience when he doth call:
> There processe, how their whole life they do spende,
> . . . .
> But, truly, we meane no person perticularly,
> But only to specifie of such generally.

century, the whole thought of life is colored by the influence of the physical conceptions current at the time and taking a still greater hold upon men as the range of studies became broader and interest in the mysteries of life keener. The thought and language of the age were impregnated with the thought and language of the physical sciences, especially the science of medicine, exactly as the literature of the nineteenth century has been universally influenced in theory and expression by the scientific conceptions of evolution.

An indication of the interest in medicine is seen in the great number of medical tracts appearing in English during the sixteenth century.[1] Elyot's *Castle of Health* and the works of Boorde, Bullein, Recorde, and Vicary were especially well known. Bullein's *Dialogue against the Fever Pestilence* reveals a physician studying the diseases of society along with his study of the pestilence, and the social evils are of primary interest. The physician Rabelais in France was one of the great anatomists of life and its evils, and his influence penetrated to England early. The ideas and the language of such works were speedily reflected in the literary treatment of life. As the didactic purpose of much of the contemporary literature is indicated in the frequent use of the word mirror, so the analytic tendency finds expression in the various titles that use anatomy.[2] The interesting fact in connection with the popularity of these titles is that they are used by the very men who apparently influenced Jonson most in his early life, and gave him his conception of humour—Lyly,

[1]Cf. the list in *The Cambridge Hist. Eng. Lit.*, Vol. III, pp. 560, 561. It could probably be greatly extended.

[2]The most notable works embodying the idea in their titles are given by Mr. McKerrow (*Works of Nashe*, Vol. IV, p. 3): Anthony de Adamo, *An Anatomi, that is to say a parting in peeces of the Mass*, 1556; Rogers, *A philosophicall Discourse, entituled, The Anatomie of the Minde*, 1576; Lyly, *Euphues. The Anatomy of Wyt*, 1579; Stubbes, *The Anatomie of Abuses*, 1583; Greene, *The Anatomie of Lovers Flatteries*, an appendix to *Mamillia*, 1583; Greene, *A maruelous Anatomie of Saturnistes*, a part of *Planetomachia*, 1585; Greene, *Arbasto, The Anatomie of Fortune*, 1584; Nashe, *The Anatomie of Absurditie*, 1589. Compare also Gascoigne, "The Anatomye of a Louer," 1575, (*Poems*, ed. Hazlitt, Vol. I, p. 35); *Valour Anatomized*, doubtfully ascribed to Sidney (cf. *D. N. B.*); Harington, *Anatomie of the Metamorphosed Ajax*, 1596; *Maroccus Extaticus. Or, Bankes Bay Horse in a Trance . . . Anatomizing some abuses and bad trickes of this age*, 1595; "The Anatomie of Alchymie," Epistle VII of Lodge's *Fig for Momus*, 1595. The word anatomy was equally popular in titles during the early part, at least, of the seventeenth century.

Greene, and Nashe. In Asper's statement of his satiric purpose in the induction to *Every Man out,* Jonson himself uses both mirror and anatomy together with scourge, the word most suggestive of the attitude of the formal satirists (cf. p. 151 *infra*). Moreover, much of the literature of the time shows an acquaintance with medical lore. Medical writers are quoted; Nashe and Greene and other writers draw more or less on medicine for terms and figures. The physician occurs in Jonson's *Magnetic Lady,* and there is much medical jargon in the play, as for instance in the purge for a purse prescribed for Sir Moth Interest (III, 4). More to the point is the fact that in the early plays Jonson often uses figures from medicine in analyzing character. In *Every Man in* (II, 1, p. 19) jealousy is discussed as a disease:

> Like a pestilence, it doth infect
> The houses of the brain. First it begins
> Solely to work upon the phantasy,
> Filling her seat with such pestiferous air,
> As soon corrupts the judgment; and from thence,
> Sends like contagion to the memory:
> Still each to other giving the infection,
> Which as a subtle vapour spreads itself
> Confusedly through every sensive part,
> Till not a thought or motion in the mind
> Be free from the black poison of suspect.
> . . . .
> Well, I will once more strive,
> In spite of this black cloud, myself to be,
> And shake the fever off that thus shakes me.

Here we have a distinct humour in the Jonsonian sense treated from the point of view of bodily disease. Jonson's analysis is true to the belief of the time that from the humours certain fumes or vapours arose, and passing to the brain, affected the mind.[1] To be associated doubtless with this very idea of vapours arising from humours as determining the sanity of men is the use of vapours

[1]Cf. *Ev. M. in,* II, 1, p. 17. Astrological conceptions also play their part in the idea of humours, as in Greene's works. See *Englische Studien,* Vol. 40, pp. 332 ff. for the physiological conception of spirits and the continuance in the drama and in late seventeenth century literature of this idea. Cf. Dowden, "Elizabethan Psychology" in *The Atlantic Monthly,* Vol. 100, pp. 388 ff., for a review of the whole field to which these conceptions belong; see also Greenough and Kittredge, *Words and their Ways,* pp. 30 ff.

in *Bartholomew Fair* and elsewhere to indicate a peculiar form of quarreling and ranting. The term seems to denote a popular fad of certain classes, as humours did, and doubtless came from medical science. Naturally, also, in close connection with the idea of humours which had taken such a hold upon the age in its study of man physically and mentally, went the purge, the recognized medical treatment for excess of humour. It is needless to quote examples from Jonson, whose whole treatment is illustrative and who constantly uses the term, as in "purge of purse" above. The purging of humours is especially conspicuous, of course, in the final adjustment at the close of the early humour comedies.

A curious side of this anatomical and humour lore is to be found in some odd conceits of the sixteenth century. In Crowley's *One and Thirty Epigrams,* 1550, "Of Vayne Wryters, Vaine Talkers, and Vaine Hearers" (E. E. T. S., E. S., No. 15, ll. 1389 ff.), we are told how the writer's head is opened and the talker stirs his brains with a stick. Examples from Nashe,[1] especially from his controversial works, are numerous, and several of them go to show that, though Jonson's use of the purge in *Poetaster* was derived from Lucian, such concrete representations on the stage were not without precedent in the English drama. In *The Returne of Pasquill* (*Works,* ed. McKerrow, Vol. I, p. 92), there is mention of an old play in which Divinity had been "poysoned . . with a vomit which he [*Martin*] ministred vnto her, to make her cast vppe her dignities and promotions." A passage a few pages farther on (p. 100) reads: "This [*Vetus Comœdia*] is she that called in a counsell of Phisitians about *Martin,* and found by the sharpnes of his humour, when they had opened the vaine that feedes his head, that hee would spit out his lunges within one yere." In *A Countercuffe giuen to Martin Iunior* (*Works,* Vol. I, p. 59), we have a reference to "the Anotamie latelie taken of him [*Martin*], the blood and the humors that were taken from him, by launcing and worming him at *London* vpon the common Stage." In *Strange Newes,* Nashe says of Harvey (*Works,* Vol. I, p. 295):

[1]In Vol. V, pp. 34-65 of his *Works of Nashe,* Mr. McKerrow throws considerable doubt on Nashe's authorship of any of the Martin Marprelate tracts that are usually ascribed to him.

> ***The tickling and stirring inuectiue vaine, the puffing and swelling Satiricall spirit* came vpon him, as it came on *Coppinger* and *Arthington*, when they mounted into the pease-cart in Cheape-side and preacht: needes hee must cast vp certayne crude humours of English Hexameter Verses that lay vppon his stomacke; a Noble-man stoode in his way, as he was vomiting, and from top to toe he all to berayd him with *Tuscanisme*.**

The age, then, was full of the ideas of medicine, and humours especially struck the fancy of writers. As humour had already acquired its various figurative meanings, it is easy to see how this interest in medical lore caused a continually widening use of the word. I have shown, I think, how naturally the word may have developed its various meanings in England itself, and how much a part of the age was the interest in humours; it remains to show definitely the development of the Jonsonian use at the end of the sixteenth century through such writers as Fenton, Lyly, Greene, Nashe, and Lodge.

First, however, it is necessary to note that Professor Spingarn (*Literary Criticism in the Renaissance*, pp. 88, 89) would trace this use of the term to Italy, connecting it with the conception of character treatment which according to him grew largely out of the Renaissance idea of decorum. As evidence he cites Salviati's definition of humour (in *Del Trattato della Poetica*, a MS. lecture of about 1586) as "a peculiar quality of nature according to which every one is inclined to some special thing more than to any other." But the use of the derived meanings of humour in England much earlier than the manuscript lecture of Salviati, the presence of forces that would naturally tend to develop such a use, and finally the great vogue of the idea in England toward the close of the century render it improbable that Italy is to be held responsible for the conception. Professor Spingarn's view neglects these important phenomena. Indeed, both the conception of humours and the corresponding treatment of character may well have been independent of foreign influences, though doubtless Italian and classic ideas had the effect of crystallizing native tendencies. It must be remembered that, after the first impulse had been received, the Renaissance spirit often worked alike in different countries of Europe without any necessary dependence of one literature upon another, for all Europe was feeling the same impulses and finding in classic literature the same sources of inspiration, releavening the medieval thought, which in itself had been akin throughout Europe. And this may be said without forgetting the great indebtedness of all Europe to Italy.

My own purpose is to trace the rise of the humour conception in England, and I have paid rather slight attention to the ultimate source except as it may be English. Since, however, the first work in which I have found the term humour used freely is *The Tragicall Discourses* of Fenton, a series of stories derived from Bandello through the French of Belleforest, a word seems necessary in regard to the possible foreign influence on Fenton's use of humour. The Italian of Bandello is not accessible to me, but, as Fenton himself says that he translated from the French (*Tragicall Discourses,* Tudor Translations, Vol. I, p. 7), there is no especial reason to believe that the Italian originals of his stories influenced him directly. In this work of Fenton, which appeared in 1567, humour is employed rather constantly in a sense not differing greatly from Jonson's. Indeed, humour is such a favorite with Fenton that often he adds to his original a passage of which it is the central word and conveys the central idea. Belleforest in the *Histoires Tragiques,* from which Fenton drew his stories, uses *humeur* occasionally, but too rarely to account for Fenton's fondness for the word.

In order to compare Fenton's work with Belleforest's in this respect, I have chosen as typical of Fenton Discourses I, II, IV, and VII. Jealousy is treated in the fourth discourse, and the word humour is frequently applied to it. The seventh is the famous "Countess of Celant" story. In these four discourses of Fenton, humour is used figuratively about thirty-five times. In the corresponding stories of Belleforest (numbers 21, 22, 10, and 20 respectively), *humeur* occurs three times with what approaches a figurative meaning, but the three uses are practically alike. The first of these examples is found in the following passage, which is not translated by Fenton: "Plein de quelque humeur melancholique, qui luy trouble le cerueau."[1] Thus only in two cases could Belleforest have suggested to Fenton the derived use of the word humour during the course of these four stories.

[1]Belleforest, *Histoires Tragiques,* Rouen, 1603, Vol. I, p. 417. Compare Fenton, *Trag. Disc.,* Vol. I, pp. 177, 178.

Moreover, in both of those cases Fenton employs the word in a way that is far more suggestive of the Jonsonian application to disposition or inclination. Belleforest evidently conceives of the physical humour as affecting the mental state, but in none of the three examples does *humeur* stand for the disposition or inclination itself. What seems to be with Fenton a constant tendency to look at character from the point of view of an inclination or a primary quality of disposition is indicated by the change he has made in translating the two passages in which both he and Belleforest use humour. Belleforest's "l'humeur, qui brouillassoit la raison" (Vol. I, p. 419) becomes in Fenton "the disposition . . . overcharged wyth a mad humor of wrong conceites" (Vol. I, pp. 179, 180), where the word disposition gives the idea a new significance, and humour becomes much more figurative in application. Again, in "manie, procedant d'vne humeur trop melancholique" (Vol. II, p. 204), Belleforest uses *humeur* in practically the physical sense, though with a suggestion of the influence on character; but Fenton's translation—"humor of madnes, proceding of a vaine braine" (Vol. I, p. 88)—transfers humour to the phrase indicating mental state and so gives the word far greater significance for disposition or character bent.

The significance of the word humour in Fenton's interpretation of character, and his fondness for expanding his original by the addition of phrases containing the word will appear from the following parallels between Belleforest and Fenton:

Fenton, *Tragicall Discourses*	Belleforest, *Histoires Tragiques*
For yf the desyre of thy litle livynge in the countrey, and glisteringe shewe of thy greate house . . . had not sturred up the covetous humour of that ravenouse marchaunte (Vol. I, p. 33).	Si tu n'eusse encor ce petit domaine que tu as aux champs & ceste spacieuse maison en ville, personne n'eust enuié ton estat (Vol. II, p. 146).
For how canne a man lay a more sewer foundation of perpetuall glorye, then in correctinge the humoure of hys fowle appetite and conquerynge the unbridled affections of the wilful mind (p. 40).	Et quelle plus grande gloire peut acquerir l'homme qu'en vainquant soy mesme, & chastiant ses affections (p. 157).

Wherin, I fedd the hongry humor of my affection with such alarams and contraryetie of conceites, that havinge by thys meane loste the necessary appetite of the stomake, etc. (p. 76).	Ie me consumoy de sorte, que perdant l'appetit, etc. (p. 195).
And he that in the choice of his wyfe respectes chieflye her beautie and greatnes of porcion . . . escapeth seldom without a sprit of grudge or cyvill discension disturbynge hys quiet, wyth a continuall humour of frettynge disposition feedynge hys mynde (pp. 79, 80).	Il n'echape gueres souuent le malheur qu'vn esprit de dissention ne se brouille parmy leur mesnage (p. 198).
How can he be acquited from an humor of a frantike man, who, etc. (p. 164).	Mais qui seroit ce fol, que voudroit, etc. (Vol. I, p. 406).
Wherin he suffered himselfe to be so much subject and overcome with the rage of this follie, that, according to the jelowse humor of th' Ytalyan, he thoughte every man that loked in her face, etc. (p. 176).	Fut si estrange sa folie, qu'il luy sembloit que tous ceux qui la regardent, etc. (p. 406).
Neyther hath this folyshe humor of jelowsy so much power to enter into the hart of the vertuous and wise man; who neyther wyll give his wife such cause to abuse herselfe towardes hym, nor suspect her wythout great occasyon (p. 177).	Le vertueux & prudent homme ne soupconnera iamais rien sans vne preuue euidente (p. 417).

Four of Fenton's stories are also translated by Painter in his *Palace of Pleasure,* and it is interesting to study the difference between the two translations in regard to the use of humour. The stories are Discourses I, VII, XI, and XIII of *The Tragicall Discourses,* corresponding, according to the original edition, to numbers XXX, XXIV, XXVII, and XXIX, respectively, in the Second Tome of *The Palace of Pleasure.* In Fenton's translation of these stories, humour occurs in the transferred sense at least twenty-five times; in Painter's, the word does not occur at all except in the physiological sense.[1] Two of these stories I have already compared with Belleforest's versions and have found that in the French humour is not used at all except in a physiological sense. Some parallel passages taken from the "Countess of Celant" story in Belleforest, Painter, and Fenton will show the relation of the three with regard to the interest in humours.

Belleforest	Painter	Fenton
Cognoissant son inclination (Vol. II, p. 76).	Knowing hir inclination (Vol. III, ed. Jacobs, p. 45).	Not ignorant of the humor of her inclination (Vol. II, p. 4).
Ces Mantoüans, qui ont tousiours quelque martel en teste? (p. 83).	The Mantuanes, whose suspicious heads are ful of hammers working in the same? (pp. 49, 50).	The Mantuans, whose heades are the common fordge whereupon the humour of frettynge jelousye doth alwaies beate? (p. 11).
Le Comte . . . batant les buissons, tandis que la proye estoit preste a sortir, luy dit (p. 86).	The Counte . . . beating the Bushes vntill the praye was ready to spryng, replyed (p. 51).	Th'erle . . . fedynge the humor of his fortune, judged yt no point of good husbandry to loase his frute . . . but beatinge the bushe as the birde was readie to go oute, recharged her with seconde admonishement (p. 14).
De mesme se resolut d'y mettre ordre, & luy fermer le pas auant qu'elle eust gaigné la campagne (p. 89).	Whereuppon hee resolued to take order and stop hir passage before she had won the field (p. 53).	Wherefore, he accompted it an acte of wisedom, to take up the vaine that fedd those humours, and stop her course afore she gained the plaine feelde (p. 16).
Toutesfois parloit-il au plus loin de ce qu'il en pensoit (p. 107).	Notwithstandyng, he sayde more than he ment to do (p. 63).	Saith he . . . feedyng her humour wyth franke wordes, dissimulynge, notwithstandynge, that which he thought (p. 34).

[1]Cf. Jacobs's edition, Vol. III, pp. 172, 178, 229, 316 for this use. With the last passage compare the corresponding one in Fenton (Vol. I, p. 65), where humour is used in the same sense.

Ce ieune Comte . . . se retira de ceste emprise, & osta de sa teste toute l'affectio*n* amoureuse . . . Et à fin qu'il n'eust occasion de s'y amuser, & que la presence ne le surprist derechef, & ne le rendist encor poursuyuant de celle qui l'auoit requis & poursuyui, il se retire à Mila*n* (p. 108).	The yong Earle . . . forbare approche vnto hir house, and droue out of his heade al the Amorous affection. . . . And to the ende he might haue no cause to thinke vpon hir, or that his presence should make hym slaue againe to hir that first pursued him, he retired in good time to Millan (p. 64).	The erle . . . checked the humour of hys accustomed desyer. . . . And because he woulde aswell remove the cause as take awaye the disease, ferynge leaste eyther the viewe of her presence, or some force of newe charme, mighte eftesones enchante hym and sett abroche the humor of former desyers, he retired immediatlye to Myllan (p. 36).

These passages indicate Fenton's predilection for the word humour and at the same time the number of shaded meanings that the word has for him.[1] The very fact, also, that he has often wrested the wording of his original in order to bring in humour, suggests his tendency to interpret character from the point of view of medieval science. Moreover, his attitude to his material seems to be more consciously analytic, didactic, and moral than Belleforest's, despite Belleforest's, or rather, perhaps, Bandello's, love for pointing a moral. Fenton's especial importance for Jonson, indeed, lies not in his use of humour alone, but in his use of the word along with a seriousness of purpose and a conception of character that connect him with Jonson. Fenton's Epistle Dedicatory to Lady Mary Sidney proclaims the seriousness of his message, and also suggests strongly a program of humours. After declaring that his purpose in selecting the stories for translation has been to present examples of virtue to be followed and of vice to be shunned, Fenton continues (*Tragicall Discourses,* Vol. I, pp. 7-9):

My seconde endevor was bent to observe the necessitie of the tyme; chiefly for that, uppon the viewe and examples of oure auncesters lyves, the fraile ymps of this age maye finde cause of shame in theyr owne

[1]Besides the passages that I quote, these six stories from Fenton show the use of humour on the following pages: Vol. I, pp. 23, 24, 37, 38, 45, 55, 77, 89, 90, 92, 110, 126, 128, 180, 184, 190; Vol. II, pp. 6, 174, 189, 239, 247, 259, 267, 291.

abuses . . . the Historians of olde tyme (in theyr severall recordes of the actes, conquestes, and noble attemptes, of Princes and greate men) have lefte oute nothynge servyng for the ornamente and institution of mannes lyfe; not forgettynge to sett oute also in naturall coollers theyr tyrannye, and other vices, wythe contempte of vertue . . . they allure, by traines of familyaritye, every succession, to embrace and beholde, as in a glasse, the undoubted meane that is hable, and wyll, brynge theym to . . . perfection in vertue. Whyche, also, moved me to use a speciall discrecion in coollynge oute suche examples as beste aggreed wyth the condicion of the tyme,[1] and also were of moste freshe and familyar memorye; to the ende that, wyth the delyte in readynge my dedication, I maye also leave, to all degrees, an appetitt and honeste desyere to honor vertue and holde vice in due detestation. And, albeit, at the firste sighte, theis discourses maye importe certeyne vanytyes or fonde practises in love, yet I doubte not to bee absolved of suche intente by the judgement of the indifferent sorte, seinge I have rather noted diversitie of examples in sondrye younge men and women, approvynge sufficientlye the inconvenience happenynge by the pursute of lycenceous desyer, then affected in anye sorte suche uncerteyne follyes. For heare maye bee seene suche patternes of chastetye, and maydes so assured and constant in vertue, that they have not doubted rather to reappose a felicitye in the extreme panges of death then to fall by anye violent force into the daunger of the fleshelye ennemye to theyr honour. In lyke sorte appeareth here an experience of wounderfull vertues in men; who, albeit hadd power to use and commande the thinge they chieflye desyered, yet, bridlynge wythe maine hande, the humour of theyr inordinate luste, vanquished all mocions of sensualytye, and became maisters of theym selves, by abstaynynge from that whereunto they felte provocation by nature. Who desyereth to see the follye of a foolishe lover, passionynge hymselfe uppon creditt, the impudencie of a maide, or other woman, renouncynge the vowe of her fayth or honor due to virginitie, the sharpp pennance attendynge the rashe choice of greate ladyes in seekynge to matche in anye sorte wythe degrees of inferior condicion; or who wisheth to bee privie to th' inconveniences in love, howe he frieth in the flame of the fyrste affection, and after, groweth not onelye colde of himselfe, but is easelye converted into a contrarye shapp and disposition of deadlye hate—maye bee heare assisted wyth more than double experience touchinge all those evills. . . . And who takes pleasure to beholde the fyttes and panges of a frantique man, incensed to synister conceites by the suggestion of frettynge jelouzye, forcynge hym to effectes of absolute desperation; the due plage of disloyaltye, in both kyndes, with the glorye of hym who marcheth under the enseigne of a contrarye vertue; a man of the churche, of dissolute lyving, punished with publike reproche; or the villenie of the greedye usurer,

[1]With this expression and the similar one in the first line of this quotation from Fenton compare Jonson's demand that literature be "after the fancie of the tyme" (p. 8 *supra*).

makyng no conscience to preferr oppen perjury in suppressynge th' innocent cause,—maye fynde here to satisfye his longynge at full. . . . I, with the tormentes that pinched here suche as labored in a passion of follye and fond desyer, maye worke a terror to all those that hereafter unhappelye syp of the cupp of suche ragynge infection.

This rather full quotation sets forth Fenton's general plan and shows his accord with the didactic purpose of literature in his age. He chooses examples that fit "the condicion of the tyme," and his purpose is to reform men, to bring them out of their evil humours. To a much greater extent than Jonson he sets the ideal beside the evil; and both men represent the punishment of vices. The program for the treatment of life which Fenton here puts before himself is much like Jonson's, and many evils that would come under the head of humours are included. The term humour occurs in the quotation only once, and then is applied to lust as a provocation of nature, a sense much nearer to the physical meaning than the ordinary use but agreeing with Jonson's definition. Other words are also used indicative of the inclination of men to vice and folly; as, disposition, condition, motion, provocation of nature, infection.

More significant for Fenton's conscious choice of the word humour in connection with the treatment of character is the way in which he has translated the arguments of the stories. These arguments give, not the gist of the story, but the theme and the moral, and, as each story is a study of an inclination or a vice, Fenton has naturally had many opportunities to add the word humour. Indeed, some of the vices and follies mentioned in the Epistle Dedicatory are here called humours by Fenton.[1] One of the most interesting of these arguments is that of Discourse II, which contains an elaborate comparison of the bodily humours with the inclinations of the mind.[2] The comparison suggests that in Jon-

[1]The moralizing openings, or *sommaires*, of the separate stories in the *Histoires Tragiques*, which Fenton in translating has called arguments, often show a close kinship in ideas to the Epistle Dedicatory of *The Tragicall Discourses;* so that, even if the original may not explain Fenton's use of humour, the critical opinions of Bandello doubtless did have an influence on Fenton's ideals.

[2]Here even Belleforest uses *humeur* in a more or less figurative sense. The passage in which the word occurs is one of the two discussed above (p. 47). The other uses of humour which I quote from the arguments have been added by Fenton.

son's definition, and the argument closes with a conception akin to Jonson's famous conception of the mental state that produces evil.

Meates . . . albeit . . . good of theimselves, yet, being swallowed in glottonous sorte, they do not only procure a surfeyt with unsavery indisgestion, but also, converting our auncient healthe and force of nature into humors of debylytie destillinge thorowe all the partes of the bodye, do corrupte the blodde which of itselfe afore was pure and without infection. Even suche is the disposition of love, whose effectes, directed by reason . . . be not suche enemies indeede to the quiet of our lyfe, as necessary meanes to reforme the rudenes of our owne nature. . . . But who . . . without advise or judgemente, will throwe himselfe hedlonge into the golphe of a folishe and conning phantasye, escapes hardly without the rewarde whiche that frantike passion yeldeth ordenarely to suche as are unhappelye partakers of suche infection.

Then, after mentioning such examples of uncontrolled passions as ought to teach men "to restraine the humor of their owne madnes," Fenton adds:

With what enamel so ever they seke to guild and colour such vices, yet can they not be excused of an humor of madnes, proceding of a vaine braine, exposing frutes according to the spirit or guide that possesseth them.

The following are some additional examples of Fenton's use of humour in the arguments prefixed to the discourses:

How can he be acquited from an humor of a frantike man, who, without any cause of offence in the world, committes cruel execution upon his innocente wife [through jealousy] (Vol. I, p. 164).

I have preferred this example of an Italian countesse, who, so long as her first husband (not ignorant of the humor of her inclination) [to lust], etc. (Vol. II, p. 4).

Amongest all the passions which nature sturreth up to disquiet the mind of man, there is none of such tyrany or kepes us more in awe then the detestable humor of covetousnes, and raging appetyt of whoredome (*ibid.*, p. 130).

Albeit he was younge, ful of wanton humors, and nothing degenerating from th' Ytalyan inclynacion touching the desier of the fleshe, etc. (p. 131).

Checked the humor of his former apetit [of lust] (p. 132).

For, albeit the sondrie enormities growing daily amongest us by the unbridled humour of oure affection, which we commonly cal love, argue the same to bee a passion of moste daungerous and perverse corrupcion, etc. (p. 214).

Albeit it [love] be an infection of it selfe, yet it serves also as a contrepoison to drive out another venym . . . not meaning for all this to perswade that it is of necessitie we make ourselves subject altogether to this humor of good and evill disposicion (p. 214).

Th' experience is not straunge, nowe a dayes, what humor of rage doth directe our fraile youth, governed by the planet of love (p. 238).

Fenton's use, then, is clearly anticipatory of Jonson's. The fact that Fenton restricts himself almost entirely to a study of love narrows his field, but the various phases of the passion—love, lust, jealousy—are several times spoken of as humours. Jonson calls love a humour in *The Case is Altered* (II, 2), and in the passage quoted above (p. 36) from *Cynthia's Revels* Phantaste discusses in detail the phases of the humour love. Lust is handled rather sparingly in Jonson, but appears in Volpone and Epicure Mammon. Jealousy Jonson constantly treats as a humour, dealing with it in Kitely, Corvino, and Fitzdottrel, in Corvino, at least, with almost tragic force. Not only the narrowness of Fenton's field but his bent toward the tragic make comparison with Jonson difficult. Fenton's program of the tendencies to be reprehended includes much more serious evils than Jonson's. Humour with the translator of *The Tragicall Discourses* carries no comic significance, the inclination being considered so forceful a passion as to call for the terms madness, rage, etc. But in intention and conception Fenton's attitude to character and his treatment of humours is practically the same as that indicated by Jonson's definition. There are some distinctions to be made, however, in the use of the word. Fenton does not give the term humour so broad a significance as Jonson does, having seemingly the physical side always closely associated with it. Hence it is that with Fenton disease, infection, and similar terms are more frequently synonyms of humour than in later writers. Fenton, for instance, certainly thinks of actual bodily humours when he says, "Love is an humor of infection derived of the corrupte partes in our selves" (Vol. I, p. 89). The examples which I have quoted show that he does not wander far from this physical meaning, and they contain no hint of the use of humour to cover a fad. Furthermore, Fenton apparently does not yet feel that the word carries its true figurative meaning alone, and he usually adds a reinforcing word, as in "the humor of her inclination," "humor of madnes," "humor of . . . disposicion," "humour of oure affection."[1] All this suggests a lack of confidence in such a use of the word and would seem to indicate that humour in the derived sense is just taking hold on the language in Fenton's time.

Considering the early date, even though there is no evidence that Fenton's work had great influence, his tendency towards a critical program is very important as indicative of consciously new trends. He connects the medieval idea of the moral purpose of character drawing and of story telling with the keen analysis of actual life and the newly developing literary art of the Renaissance. He has a program that is clearly perceived, extensive, and definite; it involves a moral application of his stories and characters; accordingly, strict attention is given to a single idea in characterization; humour is the word used to indicate the phases of character studied; and the relation of his work to the condition of the time is stressed. In much he is indebted to Bandello, but he makes a great advance himself in the emphasis that he lays through his own employment of humour upon the critical analysis of character. In all of these respects he is a clear forerunner of Jonson. Mere translator though he was, his work was of a kind to be of vital importance in helping the medieval English attitude to character treatment to persist without a serious break under new critical conditions and even in connection with romantic fiction.

By the time that the word humour and the conception of character treatment which it involves had made its beginning in English thought, a very kindred conception of art in characterization had entered from the classics in the idea of decorum. I have already expressed my dissent from Professor Spingarn's view that the humour conception was derived largely from the conception of decorum. The two ideas are doubtless related, however, and inevitably interacted on each other. From the very opening of the Renaissance, in my opinion, the classics exercised their influence on the attitude to character treatment and on literary art, an influence that gathered force. But until criticism developed conscious theory, it worked through the native art rather than became a substitute for it. The attitude of the Renaissance that gave

[1]In some cases this reinforcing word is no doubt due, however, to the fact that Fenton adds humour to the word that Belleforest had already used to indicate bent or inclination.

the name humanism to the study of the classics and under the principle of decorum emphasized a dominant trait in character portrayal undoubtedly furnished a powerful stimulus to the transfer from the portrayal of character through abstractions to the vivid picturing of types of folly drawn from real life. As typical of the attitude of Renaissance classicists to the art of characterization, Wilson and Sidney may be chosen, representing a stretch of about fifteen years of time on either side of Fenton's work. Wilson belongs to the school of Ascham and Cheke, a school of men who were thorough classicists and yet English in temper and ready champions of pure English diction and of native traditions. Apparently under the influence of this loyalty to English ideals and traditions, Wilson uses contemporary types rather than classic to illustrate the classic ideal of characterization. Sidney represents a more exact adherence to classical and Italian theories of criticism with far less regard paid to native art, though his attention to moral symbolism is almost medieval.

Wilson in discussing "description" (*The Arte of Rhetorique,* pp. 178, 179) deals with the method of handling characters in oratory. Under the marginal heading "Diuersitie of natures" he says:

> Men are painted out in their colours. . . . The Englishman for feeding and chaunging for apparell. The Dutchman for drinking. The Frenchman for pride & inconstance. The Spanyard for nimblenes of body, and much disdaine: the Italian for great wit and policie: the Scots for boldnesse, and the Boeme for stubbornesse.
>
> Many people are described by their degree, as a man of good yeares, is coumpted sober, wise, and circumspect: a young man wilde and carelesse: a woman babling, inconstaunt, and readie to beleeue all that is tolde her.
>
> By vocation of life, a Souldier is coumpted a great bragger, and a vaunter of himself: A Scholer simple: A Russet coate, sad, and sometimes craftie: a Courtier, flattering: a Citizen, gentle.

Then he discusses the conventions even for historical personages, apparently using "comelinesse" as a synonym for decorum:

> In describing of persons, there ought alwaies a comelinesse to bee vsed, so that nothing be spoken, which may bee thought is not in them. As if one shall describe Henry the sixth, he might cal him gentle, milde of nature, led by perswasion, and readie to forgiue, carelesse for wealth, suspecting none, mercifull to all, fearefull in aduersitie, and without forecast to espie his misfortune. Againe, for Richard the third, I might

bring him in, cruel of heart, ambicious by nature, enuious of mind, a deepe dissembler, a close man for weightie matters, hardie to reuenge, and fearfull to lose his high estate, trustie to none, liberall for a purpose, casting still the worst, and hoping euer the best.

While the emphasis in these passages is on the social type, so that nationality, class, or vocation is stressed as in medieval art, or else on the historical individual, the demand so early in the century for the treatment of character according to a fundamental trait is significant for the development of humours as well as for such later kindred studies as Shakespeare's Richard III or Hotspur. In Wilson's connection of the fundamental trait with definitely marked social types we see every opportunity for the social types of Chaucer's *Prologue* and the abstractions of the morality to fuse, and out of the fusion to gain greater individuality for the social type through the study of man's inner nature and greater verisimilitude for the abstraction through its connection with life.

Sidney's discussion of the problem of character treatment shows a far better formulation of principles than Wilson's or Fenton's. Though he has gained this greater definiteness by attention to classic and Italian criticism and literature rather than English, his utterances have some significance for the humour conception.[1] Indeed, most of Sidney's critical ideas are important for Jonson. Sidney's defense of the dramatic unities, his arraignment of the absurdities of romantic plays, his stress on the moral function of literature, his classic principle that "comedy is an imitation of the common errors of our life" (p. 28), doubtless influenced Jonson's theories as well as those of other Elizabethan writers. It is antecedently probable, too, that Sidney's principle of emphasizing the fundamental trait in character in order to convey the moral lesson, reinforced the tendencies of Jonson's work. The following passages show Sidney's attitude to the portrayal of character:

[1]Professor Spingarn's best statement of his view of the connection between Sidney and Jonson's humour treatment is as follows: "Even the conception of 'humours' and of their function in comedy, in the induction to *Every Man out of his Humour*, is in a measure the adaptation of a fashionable phrase of the day to Sidney's theory of comedy, though the genius of Jonson has intensified and individualized the portrayal of character beyond the limits of mere Horatian and Renaissance *decorum*." *Critical Essays of the Seventeenth Century*, Vol. I, p. xv. In this same connection Professor Spingarn gives references to the passages that I quote from Sidney.

> This doth the comedy handle so, in our private and domestical matters, as with hearing it we get, as it were, an experience what is to be looked for of a niggardly Demea, of a crafty Davus, of a flattering Gnatho, of a vain-glorious Thraso; and not only to know what effects are to be expected, but to know who be such, by the signifying badge given them by the comedian (*The Defense of Poesy*, ed. Cook, p. 28).
>
> But I speak to this purpose, that all the end of the comical part be not upon such scornful matters as stir laughter only, but mixed with it that delightful teaching which is the end of poesy. And the great fault, even in that point of laughter, and forbidden plainly by Aristotle, is that they stir laughter in sinful things, which are rather execrable than ridiculous; or in miserable, which are rather to be pitied than scorned. For what is it to make folks gape at a wretched beggar or a beggarly clown, or, against law of hospitality, to jest at strangers because they speak not English so well as we do? what do we learn? . . . But rather a busy loving courtier; a heartless threatening Thraso; a self-wise-seeming schoolmaster; a wry-transformed traveller: these if we saw walk in stage-names, which we play naturally, therein were delightful laughter and teaching delightfulness (*ibid.*, pp. 51, 52).

The idea is even expressed for tragedy (p. 28) where Sidney speaks of tragedy as making "tyrants manifest their tyrannical humours." The use of humour here, though in connection with tragedy and perhaps unconscious, is still interesting as showing at least the assimilation of Sidney's conception of character with the idea of inclination or bent. In another passage (pp. 16, 17), the abstract moral significance that lies back of the poet's treatment of character is illustrated by a large number of examples, drawn, with one exception, from the classics.

To my mind, however, Sidney's idea of moral symbolism in the portrayal of character and of consistency in treatment, or decorum, is not the same thing as the native idea of humours. It is similar, but accessory rather than essential to that ideal of character treatment in accordance with which Nashe and Lodge built up realistic sketches of English follies in the framework of the Seven Deadly Sins, and Jonson created characters, like Juniper and Brisk, by following lines of treament conventionalized for English types. Sidney seems to me not true enough to English art, not sufficiently imbued with the English spirit. His preference for classic examples marks a break with native tradition. For men like Fenton and Nashe with their eyes on actual life, classic types are of secondary interest. At any rate, in Sidney's discussions there is not the same native color or range of types or definite inclination toward an intimate study of English life that we find in Fenton, in Nashe, in Lodge later, and finally in Jonson. It is to these men with something of Jonson's provincial temper rather than to men like Sidney with his close attention to classic ideals and characters that we are to look for the development of the word humour and of the English types portrayed by Jonson under the conception of humour.

The first of these predecessors of Jonson to be mentioned is Lyly, who, though Italianate in many phases of his art, shows a strong prejudice for things English. It is in Lyly's *Euphues,* a dozen years after Fenton, that I have noted the next free use of humour in Jonson's sense to denote inclination. In spite of the fact that Jonson satirized Euphuism[1] along with other excesses in diction, there is reason for believing that *Euphues* may have attracted his more serious attention. Certainly the story shows the ordinary seriousness of purpose in treating characters and manners which prepares for Jonson. The ideal elements of character in Euphues are set over against the follies of Philautus, or self-love; and other phases of folly than those due to self-love are satirized and anatomized. In many instances it is follies of the same type, those arising from self-love, pride, pretension, that attract Jonson's rebuke; *Cynthia's Revels* has for its subtitle *The Fountain of Self-Love.*

In *Euphues* (*Works of Lyly,* ed. Bond, Vol. I, p. 196) there is a passage in which a number of character tendencies are denominated humours:

> But this I note, that for the most part they [would-be wits] stande so on their pantuffles, that they be secure of perills, obstinate in their owne opinions, impatient of labour, apte to conceiue wrong, credulous to beleeue the worst, ready to shake off their olde acquaintaunce without cause, and to condempne them without colour: All which humors are by somuch the more easier to bee purged, by howe much the lesse they haue festred the sinnewes.

Some other passages in which humour is used in *Euphues* with a kindred meaning are as follows:

[1]*Every Man out,* III, 1, gives in the term "anatomy of wit" applied to Saviolina the subtitle of *Euphues.* Cf. Koeppel, *Ben Jonson's Wirkung,* etc., for a list of echoes of *Euphues* in Jonson's works.

Althoughe these ensamples be harde to imitate, yet shoulde euery man do his endeuour to represse that hot and heady humor which he is by nature subiecte vnto (*Works,* Vol. I, pp. 278, 279).

My trust is you will deale in the like manner with *Euphues,* that if he haue not fead your humor, yet you will excuse him, etc. (*Works,* Vol. II, p. 10).

Those that . . . follow their own humour, and refuse the Phisitions remedy (*ibid.,* p. 33).

I see thy humor is loue, thy quarrell ielousie. . . . There is nothing that can cure the kings Euill, but a Prince . . . nothing purge thy humour, but . . . libertie (p. 95).

Then as one pleasing thy selfe in thine owne humour . . . thou rollest all thy wits to sifte Loue from Lust (p. 98).

But to wrest the will of man, or to wreath his heart to our humours, it is not in the compasse of Arte (p. 114).

If thy humour be such that nothing can feede it but loue, etc. (p. 156).

There can be nothing either more agreeable to my humour, or these Gentlewomens desires, then to vse some discourse (p. 163).

So that Nature might be sayd to frame vs for others humours not for our owne appetites (p. 165).

It is evident that Lyly uses humour with a much more assured application to character and in a greater number of shaded meanings than does Fenton. In these examples the word is applied to follies constantly, and has been extended to cover a momentary desire. There is even a suggestion, in the first passage quoted, of a list of humours and hence of the extension of the term to cover a fairly broad field of evils, while the word purge is used for the cure of these evils.[1]

Just as Jonson, while satirizing a fashion set by Lyly, may yet have owed something to Lyly's studies in character, so he may have been influenced toward his treatment of humours by Gabriel Harvey, whose affected diction was very probably satirized in Juniper of *The Case is Altered,* as Hart has shown.[2] The vocabulary of Juniper certainly indicates Jonson's familiarity with Harvey's works. Humour is a favorite word with Harvey. As early as 1579 he uses it several times in letters to Spenser in connection

[1]Lyly's dramas will be taken up later under a discussion of the dramatic treatments of humours.

[2]See p. 94 *infra..* Hart has pointed out the fact that Harvey's use of capricious is satirized in *The Case is Altered.* Harvey uses capricious nature, witte, veine, and humour. For this last phrase see *Works,* ed. Grosart, Vol. II, p. 54.

with follies that are indicative of temperament or character. For example, he writes:

But to let Titles and Tittles passe, and come to the very pointe in deede, which so neare toucheth my lusty Trauayler to the quicke, and is one of the prædominant humors *that* raigne in our co*m*mon Youths (*Works of Harvey,* Vol. I, p. 25).

Credite me, I will neuer linne baityng at you, til I haue rid you quite of this yonkerly, & womanly humor (*ibid.,* p. 26).

The conception of humour in the physical sense as influencing mental attitude is set forth in a passage from another of these letters:

All philosophye saith that the temperature and disposition [and] inclination of the mindes followythe the temperature and composition of the bodye. Galen, &c. (*ibid.,* p. 150).

It is especially in the quarrel with Nashe a dozen years later that Harvey makes the word humour do valiant duty:

This Martinish and Counter-martinish age: wherein the Spirit of Contradiction reigneth, and euerie one superaboundeth in his owne humor, euen to the annihilating of any other, without rime, or reason (*Foure Letters,* 1592; *Works,* Vol. I, p. 203).

Fie on grosse scurility, and impudent calumny: that wil rather goe to Hell in iest, then to heauen in earnest, and seeke not to reforme any vice, to backebite, and depraue euery person, that feedeth not their humorous fancy (*ibid.,* p. 204).

No man loather then my self, to contend with desperate | malecontents: or to ouerthwart obstinate Humoristes (*ibid.,* pp. 214, 215).

Euery Martin Iunior, and Puny Pierce, a monarch in the kingdome of his owne humour (*ibid.,* p. 233).

Indeede what more easie, then to finde the man by his humour, the Midas by his eares, the Calfe by his tongue, etc. (*Pierces Supererogation,* 1593; *Works,* Vol. II, p. 215).

That humorous rake, that affecteth the reputation of supreme Singularity (*ibid.,* p. 277).

With certain phrases in these attacks on Nashe compare Jonson's description of Puntarvolo as "wholly consecrated to singularity," and of Carlo Buffone as a "scurrilous and prophane jester; that . . . will transform any person into deformity. . . His religion is railing." Other phrases scattered throughout *Every Man out* and *Cynthia's Revels,* especially those dealing with the impudence of Carlo and Anaides, with fierce jesting, with backbiting, and so on, remind one of Harvey's characterization of Nashe.[1]

These three writers, Fenton, Lyly, and Harvey, represent three stages in the use of the term humour, covering a period of twenty-five years. Fenton employs the word to indicate disposition or characteristic inclination, but keeps near to the literal meaning and applies the term to seriously vicious tendencies. With Lyly the word is applied to follies, and Harvey about the same time shows the same use. By the time of Harvey's attacks on Nashe, however, humour in the figurative sense has become so common that the words humorous and humorist have been adopted to describe persons possessed of a humour, and humour has been extended to indicate an affectation, as the later examples from Harvey show. Both the derivatives appear frequently in Jonson's work, and humour as an affectation is constantly used by Jonson for purposes of satire. The last passages from Harvey are contemporaneous with the use of the term by Greene, Nashe, and many others; and by this time the idea of humours had reached a pretty full expansion in didactic prose.

During the years 1580 to 1592 Greene wrote a large number of stories in which—especially in those of his middle and late periods—the word humour occurs from time to time in various senses approaching Jonson's use. Some of these stories are merely studies of types embodying characteristic mental attitudes or moral inclinations. In *Planetomachia* (1585), for instance, Greene studies the influence of some of the planets upon the individual in developing one dominant trait that leads to evil. The control of particular planets over certain of the physical humours is discussed, and then Greene takes up the relation of these planets and humours to the "affections" of men. This idea of planetary influence is prominent with Lyly, Nashe, and others in the study of manners through the emphasis of one dominant humour or inclination in the individual; but it does not affect Jonson. Equally interesting is *Alcida: Greenes Metamorphosis* (1588), where Fiordespine's pride in beauty, Eriphila's wit and fickleness, and Marpesia's inability to keep a secret are studied as examples of social vices due to ab-

[1]The well-defined theories of the Renaissance on wit, jesting, etc., out of which these resemblances spring, are discussed in connection with Carlo Buffone of *Ev. M. out.*

normal or unwholesome bent in character. This work shows the influence of Lyly's *Euphues* with its study of the evil and the virtuous qualities of youth. In the slightly earlier *Euphues, his Censure to Philautus* (1587), Greene deals with passion, wisdom (or craft), fortitude, and liberality in a way which shows a greater indebtedness to Lyly, but the stressing of the qualities of youth as social is less marked than in *Alcida,* and so the work is less important as a force leading to Jonson. *The Farewell to Follie* (1591) contains several stories, in each of which is presented one supreme quality whose effect is ruinous. So this conception of character study enters into a number of Greene's works, though it is not always so completely the basis as in the stories mentioned above. His treatment of the unhealthy tendency in character is broad and embraces the deadly as well as the foolish or frivolous, for his stories are often tragic.

In a number of these studies of character, humour is applied to a quality or mood. In *Penelope's Web* (1587), Greene speaks of the "humorous perswasions" of Penelope's suitors (*Works,* ed. Grosart, Vol. V, p. 150) ; of the maid's willingness "to content her Ladies humour by beguyling the night with prattle" (p. 154) ; of "the chollericke humour and froward disposition of men" (p. 164) ; and of Saladyne's being "tickled with an inconstant humour" (p. 170). *Philomela* (1592) shows a closer approach to Jonson's use, especially in the treatment of jealousy. There is a rebuke for this "humor of iealousie" (Vol. XI, p. 120) and for the "disposition of a gelous man that woulde hazard the honour of his wife to content his owne suspitious humour" (p. 143). Later we read that his "Ielious humor was satisfied" (p. 183). In the same story there occur the phrases "amorous humour" (p. 173) and "passionate humour" (p. 142). In the *Vision* (1592) it is again jealousy to which the term humour is applied. The phrases "iealious humor" (Vol. XII, p. 230), "pestilent humor" (p. 239), and "féede his humour" (p. 247) are all used with reference to jealousy.

One of the most important writers of this "humour school" is Nashe. Some curious concrete representations of humour as indicative of the interest in the subject have been mentioned above. It is noticeable that most of these examples are quoted from Nashe. There are many uses of the term in his works, too many to dwell upon in view of the space already given to a study of the developing use of the word. It will be sufficient to quote Nashe's most characteristic passages and give reference to some of the others. One of his most important passages occurs in *Pierce Penilesse,* 1592, (*Works,* ed. McKerrow, Vol. I, pp. 219, 220):

> Some men there be that, building too much vpon reason, perswade themselues that there are no Diuels at all, but that this word *Dæmon* is such another morall of mischiefe, as the Poets Dame Fortune is of mishap: . . . so vnder the person of this olde *Gnathonicall* companion, called the Diuell, we shrowd all subtiltie masking vnder the name of simplicitie, all painted holines deuouring widowes houses, all gray headed Foxes clad in sheepes garments; so that the Diuell (as they make it) is onely a pestilent humour in a man, of pleasure, profit, or policie, that violently carries him away to vanitie, villanie, or monstrous hypocrisie: vnder vanitie I comprehend not onely all vaine Arts and studies whatsoeuer, but also dishonourable prodigalitie, vntemperate venery, and that hatefull sinne of selfe-loue, which is so common amongst vs: vnder villanie I comprehend murder, treason, theft, cousnage, cut-throat couetise, and such like: lastly, vnder hypocrisie, all Machiauilisme, puritanisme, and outward gloasing with a mans enemie, and protesting friendship to him that I hate and meane to harme, all vnder-hand cloaking of bad actions with Common-wealth pretences; and, finally, all Italionate conueyances, as to kill a man, and then mourne for him, *quasi vero* it was not by my consent, to be a slaue to him that hath iniur'd me, and kisse his feete for opportunitie of reuenge, to be seuere in punishing offenders, that none might haue the benefite of such meanes but my selfe, to vse men for my purpose and then cast them off, to seeke his destruction that knowes my secrets; and such as I haue imployed in any murther or stratagem, to set them priuilie together by the eares, to stab each other mutually, for feare of bewraying me; or, if that faile, to hire them to humor one another in such courses as may bring them both to the gallowes. These, and a thousand more such sleights, hath hypocrisie learned by trauailing strange Countries.

This selection is especially valuable because the word humour is used for a long series of vices or follies which, as Nashe says, carry the man away, and these evils are classified under three heads that might well cover Jonson's program. Of the humours that Nashe mentions under vanity, Jonson satirizes especially vain studies, dishonorable prodigality, and self-love; of the comic motives mentioned under villainy, Jonson deals also with covetise and cozenage; and of those mentioned under hypocrisy, Jonson satirizes especially Puritanism. The many phases of Machiavellism which Nashe enlarges upon so fully are rather foreign to Jonson's treatment of hypocritical friendship, but similar studies do occur in Angelo of *The Case is Altered,* Carlo of *Every Man out,* Tucca of *Poetaster,* etc. Some of the vices that Nashe enumerates can also be paralleled in the tragedies of Jonson.

A second passage of some importance is from *The Terrors of the Night* (1593). It is extremely interesting as filling in the list of humours given in the passage from *Pierce Penilesse,* and as making Nashe's program of humours more nearly equivalent to Jonson's. Of course a number of typical social evils that are treated by Jonson are analyzed elsewhere in Nashe's works, but my interest here lies in the use of the word humour for these types. The passage reads (*Works,* Vol. I, p. 353):

> As for the spirits of the aire, which haue no other visible bodies or form, but such as by the vnconstant glimmering of our eies is begotten; they are in truth all show and no substance, deluders of our imagination, & nought els. Carpet knights, politique statesmen, women & children they most conuers with. Carpet knights they inspire with a humor of setting big lookes on it, being the basest cowards vnder heauen, couering an apes hart with a lions case, and making false alarums when they mean nothing but a may-game. Politique statesmen they priuily incite to bleare the worlds eyes with clowdes of common wealth pretences, to broach any enmitie or ambitious humor of their owne vnder a title of their cuntries preseruation. To make it faire or fowle when they list to procure popularity or induce a preamble to some mightie peece of prowling, to stir vp tempests round about, & replenish heauen with prodigies and wonders, the more to ratifie their auaritious religion. Women they vnder-hand instruct to pownce and boulster out theyr brawn-falne deformities, to new perboile with painting | their rake-leane withered visages, to set vp flaxe shops on their forheads when all their owne haire is dead and rotten, to sticke their gums round with Comfets when they haue not a tooth left in their heads to help them to chide withall.
>
> Children they seduce with garish obiects and toyish babies, abusing them many yeares with slight vanities. So that you see all their whole influence is but thin ouercast vapours, flying clouds dispersed with the least winde of wit or vnderstanding.

A passage occurring a page or two earlier may also be quoted here (pp. 351, 352):

> Those spirits of the fire . . . bee by nature ambitious, haughty, and proud, nor do they loue vertue for it selfe any whit, but because they would ouerquell and outstrip others with the vaineglorious osten-

tation of it. A humor of monarchizing and nothing els it is, which makes them affect rare quallified studies.[1]

In the passage from *Pierce Penilesse* general classes of humours are discussed; in those from *The Terrors of the Night* Nashe gives specific types, applying the word humour to them several times. There is the humour of the cowardly soldier, as in Bobadill; the humour of the politic statesman, as in Sir Politick Would-be; the more general humour of women who paint, pad, and wear false hair, as in Mistress Otter; and the "humour of monarchizing" or of "vaineglorious ostentation," as in Brisk and numerous other Jonsonian characters.

Various other types, tendencies, and follies are spoken of as humours in Nashe's works. For instance, in *Pierce Penilesse* alone there are the following examples, besides those given above, most of them being pretty nearly akin to Jonson's uses in his analyses of character:

Malecontent humor (Vol. I, p. 157).

Hee will bee humorous, forsoth, and haue a broode of fashions by himselfe (p. 169).

A yoong Heyre . . . falles in a quarrelling humor with his fortune (p. 170).

The Italian is a more cunning proud fellowe, that hides his humour [of pride] far cleanlier (p. 176).

This [the craze for antiques] is the disease of our newfangled humorists, that know not what to doe with their welth (p. 183).

He hearing me so inquisitiue in matters aboue humane | capacity, entertained my greedie humour with this answere (p. 218).

Yet newfangled lust . . . brought him out of loue with this greedy, bestiall humour (p. 223).

The Foxe . . . grew in league with an old Camelion, that could put on all shapes, and imitate any colour . . . that with these sundrie

[1]In this same connection (Vol. I, pp. 354-357) Nashe has a discussion of physical humours—still considered in relation to the spirits of fire, air, and earth—and of the influence of these humours on the mind, especially as conducing to phantasy, dreams, etc. Nashe seems to have been especially attracted in these years to the science and associated superstitions of the day; and, consequently, he is constantly connecting the science and manners of the age by turning from the physical side to the moral and mental inclinations of men, and especially to social evils. Nashe expresses the same idea of the influence of an excess of one physical humour on the mind that Fenton, or Bandello, and Harvey do. He says, for instance, in one place (p. 370), "No humor in generall in our bodies ouer-flowing or abounding, but the tips of our thoughts are dipt in hys tincture."

formes, (applyde to mens variable humors) he might perswade the world, etc. (p. 224).[1]

A great number of Jonson's characters might have been suggested by Nashe's studies and especially by *Pierce Penilesse.* To my mind, no writer of the sixteenth century before Jonson, not even Chapman in his *Humorous Day's Mirth,* formed a more definite idea of humour as applied to character or organized a more definite system for the study of various follies than Nashe.[2] The one passage from *Pierce Penilesse* that was quoted at length alone suggests an extensive and organized *comedie humaine* of humour types. There is little doubt, I think, that Nashe was one of the most potent influences in Jonson's work. When we come to a discussion of the early plays separately, a number of resemblances between the work of the two men will give added strength to this idea.

Nashe's plan, as shown in the whole of *Pierce Penilesse,* of classifying and studying comprehensively social follies, was continued by Lodge in *Wits Miserie.* Lodge's importance for Jonson lies not so much in his contribution to the conception of humours, for his use of humour is more or less casual, but in his development of the character sketch of the Theophrastan type, a matter which calls for separate notice later. Lodge's use of humour in *Wits Miserie,* however, is almost altogether in the characteristic Jonsonian sense. I have noted the following examples:

This humour [of dicing] must be satisfied (Hunterian Club, p. 41).

As some poetical humor inspires me (p. 55).

In what blindnesse and error that miserable man is, that suffereth himselfe to bée conquered by this cursed humor [of envy] (p. 58).

[1]The following are some additional uses of humour in Nashe, apparently not so important for the development of Jonson's conception and yet showing a variety of meanings; as, essential bent of character, momentary mood, affectation: Vol. I, pp. 7, 114, 311, 320, 375; Vol. II, pp. 262 and 298; Vol. III, pp. 26, 30, 89, 102, 120, 134, 149, 151, 368, etc.

[2]The interest in the organization and classification of follies evidenced in Nashe is also seen at times in Jonson's humour plays. At the opening of *Every Man out,* Asper runs over a list of evil-doers according to profession, the strumpet, ruffian, broker, usurer, lawyer, courtier, with "their extortion, pride, or lusts." And in the Palinode at the end of *Cynthia's Revels,* the play that practically closes the stricter humour studies, Jonson mentions a large number of foolish fashions and customs that he has attacked most severely, and groups them under certain kinds of humours, such as swaggering, affected, fantastic, simpering, and self-loving humours. The various humours of lovers are also analyzed in *Cynthia's Revels* in Phantaste's speech, quoted above, about her "Book of Humours."

If he counsel any man in his owne humor [of malice], he laboreth, etc. . . . Flie this fiend and his humor (p. 59).

Humor of impatience (p. 64).

He will not . . . affect anie learning that féedes not his humor (p. 72).

Féed him in his humor [of immoderate joy], you shall haue his heart (p. 84).

Willing that the Ciuill world . . . should be infected with his humor [of idleness] (p. 94).

The ordinarie seate of this humor [pusillanimity] is in the sensualitie of the heart (p. 97).[1]

After 1596, the date of *Wits Miserie*, or even after *The Terrors of the Night* of 1593, it is useless to attempt any record of the growing use of the word humour, though I shall revert to the matter in connection with Jonson's forerunners in the drama. Humour occurs frequently in Dickenson's *Arisbas* (1594), in Breton's *Wits Trenchmour* (1597), etc. It occurs in what seem to be the earliest formal satires, Donne's (*ca.* 1593). Indeed, the term is quite as well suited to a study of folly in satire as in comedy, and we find Guilpin in *Skialetheia* (1598) and Rowlands a little later in his satires stressing the word as much as Jonson does in his work of the same period. Isolated examples of the use of the word are met in a great number of the writers, early and late, of the last quarter of the sixteenth century, but above only those writers could be considered who used the word humour frequently and to cover, as it were, a series of follies and evils.[2]

With the word humour in the Jonsonian sense already in great vogue, and with Jonson's scheme for the treatment of character already established in literature, we have in the character sketch of the so-called Theophrastan type a further contribution to the development of Jonson's satiric comedies. The character sketch in some form, of course, exists all the way through English literature. Chaucer's *Prologue* consists of character sketches, and its

[1]Outside of *Wits Miserie* the word humour is rare in Lodge's works. There are, however, some scattering uses of it, as in *Margarite of America*, Hunterian Club, pp. 18 and 50, and in the early *Forbonius and Prisceria*, p. 62.

[2]I have naturally not attempted to find every instance of the use of the word in any writer. In some, as in Greene, I have left many instances of the use unrecorded.

influence must have been fairly extensive. For example, late in the sixteenth century *Greenes Vision* and *The Cobler of Canterburie* have a number of character sketches in verse directly imitative of Chaucer. *The Ship of Fools, The Fraternitye of Vacabondes,* Harman's *Caueat, The Hye Way to the Spyttel Hous,* and other works of the sixteenth century show the descriptive method of outlining a character briefly. They often stress the essential quality of the type that is treated, but in the main the tendency is to deal with social classes or with individual traits that are external. Often, as in *The Ship of Fools,* the actions of characters are stressed rather than the qualities. The Theophrastan character sketch is a different thing, however, different usually in method of approach but especially in art. It describes a type which represents, not the social group, but the dominant mental or moral trait in the individual. This character tendency as applied to the individual is almost exactly the "humour" of Jonson's satiric comedy,[1] and the character sketch very readily came into use in satire on humours. Moreover, in its art the Theophrastan character sketch is preeminently suited to the satiric purpose of the comedy of humours. It is in prose, succinct, and pointed in analysis; there is a satirical or ironical turn to it; and the language often becomes aphoristic, or epigrammatic, or antithetical. In its compression it resembles the poetic epigram, which is a corresponding growth and contributed largely to the hold that the character sketch took upon the comedy of humours. Through the two influences the brief satiric analysis of character became associated with the study of humours.

Jonson himself has often been considered an innovator in the use of the Theophrastan character sketch. He was obviously, however, following in the steps of others, especially of Lodge. Indeed this type of character sketch was introduced into English literature much earlier than many have supposed, as early at least as 1576. In this year was published *The Mirror of Mans lyfe, Englisht by H. K[erton]* (from the Latin of Lotharius, afterwards Innocent

[1]Harris, *Mod. Lang. Notes,* Vol. X, pp. 44-46, "The Origin of the Seventeenth Century Idea of Humours," calls attention to this kinship, but, failing to recognize the complex nature of the origin, he overstresses the influence of Aristotle's analyses of character and of the sketches of his pupil Theophrastus.

III).[1] The work is chiefly a religious treatise, but there are several treatments of character that show the point of view and the art of the Theophrastan sketch. They occur in Book II, Chapter 13, "The properties of a Couetous man"; Chapter 24, "Of the Ambitious man"; Chapter 28, "The properties of a proude man," continued in Chapters 30-32; and Chapter 34, "Of the properties of arrogante men." These chapters are really short paragraphs, terse and direct in treatment of topics. The analysis of character is just in Jonson's manner, though the influence of the Bible is often to be detected. Of the proud man it is said: "He is rashe, bolde, boasting, arrogant, soone moued, and very importunate" (Chap. 28), and "The proude man . . . thinketh the party to whom he vseth speeche, thereby to reape profite and great commoditie: but if with curtesie hee embrace any man, hee presumeth his countenance, to gaine hym great credite. He seldome vseth any friendly affection, but alwayes imperiously dothe shewe his authoritie. His Pryde, his arrogancie, and·hys disdaine, is of more force wyth hym, than courage, or manhoode" (Chap. 32). Probably not long after the appearance of *The Mirror of Mans lyfe,* Ulpian Fulwell published *The First Parte, of the Eyghth liberall Science: Entituled, Ars adulandi, the Arte of Flatterie,*[2] which contains character sketches exactly in the Theophrastan manner. The characterizations of Pierce Pickthanke and Drunken Dickon suggest in some points Carlo Buffone and Shift of *Every Man out* and will be taken up later. Even earlier than the work of Kerton and Fulwell, Bullein's *Dialogue against the Fever Pestilence,* 1564, shows one or two close approaches to the same treatment. The new character sketch appears occasionally, too, in the work of Harvey, as the passages quoted above go to show, and Lyly and Greene in their prose works characterize their personages very nearly at

[1]Cf. Schelling's *Life and Writings of George Gascoigne,* Univ. of Penn. Publ., pp. 96 f., where the statement is made that Gascoigne translated the same work in the same year and made it a part of his *Droome of Doomes Daye.* Gascoigne described his original as "written in an old kynde of caracters." See the portion of the dedicatory epistle quoted by Prof. Schelling.

[2]The work, which is said to have been newly corrected, is assigned by Corser to the year 1579. My acquaintance with it is only through the extracts in Corser's *Collectanea Anglo-Poetica,* Part 6, pp. 389 ff. The word humour occurs incidentally in these extracts and in *The Mirror of Mans lyfe,* but is not used for the folly of the character analyzed.

times in the epigrammatic way of the Theophrastan sketch. The character sketches of *Pierce Penilesse* and *The Terrors of the Night* that might be called Theophrastan are not separated from the fluent thread of Nashe's story, but their art is just that of Jonson's rapid, pointed, and satiric treatment of character. In the drama, also, as in the early play of *Jack Juggler,* the description of character without portrayal through action supplies similar character sketches.

Indeed, the Theophrastan type of sketch can be called new in English literature only as it becomes a consciously cultivated artistic form, and is found complete and detached. As such it is most fully developed among the writers before Jonson by Lodge, whose *Wits Miserie* is composed very largely of brief, distinct delineations of character. His sketches are no more brilliant or pointed than those of *Pierce Penilesse* and of several other works of Nashe, but the method is more obvious. Taking the most brilliant sketches of Nashe, Lodge has seemingly built up the whole of *Wits Miserie* on the model of them. Both Nashe and Lodge were presumably influenced by Theophrastus himself. In 1592 Casaubon had brought out his *Theophrasti Characteres Ethici,* which doubtless soon became known to English humanists. Indeed, Lodge's knowledge of Theophrastus can hardly be doubted.[1]

It was Professor Penniman who first noted the fact that *Wits Miserie* has a great number of parallels to Jonson's character sketches. In the introduction to his edition of *Poetaster* and *Satiromastix,* to appear shortly in the Belles-Lettres Series, Professor Penniman says: "*Wits Miserie* with its satirical characterization of the 'Devils Incarnat' of the age suggests Jonson's early comedies, in which several of the very 'Devils' described by Lodge are made to play important parts. . . . Sometimes the same 'Devil' appears in several characters, and sometimes several 'Devils' inhabit the same character."[2] These parallels to Jonson's work will be taken up in connection with the separate plays; here I am interested in the character sketch only as a part of the study of hu-

[1]There is one mention of him in *Wits Miserie* (p. 20).

[2]I am under the greatest obligation to Professor Penniman for calling my attention, through personal correspondence, to this relationship between Lodge and Jonson, and for the exceptional kindness of allowing me to see his manuscript before publication.

mours, and especially in the fact that Jonson got not only the method of characterization from Nashe and Lodge primarily, but also enough details to show us what his models were.

So far I have dealt only with the non-dramatic works that might have contributed either directly or indirectly to the development of Jonson's satiric comedy. Before the appearance of *Every Man in,* however, there are a number of plays embodying the same conception of character treatment. In the drama as in prose literature it is not worth while attempting to chronicle all the uses of the word humour before Jonson. As the term became more popular, many men utilized it in its various meanings, probably without any consciousness of the fact that they were using it. It is only in the dramas where the word is employed, on the one hand, with a certain affectation or consciousness, or, on the other, for a study of typical character tendencies that the use becomes important for the very definite humour program of Jonson.[1]

In the drama as in fiction, Lyly seems to be one of the very earliest writers to study the inclinations of individuals systematically and to apply the word humour to these inclinations. His plays show transitional phases in the idea of humour. He uses the word, not as Jonson does, for a folly alone, but at times with a sense of the physical meaning; again with a view to what is fundamental and permanent in man's make-up; often with as much tragic as comic force, as in *Midas;* and, in *The Woman in the Moon,* with application to varying moods of one character under the influence of the planets.

In *Midas,* entered on the Stationers' Register 1591 and assigned to the year 1589 by Bond, three characters at least are studies exemplifying the supremacy of one passion, besides Midas with his passion for gold. These are the three councillors of Midas: Eristus, whose bent is toward love; Martius, who is eager for conquest;

[1]Typical early uses of the word are to be found in *The Arraignment of Paris,* III, 1, l. 22; *Two Italian Gentlemen,* l. 181; *Orlando Furioso,* l. 120; *James IV,* I, 2 (l. 439), II, 2 (l. 1111); *Pinner of Wakefield,* II, 1 (l. 305); *Endimion,* I, 3, l. 7, and III, 4, l. 10; *Love's Metamorphosis,* III, 1, l. 81; *Coblers Prophesie,* III, 1, l. 22, and III, 3, l. 8; *Three Lords and Three Ladies of London,* Hazlitt's *Dodsley,* Vol. VI, p. 442; *Leir,* ll. 183, 583, and 742; *Taming of a Shrew,* Shakespeare's Library, Part II, Vol. II, pp. 512 and 520. There are a number of interesting uses of humour in *The Spanish Tragedy* and *Soliman and Perseda;* cf. Crawford's *Concordance to the Works of Kyd* in Materialien.

and Mellacrites, whose sole desire is gold. The word humour is used only a few times; but in II, 1, l. 12, Eristus says of himself, "Men change the manner of their loue, not the humor," and in ll. 64 ff. Martius, in condemning the neglect of martial pursuits, says of the other councillors, "Since this vnsatiable thirst of gold, and vntemperat humor of lust crept into the kings court, Souldiers haue begged almes of Artificers, and with their helmet on their head been glad to follow a Louer with a gloue in his hatte." In the same scene Sophronia, the daughter of Midas, and like Crites the type of the well-rounded and balanced character, says of the thirst for gold displayed by Midas and Mellacrites, "The couetous humor of you both I contemne and wonder at, being vnfit for a king" (ll. 38, 39). The whole scene is a study of humours, in which each character with a dominant inclination urges his own desire in contempt of other interests, and in which through Sophronia the necessity for temperance and balance in desire is emphasized.

In *The Woman in the Moon,* licensed in 1595 and assigned by Bond to the years 1591-1593, there is a more extensive treatment of humours, but here the study deals with the influence of the planets in giving a single character, Pandora, different passions or humours at different periods. Bond sees in *The Woman in the Moon* some influence of *Planetomachia,* one of the early works in prose representing Greene's interest in the study of character bent (cf. *Works of Lyly,* Vol. III, pp. 235 f.). The successive passions dominating Pandora are called humours, and the whole play is a study of the follies arising from a lack of balance. First, under the influence of Saturn, Pandora becomes melancholy and behaves somewhat like Fallace of *Every Man out.* Music is proposed to "sift that humor from her heart" (I, 1, l. 221). Then Jupiter fills Pandora with "Ambition and Disdaine," making her display the humour of Jonson's court ladies. Pandora herself applies humour to this mood of hers (II, 1, l. 111). Mars, Sol, Venus, Mercury, and Luna in turn hold sway over her, and under each spell she acts as one of Jonson's humour types might act if dominated by the same inclination. In her final choice, Pandora says to the planets (V, 1, ll. 303 ff.):

> Thou madst me sullen first, and thou *Ioue,* proud;
> Thou bloody minded; he a Puritan:

> Thou *Venus* madst me loue all that I saw,
> And *Hermes* to deceiue all that I loue;
> But *Cynthia* made me idle, mutable,
> Forgetfull, foolish, fickle, franticke, madde;
> These be the humors that content me best,
> And therefore will I stay with *Cynthia.*

Such a list of inclinations or humours, and the detailed study that Lyly gives each is a long step toward the humour comedy of Jonson. This treatment corresponds pretty well in time to Nashe's conception of a definite program of humours, and, while not so extensive as Nashe's list, it is equally important because of its early place in the drama of humours.

Probably before this last comedy of Lyly had been produced, there had appeared on the stage the old play, *Sir Thomas More,* which contains a few scenes very suggestive of the later humour plays. The overweening justice Suresbie and the perverse and irascible servingman Faulkner are put out of their humours by More in exactly Jonson's style. Faulkner twice uses humour with distinct reference to his follies. He vows to have his hair cut only "when the humors are purgd, not theis three years" (III, 2, ll. 125 f.), and defies consequences "so it bee in my humor, or the Fates becon to mee" (III, 2, ll. 317 f.).

By this time the idea of humour was general in the drama. One need only consult Bartlett's *Concordance* or Schmidt's *Shakespeare-Lexicon* to see how common the word is in Shakespeare's plays of the period. It was also becoming more usual to look at the character of men from the point of view of a prevailing tendency rather than from that of social cleavage. Marlowe, especially, carried this attitude into tragedy, and each of his great tragedies turns upon the overmastering passion of the hero, which leads to tragic consequences.

Jonson's immediate predecessor in the comedy of humours is of course Chapman. In his *Blind Beggar of Alexandria,* 1596, several of the characters are humour types, and the word humour occurs frequently in the early part. *The Comedy of Humours,* which is supposedly Chapman's *Humorous Day's Mirth* (cf. Fleay, *Biographical Chronicle of the English Drama,* Vol. I, p. 55), was a favorite on the stage in 1597, and illustrates the use of humour in the titles of plays to attract attention. The title may even have been that of another play and not of Chapman's, for the word humour quickly became popular in titles.[1] The close relation of *An Humorous Day's Mirth* to some of Jonson's plays will be noticed later. Chapman's *Fount of New Fashions,* 1598, which is now lost, may also have been very intimately related to the satirical humour school that was rising. The title at least suggests Jonson's *Fountain of Self-Love* (or *Cynthia's Revels*).

Meanwhile, possibly in 1597 with *The Case is Altered* and certainly by 1598 with *Every Man in,* Jonson had begun tentative studies in humour comedy. These plays belong to the period when Jonson had recognized the field for his genius after the production of *A Tale of a Tub* and before Nashe and Lodge, on the one hand, and the contemporaneous craze for formal satire, on the other, had definitely turned him toward a formal plan of analysis and satire. In these experimental plays, especially in *Every Man in,* humour is a favorite word, the characters are approaching decidedly the humour type, and some influence of satire is developing. But it is only in 1599 that the mode is fully established. Indeed, Jonson marks the distinction by giving the name "comical satire" to *Every Man out, Cynthia's Revels,* and *Poetaster.*

[1]The reference in *The Case is Altered* to some play as having "nothing but humours . . . nothing but kings and princes in it" (I, 1) was probably added after humour plays became the vogue (see p. 91 *infra*). Still the language would not be inappropriate to an early reference to *An Humorous Day's Mirth,* for in a general sense "princes" might fit the characters belonging to the French nobility who appear in the play with the king and queen.

CHAPTER IV

A TALE OF A TUB

That *A Tale of a Tub* was written during Elizabeth's reign is now pretty generally recognized. The question of the exact date, however, is still debated. Fleay, followed by Schelling, assigns the date 1601, seeing in the reference to the constable as Old Blurt an echo of *Blurt, Master Constable.*[1] Small, in *The Stage-Quarrel* (p. 15), has given about the best argument against connecting this reference with Middleton's comedy: the expression, he shows, is proverbial, and *A Tale of a Tub* could hardly have been written by Jonson at a time when he was producing his great comedies.[2]

Outside of Blurt, the various references or apparent references in *A Tale of a Tub* to English works are all to works earlier than 1597, the date suggested by Small. *The Pattern of Painful Adventures* is mentioned in III, 5 (p. 465). Turfe's choice of the clown Clay and cloth-breech in preference to Squire Tub (I, 2, p. 444), and a number of allusions throughout to velvet as distinguishing Lady Tub seem to be reminiscent of Greene's *Quip for an Upstart Courtier.*[3] In II, 1 (p. 453) Bungay's dog is mentioned, and in IV, 5 (p. 474) Friar Bacon and Doctor Faustus. The last line of III, 4 possibly refers to Gascoigne's *Supposes,* all the more as the passage indicates the vague similarity of *A Tale of a Tub* to the *Supposes* and as Jonson got part of the plot of *The Magnetic Lady* from that play. There are also references to Sir Bevis and Guy in III, 3, and to Fabyan in I, 2.

But the strongest reason for assigning *A Tale of a Tub* to an early date is found in the nature of the work itself. Unless the play belongs to the decadence of Jonson's art, it inevitably suggests his apprenticeship. It does not seem appropriate to the year

[1]Fleay, *Biog. Chron. English Drama,* Vol. I, p. 370; Schelling, *Eliz. Drama,* Vol. I, p. 326; for the reference to Blurt see *A Tale of a Tub,* II, 1, p. 450.

[2]I might add to his evidence the fact that *The Life and Death of Captain Thomas Stukeley* has a Blurt who is a bailiff, and, while the play seems to have been first printed in 1605, it may have been written much earlier. Cf. Simpson, *School of Shakspere,* Vol. I, pp. 153, 154.

[3]Fleay sees here references to the morality *Cloth Breeches and Velvet Hose* of 1600. Cf. *Biog. Chron. English Drama,* Vol. I, p. 370.

1601, when Jonson's ideals in comedy were altogether opposed to such work. The stage quarrel, too, was then at its height, and yet *A Tale of a Tub,* in my opinion, takes no part in it. But the play is a fairly good antecedent to *The Case is Altered* and *Every Man in his Humour*; and it shows some motives more fully developed in Jonson's other plays. Besides, as will be shown later, it is closely akin to a whole group of plays that went out of fashion just at the opening of the seventeenth century.

The play in its present form was licensed for the Blackfriars in 1633 and was included by Sir Kenelm Digby in the second folio of Jonson's works. Jonson himself would perhaps have withheld the play from print. Indeed, it must have been due to the poverty of his old age, to the small success of his attempts at new plays, and to his fierce desire to put Inigo Jones among clowns that he revived the play at all. An additional reason for his passing favorably upon this early effort is perhaps to be found in the fact that his attitude toward what furnished legitimate comic material had been modified during his later career; and, indeed, as early as *Bartholomew Fair* he had turned to a type of play nearer akin to *A Tale of a Tub* than were the plays which had been written between the two, and had, moreover, worked out a critical defense of *Bartholomew Fair,* as Drummond tells us. Many antimasques show Jonson's interest in the clowns and rogues of England, particularly during the second half of his literary career. The same interest is to be traced in *The Staple of News* and *The Magnetic Lady,* and the latter play, especially, shows some kinship to *A Tale of a Tub. The Sad Shepherd* with its Robin Hood and Robin Goodfellow is a return to themes most popular in the English drama at the time when *A Tale of a Tub* must have been first written. Indeed, the strongest evidence against an early date for *A Tale of a Tub* is the fact that the weakening of Jonson's power as a dramatist and his growing fondness for treating the peasantry might well prepare us for just such a play as *A Tale of a Tub* at a late period in his life. For instance, the two parts of *Love's Welcome,* which are very closely related to this play through characters and scenes, were presented in the years 1633 and 1634, at the very time of the revival of our play.

Accepting *A Tale of a Tub* as early work of Jonson that was later revised, we can determine the changes with comparative ease, not only by means of the satire against Inigo Jones, but also by means of the decided difference of tone and attitude in the handling of the clowns. Fleay (*Biographical Chronicle of the English Drama,* Vol. I, pp. 370, 371, and 386) has pointed out the new material. It consists of the short scene, IV, 2; about fifty lines inserted in V, 2, from "Can any man make" to "trust to him alone"; and from "I must confer" in V, 3 to the end of the play. The added material does not have any value for the plot, and usually fails to harmonize with the rest of the play. In IV, 2, In-and-In Medlay, the joiner or cooper, is described in such a way as to be easily identified with Jones; and, though the constable is elsewhere throughout the play spoken of as the Queen's man, he is here twice called the King's man. The second addition,—in V, 2,—which also concerns Medlay as Jones, belongs to the preparation for the puppet-show rather than to the plot of the play. The first few lines of the scene, with their reference to the Queen, are evidently a part of the old draft of the play. From the entrance of Tub and Hilts to the entrance of Lady Tub with Dame Turfe and others would mark the inserted matter if we consider with Small (*Stage-Quarrel,* p. 176) the use of the word joiner as indicating the distinction between Medlay as Jones and Medlay as the cooper. This distinction will not hold, I believe. In I, 2, Medlay the cooper chooses as his song for the brideale the *Jolly Joiner,* "for mine own sake," as he says; while in V, 2, when Jonson, not content with satirizing Jones as In-and-In Medlay, must also bring in the name of Vitruvius,[1] he speaks of Vitruvius as a London cooper. The insertion in this scene, then, probably does not begin with the entrance of Tub and Hilts, but, as Fleay asserts, about twenty lines farther on. After Hilts has introduced Tub to the clowns, Tub says,

> I long, as my man Hilts said, and my governor,
> To be adopt in your society.
> Can any man make a masque here in this company?

The sudden break at "Can any man make a masque?" seems to me

[1]The use of the name Vitruvius may have been suggested by a very complimentary epigram on Inigo Jones in Davies' *Scourge of Folly;* it has the title, *To my much esteemed Mr. Inego Iones, our English Zeuxis and Vitruuius.* Epig. 157. Davies praises Jonson in the preceding epigram.

to be unnatural, and to indicate that Jonson inserted the section crudely into the play. From this point to the entrance of Lady Tub the satire on Jones is clear, but upon her entrance the action of the play is resumed. About fifty lines, then, or at most seventy-five, were inserted here, and very little more in IV, 2.

The actual plot closes in V, 3, with Tub's graceful acceptance of the situation and his welcome of the company to a wedding supper; and here the play ended as acted at court. It is uncertain whether the remainder of the play in its present form—the part dealing with the preparation and presentation of the puppet-show—is an addition or merely a substitute for some other entertainment in the older version. Small (*Stage-Quarrel,* p. 176) came to the conclusion that there was originally a masque presented by Diogenes Scriben. This does not seem improbable. The conjecture is tempting that *Love's Welcome at Welbeck,* presented in 1633 and dealing with clownish sports in honor of a marriage, was an outgrowth of the discarded ending of *A Tale of a Tub;* but a number of minor points, as the fact that Awdrey's wedding occurs in February, a month unfavorable to outdoor sports, discountenance such a theory.

For a play of its type *A Tale of a Tub* is well plotted, and, outside of the additions satirizing Jones, there is almost nothing that seems useless or inharmonious. On the other hand, the treatment of Medlay in the inserted matter is inconsistent with his character as shown in the rest of the play. Elsewhere he is the most inconspicuous of the clowns. He speaks only a few lines in the reflections of the "four wise masters," and only once does he make a speech of more than a line or two. These few sentences from him, however, show that he is the least distinctive of the group, and that he has a faculty for blundering in the use of words. As Jones, Medlay is described rather fully, occupies the attention of his group of clowns, and has pet words, which he uses with affectation and a pretense at precision. It is possible, of course, that Jonson revised the play considerably or added scattered passages, but the indications are against it, for in case of considerable revision the use of the word queen would have been corrected and Medlay's character would have been developed early in the play in a manner suitable for satire against Inigo Jones.

A Tale of a Tub as a whole, then, may be regarded as an Elizabethan product, and a study of its relations to other plays shows that it belongs to the type of comedy that immediately preceded the comedy of manners. If the early date of *A Tale of a Tub* is accepted, we see Jonson at the very opening of his career studying and imitating the most thoroughly indigenous types of English comedy, the country bumpkin, the country squire, the constable, the sturdy servingman. In plot, too, the play shows the trend that native English comedy was taking in its strivings for structural unity and vigorous action. It is true that no direct source for *A Tale of a Tub* has been found, so that Jonson was here exhibiting his independence in literary work, but enough parallels can be shown to indicate the influence of contemporary literature and to strengthen the probability that the play was produced before the close of the sixteenth century. In citing these parallels I hope it will be clearly understood that I am making no pretense at dealing with sources; my object is merely to suggest literary conventions or trends that probably influenced Jonson.

The connection of many of the characters in *A Tale of a Tub* with types in the early English drama has been indicated by Eckhardt in *Die lustige Person im älteren englischen Drama.* The fact that these types represent conventional modes of treatment rather than first-hand studies of life is noticeable even in Jonson's work. The stage type is conventional; color is given by realistic touches drawn from the observation of life. For Jonson's play some parallels in character treatment that seem to me worth particularizing will be noticed in the study of plot motives, and some independently.

The development of these characters naturally came before the development of plots suitable for presenting them. In morality and then in chronicle play, the wit, resourcefulness, and energy of English rogues and democratic yeomen, the individuality and picturesqueness of men and women of low life, with their characteristic occupations, amusements, and foibles, were early utilized. But even when Latin comedy began to teach English dramatists how to handle their characters through organized plot and thus give full force to the presentation, the tendency remained to give only in episodic form what was genuinely English or belonged to low life. The romantic comedy often emphasized this tendency. At the same time the attempt to write plays dealing with native life and tradition became more frequent. Methods of plotting, accordingly, had to be invented or borrowed. The weakness of early efforts is apparent in such a play as *Friar Bacon and Friar Bungay.* An advance was made when the plots dealt more and more with one situation and one line of interest; but incident and action were increasingly demanded in the drama, and it was difficult to sustain action through a whole play developing only one motive. Complication, then, along with unity was secured by repeating and varying one situation again and again, apparently with little idea of utilizing various events all for one end.

In *A Tale of a Tub* the intrigue that sets the events into motion concerns itself with the country girl Awdrey, who is on the point of being married by her parents to the man of their choice. Other lovers interfere. The conflict to control the girl is doubtless from Latin comedy at bottom, but the handling is purely English. The scenes shift back and forth across the fields of Finsbury, and first one side and then another seems to win the victory in the ups and downs of the conflict. The rapidity of action does not depend upon the multiplicity of elements entering into the final result, all of which must be shaped to one end as in *The Silent Woman,* but upon a kaleidoscopic combination and recombination of the same elements. As one party gains, the other falls, only to be thrown into the ascendency in a moment. The girl is merely tossed back and forth.

This see-saw rather than a steady advance in plot was common in the drama, especially at the end of the sixteenth century. In all the plays of this class, whether accidentally or not, the treatment of clowns is prominent, and often folk customs and supernatural elements from folk-lore enter in. As regards action, the type of drama seems to have secured its hold through *Menaechmi,* further developed by Shakespeare in *The Comedy of Errors,* where accident and the confusion of identity result in first one combination and then another in the tangled maze of incidents. Certain romantic comedies, also, such as *Common Conditions, John a Kent and John a Cumber, Mucedorus,* and *Midsummer Night's Dream,* seem to lead definitely toward *A Tale of a Tub.* Dissimilar as these plays are, there are some elements common to them and Jonson's play. In each, for instance, a girl is the center of the action, and the scenes shift back and forth in the open.

Common Conditions (1576) shows most clearly the connection of such plotting with the metrical romances, where the action is dependent upon the continual formation of situations of adventure that do not lead toward the dénouement and that often close with results contrary to the final solution. In this play the passing of the girl from one hand to another as the pursuit sweeps through a series of confused windings in the open furnishes the adventure and the intrigue. *Mucedorus* (printed in 1598), itself derived in part from the *Arcadia,* represents the same wanderings in field and wood that we have in *Common Conditions.* Here again there is a series of adventures akin to the romances, but Amadine is the center of all as is Awdrey, fortune favoring first Segasto, the father's choice, then Mucedorus, then Segasto again through the banishment of Mucedorus, then the wild man of the woods, and finally Mucedorus. One notable passage of *A Tale of a Tub* (III, 1, p. 457) has been traced to Mouse of *Mucedorus* (I, 4, ll. 128-130) and Bullithrumble of *Selimus* (ll. 1977 ff.).[1] Clay says almost in the exact words of Mouse:

> I have kept my hands herehence from evil-speaking,
> Lying, and slandering; and my tongue from stealing.

The closest connection, indeed, between *Mucedorus* and *A Tale of a Tub* is in the clowns Mouse and Puppy. Both are prone to fear and superstition. Mouse fears that the bear is the devil in disguise; Puppy cries out at the terrible apparition of the devil when he sees Clay in the straw of the barn. Both clowns make nonsensical answers by giving the most literal and obvious answers. Both are largely concerned with eating. Bullithrumble, also, with his fear of devils, his love of eating, etc., belongs to the same subdivision of the great class, and all three clowns are evidently related.

The Two Italian Gentlemen[2] (1584) shows little similarity to *A Tale of a Tub* in the cause and form of the shifting action, but it sets forth a complicated love intrigue in which ups and downs and varied combinations succeed each other rapidly. The presence

[1]Eckhardt, *Die lustige Person,* p. 325. The passage is, of course, derived by perversion of language from the English liturgy.

[2]Cf. *Collections* of the Malone Society (Vol. I, pp. 218 ff.) for evidence that establishes a claim for Chapman's authorship of *Two Ital. Gent.* that is stronger than Munday's perhaps.

here of two girls,[1] who are themselves, unlike Awdrey, active in the intrigue, renders the action still more complicated, while the confusion of night scenes adds to the general medley characteristic of plays of the type. The love affairs of the maid Attilia, also, who is shifted from pedant to soldier, and the arrest of Crackstone just when he believes himself about to succeed in his intrigue to marry Victoria are suggestive of *A Tale of a Tub.* A second play of Munday's, *John a Kent and John a Cumber* (*ca.* 1595), is nearer in many respects to *A Tale of a Tub.* Though it differs greatly in the types and combinations of the central characters, it has as the exciting force the plan of fathers to marry off, against their will, daughters already secretly betrothed. In the conflict arising for the possession of the girls—here again there are two girls and both are active intriguers—success falls first to one party and then another, while the intriguing forces combine, dissolve, and recombine, shifting the scenes back and forth from castle to wood and town as in *A Tale of a Tub.* Here, however, the interest is centered in the contest of two magicians on the opposing sides. The clowns Tom Tabrer, Turnop, and Sexton Hugh, with their pageant for Morton and Pembroke, though nearer to the clowns of *Love's Labour's Lost* and *A Midsummer Night's Dream,* are not unlike those of *A Tale of a Tub.* Sexton Hugh and Turnop have names reminding one of Chanon Hugh and Margery Turn-up in *A Tale of a Tub,* the last of whom is merely mentioned (II, 1, p. 454). With Munday's clowns as with Jonson's, the drollery arises partly from the respect of others for the superior wisdom of the chief clown.[2] The dramatic and play instinct of the rustics, too, is exhibited. To an extent the same pursuit in the open and the same alternation of situation is found in *A Midsummer Night's Dream,* which also deals with the love intrigues of two girls; and the drolleries of the clowns are very much

[1]The Italian original of *Two Ital. Gent.*—Pasqualigo's *Il Fedele*—I have not seen, but Fraunce's *Victoria,* which is said to be closer to this Italian play than is *Two Ital. Gent.* (cf. *Mod. Lang. Rev.,* Vol. III, pp. 177 ff.), is not so clearly a forerunner of *A Tale of a Tub* as is the English play, since the principal intrigue in *Victoria* is for a married woman's favors and not for marriage.

[2]Cf. *A Tale of a Tub,* I, 2, p. 444, where Puppy says of Turfe:

> He's in the right; he is high-constable,
> And who should read above 'un, or avore hun?

in the tone of Jonson's play. Shakespeare's play is not so close to the general type, however, for the cross wooings are of a different sort.

In *Mother Bombie* (*ca.* 1590) there are some motives akin to those of *A Tale of a Tub.* The plan of fathers for a marriage of their children is thwarted, and, through the intriguing of the pages, matches seem on the point of being made, only to be unmade. The foolish and vulgar girl who plays a part in the marriage intrigue of *Mother Bombie* is also characterized in many places like Awdrey of *A Tale of a Tub.* In *Wily Beguiled,* again, we have the exciting force of a father's plan for the marriage of his daughter, and the intrigue that upsets it. This play, though not printed till 1606, is by common consent placed much earlier; by Professor Schelling before 1595, and by Fleay in 1596 or 1597.[1] There are three rival suitors, but the alternation is not so marked as in some other plays of the group. Churms dupes the father of the girl and both the rival suitors, promising each to work in his interest and meanwhile trying to marry the girl himself. In types of character the play is somewhat akin to *A Tale of a Tub.* Like Justice Preamble, Churms, the lawyer, while he is plotting to win the girl, gets possession of the father's money by trickery. Robin Goodfellow, the ally of Churms, is the means of revealing the lawyer's intrigues to the noble suitor, as Miles Metaphor is in *A Tale of a Tub.* Similarities in these minor points may be called accidental, for the detailed treatment of characters and situations differs widely.

Two plays very dissimilar to *A Tale of a Tub* and yet showing something of the same dramatic art are *Look About You* and *Two Angry Women of Abington.* They may have come after *A Tale of a Tub,* though some students of the drama have assigned to both of them dates that would in all probability place them before Jonson's play. At any rate, they indicate the extension of the type of study seen in *A Tale of a Tub.* *Look About You* is worth mentioning merely because it shows the same fondness that we

[1]Cf. Schelling, *Eliz. Drama,* Vol. I, p. 319; Fleay, *Biog. Chron. Eng. Drama,* Vol. II, p. 159; Ward, *Hist. Eng. Dram. Lit.,* Vol. II, p. 612. The induction certainly seems to contain a number of references to the satiric comedies of the end of the century, and some echoes of Marston; but the body of the text was probably early enough to influence Jonson in *A Tale of a Tub.*

find in Jonson's play for quick transference of scene from point to point around London, for surprising complications in the course of an intrigue, and for the rapid alternations of successes and failures. The story, however, is a cross between rogue tale and chronicle, and has little kinship with *A Tale of a Tub*. In *The Two Angry Women of Abington,* there is again the plotting of a father for the marriage of a daughter. Here the intrigue is different, since the mothers are pitted against the fathers, and there are no rival suitors; but the types of character, the shifting of scenes in the fields, and the pandemonium of adventure are worth noting.[1] The girl, like Awdrey, is vulgar and ready for any marriage. Nicholas, or Proverbs, and Miles Metaphor are companion studies, and Dick Coomes is the bold, testy servingman, like "resolute" Basket Hilts.

Englishmen for my Money (1598) may be mentioned, also, as belonging to the type. Here the father has three daughters and plans to marry them all to foreign suitors instead of the Englishmen with whom they are in love. The girls, who are active in the plot against their father, pass first to the foreigners, then to the lovers, and back to the foreigners, the Englishmen, of course, winning finally. The same miscarriage of plans and preponderance of accident that is characteristic of *A Tale of a Tub* occurs here. As in *The Two Italian Gentlemen* and *The Two Angry Women of Abington,* night scenes add to the confusion.

In "Simon Eyre," one of the tales in the first part of Deloney's *Gentle Craft* (1597), there are two chapters (III and V) that give a story typical of the interest at the time in the comic love intrigues of prentices and such underlings of society. The lovers are treated unromantically as in *A Tale of a Tub,* and exhibit the same rough humor and ready craft. The work was probably too late to affect *A Tale of a Tub,* but it furnishes a non-dramatic example of a type somewhat akin to Jonson's play. Haunce, the Dutchman, by a false tale turns Florence from a meeting with John, the Frenchman, at Islington, where they are to have a feast; and Haunce and Florence go to Hogsden. Having destroyed the intimacy of John and Florence, Haunce becomes the accepted

[1]The pastoral play, of course, shows some of this same dramatic see-saw and base-playing and circuitous love intrigue, as in *The Faithful Shepherdess.*

suitor of the girl. Later, with the help of Nicholas, a new rival, John gets vengeance by breaking up a little merrymaking on the part of the two lovers and showing Haunce up in an unfavorable light. Still Haunce wins the girl, and a time is set for the marriage secretly. Nicholas and John succeed in getting the Dutchman so drunk that he can not appear at the wedding, and Nicholas rushes off to play the bridegroom. John circumvents Nicholas, however, by having him arrested on a criminal charge, and himself meets the girl. It is just at this moment that John's French wife appears on the scene. Nicholas finally wins because he is English. In *A Tale of a Tub* we have the same shifting scenes in the suburbs of London. Here as in "Simon Eyre," while the parson presumably waits at the church, the girl passes from suitor to suitor. In Jonson's play, too, a rival suitor delays the marriage by throwing the bridegroom under suspicion of having committed a robbery, and finally a pretended legal summons calls Tub away as he is about to win out. When Tub once more has the girl in his possession, he is hurried off by his mother, as John is borne away by his wife. Martin, the dark horse, finally wins the girl.

Some minor incidents of *A Tale of a Tub* find parallels in plays belonging to the end of the sixteenth century.

In *A Tale of a Tub* Chanon Hugh first offers to secure Awdrey for Squire Tub, and later accepts a larger bribe from Preamble for working in his interest. Hugh becomes the intriguer and manipulator of the action, only to be outwitted at last. The part of Hugh seems commonplace; if it occurred in only one play, it might be ascribed to accident.[1] But it occurs in a number. In *Supposes,* for instance, there is the most natural use of the motive. A parasite offers help, for profit of course, to rival lovers in turn. In *Grim, Collier of Croyden*[2] Shorthose, like Hugh a parson, ac-

[1]This motive may have come from the parasite or Roman slave. In *Misogonus* the slave pretends to be faithful to both father and son. Of course the treatment of such "two-faced" characters was frequent. Ambodexter is a favorite name for them. Cf. *Cambises;* Bullein's *Dialogue against the Fever Pestilence;* Stubbes's *Anatomy of Abuses,* Part I, p. 141, and Part II, p. 7, where the name Ambodexter is applied to the Jesuits; *Pierce Penilesse* and *Haue with you to Saffron-walden, Works of Nashe,* ed. McKerrow, Vol. I, p. 162, and Vol. III, p. 105; *Quip for an Upstart Courtier, Works of Greene,* Vol. XI, p. 252; etc.

[2]In this play the Devil says of his wife: "Though she be a shrew, yet is she honest" (Hazlitt's *Dodsley,* Vol. VIII, p. 429). Drummond's

cepts bribes of two lovers of Joan, the miller and the collier, but attempts to thwart each and secure the girl for himself. These characters are clowns of the type found in *A Tale of a Tub*. In *Satiromastix* Tucca takes toll of Prickshaft and Shorthose (who has the same name as the parson of *Grim*) to secure Widow Minever for each, and yet would win her for himself.[1] These last two plays would, of course, come after the date to which I should assign *A Tale of a Tub*.

In making the constable Turfe the central dupe of *A Tale of a Tub* and grouping around him Medlay, Clench, and To-Pan, as his headborough, petty constable, and thirdborough, Jonson has given us our most extensive burlesque of the constable. The interest in constables began early. A stupid and credulous cobbler who is constantly being played upon serves as officer in *The Famous Victories of Henry V*. In *Endimion* (IV, 2) there are a head constable and some watchmen who discuss their duty with learned reasons and whose "wits are all as rustie as their bils." In *Leir* (scenes xxvii and xxix of the Malone Society reprint) we have among watches the same sort of nonsense in the way of formal reasoning. In *A Tale of a Tub* the assistants of Turfe, like these watchmen and the immortal Dogberry and Verres, fall into learned arguments;[2] and, as in *Endimion*, an appeal is made to the constable as final authority (I, 2).[3] Dull of *Love's Labour's Lost* (I, 1), who like To-Pan is a tharborough, and whom Holofernes describes with the words, "Twice-sod simplicity" (IV, 2), is guilty of the same misuse and misunderstanding of words that we find in *Much Ado* and *A Tale of a Tub*. In fact, *Love's Labour's Lost* and *A Tale of a Tub* reflect upon the stage the great interest in diction that possessed the English at the time.[4] For Jonson as yet the satire is humorous; soon it becomes deadly.

account of Jonson's famous remark about his wife has almost the same wording.

[1]Cf. l. 1158, etc. In *Magnetic Lady* Parson Palate is retained by Practice to help him win Pleasance, but later marries her to Compass, though not without pretense of objection.

[2]*Much Ado* may have been drawn from an old play which possibly dealt with these types. Cf. Furness, *Much Ado*, in *Variorum Shakespeare*, pp. xx-xxii.

[3]The discussion of the question whether "verse goes upon veet" may be a satiric thrust at Gabriel Harvey's ideals of verse.

[4]Cf. G. Gregory Smith, *Eliz. Crit. Essays*, Vol. I, pp. lv-lx.

In *A Tale of a Tub* (V, 2), when Turfe comes home to find that he has been beguiled of his daughter and of his money as well, he cries out,

> I am cozened, robbed, undone: your man's a thief,
> And run away with my daughter, Master Bramble,
> And with my money.
> . . . .
> My money is my daughter, and my daughter
> She is my money, madam.

The passage, of course, suggests at once *The Merchant of Venice* (II, 7). In *Wily Beguiled,* also, the father, like Shylock a miser, when he finds that Churms has tricked him out of money and has eloped with his daughter, cries out (Hazlitt's *Dodsley,* Vol. IX, p. 319), "I am undone, I am robbed! My daughter! my money! Which way are they gone?" In Greene's *Never too Late* (*Works,* Vol. VIII, pp. 56, 57) we have the same situation. Fregoso "cried out as a man halfe Lunaticke, that he was by *Francesco* robde of his onely iewell." Then follows his complaint to the mayor that he has lost both daughter and plate. The resemblance here, however, seems to be merely accidental. *The Case is Altered* (cf. p. 102 *infra*) contains a scene of the same kind, which is nearer *The Merchant of Venice* than is the situation from *A Tale of a Tub*.

Finally, Miles Metaphor's report (III, 4) to his master after the failure of his first mission to get Awdrey recalls Falstaff's account to the Prince of how he was robbed of the money which he had helped to take from the travelers (*I Henry IV,* II, 4).

Many parallels to Jonson's title have been traced.[1] The best illustration of its meaning is to be found, I think, in Gascoigne's *Certain Notes of Instruction* (1575): "If you . . . neuer studie for some depth of deuise in the Inuention, and some figures also in the handlyng thereof, it will appeare to the skilfull Reader but a tale of a tubbe." The title, then, is a confession of the slightness of the work in Jonson's estimation.

[1]Cf. 5 *N. and Q.*, Vol. XI, p. 505; Vol. XII, pp. 215 f.; Ward, *Hist. Eng. Dram. Lit.*, Vol. II, p. 379, note; Harvey, *Pierces Supererogation, Works*, Vol. II, p. 213; *D. N. B.*, Vol. 38, p. 436; etc. The meaning is quite clear in a number of the passages using the term. The best illustration outside of Gascoigne is found, perhaps, in Wilson's *Arte of Rhetorique*, p. 101.

On the whole there is little in common between *A Tale of a Tub* and Jonson's other work, and the play leads forward very little toward Jonson's characteristic comedy. It is rather primitive in most respects. Here and to a slightly less extent in *The Case is Altered,* the interest in incident is dominant, whereas in the four comedies that followed incident is neglected. Besides the primitive type of plot in the play, almost all the characters represent in some details the old conventions of vice, fool, and clown. Jonson, however, handles these types, not with the spirit of abandon and delight that is customary in the older drama, but with obvious satire and burlesque. The tone of the play, in other words, is often characteristic of Jonson, but in material and type *A Tale of a Tub* looks backward.

CHAPTER V

THE CASE IS ALTERED

The Case is Altered was probably written after *A Tale of a Tub.* Certainly in general structure it represents an advance over the more or less primitive Elizabethan type exemplified in *A Tale of a Tub,* although the superior art of moving steadily forward in plot may have been due to the borrowing from Plautus. Furthermore, as far as the internal evidence of style and thought is concerned, the play seems to stand between *A Tale of a Tub* and *Every Man in his Humour.* Especially is this true of the tentative studies of humours in *The Case is Altered,* for in *A Tale of a Tub* the treatment of types is in no case from the point of view of humours and the word humour occurs only once, while in *Every Man in* the idea of humours is dominant. Again, the play represents a point in the development of his satire where Jonson has passed beyond the unmixed burlesque of *A Tale of a Tub* and has not yet reached the broader scope of his satiric treatment that begins with *Every Man in.* Clownish figures still furnish a large part of the humor in *The Case is Altered,*—indeed this form of humor is present in all of Jonson's comedies,—but they share the stage with the more pretentious social types. That finer humour of Jonson's that springs from a satirical marshaling of the insistent follies of the higher social types is scarcely felt, however, except in the impatience of Ferneze. But here again we need to be cautious in drawing conclusions, for this play is anomalous to some extent on account of its romantic tendency and its Plautine influence. The reliance on Plautus in *The Case is Altered* is very great, while in *Every Man in* Jonson has seemingly learned to handle Plautine elements with the utmost freedom. In fine, the general spirit of the play is more Jonsonian than that of *A Tale of a Tub,* but far less so than that of *Every Man in,* which represents the maturing of Jonson's peculiar powers.

A statement in *The Case is Altered* (I, 1) that Antonio Balladino is "in print already for the best plotter" furnishes the most perplexing element in assigning the play a date before that of *Every Man in.* Anthony Munday is of course satirized as Antonio Balladino, and the reference is quite clearly to the passage in *Palladis Tamia* (entered on the Stationers' Register September 7, 1598, and published the same year) in which Munday is called "our best plotter." Yet in *Lenten Stuffe* (entered on the Stationers' Register January 11, 1598-9, and published in 1599), Nashe asks, "Is it not right of the merry coblers cutte in that witty Play of *the Case is altered?*" (*Works*, ed. McKerrow, Vol. III, p. 220)—a clear reference to Jonson's play and to the character of Juniper. *Lenten Stuffe* was in all probability completed when it was entered on the Stationers' Register, and it hardly seems possible that in the four months from September 7 to January 11 Meres's work was published, Jonson's play written and probably acted, and Nashe's work prepared, with time for Jonson to make a reference to Meres and Nashe to Jonson. The hypothesis that the passage satirizing Munday was added after the first production of *The Case is Altered* seems most reasonable. (The play as we know it was not published till 1609). To the support of this hypothesis Mr. Crawford has brought some very suggestive evidence recently (10 *N and Q.*, Vol. XI, pp. 41, 42). He shows that four passages from *The Case is Altered* are quoted in Bodenham's *Belvedere,* and that, while the book represents Bodenham's selections, the editing of the quotations was undertaken by A. M., who is with little or no doubt Anthony Munday, seemingly the originator of the plan for the volume. Mr. Crawford argues that Munday would not have quoted from *The Case is Altered* in 1600 if in the form then current the play had held him up to ridicule, and, consequently, that the scene in which Munday is satirized was altered after 1600 or after the compilation of *Belvedere.* It is true that the authors' names are not affixed to the quotations in *Belvedere,* but, according to Mr. Crawford's idea, Bodenham probably gave the source with each selection in handing over the material to A. M., since a list of authors quoted is given in the preface. Thus Munday probably did not include quotations from Jonson's play unwittingly. The fact, also, that Antonio appears only in one scene gives color to the theory that the part of the "pageant poet" was a later insertion. It is reasonable to suppose, then, that *The Case is Altered* was on the stage by the end of 1597 or early in 1598.

For a study of the English influence on Jonson, the plot of *The Case is Altered* apparently offers little that is of interest. Its important elements are frankly classic—a combination of incidents from the *Captivi* and the *Aulularia* of Plautus. From the *Captivi* Jonson has drawn the story of Ferneze and his two sons, Paulo and Camillo. The capture of Paulo in war (III, 1); the capture on the other side of the noble Chamont and of Camillo, the long lost son of Ferneze, who as Gasper attends Chamont; the exchange of names between the two prisoners of Ferneze (III, 3); the dispatch of the supposed Gasper, really Chamont, to negotiate for the exchange of Chamont for Paulo (IV, 2); the discovery that the noble prisoner, through the exchange of names, has been allowed to depart; the torture of the remaining prisoner, who is really the son of Ferneze (IV, 5); the return of Chamont with Paulo; and the discovery of the tortured prisoner's identity—are incidents taken from the *Captivi*. From the *Aulularia* comes the miser story, though often considerably modified. Here Jonson got the material or suggestions for the soliloquy of Jaques on the source of his gold (II, 1); for his instructions to Rachel to watch the house (II, 1); for his constant return in anxiety to the hiding place of his gold; for the scene between Jaques and Christophero, and Jaques and Ferneze (III, 1) even to the details that Jaques is suspicious of their motives in greeting him and in suing for his supposed daughter's hand, that they misinterpret his anxiety, that Jaques leaves several times to inspect his gold, that he declares his daughter has no dowry, and that he rejoices at their departure; for Jaques's removal of his gold to a new place (III, 2); for Onion's hiding in a tree; for Jaques's search of Juniper (IV, 4); and finally for the outcry of Jaques over his loss. The characterization of Jaques, also, is largely derived from the *Aulularia,* and Rachel is suggested by Phædra—whom we only hear of in Plautus—and as guardian of the home by Staphyla. Besides, some of the details in the treatment of Onion are drawn from this play.

The two plots are joined first of all by the romantic love of Paulo and Rachel, though other suitors of the girl, especially Ferneze himself, serve to unify the action of Jonson's play. A second link is found in the motive of the stolen child. Instead of being stolen by a fugitive slave, as in the *Captivi,* Camillo has been lost in warfare; but this motive from the *Captivi* is engrafted on the miser story, for Jaques—unlike the miser of the *Aulularia,* who really has a daughter and whose gold comes to him from his grandfather—has stolen his supposed daughter and his gold. The girl proves to be a sister of Chamont, so that Ferneze's discovery of his lost son is duplicated by Chamont's discovery of his lost sister.[1]

To all this classic material Jonson has added the characters Angelo, Francisco, Maximilian, the two daughters of Ferneze, and the pages. For Strobilus of the *Aulularia* and minor figures of the servant class in Plautus's two plays, Jonson has given us Valentine, the traveler; Antonio Balladino, the poet; Juniper, the cobbler; Onion, the groom; Christophero, the steward; and four other servants of Ferneze. He has also added, along with many minor details, the treatment of Paulo's love for Rachel; of Angelo's perfidy; of Aurelia's love affair; of the memory of Ferneze's wife; of Maximilian's responsibility for Paulo; and of the action of the pages and clowns except in relation to Jaques.

Not only in the additional elements of his plot does Jonson show evidences of English influence, but also in the treatment of characters drawn from Plautus, not excepting Jaques, who is the most thoroughly Plautine of the figures. These evidences, be it repeated, can not in any case be flatly called proofs of direct borrowing. Their value lies in the indication of conventional lines of treatment and in the suggestion they give of Jonson's minute study of the contemporary drama. Conventions of both romantic and popular drama are to be traced in *The Case is Altered,* and this fact is an excellent indication of the experimental nature of the play. In *A Tale of a Tub* Jonson had tried his hand with the ordinary comic stage types, and must have been little satisfied with the results of his burlesque treatment. The comedy of manners had not yet justified itself by producing pure masterpieces, and Jonson in *The Case is Altered* turned to the only dignified or artistic comedy that the stage afforded, the romantic comedy. He modified his romanticism considerably, however, and elevated the clownish figures, or rather added potency to the treatment of them. The whole group of servants gives Jonson his outlet for satire, but especially Juniper, who serves for the satire on current follies and absurdities in the affectation of elegant speech. Of the serious

[1]Most of these details have been pointed out by Gifford in his notes to the play and by Koeppel in his *Quellen-Studien zu den Dramen Ben Jonson's,* etc.

characters, also, certain ones are more than the conventional figures in romantic comedy. Ferneze and his two daughters, especially, have been utilized as essays in the study of humours.

With the object of the satire and the source of the material involved in the treatment of Juniper, the late Mr. H. C. Hart has dealt rather fully. He has shown[1] that most of the words misused by Juniper in his affectation and pomp may be traced to Gabriel Harvey's works. Though it can scarcely be doubted that Jonson had Harvey's vocabulary in mind, the attack is apparently not personal; at any rate there seems to be no special malice in the treatment. In attacks on Latinized vocabularies it was seemingly conventional to use Harvey's as the typically bad one. Harvey's training in rhetoric and logic and his reliance on Renaissance rules for style naturally led him into a mechanical formality and pomposity that furnished a ready point of attack. Supposedly his vocabulary is ridiculed in *The Old Wives' Tale* and *Pedantius,* and his inflated diction plays a large part in Nashe's several satires against him. It is noticeable that Jonson does not use the same Harveyisms that Nashe uses; probably, indeed, he deliberately avoided doing so, and turned to Harvey's works for a new stock of terms to carry on the travesty begun by Nashe. Moreover, it must be remembered not only that many of Harvey's terms had come into pretty general use by the time of *The Case is Altered,* but that Harvey's works still leave a fairly large proportion of Juniper's perversions unaccounted for, so that Jonson must have drawn also upon the general literature of his day. In fact, numbers of new terms were doubtless passed upon and discountenanced by the more conservative writers, and in all likelihood each student like Jonson had a list of condemned neologisms to air. The influence of Nashe on Jonson's attitude to neologisms, again, was probably considerable.

Aside from the possible element of personal satire involved in Juniper's diction, his characterization as the cobbler, the most important comic figure of the play, associates him with a type popular in contemporary drama and prose literature. From the beginning, the shoemaker in literature seems to represent the sturdier yeoman class, democratic in spirit, independent in attitude, and boldly self-reliant. He is never utterly stupid, a purely burlesque

[1] 9 *N. and Q.*, Vol. XI, pp. 501 f., and Vol. XII, pp. 161 f., 263 f., 342 ff., and 403 ff.

figure like the constable.[1] In *The Pinner of Wakefield* he drinks with the English king himself and is granted special privilege by him, clearly in anticipation of the sturdy characters of *The Shoemaker's Holiday;* in *The Cobler of Canterburie* he becomes a satirist and an author; in *The Coblers Prophesie* he acts as mouthpiece of the gods; and in the folk romances of Deloney and Dekker he has equally important rôles. The shoemaker of *Locrine* is a burlesque type, but not a stupid one; in fact, his "witty" language, as will be shown, furnishes our best preparation for Juniper.

The most important phase in the treatment of the shoemaker as a type is found in this "witty" or picturesque language, and here again the type is quite distinct from the constable or watch, the second clownish figure in which Jonson and others of the period deal with perversion of language. There are two sides to the cobbler's speech. One has to do with the use of a pretentious and perverted vocabulary, including picturesque epithets, resounding proper names, and often words uttered in chaos for mere sound. The other is concerned with vivacity of speech—quick phrasing, range of figures, slang, abrupt shifts in construction. In general, it seems to me that in the plays exalting the yeoman, such as *The Pinner of Wakefield,* there is a tendency to give to his speech as he faces kings, nobles, or what not a certain boldness and decisiveness that result in sweep and terseness. The speech that was developed in the later drama as appropriate to such characters seems also to show the influence of the meter which was often used for comic characters all the way through the early drama. This type of verse with its short, rapid lines may have had something to do with the jerky phrasing of Juniper. Vice, fool, artisan, and rustic employ it, and along with the nonsense of these characters there often goes a use of ribald speech, homely figures, abusive and odd epithets, alliterative plays upon words, and a misuse of Latin words in particular. It is but natural that the doggerel verse should have its effect upon the prose that succeeded it as the proper speech for characters of this type. Will Cricket of *Wily Beguiled* speaks both doggerel verse and doggerel prose, and the same mixture appears elsewhere in the drama before Jonson. Doggerel

[1]An exception to this is found in John Cobler of *The Famous Victories of Henry V*, who is both cobbler and, as he says, a "bad officer" of the constable.

verse, indeed, is utilized in many fairly late plays. Munday used Skeltonic meter in *The Downfall of Robert Earl of Huntington,* and Jonson used it at a much later period in some of his anti-masques. Into prose went also the love of slang, abuse, plays upon words, and varied forms of misuse of words. The characters who twist the pronunciation of Latin words are numerous, and as early as *Mankind* sport seems to be made in the drama of Latinized vocabularies (cf. *Macro Plays,* E. E. T. S., p. xviii). In the middle of the sixteenth century the critical discussion of borrowed terms and the contradictory opinions held on the subject induced writers to pay excessive attention to diction both for satiric and for humorous purposes. The influence of this trend is very evident in all of Jonson's early plays. Two ways of treating Latinized vocabularies are especially marked: one consisted in the burlesque use by clowns, fools, etc.; the other, in the pedantic use. Jonson renders the pedantic use more ludicrous by adding the vocabulary of Harvey to the clownish diction of Juniper.

Both phases of the shoemaker's language, its perversion and its raciness, seem to develop naturally from *The Coblers Prophesie* to *Locrine*[1] and on to *The Case is Altered.* Ralph of *The Coblers Prophesie,* like Juniper, is the chief clownish figure in a play half satiric in nature, though his part is more important for the serious plot. The amount of perverted language used by Ralph is small, for his speech is largely made up of prophecies inspired by Mercury. But at times he is just in Juniper's vein. When his wife chides him for singing love songs, his reply is (I, 1, ll. 57, 58):

> Content your selfe, wife, tis my own recantation;
> No loue song neither, but a carrol in beauties condemnation.

The Latinized vocabulary, the delicate shift in the form of words, and the haunting sense of the real meaning all suggest Juniper. The prophecies which Ralph utters illustrate the other side of his language. They are written in the short, rapid lines of which I have spoken, and are full of figures and nonsense verse.

In *Locrine* the speech of the shoemaker Strumbo shows some of this tendency to rapid phrasing, though here the gentleman's elegance of diction rather than the clown's vigor is in the ascendency.

[1]Whatever the relative dates of these two plays, the cobbler part in *Locrine* is the more advanced for our purposes.

At the same time the language reveals just the perversion that makes it an excellent burlesque or parody and so prepares for Juniper. In I, 2, Strumbo appears at his best as a pompous speaker. The language is a lover's jargon that in balancing of phrases often suggests the rhetorical tricks of the day rather than Juniper's speech, as I have indicated, but the scene shows Strumbo, to use his own expression, provided with "a capcase full of new coined wordes":

Either the foure elements, the seuen planets, and all the particuler starres of the pole Antastick, are aduersatiue against me, or else I was begotten and borne in the wane of the Moone, when euerie thing as *Lactantius* in his fourth booke of Constultations dooth say, goeth asward.[1] I, maisters, I, you may laugh, but I must weepe; you may ioy, but I must sorrow; sheading salt teares from the watrie fountaines of my moste daintie fairie eies, . . . in as great plentie as the water runneth from the buckingtubbes, or red wine out of the hogs heads: for . . . the desperate god *Cuprit*, with one of his vengible birdbolts, hath shot me vnto the heele: so not onlie, but also, oh fine phrase, I burne, I burne, and I burne a, in loue, in loue, and in loue a. Ah, *Strumbo*, what hast thou seen? not *Dina* with the Asse *Tom?* Yea, with these eies thou hast seene her, and therefore pull them out, for they will worke thy bale. Ah, *Strumbo*, hast thou heard? not the voice of the Nightingale, but a voice sweeter than hers. Yea, with these eares hast thou heard it, and therefore cut them off, for they haue causde thy sorrow. . . . Oh my heart! Now, pate, for thy maister! I will dite an aliquant loue-pistle to her, and then she hearing the grand verbositie of my scripture, will loue me presently.

The letter follows, and Strumbo exclaims on it, "Oh wit! Oh pate! O memorie! O hand! O incke! O paper!" Later in the scene, after Strumbo has addressed Dorothie in a speech with such Juniperian nonsense as "Oh my sweet and pigsney, the fecunditie of my ingenie," etc., she complains, "Truly, M[aister] *Strumbo,* you speake too learnedly for mee to vnderstand the drift of your mind, and therfore tell your tale in plaine termes, and leaue off your darke ridles." Strumbo answers, "Alasse, mistresse *Dorothie,* this is my lucke, that when I most would, I cannot be vnderstood; so that my great learning is an inconuenience vnto me."

[1]The mixing of a pseudo-scientific jargon with nonsensical learned references, as in the opening of this scene from *Locrine,* is the trick that makes Clove's first speech in *Every Man out,* III, 1, distinctive in its method of perverting speech.

Just such rhetorical tricks of balance, exclamation, interrogation, and figurative language as are used here by Strumbo and are attacked by Shakespeare in *Love's Labour's Lost* are treated elaborately in Wilson's *Arte of Rhetorique.* They occur at times in Juniper's speech, but are secondary to inkhornism and slang. Jonson was doubtless too careful of decorum to make Juniper a rhetorician. What is of interest for Juniper is the fact that Strumbo is represented as a shoemaker who pours forth language tortured with excess of ornament, stilted diction, and torrents of phrases. A number of similar details, moreover, are to be found in the two studies; as when Juniper boasts (II, 4), "O ingle, I have the phrases, man," etc., or Maximilian asks, after a speech of Juniper's (I, 2), "Doth any man here understand this fellow?" and later declares, "Before the Lord, he speaks all riddle I think,"—all of which is fairly close in thought and even in wording to phrases of Strumbo's speech just quoted. Juniper himself is not a lover, though he does undertake to woo Rachel for Onion. Love is treated in the two plays in much the same tone and spirit. Indeed, Onion's exclamations as they approach Rachel (IV, 4) correspond to one phase of Strumbo's speech, but the *oh's* of love poetry and prose are frequently satirized in the period.

Jonson's work in Juniper is thoroughly characteristic of him. The treatment of Ralph and Strumbo which I have indicated is not sustained, but Juniper is consistent to the end. In fact, he is practically a new figure, for only suggestions or faint hints of him lie in the forerunners of his type. For instance, in neither Ralph nor Strumbo are Juniper's chaotic phrases, full-sounding proper names, and unique words of address more than foreshadowed in the dimmest fashion. Strings of epithets, often chaotic and usually bound together by alliteration, are common in the drama, as in the speech of Will Cricket of *Wily Beguiled,* but they do not prepare us for Juniper's wealth of phrases, for the whimsical, fresh, and high-sounding epithets that he applies to his fellows, or for the buoyancy and good spirit in his application of them. These characteristics are perhaps best suggested in some of Falstaff's good-humored, whimsical speeches in *I Henry IV,* which was probably written before *The Case is Altered.* At any rate, Falstaff's language here reveals the possibilities that lie in the epithet as a device for the portrayal of comic character. The mixture of heartiness and insulting effrontery in Falstaff's addresses to his social and moral superiors certainly appears in Tucca, whether there is any influence of the character on Juniper or not.

A minor convention, but perhaps a more obvious one, has to do with the way in which the shoemaker is introduced on the stage. He is usually introduced sitting on his stool at work and singing. In the opening scene of *The Case is Altered,* Juniper is discovered, "sitting at work in his shop, and singing." The song gives the tone of the characterization of Juniper, for it is close enough to the pretentious ballad to furnish an excellent parody. Scene 3 of Act IV in *The Case is Altered* opens similarly. Ralph of *The Coblers Prophesie* enters during the first scene "with his stoole, his implements and shooes, and, sitting on his stoole, falls to sing." His song, with its jingling refrain, suggests a parody of the popular love ballad. Scene 2 of Act II in *Locrine* opens with the stage direction, "*Enter* Strumbo, Dorothie, Trompart, *cobling shooes and singing*"—a song of the cobbler's merry life. In *The Pinner of Wakefield* (IV, 3) a shoemaker is introduced "sitting vpon the stage at worke," though there is no mention of his singing. The singing of cobblers, however, is apparently an accepted convention in all the literature that utilizes the type during the period around Jonson. The shoemakers of *The Cobler of Canterburie,* of Deloney's *Gentle Craft,* and of Dekker's *Shoemaker's Holiday* are all fond of singing, and in *Wily Beguiled* (Hazlitt's *Dodsley,* Vol. IX, p. 293) there is mention of "an honest Dutch cobbler, that will sing *I will noe meare to Burgaine go,* the best that ever you heard."

The cobbler was a favorite figure in literature, as has been indicated. Besides the works mentioned, he appears, for instance, in the early *Knack to Know a Knave,* and *The Cobler of Queenhithe* (1597) has been lost. Dekker later, especially in Simon Eyre and Firk, has carried on the convention of the cobbler's speech. Eyre uses the rapid phrases, picturesque epithets, and high-sounding proper names of Juniper.[1] With Tucca of *Poetaster* Jonson returned to the type of speech, and Dekker followed with his Tucca. Shakespeare had been sufficiently attracted by the vogue to open *Julius Caesar* with a shoemaker scene, in which the language takes

[1]Cf. Stoll, *Mod. Lang. Notes,* Vol. XXI, pp. 20-23 for the influence of Juniper on Simon Eyre.

the form of puns. The picturesque speech that culminated in Juniper and Eyre passed to characters other than the shoemaker, and appears in Murley of *Sir John Oldcastle,* in the Host of *The Merry Wives of Windsor,* and in the Host of *The Merry Devil of Edmonton.* Some phases of the type of speech are found in characters of many later plays, as in the leader of the mob in *Philaster.*

Onion belongs to no such distinct type as Juniper. As a clownish household servant his lines of affiliation are too extensive to be traced. The characterization of Onion includes a number of distinct features. He is enamored of Antonio Balladino, being as right of his "humour as may be, a plain simple rascal, a true dunce," and loves his type of play (I, 1); in language he is an understudy to Juniper, and his efforts at serious speech result in illogical juxtapositions; he plays upon his name (IV, 3 and 4); as a lover, he uses ecstatic nonsense made of phrases beginning with *oh's* (IV, 4); he seeks others to help him in his love making (II, 2 and IV, 3); he is expert at the cudgels, but is beaten by a novice (II, 4); like Sogliardo, he is instructed in court graces (IV, 1); he has acquired officiousness with his office (I, 1); of him his master says, "He'll bandy with me word for word; nay more, put me to silence," but he quickly repents (I, 2); finally, finding the gold of Jaques, he turns gentleman and uses it to dress elegantly and to drink (V, 2). Throughout the play he is the foil to Juniper. The name of Onion is used for a friar in the *Decameron,* and was borrowed for one in *Tarlton's News out of Purgatory.* Onion's love-making has already been compared with that of Strumbo. His overthrow in cudgel play belongs to folk literature, though I do not know of any exactly similar scene. In the ballads Robin Hood unexpectedly meets his match in popular heroes, and the shoemakers in *The Pinner of Wakefield* are overcome by the popular George-a-Greene. A hint of Onion's independent attitude toward his master may have been drawn from the *Aulularia,* but the characterization is that of an English servingman. Pride in his office and bullying of his master are the new turns. In Basket Hilts of *A Tale of a Tub* Jonson had already treated a character similar to Onion in this respect, and in Waspe of *Bartholomew Fair* he afterwards developed the type fairly freshly. The scene in *The Case is Altered* where Onion turns upon Ferneze and Maximilian in anger, defies them, and accepts his dismissal scornfully, only to repent immediately and send Juniper to intercede (I, 2), is much like an incident in *Sir Thomas More,* a play that probably influenced Jonson in other work. Faulkner, the servant of Morris, is so proud and insistent that he will be tried before no one but More; he is almost as bold in speech to More as Onion is to Maximilian; his speech and manner, like Onion's, are nonsensical and affected, though Faulkner is a punster; at his last appearance he bandies words with his master, as Onion does, welcomes his dismissal, repents at once, and is restored to favor by the indulgent Morris. The last episode dealing with Onion, wherein he uses his new-found wealth to deck himself out and ape a gentleman, shows a commonplace resemblance to a part of *James IV.* In IV, 3 of *James IV,* Slipper, who like Onion plays upon his name, and who has all the clown's conventional quips, cranks, and affectations of speech, having gotten money dishonestly, has tradesmen to make a gentleman of him, content to spend all for one fling.

Valentine is a traveler only faintly sketched. He seems to be one of the earliest examples of his type upon the stage, and is probably drawn from non-dramatic literature. Later the opening of a drama with the return of one from his travels became popular, as in *The English Traveller, A Fair Quarrel, The Wild Goose Chase,* etc., though the part of the returned traveler is usually played by the master rather than by the servant. The conventional satire on the boasting of the traveler is lightly touched in *The Case is Altered.* In V, 2, Valentine starts to tell of the wonders of Mesapotamia in order to "gull these ganders," but is promptly side-tracked. In II, 4, he holds the center of the stage for a short time while he discusses the customs of Utopia, especially in regard to theatres. The whole manner of this passage is that of the popular dialogue of the time, such as Stubbes's *Anatomy of Abuses.* Under cover of the name Utopia, Jonson satirizes the follies of the time,[1] and praises England as the ideal land, while the questioners are merely puppets suggesting the line of talk. According to Hart (*Works of Ben Jonson,* Vol. I, p. xxx), Valentine "foreshadows, in a transient manner, Asper of *Every Man out of his Humour* and Crites of *Cynthia's Revels;* that is to say, he is Jonson him-

[1]The satire which Jonson puts in the mouth of Valentine on the posing dramatic critic is slightly anticipated in Hall's *Virgidemiarum,* I, 3.

self." As evidence he cites the repetition of Valentine's ideas in Asper. To my mind, however, this means merely that in *The Case is Altered* Jonson has expressed some of his ideas on stage conditions through the mouth of one of his characters. Appropriately enough, it is the traveler, as the scene is laid in Italy.

In the incidents connected with Jaques, *The Case is Altered* follows Plautus closely; but the characterization is fresh, and English sources may have contributed to it. The niggardliness of the Plautine miser, his hoarding of disgusting trifles, etc. are not found in Jaques. We hear of his threadbare coat, but Rachel is well dressed. The central point of Jaques's character is a worship of his gold, a glorification of it. With Plautus the imagination of the miser is not fired by his gold, his affection is not awakened so fully as in the case of Jaques. The spirit of Jonson's treatment is thus somewhat suggestive of Renaissance influence. Some parallels, indeed, exist in English literature. Avarice of *Respublica,* for instance, resembles Jaques in the worship of money. This old play does not seem to have been published and may not have been known by Jonson. On the other hand, it may be typical of a treatment found in plays lost to us or in literature that I have not connected with *The Case is Altered.* The relation between Jaques and Avarice could not be very close, and yet the crude characterization of Avarice has several distinct suggestions of Jonson's miser as well as a number of details that are found in Plautus also. Most of all, Avarice's adoration of his gold and his affectionate address to it suggest Jaques. In *Midas,* too, the praise of gold (I, 1) is much in the spirit of Jaques, though there are no noteworthy parallels. The elopement of Rachel, the discovery on the part of Jaques that he has lost both daughter and gold at the same time, and his confused cries over his child and his money (V, 1) furnish, as has often been noted, a parallel to Shylock and Jessica in *The Merchant of Venice.* Parallels to this scene are pointed out under *A Tale of a Tub* (p. 88 *supra*), in which there is a similar situation.[1]

The other characters in *The Case is Altered* represent the romantic interest of the play, and some of them at the same time

[1]For a passage in *The Case is Altered* that suggests further kinship with *The Merchant of Venice,* see the discussion of *Every Man out,* p. 165 *infra.*

furnish a basis for humour studies. Many incidents are drawn directly from Plautus and yet are changed sufficiently to give them a romantic cast, while the characterization does not depend noticeably on the Latin original. In varying from his classic sources, Jonson has often approached typical situations of the early romantic English drama. The most noticeable romantic elements are the treatment of love and friendship. In Rachel, highborn but occupying a humble position, and courted by clowns and nobles, we have a romantic situation which may be illustrated from the early English drama by *Faire Em,* whose heroine, a lady but seemingly merely a miller's daughter, is courted by her father's servant and by several gentlemen. The number of Rachel's lovers and their shifts to gain access to the girl represent the same type of treatment that has already been studied in *A Tale of a Tub.* The love of both father and son for the same girl may have been suggested by the love of uncle and nephew in *Aulularia;* the type of rivalry between father and son in *Mercator* and *Casina* is not suggestive of the romantic device or attitude of Jonson's play. The situation combined with other romantic entanglements is found in *Menaphon.* It became a notable device of the English drama. *The Wisdom of Doctor Dodipoll,* in which the love of Duke Alphonsus clashes with that of his son, is fairly near *The Case is Altered,* though the play is probably later than Jonson's (cf. p. 109 *infra*). This situation of *The Case is Altered* was possibly borrowed by Chapman for *The Gentleman Usher,* and a number of later plays have parallels,—*The Fawne, The Humorous Lieutenant, Hector of Germanie,* etc.

Common in romantic drama is the rivalry in love between two friends, and especially the falseness of one. In Angelo's betrayal of Paulo's trust, *The Case is Altered* is more closely akin to *The Two Gentlemen of Verona* than to anything else. Paulo, leaving for war, entrusts Angelo with the secret of his love for Rachel, and commends the girl to his protection. Angelo ignores the claims of friendship and determines to win her for himself. He makes a tool of the clownish suitor Christophero in effecting the escape of Rachel, who is led to believe that Paulo has summoned her to join him. With Rachel at his mercy, Angelo attempts to win her in spite of former repulses, and, failing, would force his love on her. Paulo comes in the nick of time, is a witness of his friend's perfidy, and spurns him, only to forgive the shamed Angelo forthwith. In *The Two Gentlemen of Verona* Valentine reposes the utmost confidence in Proteus. Proteus, enamored of Silvia, Valentine's betrothed, betrays him, secures his banishment, and then woos Silvia, who, like Rachel, scorns him and reproaches him for his disloyalty. Proteus uses a stupid but wealthy suitor to gain access to Silvia, pretending, like Angelo, to be working in the other suitor's behalf. When Silvia finally escapes in search of Valentine, Proteus overtakes her and presses his suit, while Valentine, unknown to both of them, overhears. At the moment when Proteus becomes dangerous, Valentine breaks in upon the scene, and Proteus, repenting immediately, is forgiven. There are a few slight resemblances of language in the two plays. Angelo says scornfully (III, 1),

True to my friend in cases of affection!

and Proteus asks (V, 4),

In love
Who respects friend?[1]

For the early part of this particular episode in *The Case is Altered, Julius and Hyppolita,* one of the suggested sources of *The Two Gentlemen of Verona,* offers a closer parallel than does the Shakespearian play. In *Julius and Hyppolita* a lover who is forced to take a long journey entrusts his beloved to his "friend and brother" and is betrayed by him, but for the rest, except in minor details, the play does not resemble Jonson's.

In contrast with the false friend is the treatment of unblemished friendship between Camillo and Chamont in *The Case is Altered.* Chamont's escape, with Camillo left as a pledge, is from Plautus, as well as the final return of Chamont. But with Plautus there is little trace of the equality in love and the perfect confidence that exists between Chamont and Camillo. In *The Case is Altered* Camillo, on the point of execution, is firm in his faith that Chamont will return to redeem him at the appointed time. The change in tone of treatment makes the situation very similar to that of the old play of *Damon and Pithias.* There is the same sacrificing friendship, the same confidence in the friend's return at

[1]The sentiment and some of the situations in both stories are suggestive of *The Knightes Tale.*

the appointed time, the same readiness to die if need be in the service of the friend, and the same fond greeting at return.

Jonson's treatment of Aurelia and Phœnixella, the two daughters of Ferneze, shows him apparently in advance of the movement in romantic comedy. Aurelia is sprightly, free-spoken, wayward in humour, and contemptuous of convention. Phœnixella is sober, modest, and altogether steadfast in conduct. Such a contrast between sisters or cousins is frequent in the later drama, as in *Much Ado, The Dutch Courtezan,* and *The Wild Goose Chase*, and something of the same thing is found in *The Taming of the Shrew*. If, as Furness has suggested (*Variorum Shakespeare,* pp. xx-xxii), there was an old play with the plot of *Much Ado,* the play may have furnished Jonson an early example of this contrasted pair of girls. The scene (II, 3) in which Aurelia and Angelo bandy words represents Aurelia as the conventional witty woman of the Renaissance, a type which is also conspicuous in Shakespearian romantic comedy (cf. p. 202 *infra*).

Maximilian, aristocratic, careful of his honor, a leader of expeditions, responsible for younger men, and seemingly of middle age, is a distinct forerunner of a favorite type in Beaumont and Fletcher's plays. Ferneze,[1] the impatient, imperious father, is also met later in such plays as *Monsieur Thomas.* For neither character can I point out a model. Ferneze, as well as his two daughters, is distinctly treated as a humour type. The pages of *The Case is Altered,* with their rascality and their apish mockery of the tricks of court—especially with their mastery of compliment—are also English types, akin to the pages of Lyly, of *Damon and Pithias,* etc. The French page Pacue, who speaks a mixture of French and English, with words ending in *a,* reminds one of Jaques in *James IV*. There is a similar use of English and French in *Englishmen for my Money.*

The wealth of motives and material found in *The Case is Altered*—romantic love, romantic friendship, mazes of love entanglement, Plautine motives of lost and stolen children, clownish fads and folk points of view, satire on word-mongery and especially on unchecked follies—exhibits nearly every current that is apparent in the drama around 1597, when experiments were being made in many lines.

[1]The name is common in drama and story. Cf. *Farewell to Folly, Law Tricks, Malcontent, Bashful Lover, Patient Grissell.*

Certain of the trends are emphasized so strongly that they become significant of the future development of Jonson. Word-mongery Jonson satirizes elaborately, but it is not yet, as in the later plays, connected with the brilliant social types who gave the folly prominence. The dominant trend of character shown in such studies as those of the miser, the imperious man, the word-monger, the sober and the vivacious girl, gives promise of Jonson's later ability to center attention, with tremendous emphasis, upon the single folly or foible of a foolish character, and yet to combine satire on the characteristics of the social type with satire on the individual trait, thus rendering the newer abstraction for more natural. In the four comedies that followed, this interest became more and more absorbing, while structurally the plays weakened through the submergence of plot in character study.

CHAPTER VI

EVERY MAN IN HIS HUMOUR

Every Man in his Humour marks Jonson's complete mastery of the comedy of manners. The satirical tone of his work, the influence of current forms of literary satire, and above all the scheme for a definite program of humours and an extensive use of character sketches reach their apogee in *Every Man out of his Humour.* But the *dramatis personae* of *Every Man in* are representatives of social follies; much of the action results from the indulgence of the individual character in the particular tendency or humour absurdity that marks him; and the *saeva indignatio* of the satirist that seems to indicate personal impatience with follies and with the concrete types representing follies is developing strength. The play is consequently far in advance of either of the two plays representing outgrown tendencies, whatever their dates may be.

Perhaps the closest link between *The Case is Altered* and *Every Man in* lies in Jonson's dependence for both plays upon the conventional situations of Plautine comedy. Brainworm's espousing the cause of the son against the father in *Every Man in,* for instance, his resourcefulness and daring in the intrigue against the father, and his manipulation of events so that the son gets possession of the girl of whom he is enamored are thoroughly Latin. In *Every Man in,* however, Jonson has not used situations and characters derived immediately from Plautine plots as in *The Case is Altered;* the resemblances to the work of Plautus are only very general and often lie in phases of treatment that had become more or less conventional in the English drama before Jonson. The duped father, the gay son, and the equally gay young friend are only dimly suggestive of Plautus. Bobadill, the boastful, cowardly soldier, is a type from Latin comedy already common in English comedy.

There are no direct sources for any large part of Jonson's plot so far as I have been able to discover. Indeed there is little plot. With *Every Man in,* incident becomes of minor importance, and here, as in the later plays of the group, the stress is on the characters. In handling these characters Jonson was undoubtedly influenced by English literature more than by Latin. Not only was there a strong general tendency in the English drama to conventionality of treatment, but enough parallels can be pointed out between *Every Man in* and contemporary works to indicate that Jonson was a close student of English literature. Indeed, in this play, as elsewhere, Jonson's ability to treat freshly what is conventional, and to surpass his contemporaries in giving consistency to interwoven motives marks his measure of independence and originality.

It is, then, chiefly the origin of Jonson's characters that we are concerned with. Of these the most interesting for their literary connections are the gulls, and they illustrate admirably the fact that often what seems newest and most distinctive in Jonson's work merely resulted from the hardening into form of plastic material found at hand. In this case, however, scarcely so much can be claimed as Jonson's share in the work; for, new as was the term gull apparently,—and newer still its application to the especial type satirized in *Every Man in,*—the character of the gull had already been elaborately analyzed in contemporary literature, as we shall see.

The Hye Way to the Spyttell Hous (*ca.* 1550) furnishes the *New English Dictionary* with its earliest example of the word gull in the derived sense (l. 427):

> [The clewners] do but gull, and folow beggery,
> Feynyng true doyng by ypocrysy.

Here the verb apparently means merely to deceive. The next instance of this use that I am able to point out is in the play of *Sir Thomas More,* which may have been written as early as 1590 (I, 2, l. 151):

> But let them gull me, widgen me, rooke me, foppe me!
> Yfaith, yfaith, they are too short for me.

Nashe uses the term both as verb and as noun, with the meaning to dupe or one easily duped. It occurs in *The Terrors of the Night* and *The Unfortunate Traveller,* both entered on the Stationers' Register in 1593, and in the epistle "To the Reader" added to the 1594 edition of *Christs Teares ouer Ierusalem.*[1] The example

[1]Cf. *The Works of Nashe,* ed. McKerrow, Vol. I, p. 370; Vol. II, pp. 179, 222, and 298.

from *The Terrors of the Night* and one from Shakespeare's *Richard III* are the first uses of the word as a noun that are cited by the *New English Dictionary*. Donne also employs the term early (line 59 of his first satire, *ca.* 1593), and Lodge uses it in *Wits Miserie,* 1596 (p. 4). In *A Tale of a Tub,* Chanon Hugh assumes a disguise "to gull the constable" (III, 5), and the word occurs both an noun and as verb in *The Case is Altered* (III, 3; IV, 3; V, 2).[1] With the last decade of the sixteenth century, then, the word gull to mean a simpleton seems to have come into vogue. Doubtless it was a slang term that suddenly sprang into popularity. In its early uses the term as a noun has reference merely to one easily beguiled and led into folly, and as a verb to the duping of such a one. This first view of the gull connects him very readily with the fool so popular in all forms of literature throughout the century; and, like many names for the fool,—dotterel, daw, rook, etc.,—gull may have had its origin in the comparison of a fool to a silly bird. The early use in *Sir Thomas More* with the synonyms widgeon and rook would suggest this, as well as a passage in *Wily Beguiled* in which goose is associated with gull (Hazlitt's *Dodsley,* Vol. IX, p. 249).[2]

True to the temper of the age, the term did not long remain so general in its application. Presumably before the word had become widely familiar, it had already begun to be restricted to a specialized type of the simpleton. It is to Sir John Davies that we are indebted for our first full length portrait of the gull as a type.[3]

[1]If *Wily Beguiled* and *The Wisdom of Doctor Dodipoll* are as early as some scholars have thought, they are among the first works using the term freely. In *Wily Beguiled* it occurs three times (Hazlitt's *Dodsley,* Vol. IX, pp. 248, 249, and 276) and as often in *Doctor Dodipoll* (once in III, 2 and twice in Act V). The date of both plays is very uncertain. *Doctor Dodipoll* in its present form seems certainly as late as the end of 1599, for in III, 2, Alberdure says:

> Then reason's fled to animals, I see,
> And I will vanish like Tobaccho smoake—

apparently a satire on the passage in *Julius Caesar* (III, 2),

> O judgment, thou art fled to brutish beasts.

The wording is almost the same as in Jonson's satire on the same passage, which is put in the mouth of Clove in *Ev. M. out* (III, 1).

[2]Cf. *N. E. D.* for this and another possible derivation.

[3]The epigrams of Davies were doubtless complete and in circulation by the end of 1596. Cf. an article by me on "The Custom of Sitting on the Elizabethan Stage" in a forthcoming number of *Modern Philology.*

Having used the word in his first epigram, Davies devotes his second epigram to a definition of it:

> Oft in my laughing rimes, I name a Gull:
> But this new terme will many questions breed;
> Therefore at first I will expresse at full,
> Who is a true and perfect Gull indeed:
> A Gull is he who feares a veluet gowne,
> And, when a wench is braue, dares not speak to her;
> A Gull is he which trauerseth the towne,
> And is for marriage known a common woer;
> A Gull is he which while he proudly weares,
> A siluer-hilted rapier by his side;
> Indures the lyes and knocks about the eares,
> Whilst in his sheath his sleeping sword doth bide:
> A Gull is he which weares good handsome cloaths,
> And stands, in Presence, stroaking up his haire,
> And fills up his unperfect speech with oaths,
> But speaks not one wise word throughout the yeare:
> But to define a Gull in termes precise,—
> A Gull is he which seemes, and is not wise.

In Epigram 47, "Meditations of a Gull," Davies reverts to the subject:

> See, yonder melancholy gentleman,
> Which, hood-wink'd with his hat, alone doth sit!
> Thinke what he thinks, and tell me if you can,
> What great affaires troubles his little wit.
> He thinks not of the warre 'twixt France and Spaine,
> . . . .
> But he doth seriously bethinke him whether
> Of the gull'd people he be more esteem'd
> For his long cloake or for his great black feather,
> By which each gull is now a gallant deem'd;
> Or of a journey he deliberates,
> To Paris-garden, Cock-pit or the Play;
> Or how to steale a dog he meditates,
> Or what he shall unto his mistriss say:
> Yet with these thoughts he thinks himself most fit
> To be of counsell with a king for wit.

In 1598, a second satirist, Guilpin, gives an epigram (number 20) of his *Skialetheia* to further study of the gull, at the same time crediting Davies with an earlier definition. Guilpin's elaborate picture of the gull, almost certainly too late to have any direct influence on *Every Man in,* is all the more interesting as showing the conventionalized conception in a work appearing in the year of Jonson's play.

TO CANDIDUS

Friend Candidus, thou often doost demaund
What humours men by gulling understand:
Our English Martiall hath full pleasantly,
In his close nips describde a gull to thee:
I'le follow him, and set downe my conceit
What a gull is: oh word of much receit!
He is a gull, whose indiscretion
Cracks his purse strings to be in fashion;
He is a gull, who is long in taking roote
In baraine soyle, where can be but small fruite:
He is a gull, who runnes himselfe in debt,
For twelue dayes wonder, hoping so to get;
He is a gull, whose conscience is a block,
Not to take interest, but wastes his stock:
He is a gull, who cannot haue a whore,
But brags how much he spends upon her score:
He is a gull, that for commoditie
Payes tenne times ten, and sells the same for three:
He is a gull, who passing finicall,
Peiseth each word to be rhetoricall:
And to conclude, who selfe conceitedly,
Thinkes al men guls: ther's none more gull than he.

Thus the gull has come to be not merely a credulous and simple-minded fool, but an affected and pretentious fool. The second line of Guilpin's epigram suggests the connection between the gull and the study of humours. As gull, like humour, became more specific and restricted in its application, it was associated with humours to indicate a fool with his particular fads and inclination. With Jonson, however, the gull represents the folly that comes not from perversion or lack of breadth of view in a man of possible worth, as in the humour types, but from shallowness of mind accompanied by pretensions to gentility, bravery, wisdom, etc., where every action of the gull merely serves to emphasize his crudeness, cowardice, or stupidity. The gulls are zanies for the humour types, as Jonson indicates in *Cynthia's Revels.*[1]

[1]Mercury says of the gull Asotus in relation to Amorphus, "The other gallant is his Zany, and doth most of these tricks after him; sweats to imitate him in everything to a hair" (II, 1). See also *Ev. M. out,*

Before attempting a comparison of Jonson's gulls with those of the epigrams quoted, it will be necessary to take up the relation of *Every Man in* to Chapman's *An Humorous Day's Mirth* (1597), where we have in Labesha a companion study of the gull. Chapman's play probably suggested as much for *Every Man in* as did anything else in the drama. First of all, it seems to be the earliest play extant in which a definite program of humours is developed. Chapman uses the word humour for his types more consistently in *An Humorous Day's Mirth* than Jonson does in *The Case is Altered* of about the same date or in *Every Man in* of later date, to indicate the fundamental folly of the individual. In fact, the full influence of Chapman's comedy is not felt till *Every Man out*. But in both *Every Man in* and *An Humorous Day's Mirth,* it is clear that the characters are studied from the point of view of humours. The one typical humour that appears in both of the plays is jealousy, a form of mental unbalance which, among the prose writers who develop the use of the word, has the name humour applied to it oftener than does any other character inclination. Labervele of Chapman's play represents jealousy in a husband, corresponding to Kitely of *Every Man in* but not very similar. In addition Chapman deals with the jealous wife in the character of the Countess Moren.[1] A further link between the two plays is found in the treatment of the gull, as I have just indicated. *An Humorous Day's Mirth* first introduces the gull into comedy, and, while Chapman does not stress the type so consistently as Jonson does, the characterization is similar. Indeed, Jonson's advances over Davies are practically all anticipated by Chapman. One of the few character sketches in *An Humorous Day's Mirth* describes "a very fine gull" (p. 36),[2] and suggests pretty clearly Fungoso of *Every Man out,* who along with Sogliardo represents Jonson's continued inter-

IV, 1, where Brisk as an imitator of courtly types is compared to a zany. Florio in *A Worlde of Wordes*, 1598, defines the word *Zane* as "a gull or noddie," and also as any "vice, clowne, foole," etc.

[1]At the end of both plays, the characters, through the manipulation of the intriguers, are made to meet at a set place, and adjustments follow the comic embarrassment. For the type of conclusion in Jonson's play, *Look About You,* though probably not earlier than *Every Man in,* furnishes another parallel.

[2]The references to Chapman's works are by page to the volume of plays, edited by R. H. Shepherd, in the Chatto and Windus issue of *The Works of Chapman.*

est in the country gull. Stephen, the country gull of *Every Man in,* seems especially to have been modeled on Chapman's Labesha, with some touches of Blanuel, another type of gull in *An Humorous Day's Mirth.* Mathew, Jonson's town gull, also shows the same characteristics, but he is more complex, approaching the popularly satirized gallant—who really lays the foundation for many of the gulls but is to be kept distinct. A good test of the kinship between Stephen and Labesha is furnished by Davies' definition of a gull. The folly, the cowardice, the "unperfect speech" filled up with oaths, the melancholy, and other characteristics mentioned by Davies appear in both Stephen and Labesha, and to an extent in Mathew and Blanuel also.

Of course the chief stress in every delineation of the gull is on his "little wit." The foolish talk of Labesha and Stephen establishes the character of each at his very first appearance, and the attitude of Martia and the Elder Knowell to them in the early scenes merely emphasizes the impression. One phase of the gull's weak wit comes out in his taking his opinions and often his words from others. It is the nature of the gull to be a copy. Stephen's speech is molded out of the words or suggestions of others, and often it amounts to a mere echo.

> *Step[hen].* Cousin, how do you like this gentleman's verses?
> *E. Know[ell].* O, admirable! the best that ever I heard, coz.
> *Step.* Body o' Caesar, they are admirable! The best that I ever heard, as I am a soldier! (IV, 1).

Blanuel in *An Humorous Day's Mirth* is called the "complete ape" in compliment. To every complimentary salutation of Lemot, Blanuel replies as an exact echo, and has no words of his own to offer. Mathew assents to Stephen's claim that the latter's sword is a Toledo, and then agrees immediately with Bobadill's contemptuous verdict that it is a "poor provant rapier" (III, 1). He also accepts a Latin phrase, *incipere dulce,* quoting it without knowledge of its double meaning (IV, 1), and pretends to understand the Latin spoken by Wellbred (III, 1). Labesha attempts to quote Latin and to soliloquize philosophically in the manner of Dowsecer. He is nonplussed by Lemot's objection to his saying, "No matter for me," and accepts the statement that it is "the heinousest word in the world" (p. 36). Stephen is convinced that he may swear by his soldiership (III, 2, p. 35), and thus his use of a commonplace phrase is determined by the approval or disapproval of others. So the gulls are played upon by those from whom they would take their cue.

An exaggerated idea of his own importance and powers is another phase of the gull's simple-mindedness. According to Davies,

> He thinks himself most fit
> To be of counsell with a king for wit.

Labesha's egoism is pervasive, and comes out in the perfect confidence that he feels in the worth of his foolish talk. Mathew "doth think himself poet-major of the town" (I, 1), and scorns Downright as a clown lacking in good manners and speech (I, 4). Stephen, also, has a good opinion of himself. "By gads-lid I scorn it," he tells Knowell, "I, so I do, to be a consort for every humdrum . . . 'Slid, a gentleman mun show himself like a gentleman. Uncle, I pray you to be not angry; I know what I have to do, I trow, I am no novice" (I, 1). A part of the gull's egoism is his love of flattery. Both Labesha and Stephen are readily played upon by flattery. Labesha is cajoled by praise of his eye, his nose, his general perfection of feature (p. 29); and Brainworm gulls Stephen with ironical praise of his leg (I, 2). Mathew, too, is flattered by Bobadill, who tells him that a company of gallants drank to him the night before (I, 4).

The gull's "unperfect speech" filled up with oaths is exemplified in both Labesha and Stephen. Labesha's first speech begins with "I protest" (p. 24), and this is one of the oaths of Stephen as well as of Bobadill and Mathew—naturally, however, for it seems to have been affected by all gallants. "Forsooth" Labesha uses repeatedly in the same scene. The word forsooth is satirized by Jonson in *Poetaster* (IV, 1), *Penates,* and *The Masque of Christmas* as a citizen's oath, and is especially appropriate for the gull of clownish type (cf. also *I Henry IV,* III, 1). Except for the first scene in which he appears, however, oaths are not conspicuous in the portrayal of Labesha. Stephen's first oaths, also, are crude—"by gads-lid," "by my fackings," etc.—until he meets Bobadill and learns to swear like a gallant. Henceforth the greater part of his speech is larded with the oaths which ravish him in the mouth of Bobadill. His use of them is part of the portrayal of his mimicry, and Jonson has heightened the absurdity of the situation by making Stephen forget them at the crucial moment.

Cowardice covered by swaggering and boasts of valor is another characteristic stressed by Davies, Chapman, and Jonson, and marks the gull as an understudy to the braggart soldier. Mathew is a coward. He protests that he will speak to Bobadill of his mean lodging, but fawns and flatters when he meets his hero face to face; he laughs at Downright's threats, pretends to be eager to meet him, and then runs away when Downright attacks two at once. Stephen's boasting and cowardice are treated more ludicrously. In the opening scenes, he plays the swaggerer, attempts to pick a quarrel with a servingman, pretends to be anxious to waylay him, manages to miss him, declares his desire to follow him, and, when a means of overtaking him is suggested, offers a trivial excuse for refusing. In many other details Stephen is revealed as a boaster who backs down at the first suggestion that his boast is called.

> *Step[hen].* Oh, now I see who he laughed at: he laughed at somebody in that letter. By this good light, an he had laughed at me—
> *E[dward] Know[ell].* How now, Cousin Stephen, melancholy?
> *Step.* Yes, a little: I thought you had laughed at me, cousin.
> *E. Know.* Why, what an I had, coz? what would you have done?
> *Step.* By this light, I would have told mine uncle.
> *E. Know.* Nay, if you would have told your uncle, I did laugh at you, coz.
> *Step.* Did you, indeed?
> *E. Know.* Yes, indeed.
> *Step.* Why then—
> *E. Know.* What then?
> *Step.* I am satisfied; it is sufficient (I, 2).

In III, 1, when the disguised Brainworm enters while Stephen is still breathing out threatenings against him for selling him the faked Toledo, the dialogue is similar.

> *Step[hen].* Oh—od's lid! By your leave, do you know me, sir?
> *Brai[nworm].* Ay, sir, I know you by sight.
> *Step.* You sold me a rapier, did you not?
> *Brai.* Yes, marry did I, sir.
> *Step.* You said it was a Toledo, ha?
> *Brai.* True, I did so.
> *Step.* But it is none.
> *Brai.* No, sir, I confess it; it is none.

Step. Do you confess it? Gentlemen, bear witness, he has confest it:—Od's will, an you had not confest it—[1]

In his rôle of dragon guarding Martia, Labesha shows the same quality of courage when he is mocked by those who converse with her in defiance of him.

Mo[ren]. Well, sirrah, get you hence, or by my troth I'll have thee taken out in a blanket, tossed from forth our hearing.

[La]be[sha]. In a blanket? what, do you make a puppy of me? By skies and stones, I will go and tell your lady (p. 27).[2]

. . . .

[La]be[sha]. . . . Go to, mistress Martia, . . . are you not ashamed to stand talking alone with such a one as he?

Le[mot]. How, sir? with such a one as I, sir?

Be. Yea, sir, with such a one as you, sir.

Le. Why, what am I?

Be. What are you, sir? why, I know you well enough.

Le. Sirrah, tell me what you know me for, or else by heaven, I'll make thee better thou hadst never known how to speak.

Be. Why, sir, if you will needs know, I know you for an honourable gentleman and the king's minion, and were it not to you, there's ne'er a gentleman in Paris should have had her out of my hands (pp. 28, 29).

The melancholy of the gull that is mentioned in the second epigram quoted from Davies characterizes the gulls of both Chapman and Jonson. Lemot describes Blanuel as retiring, after his first salutations are over, "to a chimney, or a wall, standing folding his arms," and affecting silence (p. 23). Labesha, also, has his melancholy. On account of Martia's treatment of him, he grows "marvellous malcontent," and in imitation of Dowsecer, quotes Latin and attempts to utter profound soliloquies. By a bait of cream he is soon tempted out of his pose, and "his melancholy is well eased" (pp. 39, 40). So Stephen, when his cousin introduces him into

[1]This last example is suggestive of an epigram of Sir Thomas More as given in Kendall's *Flowers of Epigrams*, pp. 176, 177. It is called "A Iest of a Iackbragger." A soldier goes out to avenge himself on a clown.

Shaking his sword the souldier sayd,
  You slaue you vsde my wife:
I did so said the clowne, what then?
  I loue her as my life.
O doe you then confesse said he?
  (by all the gods I swere)
If thou hadst not confest the fact,
  it should haue cost thee dere.

[2]Later he threatens to tell Martia's father if she mocks him.

the group of gallants and gulls, stands aside in silence, until Wellbred asks, "But what strange piece of silence is this, the sign of the dumb man?" Stephen explains himself by saying, "I am somewhat melancholy, but you shall command me, sir, in whatsoever is incident to a gentleman." Mathew's interest is aroused at once.

Mat. But are you, indeed, sir, so given to it?
Step. Ay, truly, sir, I am mightily given to melancholy.
Mat. Oh, it's your only fine humour, sir; your true melancholy breeds your perfect fine wit, sir.[1] I am melancholy myself, divers times, sir, etc. (III, 1).

The love-making of his gulls and gallants Jonson touches only lightly in *Every Man in,* whereas it is a notable point with Davies and Chapman. Except for Stephen's boast of the jet ring with its posy that Mistress Mary sent him (II, 2), the treatment of the gull as a wooer is omitted in Stephen. But Mathew is the lover studying how he shall approach his mistress, and writing, or rather stealing, poems in her honor. In the end he is discarded for Knowell. So Labesha, on account of his money, is betrothed to Martia by her father, but loses her to Dowsecer in spite of his assiduity as a lover.[2] The gull in this is again the understudy of the English braggart. Ralph Roister Doister, Crackstone of *Two Italian Gentlemen,* and Basilisco of *Soliman and Perseda* all fail in love. Further, the "good handsome cloaths" of the gull are not conspicuous in *An Humorous Day's Mirth* or *Every Man in.* Both Stephen and Labesha have some wealth—Labesha enough to make him the suitor favored by Martia's father (p. 23)—but there is no lavishness about either. Rather, a touch of parsimony belongs to them. It is not until *Every Man out* that the finery of the gulls is stressed.

Mathew shows the folly, the weakness, the egoism, the love of flattery, the melancholy, and the cowardice of the ordinary gull, but he also approaches closely the posing gallant of the day. In fact, the pretentious and make-believe man of fashion became the best known type of gull from the time of Mathew and Brisk.

[1]Whalley traces this idea to Aristotle. See his note to the passage.

[2]There are traces in Labesha of the foolish but wealthy heir desired for his money, as in *Mother Bombie, Wily Beguiled,* and numerous other plays.

Davies' conception of a gull is that of a gallant. Jonson distinguishes Stephen and Mathew as the country and the town gull. The country gull often comes of good family and has wealth back of him; his follies arise partly from crudeness. The town gull, however, with no position socially and apparently no money,—Mathew's father is a "worshipful fishmonger," and on the day covered by the play Mathew starts with two shillings in his pocket,—has still caught some of the veneer of the fashionable without the individual force that marks a natural man. Jonson keeps the two types apart also in *Every Man out.* Brisk belongs to the town and Sogliardo and Fungoso to the country. Mathew's strongest point of individuality as a gull lies in his complimenting his mistress through shallow and stolen verses. Nashe in describing the nature of an upstart in *Pierce Penilesse* (*Works,* ed. McKerrow, Vol. I, pp. 168, 169), among many details that suggest various characters of Jonson, gives one detail that is interesting for this phase of Mathew: "All malcontent sits the greasie son of a Cloathier. . . . Sometimes (because Loue commonly weares the liuerey of Wit) hee will be an *Inamorato Poeta,* & sonnet a whole quire of paper in praise of Lady *Swin-snout,* his yeolow fac'd Mistres." So Mathew, the son of a fishmonger, says, "I am melancholy myself divers times, sir, and then do I . . . overflow you half a score, or a dozen of sonnets at a sitting" (III, 1). Satire on the shallow vein, the plagiarism, and the mawkish sentimentality of the gallant's verse is, of course, exceedingly common at the end of the century. The affectation of writing verse as a part of the convention of courtly love is perhaps the point of such attacks rather than the banality of the verse. Wooing and witless poetry are emphasized in Gullio of *The Return from Parnassus,* Part I, more than in the gull Mathew. Jonson himself gives fuller attention to these follies in his satire in *Cynthia's Revels* on the evils of courtiers.

The exact analysis of character and the tabulation of qualities were characteristic of medieval literature, with its numbered vices and virtues, its comparison of the traits of animals with those of men, and so on. The mode continued in the Renaissance. Spenser's *Faerie Queene* exemplifies the classification of qualities, and Jonson's masques again and again show the same method of literary treatment. Criticism was academic, and called for fixed standards, forms, and modes. The stress on decorum in character emphasized types rather than individuals. Rhetorical studies took the form of elaborate classifications. This interest in analysis and classification may well account for the study of types in Elizabethan literature and for the recurrence of certain details in such types as the gull, the cobbler, the clown. The tendency would be all the more natural in a man like Jonson, trained in the school of classicism, and especially versed in satire, where characters are built up from a certain number of external follies. The restriction of these types to a comparatively small number; the constant repetition of even such specific types as the revenger, the malcontent, the braggart soldier, and the patient wife; and the fact that many of these types were introduced from foreign literature would all indicate not direct observation of life but literary convention. Accordingly, even though there may be only a similarity in generalized qualities and little resemblance in detail, one feels justified in saying that Jonson took over the groundwork for his gulls from Davies and Chapman and drew on life merely for touches here and there that make the types more concrete. In all ages writers had scored separately all the follies that unite in the gull, and doubtless all had existed in single individuals before characters like Mathew were portrayed; but such a grouping or such a mode of approach had not been followed. When the gull had once been fixed as a type, men saw the same character much more frequently. But it was to literature that they owed the insight, and Jonson could still go to Erasmus, and Dekker to "Grobianus" for phases of the treatment of the gull. So there followed a succession of gulls in the satire on the follies of the time. Jonson dealt with gulls in *Every Man in, Every Man out,* and *Cynthia's Revels,* varying the types only in details. As late as *The Silent Woman* he made elaborate studies of the type in Daw and La-Foole, with their pretensions to learning, to the favor of women, and to courage, and with their disgrace in wooing and in fighting. Other writers followed the type as assiduously. In Gullio of *The Return from Parnassus,* Part I, (*ca.* 1599) many details of Jonson's gulls are repeated, but wooing, writing of verse, and braggadocio are especially stressed. Emulo of *Patient Grissell* (1599) seems close akin to Brisk in his boasting and cowardice, his notable battle, etc., and to Mathew in his misfortunes in love and his sonnets in honor of his mistress, though as in Gullio the last details show the closer approach of the gull to the courtier. The *Gullinge Sonnets* of Davies, "A doozen of Gulles" at the end of *Pasquils Jests,* and *The Guls Horne-booke* furnish examples of the word as used in titles.

This view of Jonson's gulls gives a point of departure for a digression on the subject of the personal satire in Jonson's attacks. In general it seems to me that the importance of his personal hostilities in determining his literary treatment has been greatly overstressed. Preconceptions in regard to Jonson's satire on Marston, for example, have kept many close students of both writers from emphasizing sufficiently, I think, the kinship of their early work before Marston's excesses spoiled the relation. It seems entirely in keeping with what we know of the man Jonson to suppose that he would enjoy filling in a type character with details fitting some individual whom he wished to ridicule. That he undoubtedly did, but I doubt whether in any case he allowed personal satire to interfere with the moral purpose of his comedies,—the attack on typical follies as a means of upholding fundamental social laws. Even the characters who are spokesmen for Jonson embody principles. Indeed, with respect to various characters of Jonson who have been identified with this or that prominent London contemporary, the objection can be raised that they are so evidently types and so closely approach abstractions as to give one little ground, outside of contemporary references, on which to build a surmise as to identity.

Professor Penniman, for instance, in the introduction to his forthcoming edition of *Poetaster* and *Satiromastix* remarks: "While the affected courtier, the country gull, and the town gull were undoubtedly types, the particular example of them found in the characters of Gullio and Matheo as we have seen, and in Fastidious Brisk in *Every Man out,* Hedon in *Cynthia's Revels,* and Emulo in *Patient Grissell,* as we shall see, were also Daniel." But the identification of these characters with Daniel must rest upon the applicability of minor points in the satire, for every general point in their characterization is conventional. Professor Penniman of course recognizes the type underlying these figures, but he seems to me to underestimate their conventionality. Though Jonson undoubtedly satirizes Daniel frequently, the satire is incidental, I believe, as in the lines which Mathew plagiarizes, or rather parodies, from his works. It must be admitted that, if any man in public life sat for the portrait of these gulls and gallants, it would naturally be Daniel. He was connected with the court, wrote court poetry, and seemingly affected courtly or Italianate manners; he was a conspicuous figure, the center of intense admiration and even more intense hostility; and finally, on account of his being so much in the limelight, certain adverse criticisms on his work became conventionalized, and this itself suggests the possibility that his personality may have been conventionally satirized. These are the strongest grounds, however, for seeing Daniel in these early figures, and, tempting as the identification is, it seems to me unsafe to make it. I myself have attempted to follow out only the conventional lines of treatment in these plays of Jonson, and so have avoided any effort to get at what is personal. It is not out of keeping with my purpose, however, to point out that, where Jonson attacks Daniel openly in his incidental satire, the point of attack is conventional. The satire in *The Silent Woman,* II, 1, on those who compare Daniel with Spenser seems to be by way of reply to a claim of Daniel's admirers. Davison in *A Poetical Rapsody* says of Daniel that his "Muse hath surpassed Spenser" (*Cambridge History of English Literature,* Vol. IV, p. 160). Daniel's "silent rhetoric" and "dumb eloquence" are ridiculed both in *Every Man out,* III, 1, and in *The Staple of News,* III, 1. The same bit of satire is found in Davies' Epigram 45, *In Dacum*, supposedly Daniel.[1] The most notable point in the direct attack on Daniel lies in the verdict that he was after all not a poet. Jonson, apparently in a mood of intended fairness, told Drummond, "Samuel Daniel was a good honest man, had no children; but no poet." The same point is made in *The Forest,* where Jonson, in what is clearly a reference to Daniel, speaks of a rival poet as a "better verser," or "Poet, in the court-account" ("Epistle to Elizabeth, Countess of Rutland," *Works,* Vol. III, p. 272). Davies in another epigram addressed *In Dacum,* No. 30, satirizes the prosiness of Dacus, who is numbered among the poets but is none. Drayton in *Of Poets and Poesy* later says that Daniel's "maner better fitted prose." All this, however, seems to me merely an application to Daniel of a commonplace distinction of Renaissance criticism—that between the true and the false poet. Rhymer and verser are fre-

[1]But see Grosart's edition of Davies, Vol. 1, pp. cxxi f., for the claim that Dacus is not Daniel and even that "silent eloquence" is conventional. Cf. also Small, *Stage-Quarrel*, pp. 192 ff.

quently applied to the uninspired poet. Elyot in *The Governour* (Vol. I, p. 120 of Croft's edition) says: "Semblably they that make verses, expressynge therby none other lernynge but the craft of versifyeng, be nat of auncient writers named poetes, but onely called versifyers." In connection with this passage Croft refers the idea back to Quintilian and to Æneas Sylvius, and cites Puttenham. According to Drummond, Jonson "thought not Bartas a Poet, but a Verser." There is a passage, also, in *Cynthia's Revels* (II, 1) in which Mercury says of Hedon, who is the Italianate courtier and consequently a sonneteer, "Himself is a rhymer, and that's thought better than a poet." (See also *Timber,* ed. Schelling, p. 76). The expression has been used to connect Hedon with Daniel, but to my mind it is hardly necessary to read into it more than the general Renaissance distinction between poets true and false. Even where Daniel is unquestionably attacked, however, the satire seems to be expressive not so much of personal hostility to Daniel as of the critical conventions of the school to which Jonson belongs.

In the Quarto of *Every Man in,* Prospero, or Wellbred, in writing of Mathew and Bobadill,[1] says, *"I can shew thee two of the most perfect, rare, & absolute true* Gulls, *that euer thou saw'st"* (ll. 166 f.). In the revised form, however, this has been changed. Perhaps Jonson consciously refrained from classifying Bobadill with the gulls on account of his closer approach to the *miles gloriosus* type than the ordinary gull or false gallant shows. But the margin between Bobadill and the gull is a narrow one. On the one hand, the gulls, especially as they approach a station of some dignity, have taken over many traits of the braggart; they are boasters, swaggerers, cowards, and unsuccessful lovers. On the other hand, Bobadill verges upon the gull in combining with his braggadocio a gallantry which is tinsel and which he is put to his wits' end to maintain. Still Bobadill is the braggart soldier, a type but not a counterfeit or imitation as are the gulls; rather he has his independence and his power of taking the initiative. It is only when he has been beaten by Downright that he becomes a weak second to Mathew in the pursuit of vengeance.

As a bragging soldier Bobadill of course has a number of prede-

[1]For suggestions as to the origin of the name cf. 4 *N. and Q.*, Vol. VII, p. 208, and *Englische Studien,* Vol. 36, pp. 331, 332. Cf. also the British Museum catalogue for a list of authors who bore the name.

cessors in the English drama and in general literature. Graf in *Der Miles Gloriosus* has studied the type in the English drama, stressing naturally the boastfulness of the soldier. But for Bobadill I am concerned chiefly with the development of a more specific and complex character, one with marks of English gallantry. Perhaps the best evidence of the conventionality of this type with its English turn may be found in the braggarts of *The Two Italian Gentlemen* and *Soliman and Perseda,* plays showing forms of the *miles gloriosus* as crude as Pyrgopolinices, and yet furnishing a better preparation for Bobadill, absurd as they are, than do the Latin prototypes.

In Crackstone of *The Two Italian Gentlemen*[1] there are a few suggestions of Bobadill. Crackstone "braues it with the best, in euery company" (l. 22; cf. l. 63 also),[2] as Bobadill pretends to gallantry and choice of friends. He affects elegant language, but his speech is really bombastic and perverted, whereas Bobadill's language is correct and never overdone, but merely the stilted and affected speech of gallants. Both use Italian terms, and this is perhaps significant of the new elegance of the times. Comment is made on Crackstone's language (l. 1377) as on Bobadill's. Of course each braggart tells of the marvelous deeds he has accomplished, of the enemies he has slain, and each seemingly longs to fight his adversary, makes a show of being formidable, and cringes at the mere approach of danger. When Crackstone is overthrown ingloriously after his great pretense of bravery, he accepts the situation and explains it by saying (l. 1330),

T'is the Fortune of warre, lucke runnes not euer to one side.

So Bobadill explains his cowardice by saying that he was "fascinated," bewitched (IV, 7). After Crackstone's overthrow Pedante asks (ll. 1308 f.),

[1]Frangipetra, the soldier of Fraunce's *Victoria,*—which has for its source the same Italian play, *Il Fedele* of Pasqualigo, from which the author of *Two Ital. Gent.* derived his plot,—is slightly sketched, and the stress is on the pedant. Probably the braggart was as lightly touched in the original play as in Fraunce's. Cf. *Mod. Lang. Review,* Vol. III, pp. 177-181. The English dramatist added to the character and transferred to the braggart the whole episode of the pedant's love affair, so that the final result is probably an English study of the boastful soldier.

[2]The references are by line to Flügge's edition of the play in *Archiv für das Studium der neueren Sprachen und Literaturen,* Vol. 123, pp. 45 ff.

> Is this my lusty kill Cow, that will eate vp so many men at a bit,
> And when he deales with a shadowe will not stand to it?

In *Every Man in* (V, 1), when Bobadill enters his complaint that Downright has beaten him, Justice Clement exclaims, "O, God's precious! is this the soldier?" The interesting thing about this treatment of Crackstone is that so early in the history of the drama an English dramatist, either Chapman or Munday, has begun to develop the peculiar characteristics of the braggadocio gallant.

In the same way Basilisco of *Soliman and Perseda,* though he is portrayed in the spirit of nonsensical bombast and burlesque, as was the Latin soldier, shows some advances toward the English combined gallant and braggart.[1] His affected language and his oaths are only dimly suggestive of Bobadill.[2] More interesting is Basilisco's pretended gallantry, in which some of the traits of Bobadill are foreshadowed. Piston in giving a character sketch of Basilisco says, "He goes many times supperles to bed, and yet he takes Phisick to make him leane. Last night he was bidden to a gentlewomans to supper," etc. (I, 3, ll. 214 ff.). Bobadill at his first appearance tells of having been invited to dine with gallants the night before; but that morning, having no money, he condescends to let Mathew pay for his breakfast and is content to take the most frugal fare (I, 4). Both Basilisco and Bobadill show the refinement of braggardism that expresses itself not in boasts of enemies slain but in pretence to great skill in the use of arms. In I, 3, Basilisco comments on the tourney: "Their Launces were coucht too hie, and their steeds ill borne" (l. 183); and a little later,

> Prettie, prettie, but not famous;
> Well for a learner, but not for a warriour.

The same kind of expert criticism is called forth in the fencing lesson which Bobadill gives Mathew (I, 4). "A well experienced hand would pass upon you at pleasure," he tells Mathew; and later, "Why, you do not manage your weapon with any facility or

[1]Miss Winifred Smith, in *Modern Philology*, Vol. V, p. 562, traces to Italian comedy the name Basilisco and also the new trend towards inflated diction in the treatment of the type.

[2]Basilisco swears "by the marble face of the Welkin" (I, 3, l. 193 in Boas's edition) and Bobadill "by this welkin" (IV, 5). Naturally both swear upon their honor. Compare *Two Ital. Gent.*, ll. 10, 11, for Crackstone's oaths.

grace to invite me. I have no spirit to play with you," etc. This comes out more strongly in IV, 5, where Bobadill explains on the ground of jealousy the ill will borne him by professional fencing masters, and is led on by Knowell to his famous boast of how he with nineteen others chosen by an instinct peculiar to him would be a sufficient standing army for the whole realm. The cruder forms of boasting characterize Basilisco also. When he is warned that the enemy whom he is seeking has "planted a double cannon in the doore," Basilisco replies (II, 2, ll. 58 ff.):

> Thinkes he bare cannon shot can keepe me back?
> Why, wherfore serues my targe of proofe but for the bullet?
> That once put by, I roughly come vpon him.

So Bobadill instructs Mathew (I, 4), "Should your adversary confront you with a pistol, 'twere nothing, by this hand! you should, by the same rule, control his bullet, in a line," etc. Later, in his account of being the first man to enter a breach, he uses the cannon (III, 1): "They had planted me three demi-culverins just in the mouth of the breach; . . . their master-gunner . . . confronts me with his linstock, ready to give fire; I . . . discharged my petronel in his bosom, and . . . put 'em pell-mell to the sword." Finally there are some similar touches when the two braggarts begin to trim sail. Basilisco says of the page Piston (II, 2, ll. 88 ff.):

> Doubtlesse he is a very tall fellow;
> And yet it were a disgrace to all my chiualrie
> To combate one so base:
> Ile send some Crane to combate with the Pigmew;
> Not that I feare, but that I scorne to fight.

When Knowell ironically expresses fear for Downright, Bobadill answers, "If he were here now, by this welkin, I would not draw my weapon on him . . . but I will bastinado him, by the bright sun, wherever I meet him" (IV, 5). A few moments later, when Downright descends upon him and orders him to draw his weapon, Bobadill protests, "Tall man, I never thought on it till now—Body of me, I had a warrant of the peace served on me, even now as I came along," etc., and Downright immediately disarms and beats him.

Falstaff is too strongly individualized to contribute much to the study of a type. Graf, however, in *Der Miles Gloriosus* (pp. 45,

46) has pointed out a number of minor parallels between him and Bobadill. Besides these, Falstaff's "I will imitate the honourable Roman in brevity" (*II Henry IV,* II, 2) and "I will not use many words with you" (III, 2) may be worth recalling in connection with Bobadill's "I love few words" (III, 1). This affectation of brevity in speech probably arises from the accepted notion that a man of action is little given to words.[1]

Bragadino of *The Blind Beggar of Alexandria,* a brief sketch, shows the braggart soldier in the rôle of a Spanish gallant. Humour is one of his favorite words, used not as Pistol uses it but as an Elizabethan gallant would use it. His affected language is as far as Bobadill's from the mere clownish travesty of fine talking that we find in the ordinary braggart soldier. Braggart and coward though he is, there is in Bragadino's actions as in Bobadill's an approach to dignity that is new, and indeed he several times expresses a dislike of doing what is "ridiculous." Bragadino also declares, "I love few words" (p. 6). He attempts to parley with the fiery Count Hermes as Bobadill does with Downright, but will not fight. "I do not like this humour in thee in pistoling men in this sort," he tells the count; "it is a most dangerous and stigmatical humour; . . . otherwise I do hold thee for the most tall, resolute, and accomplished gentleman on the face of the earth" (p 7).[2] In this brief encounter it also comes out that Bragadino, like Bobadill, understands the virtues of a friendly pipe of tobacco.

A few minor points in the characterization of Bobadill as a gallant are interesting. In Epigram 22 Davies, after describing a gallant who strives for the newest fashions and fads, concludes,

> Yet this new fangled youth, made for these times,
> Doth aboue all praise old George Gascoine's rimes?

So Bobadill and Mathew—in the very scene (I, 4) in which Bobadill says of his boot, "It's the fashion gentlemen now use"—are made ridiculous by their praise of the old-fashioned *Spanish Tragedy.* The cavaliers who admire Harvey's works are also satirized by Nashe in a passage from *Haue with you to Saffron-walden* that

[1]In *II Henry IV* (III, 2) Bardolph and Shallow play at length with the word accommodate. This word is used by Bobadill, and Jonson in *Timber* (p. 71, ed. Schelling) mentions it as one of "the perfumed terms of the time."

[2]Bobadill speaks of himself in contrast with Downright as being "a man in no sort given to this filthy humour of quarrelling" (V, 1).

is worth quoting. Importuno says of Harvey (*Works,* Vol. III, p. 41):

> His stile is not easie to be matcht, beeing commended by diuers (of good iudgement) | for the best that ere they read.

And Piers replies:

> Amongst the which number is a red bearded thrid-bare Caualier, who (in my hearing) at an ordinarie, as he sat fumbling the dice after supper, fell into these tearmes (no talke before leading him into it): There is such a Booke of *Harueys* . . . as I am a Souldiour and a Gentleman, I protest, I neuer met with the like contriued pile of pure English.[1] O, it is deuine and most admirable, & so farre beyond all that euer he published heretofore, as day-light beyond candle-light," etc.

In like manner Bobadill and Mathew praise *The Spanish Tragedy,* a subject introduced as inconsequentially as were Harvey's works by the "thrid-bare Caualier":

> *Bob.* Well penned! I would fain see all the poets of these times pen such another play as that was. . . .
>
> *Mat.* Indeed here are a number of fine speeches in this book. . . . Is't not excellent? Is't not simply the best that ever you heard, captain?[2]

One conspicuous mark of the gallant is not wanting in Bobadill—he is a devotee of tobacco. In III, 2, we have a notable speech from him on the subject of its miraculous powers. Arber in his edition of King James's *Counterblaste to Tobacco* gives a number of quotations from various works showing the miracles attributed to tobacco.[3] One of the works cited, Frampton's *Joyfull newes* (1577), translated from French and Spanish, contains accounts of the power of tobacco to heal wounds, ulcers, scrofula, etc. (Arber,

[1]Compare Bobadill's stricture on Downright immediately after the discussion of *The Spanish Tragedy* (I, 4): "I protest to you, as I am a gentleman and a soldier, I ne'er changed words with his like. . . . He has not so much as a good phrase in his belly."

[2]Such extravagant and pointless expressions of praise seem to characterize the "little wits" of the time. Stephen, echoing Knowell's ironic judgment, seriously declares of Mathew's verses, "They are admirable! The best that I ever heard, as I am a soldier" (IV, 1). Labervele in *An Humorous Day's Mirth* pronounces some of his own verses "wonderful rare and witty, nay divine!" and "the best that e'er I heard," etc. (p. 25). Labesha says of his prospective father-in-law's speech, "I protest, sir, you speak the best that ever I heard" (p. 24).

[3]Cf. Nashe's reference in *Lenten Stuffe* to the custom of writing about the miracles of tobacco, *Works,* Vol. III, p. 177.

pp. 81-84). The passage which Arber quotes from Hariot's *Briefe and true report of the new found land of Virginia* (1588) also attributes to tobacco the power to cure by purging "superfluous fleame and other grosse humors." For Bobadill's speech the most interesting detail cited by Arber (p. 85) is from Hakluyt: "The *Floridians* when they trauell haue a kinde of herbe dryed, which with a cane, and an earthen cup in the end, with fire and the dried herbs put together, do sucke thorow the cane the smoke thereof, which smoke satisfieth their hunger, and therewith they live foure or fiue dayes without meat or drinke, and this all the Frenchmen vsed for this purpose." Compare with this what Bobadill says of the power of tobacco to sustain life: "I have been in the Indies, where this herb grows, where neither myself, nor a dozen gentlemen more of my knowledge, have received the taste of any other nutriment in the world, for the space of one and twenty weeks, but the fume of this simple only."

For the rest of Bobadill's speech, the closest parallel that I have noted is in Epigram 36 of Davies, "Of Tobacco."

Jonson	Davies
Therefore, it cannot be, but 'tis most divine. Further, take it in the nature, in the true kind: so, it makes an antidote, that had you taken the most deadly poisonous plant in all Italy, it should expel it, and clarify you, with as much ease as I speak. And for your green wound,—your Balsamum and your St. John's wort are all mere gulleries and trash to it. . . . I could say what I know of the virtue of it, for the expulsion of rheums, raw humours, crudities, obstructions, with a thousand of this kind; but I profess myself no quacksalver. Only thus much; by Hercules I do hold it, and will affirm it before any prince in Europe, to be the most sovereign and precious weed that ever the earth tendered to the use of man.	Homer, of Moly and Nepenthe sings: Moly, the gods' most soueraigne hearb diuine, ... But this our age another world hath found, From whence an hearb of heauenly power is brought; Moly is not so soueraigne for a wound, Nor hath Nepenthe so great wonders wrought: It is Tobacco, whose sweet substantiall fume The hellish torment of the teeth doth ease, By drawing downe, and drying up the rheume, ... It is Tobacco, which doth cold expell,

And Knowell adds:

This speech would have done decently in a tobacco-trader's mouth.

And cleares the obstructions of the arteries,
And surfeits, threatning death, dijesteth well,
Decocting all the stomack's crudities:

. . . .

It is Tobacco, which hath power to rarifie
The thick grosse humour which doth stop the hearing;

. . . .

O, that I were one of those Mountebankes,
Which praise their oyles and powders which they sell!
My customers would giue me coyne with thanks; etc.

Finally, Bobadill's purpose to rid the country of enemies (IV, 5) is noticeably of the nature of the projects and monopolies which Jonson worked out so fully later in Politick Would-be and Meercraft. These were matters of current satire before *Every Man in.* See *The Merie Tales of Skelton,* iv; *Mery Tales and Quicke Answeres,* 138; *Pleasant Conceites of Old Hobson,* 12; and Nashe's *Strange Newes* (Vol. I, p. 331). A succinct history of monopolies during Elizabeth's reign is given in Price's *English Patents of Monopoly.*

Thus the Plautine and the traditionary influence in the treatment of the braggart soldier undoubtedly remains in the literature of Jonson's period, but there is a growing tendency, exemplified in *The Two Italian Gentlemen* and *Soliman and Perseda,* to a treatment of the type more in accord with new conditions and new standards of manners. So in Bobadill we have a character who in certain fundamental traits illustrates the older conventions of the type, but one who has more qualities of the would-be gallant. These very qualities, of course, had quickly become conventionalized for the braggart in an age prone to borrowing. Much of the repetition in the various treatments of the type may be due to the fads that held sway in contemporary society, but the fads in literature are equally strong. When one phase of a character treatment or one mode of attack on follies had attracted attention, it was freely utilized, especially where it added to the realism of the character.

Perhaps the new type of braggart soldier was a native English type. Such men as Stukeley, for example, must have lent verisimilitude to the stage braggart. At any rate, the pretended soldier and his near kinsman the boasting traveler are especially popular objects of satire. The marvelous experiences and the marvelous exploits of men who have never left their native heath are treated again and again in the literature of the period.[1] Though on account of the sameness of literary treatment it seems quite safe to say that there is a large influence of literary conventions in these satirical portraits and sketches, they undoubtedly depicted many an upstart in England, so that as a generalized picture of manners they are true to life.

Of the other socially inferior characters of the play, Cob and Brainworm are alone strongly or distinctly characterized. Cash and Formal are not complex; in fact, they do little more than serve as foils for Kitely and Brainworm. Cob himself in a sense furnishes a foil for the comic action. The humblest of clownish types, he is yet preyed upon by the pretentious Bobadill, who lives in his house; he prepares us for the appearance of Mathew and Bobadill by his characterization of them; his clownish notions of the effect of tobacco present a sharp contrast to Bobadill's praise of its virtues; he is the only person whom Bobadill dares to attack; one scene between him and his wife furnishes an excellent burlesque of Kitely's fear of being cuckolded; he affords an opportunity for the expression of Justice Clement's mad humour; he acts as messenger, and at his house assemble the various characters duped by Brainworm. Altogether he is an effective linking device for the play. But withal there is an independent interest in his portrayal. He is more than a mere fool or merrymaker for the groundlings, representing, as he does in part, the cruder London citizen with a

[1]For this motive or slight variations on it cf. Hall, *Virgidemiarum*, Book III, Satire VII; Nashe, *Works*, Vol. I, pp. 169 and 205; Lodge, *Wits Miserie*, Hunterian Club, p. 4; *Defence of Conny-catching*, *Works of Greene*, ed. Grosart, Vol. XI, pp. 72 ff.; Bullein, *Dialogue against the Fever Pestilence*, p. 111; *Ship of Fools*, ed. Jamieson, Vol. II, pp. 66, 67; *Merry Knack to Know a Knave*, Hazlitt's *Dodsley*, Vol. VI, p. 512. But compare Theophrastus's character of the Boastful Man, who, though he has never been out of Attica, pretends to have served under Alexander, to have brought home gemmed cups, etc.

half whimsical, half serious and dignified attitude to himself and his neighbors. Cob is older than the usual clown, a married man, a housekeeper, and a water bearer,—a typical poor citizen. The same type of clown appears in Simplicity of *The Three Ladies of London* and *The Three Lords and Three Ladies of London.* In the second play, Simplicity is middle-aged, is married to Painful Penury, and has been a water bearer, as his wife now is. Both clowns represent the simpler and cruder poor man of London in contrast with characters who represent the follies or evils of London. Both clowns have their affected language, their whimsical conceits, and their marks of coarseness. Both have a shrewd perception of the follies around them, and are naively satirical in their attitude to them. Both suffer from the shams and rascalities of their superiors. In *The Three Ladies of London,* Simplicity at the opening characterizes Fraud, who preys upon him, much as Cob does Bobadill and Mathew; Fraud would beat Simplicity for expressing his views of evils, as Bobadill does beat Cob in III, 2; and later Simplicity is beaten through Fraud's rascality. In *The Three Lords and Three Ladies of London* Fraud's capture is effected through Simplicity as Bobadill is to be arrested through Cob; and, interestingly enough, Fraud is bound to a post, a type of punishment that Justice Clement in the Quarto promises Bobadill and Mathew. The kinship of the two characters emphasizes the didactic purpose underlying Jonson's work, with all of his realism and concreteness.[1] Cob seems to be an artistic treatment of the type represented in Simplicity, in People of *Respublica,* and in other clowns of the moralities.

Cob's mock genealogy and his plays upon his name have many English as well as classic precedents.[2] Two passages are given to his genealogy (I, 3 and III, 2). "Why, sir, an ancient lineage, and a princely," he tells Mathew. "Mine ance'try came from a king's belly . . . herring, the king of fish. . . . The first red herring that was broiled in Adam and Eve's kitchen, do I fetch my pedigree from, by the harrot's book. His cob was my great, great, mighty great grandfather." Later (III, 2) he cries out on fasting, because his "lineage goes to wrack; poor cobs! they smoke

[1]Cf. pp. 253 ff. *infra* for the relation of *Cynthia's Revels* to Wilson's plays.

[2]The name of Onion in *The Case is Altered* and of Peter Tub in *A Tale of a Tub* are both played upon.

for it," etc. In *James IV* (IV, 3) Slipper gives a similar mock pedigree: "A fine neate calues leather . . . is my neer kinsman, for I am *Slipper* . . . Guidwife Calf was my grandmother, and goodman Neather-leather mine Vnckle; but my mother, good woman, Alas, she was a Spaniard." Gluttony in *Doctor Faustus*,[1] also, tells of his ancestry: "My grandfather was a Gammon of Bacon, my Grandmother a hogshead of Claret wine," etc.[2]

Brainworm, the intriguer of the play, represents the slave of Latin comedy in his love of intrigue, his resourcefulness and boldness, and his duping of the father through loyalty to the son. Attention has also been called to Brainworm's likeness to the Italian zany, always intriguing by elaborate ruses and disguises "to humiliate his master's enemies and rivals."[3] But with the general foundation for the figure already laid, Jonson has filled in the characterization of Brainworm from English sources. In many details of the treatment Brainworm is the typical English coney-catcher. His first disguise is that of a common soldier begging for livelihood, and his boasted experiences furnish an interesting counterpart to Bobadill's. The soldier with the "smoky varnish" on his face pretends to have served fourteen years by land and sea, to have been wounded often and severely, to have been made a galley-slave thrice, to have seen many battles, sieges, and campaigns in various lands, and finally, coming home, to have been compelled to beg. This disguise of Brainworm's was a regular device of a coney-catcher whose line was begging. Honesty of *A Knack to Know a Knave* (Hazlitt's *Dodsley*, Vol. VI, p. 512) describes the character briefly:

[1]Quoted from the Quarto of 1604.

[2]Mouse of *Mucedorus* is the son of Rat, I, 4. Cf. also the kinship of Sly in *The Taming of the Shrew;* Pock of *All Fools*, III, 1; the personified Pint-pot of *English Traveller*, III, 4; and Ninny of *Woman is a Weathercock*, I, 2. Somewhat similar passages occur in *Like Will to Like*, Hazlitt's *Dodsley*, Vol. III, p. 335, and *Birth of Merlin*, III, 4. The sons and daughters of Christmas in Jonson's *Masque of Christmas*, and similar folk burlesques may be mentioned in this connection. In *The Silent Woman* Jonson gives a notable source for the great house of La-Foole, which much resembles that of Goosecappe in *Sir Gyles Goosecappe*, ll. 97 ff. Pilcher's name in *Blurt, Master Constable*, I, 2, is played upon just as Cob's is, and the puns are somewhat similar.

[3]Cf. the article by Miss Winifred Smith in *Modern Philology*, Vol. V, pp. 562 ff.

And cogging Dick was in the crew that swore he came from France:
He swore that in the king's defence he lost his arm by chance.

A fuller description of him is found in *The Hye Way to the Spyttel Hous* (ll. 279 ff.):

For they do were souldyers clothyng,
And so beggyng deceyue folke ouer all,

. . . .

. . . whan a man wold bryng them to thryft,
They wyll hym rob, and fro his good hym lyft.

. . . .

These be they that dayly walkes and jettes
In theyr hose trussed rounde to theyr dowblettes,
And say: good maysters, of your charyte,
Helpe vs poore men that come from the se;
From Bonauenture we were caste to lande,
God it knowes, as poorly as we stande!
And som*t*yme they say that they were take in Frau*n*ce,
And had ben there vii. yeres in duraunce;
In Muttrell, in Brest, in Tourney or Tyrwyn,
In Morlays, in Cleremount or in Hedyn;
And to theyr countrees they haue ferre to gone,
And amonge them all peny haue they none.
Now, good mennes bodyes, wyll they say then,
For Goddes sake helpe to kepe vs true men![1]

The list of places suggests Brainworm's campaigns. In many details this sketch is like Harman's picture of the type in his *Caueat for Common Cursetors,* though Harman is slightly closer to Brainworm:

Eyther he [the Ruffler] hath serued in the warres, or els he hath bene a seruinge man . . . And with stout audacyte, demaundeth where he thinketh hée maye be bolde, and circomspecte ynough, as he sethe cause to aske charitie, rufully and lamentably, that it would make a flyntey hart to relent, and pytie his miserable estate, howe he hath bene maymed and broused in the warres (*The Rogues and Vagabonds of Shakspere's Youth,* ed. Viles and Furnivall, New Shakspere Society, p. 29).
[The Upright Man—who is very similar to the Ruffler—will] stoutely demaund his charytie, eyther shewing how he hath serued in the warres, and their maymed, eyther that he sekethe seruice, and saythe that he woulde be glad to take payne for hys lyuinge, althoughe he meaneth nothinge lesse (p. 31).

[1]See Hazlitt's note to the passage, *Early Popular Poetry,* Vol. IV, pp. 38 ff.

And if they chaunce to be retained into seruice, through their lamentable words, with any welthy man, They wyll tary but a smale tyme, either robbing his maister or som of his fellowes (p. 34).

All this exactly describes Brainworm, with his war record, his weeping, his proposal to rob the elder Knowell, and his taking of service.[1]

The incident that starts Brainworm on his career as a pretended officer of the law was possibly taken from the section "How *George* serued his Hostis" in *The Jests of Peele* (*Shakespeare Jest-Books,* Vol. II, pp. 302 ff.), which were probably current before *Every Man in* was written.[2] The story is told of how Peele, having arranged for his clothes and everything in the room to be pawned by a friend, is left naked and escapes in old armor. In *Every Man in,* Brainworm makes the justice's clerk Formal drunk, and strips him of his suit, leaving him to come home later encased in "rusty armor."[3] Disguised as Formal, Brainworm fleeces Mathew and Bobadill, and then appears in the guise of a sergeant to arrest Downright, intending, he declares, to "get either more pawns, or more money of Downright, for the arrest" (IV, 7). In this, however, he is foiled. In *The Blacke Bookes Messenger,* Brown calls in a friend, who takes the guise of a constable in order to arrest the Maltman for the purpose of fleecing him, but has to resort to a subtle trick to succeed.[4] Brainworm's quick changes in disguise belong, of course, to the coney-catcher. Compare the rapid shifts of *Look About You, Dutch Courtezan, Blind Beggar of Bednal Green, Bartholomew Fair,* etc.

Of the more serious studies, Dame Kitely and Bridget are scarcely distinct enough to represent any influence. They are well characterized by Gifford in his edition of Jonson (Vol. I, p. 60).

[1]In *The Contention between Liberality and Prodigality,* 1602, probably a revised play, a Captain Welldone (cf. Wellbred) enters (III, 5) begging and excusing himself just as Brainworm does. The language is fairly suggestive of *Ev. M. in.*

[2]See p. 180 *infra* for evidence that the *Jests* were written early.

[3]Cf. also "How *George* read a Playe-booke to a Gentleman" in *The Jests of Peele* (*Shakespeare Jest-Books,* Vol. II, pp. 293 ff.) for a slightly similar episode. See also *The Devil is an Ass,* V, 1, for Pug's theft of Ambler's suit, and *Blind Beggar of Bednal Green,* II, 2, where cutpurses who shift from disguise to disguise, as does Brainworm, rob Strowd and leave him naked.

[4]In *Wits Miserie,* p. 63, Lodge says of Brawling Contention: You shall hire him for a speciall baily if you come off with an angell."

The friends young Knowell and Wellbred, one a scholar and poet and the other a high-spirited, gentlemanly gallant, have no inordinate humours or strong comic individuality; that is, they do not represent follies, although they lead a gay life. They suggest Plautine types, but on the whole are rather English. Just this pair of gentlemanly friends, loving mischief and scorning inordinate folly, became popular later, especially with Beaumont and Fletcher.[1] In *Every Man in* they play upon the gulls and the humour types and render their follies more ridiculous, a function that Lemot of *An Humorous Day's Mirth* discharges, though he reminds us more of Macilente. It is a rather new function in dramatic plotting, and was probably developed by Chapman for the exposure of the humour types. Of Wellbred, however, Kitely and Downright do not take so mild a view. In II, 1, Kitely says of him:

> He and his wild associates spend their hours,
> In repetition of lascivious jests,
> Swear, leap, drink, dance, and revel night by night.

And Downright a little later declares: "I am grieved it should be said he is my brother, and take these courses." But these two sober citizens seem to have been oppressed by the gayety of Wellbred, who is not treated in the play as lacking courage, sense, or honor.

There remain Kitely, Downright, Justice Clement, and the elder Knowell, characters with decided humours. These four certainly do not represent types so strongly as do the other characters. It is probable that Jonson, who to my mind always engrafts upon his most original work some details drawn from his vast knowledge of literature, had a number of suggestions for each of these characters, but it is not obvious here, as in the case of the soldier and the gulls, that he took over distinct outlines and merely gave new life and a new turn to what he borrowed. In these more serious characters, representing in every case a strong individuality and a rather worthy nature in spite of the predominance of some humour, we seem to have studies of life with an occasional suggestion from literature enriching the treatment. In each of the four characters

[1] *The Two Angry Women of Abington*, possibly later than *Ev. M. in*, has a faint echo of them in Francis and his friend Philip, who offers his sister to Francis in marriage.

there is something of the more wholesome middle-class life of England. There is thorough manliness in Downright and Clement, and, as opposite as their humours are, both are expressive of the English spirit of independence and self-assertion. Contrasted with these two outspoken characters are Kitely and Knowell with their kindliness of spirit and lack of driving force, in fact with a certain natural timidity in the expression of self.

Kitely is a notable study of the humour of jealousy, for, in spite of the innumerable treatments of the theme that fill all literature and especially all Elizabethan literature preceding and following Jonson, Kitely seems to be fairly distinct in the details of his action under the influence of jealousy, and free from the most common symptoms of the humour. Corvino and Fitzdottrel, Jonson's other important studies of jealousy, are really conventional treatments in comparison. They follow the conception of jealousy as a dangerous passion, whereas Kitely's diseased attitude is less weighted with tragic intensity. Under the influence of the word humour, Jonson has made what might be called a pathological study of Kitely, stressing the power of mental attitude to stir his imagination, in spite of Kitely's efforts to check his folly and his recognition of it as a disease that has taken hold upon him.

In *Greenes Vision,* there are two stories dealing with jealousy, which, though in outline very different from Jonson's treatment, are interesting because jealousy is often called a humour and there are certain analyses of it as a disease. At the end of the first story, the jealous husband, who has been drugged, has his sickness explained to him: "I will tell thee Sonne this disease is a mad bloud that lies in thy head, which is growne from iealousie, take héede of it, for if it should continue but sixe dayes, it would make thée starke mad" (*Works of Greene,* Vol. XII, p. 234). The second story opens with an account of how a merchant of wealth and position, having married a beautiful woman, grows jealous of the merchants who resort to his house, as Kitely is jealous of the gallants who frequent his house with his brother Wellbred. The two husbands soliloquize on woman's frailty at times in somewhat the same vein, and Vandermast tries to reason himself out of his humour as Kitely tries to check his. In this second story (p. 254) jealousy is described as a "canckar, that fretteth the quiet of the thoughts . . . a poyson spetially opposed against the perfections of loue." Greene adds, "The hart being once infected with iealousie, the sléepes are broken," etc. With these passages from Greene compare Kitely's soliloquy on his disease.[1]

Gifford calls attention to the parallel between Kitely's cautious approach to Cash in III, 2, and King John's sounding of Hubert in *King John,* III, 3. The parallel is striking. Both Kitely and King John set value upon an oath of loyalty, both start several times to tell their secrets, both stop and turn to flattery of the listener and to a discussion of matters not closely related to the thing in hand, and both finally entrust the close secret—King John immediately and Kitely later. Gifford speaks of Shakespeare's greater power, but the power lies in the poetry of Shakespeare. For the stage device showing caution, hesitation, and drawing back where one wishes to use another and yet fears to trust him, Jonson has surpassed the master. Some parallels in language also occur.

Jonson.

Kit[*ely*]. It shall be so.
Nay, I dare build upon his secrecy,
He knows not to deceive me.—Thomas!
Cash. Sir.
Kit. Yet now I have bethought me too, I will not.—
Thomas, is Cob within?
. . . .
Thomas—you may deceive me, but, I hope—
Your love to me is more—
Cash. Sir, if a servant's
Duty, with faith, may be called love, you are
More than in hope, you are possessed of it.
Kit. I thank you heartily, Thomas: give me your hand:
With all my heart, good Thomas. I have, Thomas,

Shakespeare.

K[*ing*] *John.* Come hither, Hubert. O my gentle Hubert,
We owe thee much! . . .
. . . .
And, my good friend, thy voluntary oath
Lives in this bosom, dearly cherishéd.
Give me thy hand. I had a thing to say,—
But I will fit it with some better time.
By Heaven, Hubert, I'm almost ashamed
To say what good respect I have of thee.
Hub. I am much bounden to your Majesty.
K. John. Good friend, thou hast no cause to say so yet:
. . . .

[1]Quoted on page 43 *supra*.
In Fenton's *Tragicall Discourses*, IV, the terms diseases and humour are applied a number of times to jealousy. The two words are practically synonymous.

A secret to impart unto you . . .
. . . .
Think I esteem you, Thomas,
When I will let you in thus to my private.
. . . .
I know thy faith to be as firm as rock.
Thomas, come hither, near; we cannot be
Too private in this business. So it is,
—Now he has sworn, I dare the safelier venture. [*Aside.*
I have of late, by divers observations—
. . . .
Thomas, it will be now too long to stay,
I'll spy some fitter time soon, or tomorrow.

I had a thing to say,—but let it go:
The Sun is in the heaven . . .
. . . .
Then, in despite of brooded watchful day,
I would into thy bosom pour my thoughts:
But, ah, I will not! yet I love thee well;
And, by my troth, I think thou lovest me well.
Hub. So well, that what you bid me undertake,
Though that my death were adjunct to my act,
By Heaven, I'd do't.
K. John. Do not I know thou wouldst?

For Downright with his proverbs, his blunt speech, and his impatience there is probably no immediate forerunner. The use of proverbs is common in clownish types, but unusual for one of Downright's social position. Studies of impatience, anger, bluntness, are also not uncommon. Jonson himself had already treated the humour of impatience in Ferneze of *The Case is Altered.* Lodge in *Wits Miserie* gives a whole section to analyzing the various phases of the deadly sin Wrath, and among many details that fit neither Ferneze nor Downright there is one passage on Impatience (p. 72) which describes Downright: "He will not stay to hear an answere whilest a man may excuse himselfe, nor endure any reading if it fit not his purpose, nor affect anie learning that féedes not his humor." Downright impatiently checks Kitely's explanations, and demands that he come to the point (II, 1); and, when Bobadill attempts to parley (IV, 5), Downright beats him incontinently. As Mathew is about to read his verses (IV, 1), Downright cries out, "Hoy-day, here is stuff!" and later, "Death! I can indure the stocks better." Wellbred explains Downright's impatience on the occasion by saying, "A rhime to him is worse than cheese, or a bagpipe." On the whole, however, the character of Downright does not seem to carry on definitely any conventional treatment of wrath or impatience. Certainly there is small ground for comparing him with Falconbridge or Hotspur, Shakespeare's studies of the irascible nature. In Shakespeare's characters, especially Falconbridge, bluntness and impatience are not the controlling factors, but merely a mask for a finer nature—secondary factors derived from spiritual honesty.

Justice Clement, also, with his mad, merry humour, his love of a jest, his good fellowship and kindly spirit, and withal his keen commonsense and his justice, is, so far as I know, a unique figure in the drama. The foolish justice was proverbial. Justice Silence had rendered him a telling stage figure about the time of *Every Man in,* and he appears in *How a Man May Choose a Good Wife from a Bad* probably not long after. The type is common in jest books also. Jonson himself takes up the character later in *Bartholomew Fair* and *The Devil is an Ass.* Clement, however, is not the foolish justice, but shrewd and whimsical. The portrayal of Sir Thomas More as a magistrate in the play of *Sir Thomas More* illustrates the type in some details very well indeed; as, for example, in his surprising use of jests when dealing with characters representing follies, in his learning and his quick parodies of pretentious language, in his readiness always to meet folly as a challenge, and in his fundamental justice and leniency.[1]

The elder Knowell, the country gentleman solicitous about his son's small follies and in sympathy with the old régime, is also to a large extent a fresh humour type. One phase of his characterization, however, shows considerable literary influence and no little skill on Jonson's part. Knowell is not an allegorical figure, but he does seem to stand for the older virtues, older morals, and the conservative tendencies of society—as Cob seems to stand for a social principle. Knowell, with his old-fashioned manners and wisdom, is contrasted with the new manners and follies of his son, and to a certain extent he furnishes a chorus or commentator on

[1]For a bit of Clement's burlesque poetry given in the Quarto (ll. 2853 ff.) Prof. Penniman points out a parallel in *Wits Miserie,* p. 23. Cf. introduction to his edition of *Poetaster* and *Satiromastix.* Gifford (Jonson's *Works,* Vol. I, p. 57, note 2) has suggested the similarity between another burlesque of Clement's and a passage in Googe's *Zodiacke.* For two earlier instances of the Justice's pun (V, 1) on the "whole realm, a commonwealth of paper" that Mathew carries in his hose, cf. Hart, 9 *N. and Q.*, Vol. XI, p. 501.

the follies of the central characters in the play. To a certain extent, also, he is a forerunner of Asper and Crites, though he is more strongly individualized than Jonson's other conservers of morals, and he scarcely expresses Jonson's own ideals so consistently as they do. As critic of the follies that Jonson is studying in *Every Man in,* Knowell represents the conservative ideals of the better middle class; Asper is a whipper of social follies, imbued with the spirit of contemporary satire; and Crites is the critic whose own ideal character renders him the judge of the types of ignorance and folly. The significance of these characters is much more evident, of course, in Asper and Crites than in Knowell, but to my mind Knowell in one phase of his characterization continues Jonson's idea of a commentator which had its inception in Valentine of *The Case is Altered.* Knowell's function as the conserving social force comes out in his numerous soliloquies and in his rebukes of folly. His tendency to moralizing becomes, like Macilente's envy and possibly Asper's harshness, a humour, while Crites represents a contrast to humours. Yet in each case the type is that of the moralizer.

Knowell soliloquizes on his scholarly son's pursuit of "idle poetry" (I, 1); on his son's choice of a companion (I, 1); on the method he shall pursue in dealing with his son (I, 1); and, in the Folio, on the evils in the modern system of rearing children (II, 3). Instead of this last soliloquy, the Quarto has one on the proper sway of reason over man. In I, 1, Knowell rebukes Stephen for quarreling and for extravagance, and gives him a moral lecture embracing well-known maxims of conduct; and in II, 3, the begging soldier's degenerate, servile type of life falls under his censure. Otherwise Knowell's participation in the play is slight except for the trick played upon him by his own son, though the fact that he follows Edward Knowell to London gives a motive for much of the action.

A father's soliloquy on the course of his son, in spirit much like those of Knowell in the opening scenes, may be found in Lodge's *Alarum against Usurers* (Shakespeare Society, pp. 49, 50). In both cases the fact is mentioned that the son stood high in favor at the universities. Knowell's conviction in regard to the fruitlessness of poetry as a pursuit is very closely paralleled in some lines which Gifford quotes from the part of Old Hieronimo in *The*

Spanish Tragedy (IV, 1, ll. 69 ff.). The Folio soliloquy on fathers' training their children in evil living is drawn almost wholly from the classics, as Whalley and Gifford point out, but the ideas had become commonplace in the didactic literature of England and consequently fit well into the fatherly humour of Knowell.[1] The corresponding Quarto soliloquy (ll. 880 ff.) presents an elaborate figure of Reason placed by Nature as king over the estate of man "to haue the marshalling of our affections." The affections often rebel against

> Their liege Lord Reason, and not shame to tread
> Vpon his holy and annointed head.

This same figure, about which, however, there is of course nothing strikingly distinctive, forms the plot of Medwell's *Nature,* Part I. Nature endows man with Reason and Sensuality, but Reason is to be "chyef gyde" and to "gouerne" (ll. 99 ff.). Immediately Sensuality raises a revolt, and man rebels against Reason, going so far as to smite him on the head (ll. 1155 ff.).[2]

More interesting for its conventionality than any of these soliloquies is the passage in which Knowell lays down five rules of conduct for the guidance of Stephen (I, 1). The advice is similar to that which Polonius later gives to Laertes. Knowell warns Stephen against spending money on baubles and on foolish companions; against invading every place; against the use of flashing bravery; against living beyond his income; and against standing upon a gentility of birth rather than of deeds. Similar advice, usually of a father to a son, is to be found frequently in English literature of this period,[3] and to trace such lists of maxims would

[1]Cf. Babington, *Ten Commandments,* quoted in the introduction to the New Shakspere Society edition of Stubbes's *Anatomy of Abuses,* p. 82*; Wager, *The Longer thou Livest,* ll. 114 ff. and 1012 ff.; Lodge, *Fig for Momus,* Hunterian Club, pp. 33 ff.; Lyly, *Euphues, Works,* ed. Bond, Vol. I, pp. 185 and 244; Northbrooke, *Treatise against Dancing,* etc., Shakespeare Society, pp. 11, 12; etc.

[2]Cf. pp. 161 f. *infra* for parallels between the second part of *Nature* and *Every Man out.*

[3]Cf. *Euphues, Works of Lyly,* Vol. I, pp. 189 f. (repeated in almost the same form on p. 286); Vol. II, pp. 16 f., 149, 187 f.; Lodge, *Rosalind,* near the beginning; Lodge, *Euphues his Shadow,* Hunterian Club, p. 13; *Margarite of America,* Hunt. Club, pp. 18, 19; *Fig for Momus,* Hunt. Club, p. 59; *Alarum against Usurers,* Shakespeare Society, p. 75; Greene, *Carde of Fancie, Works,* ed. Grosart, Vol. IV, pp. 21, 22; *Mourning Garment,* Vol. IX, pp. 137 ff.; Breton, *Wits Trenchmour,* pp. 14 and 18.

be a hopeless task. The study of the ultimate sources of these lists has, so far as I know, been undertaken most fully by Fischer in his edition of *How the Wyse Man Taught hys Sone* (Erlanger Beiträge, Band I, Heft II, pp. 11 ff.), where he traces a large number of such precepts from Cato on through Old and Middle English.[1] Account must also be taken of the Italian courtesy books, the name of which was doubtless legion and which extended to all lengths and covered all phases of conduct. Knowell, for example, makes gentility a matter of the individual man, an idea which is rather fully dealt with in *Euphues* (*Works of Lyly,* Vol. I, pp. 316 ff.). The discussion of nobility of birth along with rules of conduct is frequent in Italian courtesy books, where sometimes the view of Jonson and Lyly is expressed, and sometimes that which lays chief stress on birth and wealth, as in Castiglione's *Courtier.*[2] Doubtless all of Knowell's wisdom was derived from the moral and educational treatises of the Renaissance, which were largely Italian, though much of his moralizing may have been familiar to Jonson in the classics also.

Knowell's whole attitude of loyalty to the older standards of morals and manners is illustrated by Greene's *Quip for an Upstart Courtier* (*Works,* Vol. XI, pp. 233 ff.), where Cloth-breeches praises the simplicity of the older régime in England in contrast with the régime of present day upstarts. In *Two Angry Women of Abington,* also, Coomes praises the old sword days as opposed to the modern rapier days (II, 4).

In turning with *Every Man in* from the recognized types of comedy to a serious program of satire on humours, Jonson sets forth rather definitely in the prologue his critical and moral purpose. It has frequently been pointed out that the critical ideas expressed

[1]Förster, *Engl. Stud.*, Vol. 36, pp. 1 ff. prints a Middle English version of Cato's maxims. A large number of texts are printed in *The Babees Book*, etc., E. E. T. S., No. 32, and in *Queene Elizabethes Achademy*, etc., E. E. T. S., E. S., No. 8. In this last volume Dr. Furnivall prints one poem giving a mother's advice to a daughter. The advice of a mother to her daughter occurs in Phillip's play of *Patient Grissell.* In *James IV*, I, 1, ll. 151 ff., the father advises the daughter.

[2]Cf. also Rossetti, *Essay on Early Italian Courtesy Books*, E. E. T. S., E. S., No. 8, pp. 12 and 56; Holme, *Mod. Lang. Review*, Vol. V, pp. 145 ff.; Stubbes, *Anatomy of Abuses*, pp. 42, 43 and notes, where classic parallels are given. Einstein, *Italian Renaissance in England*, pp. 61 ff. gives what is perhaps the clearest and best discussion of the conflicting ideals in regard to nobility.

in the prologue were generally current among students of criticism in the Renaissance.[1] The ideas and even the wording are often paralleled in Sidney's *Defense of Poesy*.[2] Almost the same objections, however, to the absurdities of romantic plays were expressed by Sidney's predecessor, Whetstone, in the dedication of *Promos and Cassandra;* and about the time that *Every Man in* was written, and almost certainly before the prologue was written, these ideas were dramatized in the notable critical induction of *A Warning for Fair Women*, printed in 1599.

[1]Cf. Gifford, *Works of Jonson*, Vol. I, p. 2; Penniman, *The War of the Theatres*, pp. 14 ff.; Smith, *Eliz. Crit. Essays*, Vol. 1, pp. xxxi ff., and especially p. xliii; Spingarn, *Crit. Essays of the Seventeenth Cent.*, Vol. I, pp. xiii ff.

[2]Cf. especially the parallels cited by Professor Spingarn.

CHAPTER VII

EVERY MAN OUT OF HIS HUMOUR

The years 1598 and 1599 were notable in the production of satire. Early in the decade such prose works as Greene's *Quip,* Nashe's *Pierce Penilesse,* and Lodge's *Wits Miserie* marked a definite advance in one phase of the satiric movement. At the same time verse satire was coming into popularity. Donne's satires seem to have been written about 1593; Campion's *Poemata* (in Latin) and Lodge's *Fig for Momus* date from 1595; and Davies' *Epigrammes* were produced about the same time. But the real satiric outburst began in 1597 with Hall's *Virgidemiarum.* In 1598 appeared Marston's *Metamorphosis of Pygmalion's Image and Certain Satires,* the same author's *Scourge of Villainy,* Guilpin's *Skialetheia,* Bastard's *Chrestoleros,* and Rankins' *Seaven Satyres.* Early in 1599 appeared Middleton's *Micro-Cynicon,*[1] and during the course of the year Weever's *Epigrams in the Oldest Cut and Newest Fashion.* The vogue was met by an order of June 1, 1599, restraining satires and epigrams, which singled out as especially obnoxious the works of Hall, Marston, Guilpin, and Middleton. The satirical poems and the collections of satires and epigrams that appeared during the next two years, notwithstanding, speak for the strength of the movement. The influence of this school of formal satire on Jonson is to be felt in *Every Man in* of 1598, but in 1599[2] he produced the first of his comical satires, *Every Man out of his Humour,* a play that transfers to the stage the whole tone, spirit, and range of the popular contemporary satire.

The changes from *Every Man in* to *Every Man out* are clearly marked, but not sweeping. In both plays some of the broader phases of didacticism or of the older forms of satire are blended

[1]I use Middleton's name for convenience although Middleton's authorship has been doubted by some and Moffat's suggested. Cf. *Cambridge Hist. Eng. Lit.*, Vol. IV, p. 589, for example.

[2]The Folio states that the play was acted in 1599. For Jonson this does not mean the beginning of the year 1600. Cf. Thorndike, *Influence of Beaumont and Fletcher on Shakespeare*, p. 17. *Ev. M. out* was doubtless finished toward the end of 1599, after the production of *Julius Caesar.*

with the new satire. For the quick dissection of follies, *Every Man out* has seized upon the character sketch, which goes back to earlier English prose but connects closely with the popular epigram also. The critical ideas of Jonson have developed into a definite system, and are expounded. With *Every Man out,* also, humour assumes for him a much more exact meaning, and, according to the definition which he gives, is more consistently representative of inner character. Many of the character types of *Every Man in* are carried over into *Every Man out,* though the characterization is more completely from the point of view of humours. Brisk continues the type illustrated in Mathew, but with a more vigorous personality. He is much more clearly the gallant and less the gull. His boasts of his prowess and his function as model for the true gull Fungoso connect him with Bobadill of *Every Man in.* The country gull Stephen has developed into Fungoso and Sogliardo, both of whom are clearly individualized. Like Stephen, they ape the fashion of gallants, but each follows in a different way the follies of London life into which they are plunging. As studies of a citizen and his wife, Deliro and Fallace stand in definite contrast to Kitely and his wife, while Fido is a colorless repetition of Cash. In general, the characters of *Every Man out* represent more clearly than do those of *Every Man in* various phases of the affected gallantry and singularity which the contemporary satirists were attacking. While the types are almost as varied as in *Every Man in,* they all belong to a narrower sphere, the world of the posers and spendthrifts, with those who heap money for them, like Sordido, or those who are used by them, like Deliro, or those who prey upon them, like Shift. Consequently, the types are rather more specific than in *Every Man in,* representative of more definite follies. So for Knowell, the respectable, moral gentleman of the suburbs of London, there appears Puntarvolo, "consecrated to singularity," and as antiquated in his affectation of the forms of chivalry as Knowell is in his moralizing. Instead of Bridget with her respectability despite the fact that Mathew is her servant, appears Saviolina, as foolish as her servant Brisk. Instead of Brainworm, a mixed type of Roman slave and English coney-catcher, appears Shift, also a pretended soldier, a beggar, and a rogue, but one whose path lies close to that of the gulls and pretended gallants. The clown Cob has been dropped, and the rustic Sordido, brother and father of the two gulls, has been added. Downright with his humour of impatience has given place to a new type of scourger, Carlo, the "profane jester," who "will transform any man into deformity." Knowell and Wellbred, the pair of gallants of a respectable sort, have disappeared in this study of thoroughgoing follies, and their function of exposing the gulls and the humour types is taken by Macilente, whose humour of envy makes him an effective agent in the satiric comedy intended to lash the follies of the day. The Plautine elements in Jonson's humour plays thus drop out, and a character more suggestive of the allegorical figure of Envy in the moralities becomes the intriguer. The whole play is more English in tone. It is a gigantic burlesque of English manners, in the spirit and form of the contemporary satire, and yet close to life, as we must feel.

For a defence of his new type of play Jonson has made use of the machinery of induction and chorus. The fashion of setting before the audience in dramatic form whatever the author wished understood as preliminary to the play had already become rather widespread in the contemporary English drama. The device took many forms. A character typical of some period in the past or one representing a source might be chosen, as in the case of Skelton in Munday's *Downfall of Robert Earl of Huntington,*[1] or of Higden in what is probably an old play, *The Mayor of Queenborough*. In other inductions the characters often represented the tone or quality of the play. The atmosphere enveloping *The Spanish Tragedy* is typified in the Ghost and Revenge, who comment as they sit by. More dramatic is the opening of *Soliman and Perseda,* where Love, Fortune, and Death contend as to who shall control. The contest motive for revealing the tone of a play was popular. Tragedy prevails over Comedy and History in *A Warning for Fair Women,* and the tone suggested by the victory of Tragedy dominates the play as thoroughly as Asper's spirit pervades *Every Man out.* Tragedy, indeed, speaks somewhat in the manner of Asper; and the criticism of absurd plays suggests the prologue to *Every Man in.* An excellent counterpart to *A Warn-*

[1]Jonson has followed in *Ev. M. out,* in *Cynthia's Revels,* and elsewhere Munday's device of introducing into the induction the actors of the play.

ing for Fair Women is found in *Wily Beguiled,* where the title Spectrum is spirited away by Juggler, and fun prevails.[1]

More closely allied to the special type of induction adopted in *Every Man out* is the device of a group of plays in which the attitude of an audience is represented through actors who take the rôle of spectators. Indeed, the presenter and the critic were already established upon the English stage, though the treatment had usually been humorous and satirical rather than serious and judicial. In *The Old Wives' Tale* the clowns are diverting comic figures, but their importance lies in furnishing for the play a presenter and a chorus of Jonson's type. Madge, who starts the folk-tale taken up by the play, is presenter, and embodies the spirit of the play somewhat as Asper does in *Every Man out.* Peele was satirizing the hurly-burly of romance as much in the presenter of his potpourri of folk-lore and romance as in the play itself. Associated with Madge are Fantastic and Frolic, two sympathetic spectators, who express their interest by occasional questions and remarks—not critical, however. In *The Taming of a Shrew,* the part of Sly, less fully developed by Shakespeare in *The Taming of the Shrew,* not only introduces a humorous element but again gives the occasion for some ironical satire on the tastes of such spectators as Sly. Undoubtedly, too, the humorous purpose in presenting a spectator on the stage is uppermost in *Summer's Last Will and Testament,* but the humor arises largely, as in the case of Sly, from the satire on the dramatic taste of the common clown, to whom neither poetry nor a serious study of character can appeal[2]—for Nashe's use of folk-lore has the interest both of poetic fancy and of moralizing and philosophizing on the part of the allegorical characters. Summer, with his mockery of all that is most serious in the play, typifies the limitations of the audience. Through the device, Nashe is enabled at once to stress his more critical purpose and, by paradox, to suggest explanations and values. Jonson foolishly took the direct method in *Every Man*

[1]Cf. the strife of Envy and Comedy in *Mucedorus.*
Spectrum in *Wily Beguiled* is suggestive of satiric comedy. Indeed, the whole spirit of the prologue would seem to indicate that so much of the play, at least, was written after the rise of strongly satiric comedy.

[2]Cf. Wilson, *Arte of Rhetorique,* ed. Mair, p. 198, for a serious discussion of this matter.

out, but for most of his later inductions he follows Nashe in using the indirect approach. The gossips of *The Staple of News,* as well as the citizen and his wife in Beaumont and Fletcher's *Knight of the Burning Pestle,* are to my mind distinctly modeled on Nashe's device of Will Summer. Even in the enveloping action of *Every Man out,* though the method differs from Nashe's, there are several details betraying a kinship,—the mockery of prologue and author, the statement of the principle that satire is aimed not at individuals but at classes, and the attitude of superiority to ignorant critics.

The induction of *James IV,* while not so important for Jonson as that of *Summer's Last Will and Testament,* offers in its seriousness and greater directness a closer parallel to the spirit of Jonson's treatment. In Greene's play, Bohan, a cynic and scorner of the evils of life, leads Oberon to "the Gallery" to show him a picture of the follies of the Scottish court, in order that Oberon may "iudge if any wise man would not leaue the world if he could." The serious satirical purpose of Bohan as presenter, the malcontent type in him, which suggests Asper-Macilente, and the discussion of the moral between acts all connect Greene's treatment with Jonson's.

In *Every Man out* the enveloping machinery of presenter and chorus is for the purpose of defending Jonson's methods and enunciating his critical opinions. The discussion of the habits of theatre-goers (II, 4), and the ridicule of Munday's citizen type of comedy (I, 1) which are to be found in *The Case is Altered* are episodic, and satirical rather than constructive. More important for the development of Jonson's theories is the satire on false poetry in *Every Man in* and the defense of true poetry which appears in the Quarto.[1] With *Every Man out,* the criticism that before had been scattered is organized and definitely formulated as throwing light on Jonson's purposes. Asper, the presenter, stands for the ideals of satiric comedy. He is the scourger, the embodiment of the satirical spirit abroad. Often, as when he addresses the "gracious and kind spectators," he may represent the author, just as Macilente, whose rôle is taken by the actor playing Asper, is in many respects the mouthpiece of Jonson. But Asper

[1]The prologue of *Ev. M. in,* stating definitely Jonson's ideal in comedy, doubtless belongs to a period as late as *Ev. M. out,* perhaps later.

is to my mind a familiar type, the stern and fearless castigator of evils. As a scourger he contrasts with Macilente, whose hatred of folly is contaminated by a mixture of unworthy envy; and the two men stand for two types of satirists. When Macilente is cured of his humour of envy, he becomes a worthy figure of the age,—Asper again, the embodiment of a noble indignation against folly. But other matters besides the satirical purpose of the play come in for consideration, also, and questions of stage-craft needed to be discussed in a critical, judicial spirit not suited to Asper. Cordatus and Mitis are accordingly introduced as judicial observers and critics of the play as a play.

Inevitably, in presenting the ideal satirist and the ideal critic, Jonson presents his own theories for satire and his own estimate of his work. The greater egoism, of course, lies in portraying the ideal critic of his work, for in Asper as scourger Jonson might readily feel that he embodied the satirical ideals of Chapman, let us say, as much as his own. In defence of Jonson's whole attitude to his mission and his art it should be urged that the militant spirit in literature was stronger at the end of the sixteenth century than ever before or since, perhaps, though the rigidity of Jonson's intellectual nature made him carry the spirit through his whole career when once he came under the dominance of it. The age was one in which sharp social and religious cleavage made bitter polemics popular; in which the development of the ideals of individuality allowed a man to defend confidently his own views and accomplishments; and in which, paradoxically enough, the following of fixed standards and systems by certain groups rendered a poet's defence of himself a defence of the ideals of his group. Much of Jonson's egoism is thus a result of a belief in ideals rather than in self. The struggle of the newly developing classicism was one of the influences that intensified the spirit of aggressiveness and dogmatism in Jonson's group, though more potent, perhaps, was the nature of the men themselves,—Nashe, Marston, and Jonson in particular. The influence of Nashe is especially conspicuous. To my mind, he set the tone for English satire.

For the ideas expounded by Asper and the chorus, much of Jonson's material was derived from classic or Italian sources, but he has culled out what was especially applicable to English literature and had been approved by preceding critics and satirists.

The literary affiliations of Asper are, of course, to be sought first of all in formal satire, and, brief as the part is, it is remarkable how many conventions of the satirical school it illustrates. Even Asper's fashion of turning from one point to another without any organized program for venting his indignation marks him as the typical satirist. The most conspicuous exception, perhaps, is that he does not affect harshness and obscurity of language. In portraying Asper as satirist, however, it is to be remembered that Jonson was following a type of literature whose lines of treatment were very definitely marked, more so perhaps than the common influence of classicism on the writers of the school would naturally explain, though that was great enough. The satirists followed each other very closely. Nashe's *Pierce Penilesse* influenced Lodge's *Wits Miserie*. Guilpin seems to have been indebted to Lodge and Davies as well as to Marston. Donne, Hall, and Marston show clear traces of kinship. The community of ideas and methods among all these men is strikingly revealed by a cursory reading; even the recurrence of certain words, like galled, is noticeable.[1]

The chief function of the satirist was, of course, to scourge vice and folly. The evils are naturally much the same in all the satire of the period—in the satire of all periods, one might well say. I have already spoken of the classification of vices in the prose satirists, especially in connection with humours. Asper runs briefly over a list of evil-doers,—the strumpet, broker, usurer, lawyer, courtier, with "their extortion, pride, or lusts,"—and dismisses them as

> so innate and popular,
> That drunken custom would not shame to laugh,
> In scorn, at him, that should but dare to tax 'em.

He pauses long enough, however, to direct a special paragraph against the Puritan. In the second of the satires included with *Pygmalion's Image,* Marston arraigns the Puritans similarly, though his charges are more concrete and specific. Interestingly enough, Asper's speech, according to Gifford, goes back in many

[1]Similarly, when once Jonson had achieved notable success in adapting the methods of satire to the uses of comedy, the dramatists followed him as quickly as the satirists followed each other. The reaction of the drama on satire is pretty clear also. Rowlands' *Letting of Humour's Blood in the Head Vein,* for instance, seems to me to have been strongly influenced by *Every Man out.*

details to Juvenal's description of the feigned Stoics, so that we find Jonson again fitting his classic material into the mold of contemporary life. I quote the passages from Jonson and Marston for the parallelism in method.

Jonson

O, but to such whose faces are all zeal,
And, with the words of Hercules invade
Such crimes as these! that will not smell of sin,
But seem as they were made of sanctity!
Religion in their garments, and their hair
Cut shorter than their eyebrows! when the conscience
Is vaster than the ocean, and devours
More wretches than the counters.

Marston

That same devout meal-mouth'd precisian,
That cries "Good brother," "Kind sister," makes a duck
After the antique grace, can always pluck
A sacred book out of his civil hose,
And at th' op'ning and at our stomach's close,
Says with a turn'd-up eye a solemn grace
Of half an hour; then with silken face
Smiles on the holy crew, and then doth cry,
"O manners! O times of impurity!"

. . . .

—who thinks that this good man
Is a vile, sober, damned politician?
Not I, till with his bait of purity
He bit me sore in deepest usury.
No Jew, no Turk, would use a Christian
So inhumanely as this Puritan.

It is after his elaborate explanation of the true nature of humour that Asper reveals his program as presenter of the play. In reply to the remark of Cordatus that

if an ideot
Have but an apish or fantastic strain,
It is his humour,

Asper declares,—

Well, I will scourge those apes,
And to these courteous eyes oppose a mirror,
As large as is the stage whereon we act;
Where they shall see the time's deformity
Anatomized in every nerve and sinew,
With constant courage, and contempt of fear.

How far the types of folly attacked in the play coincide with the types common in satire will be seen when the individual characters are discussed separately. Much the same pictures are drawn by satirist after satirist.

As a scourger Asper shows the harsh impatience with evil and the bold defiance of evil-doers that make him the typical satirist of the age. His defence of the satirist's uncompromising sharpness which opens the induction is taken from Juvenal (Satire I), but it echoes the satiric spirit of Marston and Middleton, and even their impassioned language, more perhaps than it does Juvenal's. Marston had anticipated Jonson in the use of this satire from Juvenal, adopting its mood and some of its ideas for the second satire of his *Scourge of Villainy.* Marston's satire is, of course, much fuller than Asper's speech, but it is interesting to compare the tone of the two. The parallels scarcely illustrate what is evident enough in a comparison of Asper with the composite satirist of the age—Jonson's finer literary gift, which he shows especially in avoiding the inconsistencies and in toning down the absurdities of his predecessors. Thus Jonson says:

> Who is so patient of this impious world,
> That he can check his spirit, or rein his tongue?
> Or who hath such a dead unfeeling sense,
> That heaven's horrid thunders cannot wake?
> . . . .
> Who can behold such prodigies as these,
> And have his lips sealed up? Not I.

The following lines from the satire of Marston illustrate his use of these ideas:

> Preach not the Stoic's patience to me;
> I hate no man, but men's impiety.
> My soul is vex'd; what power will resist,
> Or dares to stop a sharp-fang'd satirist?
> Who'll cool my rage? . . .
> . . . .
> What icy Saturnist, what northern pate,
> But such gross lewdness would exasperate?
> . . . .
> O damn'd!
> Who would not shake a satire's knotty rod,
> When to defile the sacred seat of God
> Is but accounted gentlemen's disport?
> . . . .

> O what dry brain melts not sharp mustard rhyme,
> To purge the snottery of our slimy time!
> Hence, idle "*Cave*" . . .
> . . . .
> Who can abstain? What modest brain can hold,
> But he must make his shame-faced muse a scold?

Marston's "Hence, idle *'Cave,'*" and the repeated cautions of Cordatus against Asper's too great boldness[1] bring out another characteristic of the satirist, his declared recklessness of consequences, and his fearlessness of those whom he might offend. It was common with the satirists to defy the ill will of those whose folly they exposed.[2] The mood is found in the author's prologue to *Micro-Cynicon,* a work which was notorious by June 1, 1599, and which is often suggestive of Asper's type of satirist. Usually, however, the reader or hearer was also reminded aptly that to cry out was to betray oneself as hurt. Asper's medicine, he several times declares, is for the sick. Hall puts the matter very succinctly in the postscript to his satires: "*Art thou guilty?* Complain not, thou art not wronged. *Art thou guiltless?* Complain not, thou art not touched." Almost without exception, moreover, the satirists were careful to defend themselves against the imputation that they attacked individuals. The wording may vary and even the matter, but the principle holds for all. Bishop Hall's remark above is in connection with his protest against a personal interpretation of his attacks on folly. Marston's address "To him that hath perused me," at the end of *The Scourge of Villainy,* deals with the same ideas. Probably about the time of Jonson's play, Shakespeare put the protest in the mouth of the malcontent and satiric Jaques (*As You Like It,* II, 7), and it is the more significant

[1]In Nashe's *Returne of Pasquill,* the interlocutor Marforius several times urges on Pasquill the need of caution. Cf. *Works,* ed. McKerrow, Vol. I, pp. 82, 83.

[2]With Asper's—

> I fear no mood stamped in a private brow,
> When I am pleased t' unmask a public vice—

compare Marston's—

> I dread no bending of an angry brow,
> Or rage of fools that I shall purchase now (*Scourge of Villainy,* Sat. X, ll. 5, 6).

The connection is different, however.

here because it is uncalled for.[1] Jonson's fullest discussion of the matter in *Every Man out* is through Cordatus and Mitis at the end of Act II.[2] I could scarcely point to a better example of the set themes of satire than the reader will find who takes the trouble to compare the passages from these four men. Of similar tenor is the warning in the induction to *Summer's Last Will and Testament*: "Moralizërs, you that wrest a neuer meant meaning out of euery thing, applying all things to the present time, keepe your attention for the common Stage: for here are no quips in Characters for you to reade." The wording, too, is suggestive of Jonson's complaint near the end of Act II: "Indeed there are a sort of these narrow-eyed decypherers, I confess, that will extort strange and abstruse meanings out of any subject, be it never so conspicuous and innocently delivered."

But the satirist must be taken into account as literary man as well as scourger. Part of the material of the satirical school

[1]Shakespeare's so-called gloomy period of tragedies and bitter comedies probably has no meaning so far as his personal experiences and mood are concerned. The influence that determined the tone of Shakespeare's plays during this period was undoubtedly the vogue of satire, though a real mood of disillusionment, melancholy, and bitterness in the age may have helped to make satire fashionable. The drama in general came under the influence of formal satire around the year 1600. With Shakespeare the ingenuous satire on word-mongery in the early *Love's Labour's Lost* and *Much Ado* gave place about this period to such studies in the malcontent as Casca, Jaques, and finally Hamlet. *Twelfth Night* and to a greater extent *The Merry Wives of Windsor* are obviously influenced by the humour trend that was associated with satire. In *Troilus and Cressida* we find expressed the bitterer satiric spirit of Marston, who developed the malcontent. This mood of satiric pessimism reaches the extreme for Shakespeare in the tragedies. At the same time Jonson had turned from humour comedy to tragedy in *Sejanus* and had closed the period with *Volpone*, a comedy with the tone of tragedy, which echoes what is perhaps the age's darkest note of pessimism. Then the reaction against satire and tragedy set in, and the fashion in plays changed. Beaumont and Fletcher's type of play took the public fancy. Jonson shifted the emphasis of his work from satire to the more pleasing elements of plot, organization, liveliness, etc., producing the farcical *Silent Woman* and finally the uproarious *Bartholomew Fair*. About the same time Shakespeare turned again to romance, but, as Mr. Thorndike has shown, instead of following his early manner in comedy, he adopted the newer conventions of the stage.

[2]The Quarto closes with some lines by Macilente, omitted in the Folio, which recapitulate parts of the discussion in the induction. Macilente appeals for applause to those who

> are too wise to thinke themselues are taxt
> In any generall Figure, or too vertuous
> To need that wisdomes imputation.

which dealt with literary matters was naturally for the purpose of scourging follies, but much of it expressed the satirist's attitude to his own work. Asper's utterances along this line show two opposing phases. On the one hand, he expresses a complete confidence in his art, and a desire for criticism of his work, a willingness to be censured by the judicious as he is ready to spend himself for them. On the other hand, he declares his utter scorn for literary pretenders and witless critics. I have already spoken of the fact that the writers of Jonson's day felt no hesitancy in defending confidently their own work. Jonson's egoism in regard to his art is by no means unique, though it probably offends more because it seems more fundamental to the man's nature than in the case of others. Through Nashe's satires, especially those against Harvey, there runs a vein of defiant confidence that easily surpasses Jonson. Again, where Jonson challenges—

> Let envious censors, with their broadest eyes,
> Look through and through me—

half a score of other writers like Hall, Marston, and Middleton could be pointed out who fling down the gauntlet in belligerent poems defying envy or detraction. The literature before Jonson is also filled with scorn for the ignorant critic and for pretended poets and poets of other schools. Nashe in the prologue to *Summer's Last Will and Testament* takes Jonson's blunt attitude to his critics: "Their censures we wey not, whose sences are not yet vnswadled." In most of these points, Marston represents the extreme before Jonson. For line of thought and for mood, the introductory section to his *Scourge of Villainy* is often an interesting forerunner of Asper's part. Marston opens with some defiant and self-confident stanzas in which he presents his "poesy" to Detraction. His next section is addressed *In Lectores prorsus indignos,* and his resentment that ignoramuses and coxcombs should be allowed to pass judgment on his work is like Jonson's indignation at the gallant "that has neither art nor brain" and yet by his presumptuous criticism of a play will infect a whole audience. Marston then turns from unworthy critics, and addresses several stanzas to "diviner wits"—the "judicious friends" of Asper. The introduction closes with a prose section headed "To those that seem judicial Perusers," in which Marston, probably following Hall (prologue to Book III of the satires), protests that English satire should not be bound down by the convention of roughness and obscurity of language. The spirit of this section is paralleled in Jonson's discussion, through the chorus, of innovation in the laws of comedy. A few corresponding passages in the part of Asper and the works of Marston, especially the introduction to *The Scourge of Villainy,* are added to illustrate the relation between the two men.

Jonson

Yet here mistake me not, judicious friends;
I do not this, to beg your patience,
Or servilely to fawn on your applause,
Like some dry brain, despairing in his merit.
Let me be censured by the austerest brow,
Where I want art or judgment, tax me freely:
Let envious censors, with their broadest eyes,
Look through and through me, I pursue no favour;
Only vouchsafe me your attentions,
And I will give you music worth your ears.
O, how I hate the monstrousness of time,
Where every servile imitating spirit,
Plagued with an itching leprosy of wit,
In a mere halting fury, strives to fling
His ulcerous body in the Thespian spring,
And straight leaps forth a poet!
. . . .
And I will mix with you in industry
To please: but whom? attentive auditors,
Such as will join their profit with their pleasure,

Marston

Envy's abhorrèd child, Detraction,
I here expose, to thy all-tainting breath,
The issue of my brain: snarl, rail, bark, bite,
Know that my spirit scorns Detraction's spite.

Know that the Genius, which attendeth on
And guides my powers intellectual,
Holds in all vile repute Detraction;
My soul an essence metaphysical,
That in the basest sort scorns critics' rage
Because he knows his sacred parentage (*Scourge of Villainy,* "*To* Detraction," etc.).

O age, when every Scriveners boy shall dippe
Profaning quills into Thessaliaes spring (*Histriomastix,* III, ll. 197 f. Assigned to Marston).

1. But, ye diviner wits, celestial souls,
Whose free-born minds no kennel-thought controlls,
Ye sacred spirits, Maia's eldest sons—

2. Ye substance of the shadows of our age,

And come to feed their understanding parts:
For these I'll prodigally spend myself,
And speak away my spirit into air;
For these I'll melt my brain into invention,
Coin new conceits, and hang my richest words
As polished jewels in their bounteous ears.

In whom all graces link in marriage,
To you how cheerfully my poem runs!

3. True-judging eyes, quick-sighted censurers,
Heaven's best beauties, wisdom's treasurers,
O how my love embraceth your great worth! (*Scourge of Villainy, In Lectores*, etc., ll. 81 ff.).

I may repeat here that to my mind the hostility between Jonson and Marston may often have been overstressed. The connection of the two men which resulted in the literary partnership of *Eastward Hoe* probably began early. Jonson, Chapman, and Marston shared very similar impulses and carried on very similar studies, perhaps exchanging ideas and ideals in social intercourse. Certainly both Marston and Chapman seem to have given Jonson suggestions for *Every Man out.* Jonson and Marston, however, were just the men to quarrel frequently, in spite of all bonds of fellowship. Jonson's statement to Drummond that he had many quarrels with Marston seems to me out of keeping with a long continued enmity between the two men; it suggests, rather, constant intercourse. Marston's dedication of *The Malcontent* to Jonson and the collaboration of the two in *Eastward Hoe* after *Poetaster* and *Satiromastix* were written indicate that at least they were as ready for reconciliation as for wrath.

With regard to the part of Cordatus and Mitis in this enveloping machinery, its art is that of the dialogue so popular in the didactic literature of the sixteenth century and already utilized in *The Case is Altered* for Valentine's discussion of the stage, as it was later utilized in the Apologetical Dialogue of *Poetaster.* Cordatus and Mitis serve as prompters for Asper, and, after he leaves the stage, Mitis plays the same rôle for Cordatus in setting forth Jonson's dramatic purposes. The interlocutor is, of course, a mere figurehead. He serves to pave the way by suggesting a new idea or an objection and so furnishing a topic, but he never really offers a strong debate. The dialogues of Plato, Lucian, Cicero, and the Latin satirists may have rendered this form of literature popular in the Renaissance, but, as I have already said, the vogue was extensive in England before Jonson's time. Many of the critical utterances of Cordatus and Mitis are likewise to be traced in earlier Renaissance literature. Indeed, one is amazed at the degree to which Jonson conforms in the pettiest details to the academic rules that were gradually worked out in the Renaissance. Much of this body of doctrine can be traced to classic sources and to Italian interpretation of those sources, so that it is difficult to disentangle the English elements. I judge, however, that there were some decidedly independent trends in English literature. They often concerned very petty points, but even the petty point became fixed. A certain conventionality in the satire on Daniel comes from the use of Daniel as the stock example of the violation of principles that were upheld by the most orthodox. In different connections I have already touched upon a number of the points discussed by Cordatus and Mitis, especially the claim for independence in the form of comedy and for a certain freedom in adapting its rules. They also apply Jonson's theory of humour, which is first definitely stated in this play. Their discussion of what comedy should be—at the end of III, 1—repeats the ideas of the prologue to *Every Man in.* For these ideas Jonson may have drawn upon Whetstone, Sidney, the author of *A Warning for Fair Women,* and various others of his predecessors. Other details of Jonson's theory of comedy are taken up by the chorus, also, but usually merely by way of explaining the problems of the play or of applying the general rules given by the critical writers of the time.

Among the characters in what is properly the play, Macilente is easily the most important from the point of view of structure. He is the intriguer of the play and stands in opposition to all the other characters, observing their humours and plotting to bring about their overthrow. But, aside from his function in the plot, his dual nature makes him a complex character. He hates all follies with a justifiable hatred, and yet at the time of the play he has given away to the humour of envy.[1] It is envy that makes him a malicious intriguer, and this accounts for the care with which the Chorus explains his humour (I, 1, p. 79). As a figure

[1]His envy is spoken of a number of times. Cf. the character sketch prefixed to the play; I, 1, pp. 76, 78, and 79; IV, 1, p. 112; IV, 3, p. 112; V, 1, p. 126; epilogue, p. 140.

of envy, he connects clearly with the allegorical character of Envy in the Seven Deadly Sins. But he is, in addition, a scholar and given to reflection. In this rôle his envy takes the form of malcontent, so that he becomes one of the very earliest studies of the humour of malcontent, which was soon to attract so much attention in the drama.

In the characterization of Macilente as Envy, Jonson has followed pretty closely the conventional traits of the abstraction. The description of Envy in Passus V of *Piers the Plowman* gives an early example:

So loked he with lene chekes · lourynge foule:
His body was to-bolle for wratthe · that he bote his lippes,
And wryngynge he yede with the fiste · to wreke hym-self he thoughte
With werkes or with wordes · whan he seighe his tyme.
Eche a worde that he warpe · was of an Addres tonge,
Of chydynge and of chalangynge · was his chief lyflode,
With bakbitynge and bismer. . . .

. . . .

I wolde be gladder, bi god · that gybbe had meschaunce,
Than thoughe I had this woke ywonne · a weye of essex chese.
I haue a neighbore neyghe me · I haue ennuyed hym ofte,

. . . .

His grace and his good happes · greueth me ful sore.
Bitwene many and many · I make debate ofte,

. . . .

Awey fro the auter thanne · turne I myn eyghen,
And biholde how Eleyne · hath a newe cote;
I wisshe thanne it were myne · and al the webbe after.
And of mennes lesynge I laughe · that liketh myn herte;

. . . .

For who-so hath more than I · that angreth me sore.
And thus I lyue louelees · lyke a luther dogge,
That al my body bolneth · for bitter of my galle.
I myghte noughte eet many yeres · as a man oughte, etc.

Almost all of these details fit Macilente. Leanness is one of the most common characteristics of Envy.[1] Macilente means lean, and the leanness of the character is frequently referred to in the play.[2] Macilente also gives vent to his spleen in both works and

[1]Cf. *Ship of Fools*, ed. Jamieson, Vol. I, p. 254; *Endimion*, V, 1; *Faerie Queene*, V, xii, 29.

[2]Cf. I, 1, p. 76; IV, 2, p. 112; IV, 4, p. 115; V, 4, pp. 130 and 132; V. 7, p. 139.

words, and his malice is vengeful. The sharpness of his tongue leads Carlo to say of him, "He carries oil and fire in his pen, will scald where it drops" (I, 1, p. 76). Twice in IV, 1, Fallace accuses him of backbiting. Every fresh instance of worldly prosperity calls forth a tirade from him, and the overthrow or mishap of each separate fool is met with rejoicing. The finery of the coxcombs, like Eleyne's "newe cote," several times rouses his resentment. He takes special delight, also, in "setting debate" (IV, 3, p. 112) between Deliro and Fallace, between Carlo and Puntarvolo, between Shift and Puntarvolo, etc. Even the fact that Envy can not eat is suggested in Jonson's character. When Macilente speaks contemptuously of Carlo's fondness for pork, Carlo replies (V, 4, p. 132): "If thou wouldst farce thy lean ribs with it too, they would not, like ragged laths, rub out so many doublets as they do; but thou know'st not a good dish, thou."

The passage from *Piers the Plowman* is only suggestive of how far back the characterization of Macilente may be traced and how thoroughly conventional is the groundwork of the treatment. Parallels for Macilente as a study of Envy are to be found all the way through English literature, for the conventional traits of the abstraction remained pretty well fixed. Spenser has two treatments of Envy in *The Faerie Queene* (I, iv, 30-32, and V, xii, 29-32), which, with decided differences in detail, portray the same general disposition that we find in Envy of *Piers the Plowman* and in Macilente. In Book I Spenser says of Envy:

> But inwardly he chawed his owne maw
> At neighbours welth, that made him ever sad.
>
> . . . .
>
> Still as he rode he gnasht his teeth to see
> Those heapes of gold with griple Covetyse.

In Book V the female Envy is described as eating her own gall through sheer vexation at goodness. Spenser continues:

> For, when she wanteth other thing to eat,
> She feedes on her owne maw unnaturall,
> And of her owne foule entrayles makes her meat.

In comparing his own lot with Sordido's, Macilente complains (I, 1, p. 78),

> Meantime he surfeits in prosperity,
> And thou, in envy of him, gnaw'st thyself;

and the thought that an arrant gull like Sogliardo should have "land, houses, and lordships," wrings from Macilente the exclamation, "O, I could eat my entrails." The gnashing of the teeth is found in a quotation which Cordatus applies to Macilente (I, 1, p. 72):

Invidus suspirat, gemit, incutitque dentes.

For Macilente, especially in his malicious activity as the intriguer of a drama, the most interesting of the many treatments of Envy is perhaps to be found in Medwell's *Nature.* This play represents a dramatization of the abstract type which, its period considered, is no mean forerunner of Macilente. *Nature* furnishes nothing for Jonson's plot, but it presents in concrete form the malice of Envy as an intriguer and the same hostility between Envy and Pride which exists between Macilente and Brisk, Jonson's figure of pride.

In cam Pryde garnyshed as yt had be
One of the ryall blode
It greued me to se hym so well be sene
But I haue abated hys corage clene (Pt. II, ll. 912-915).

Whan I se an other man aryse
Or fare better than I
Than must I chafe and fret for yre
and ymagyn wyth all my desyre
To dystroy hym vtterly (Pt. II, ll. 933-937).[1]

In Medwell's play, Envy, like Macilente, shows his spitefulness toward all, and lays a special trap for Pride, as Macilente does for Brisk. Envy complains that Bodily Lust is furnished with better clothes than his, while Macilente, meanly clad, chafes at the finery of less worthy men. Pride is exactly the type of gallant seen in Brisk. He is always in advance of Man in fashion as Brisk is of Fungoso, and Fungoso's mad efforts to keep up with the style as set by Brisk recall the verdict that Pride passes on Man's array (Pt. I, ll. 1025 ff.):

It ys not the fassyon that goth now a day
For now there ys a new guyse.

[1]Cf. also the character sketch in ll. 1187 ff. Here, as in *Piers the Plowman,* Envy is described as a backbiter and detractor. This phase of Envy Jonson has not stressed in Macilente, though I have mentioned the fact that Fallace accuses him of backbiting. Spenser distinguishes Envy and Detraction (*F. Q.*, V, xii).

> It ys now .ii. dayes a gon
> Syth that men bygan thys fassyon
> And euery knaue had yt anon
> Therfore at thys season
> There ys no man that setteth thereby
> If he loue hys own honesty.

Like Brisk, Pride mortgages his land for fine clothes. He is also waited on by his page Garcio, as Brisk is by Cinedo. In all these points, however, both Pride and Brisk are doubtless merely typical gallants.

Though Macilente's tirades usually arise from pure envy, there are touches of dissatisfaction with society and of scorn for men in general which tend to make his expressions of envy broaden at times into satirical reflection on life. He is thus a forerunner of the malcontent. Many trends of contemporary literature indicate the growing popularity of the general type. Morosus was known to the age, and the misanthrope Timon and the cynic Diogenes were favorite figures.[1] A phrase in *The Defence of Conny-catching* applies aptly to Macilente: "No other humour left, but satirically with *Diogenes,* to snarle at all mens manners." Associated with malcontent was the melancholy which the age affected, as in the gulls of *Every Man in.*[2] Those who come under the influence of Saturn are often portrayed as gloomy or pessimistic. Envy is conceived of as a kindred type.[3] The satirist's affected scorn of

[1]For Diogenes see Lyly's *Campaspe,* Lodge's *Diogenes in his Singularitie, The batynge of Dyogens* (cf. *Cam. Hist. Eng. Lit.,* Vol. IV, p. 583), etc. For Timon see Painter's *Palace of Pleasure,* I, No. 28, Plutarch's "Life of Antony," etc.; cf. also Ward's *Hist. Eng. Dram. Lit.,* Vol. II, p. 178. References to the two, but especially to Diogenes, are very frequent in Elizabethan literature. Greene (*Works,* Vol. IX, p. 129) has the following passage combining the two with Morosus: "Yet was he not *Morosus,* tyed to austerne humours, neither so cinicall as *Diogenes,* to mislike *Alexanders* royalty, nor such a *Timonist,* but hee would familiarly conuerse with his friends."

[2]Cf. "melancholy malcontent" in *Wily Beguiled,* Hazlitt's *Dodsley,* Vol. IX, p. 268.

[3]For the influence of Saturn see Greene's *Planetomachia, Works,* Vol. V, pp. 45 ff.; Lyly's *Woman in the Moon,* I, 1; Rankins' *Seaven Satyres,* "Contra Saturnistam." Several of the terms used for this mood are combined in the following passage from *The Cobler of Canterburie,* p. 108 of the Shakespeare Society edition of *Tarlton's Jests,* etc.: "The enuious practises that solemne Saturnists ruminate . . . the sundrie schismes the melancholy michers do publish." Humour is also frequently combined with these terms at an early period. The phrase "melancholy humour" occurs a number of times in Greene's *Planetomachia,* 1585; cf. also *The Works of Greene,* Vol. XI, p. 213, and *The Works of Nashe,*

men and manners is, of course, the mainspring of the malcontent, and he arose with satire. The word malcontent is met frequently in the literature at the end of the century. Nashe, for example, is fond of both malcontent and *malevole*. *Pierce Penilesse* begins with an account of the "malecontent humor" into which Pierce has fallen because, though a scholar and a poet, he is poor, whereas cobblers and other clowns are well-to-do. His raging against fortune, his comparison of self with others, his envy and discontent, and even at times the wording, suggest Macilente very strongly. Greene in *Repentance* (*Works*, Vol. XII, p. 172) gives a short picture of himself as a "Malcontent," in which there are conventional details. The characterization of the type was quickly taken up in verse satire. In *Skialetheia* Guilpin twice deals with the malcontent (Epigram 52 and Satire V); and the second of the satires included with *Pygmalion's Image* contains a sketch of Bruto the traveler, clad in staid colors and exclaiming against the corrupt age, having learned only vices abroad,—an interesting first sketch by Marston of the qualities that are associated with many of the type.

Kindred studies were also appearing in the drama of the period. Bohan in the induction of *James IV*, with his scorn for the social life around him, has already been compared with Macilente. Diogenes, a related type, appears in Lyly's *Campaspe*. Two of the characters in *A Masque of the Knights of the Helmet* described in *Gesta Grayorum* are Envy and Malcontent. Dowsecer of *An Humorous Day's Mirth*, reflective and melancholy, belongs to the same general type. Doubtless some of the cynics and villains of tragedy also contributed to the vogue. Especially in and around 1599, the central year for satire, there are a number of plays reflecting the malcontent spirit of Macilente, though usually the type presented is nearer a combination of Asper and Macilente, showing the tendency in both to reflection and cynicism, but with more of the righteousness of Asper and less of the envy of Macilente. In the second scene of *Julius Caesar*, the lean Casca is portrayed with touches of the malcontent, and his use of prose

Vol. II, p. 262; compare "humorous melancholie" in Greene's *Never too Late*, *Works*, Vol. VIII, p. 127. Lodge uses humour three times in a short space for describing Envy or various phases of envy, *Wits Miserie*, pp. 57-59. Nashe's use of "malecontent humor" and Greene's use of the term for the moods of Diogenes and Morosus have also been quoted in this discussion.

represents a convention of the type. Feliche of *Antonio and Mellida* and Malevole of *The Malcontent* followed Macilente probably in quick succession. Possibly before Marston's contribution to the type, though probably later than *Every Man out,* appeared *As You Like It,* with its cynical and moralizing Jaques,[1] who desires (II, 7)

> liberty
> Withal, as large a charter as the wind,
> To blow on whom I please,

and promises,

> Give me leave
> To speak my mind, and I will through and through
> Cleanse the foul body of th' infected world.

The numerous treatments of cynical and soul-poisoned spirits that follow Asper-Macilente in all the drama of the age, including a number of Shakespeare's plays, have no value for Jonson's treatment of Macilente except as illustrating the growth of the type. In the literature preceding *Every Man out* there are, however, scattering expressions of the malcontent spirit which may have given suggestions to Jonson.

A passage in Macilente's opening soliloquy may be compared with Shakespeare's twenty-ninth sonnet.

Jonson	Shakespeare
When I view myself,	When, in disgrace with fortune and men's eyes,
Having before observed this man is great,	I all alone beweep my outcast state,
Mighty, and feared; that loved, and highly favoured;	And trouble deaf Heaven with my bootless cries,
A third thought wise and learned; a fourth rich,	And look upon myself, and curse my fate,
And therefore honoured; a fifth rarely featured;	Wishing me like to one more rich in hope,
A sixth admired for his nuptial fortunes:	Featured like him, like him with friends possess'd,
When I see these, I say, and view myself,	Desiring this man's art, and that man's scope, etc.
I wish the organs of my sight were cracked; etc. (I, 1).[2]	

[1]Like Macilente and others of the type, Jaques has just returned from travel when the play opens.

[2]Cf. *Antonio and Mellida,* Pt. I, III, 2, ll. 42 ff. for a passage probably imitated from Jonson but different in spirit.

In *Histriomastix,* when Chrisoganus comes under the sway of Envy, he falls into a soliloquy that is just in Macilente's vein (IV, ll. 132-158). Simpson, in his edition of the play, has compared the soliloquy with Macilente's opening speech, declaring that "the general tone and purpose of the two speeches are identical, though Jonson's is infinitely the better." The passage from *Histriomastix* belongs to the portion of the play assigned to Marston, and the part of Chrisoganus has commonly been accepted as a compliment to Jonson. I shall have occasion in a later chapter to revert to the matter of the relation between *Histriomastix* and the work of Jonson.

In II, 2, ll. 11 ff., Macilente protests,

> I see no reason why that dog called Chance,
> Should fawn upon this fellow, more than me:
> I am a man, and I have limbs, flesh, blood,
> Bones, sinews, and a soul, as well as he:
> My parts are every way as good as his;
> If I said better, why, I did not lie.

This is repeated from *The Case is Altered* (III, 1), where Angelo says:

> 'Sblood, am not I a man,
> Have I not eyes that are as free to look,
> And blood to be inflamed as well as his?
> And when it is so, shall I not pursue
> Mine own love's longings, but prefer my friend's?

Both passages seem inspired by Shylock's speech in *The Merchant of Venice* (III, 1): "Hath not a Jew eyes? hath not a Jew hands, organs, dimensions, senses, affections, passions? . . . and if you wrong us, shall we not revenge?"[1]

In the opening pages of *Pierce Penilesse,* which I have already spoken of as picturing Pierce's "malecontent humor," there is a passage that in ideas and turn of expression is somewhat similar to the one just quoted from Macilente: "Thereby I grew to consider how many base men that wanted those parts which I had, enioyed content at will, and had wealth at command: . . . and haue I more wit than all these (thought I to my selfe)? am I better borne? am I better brought vp? yea, and better fauored?

[1]Cf. *The Witch of Edmonton,* II, 1, for the same idea.

and yet am I a begger?" With this passage compare also the speech in *Every Man out* (II, 2, p. 93) beginning,

> I fain would know of heaven now, why yond fool
> Should wear a suit of satin? he? that rook.

Macilente's sharp and satiric vein is brought out in Carlo's characterization (I, 1, p. 76): "He carries oil and fire in his pen, will scald where it drops: his spirit is like powder, quick, violent; he'll blow a man up with a jest: I fear him worse than a rotten wall does the cannon; shake an hour after at the report."[1] Later (IV, 4, p. 115) Carlo calls him "the pure element of fire, all spirit, extraction," and adds that he "walks up and down like a charged musket." Guilpin had already used similar language in describing the satiric spirit of the age (*Skialetheia, Satyra prima*):

> How now my *Muse* . . . .
> . . . .
> Thys leaden-heeled passion is to dull,
> To keepe pace with this Satyre-footed gull:
> This mad-cap world, this whirlygigging age:
> Thou must haue words compact of fire & rage:
> Tearms of quick Camphire, & Salt-peeter phrases,
> As in a myne to blow vp the worlds graces,
> And blast her anticke apish complements.

Clothes have no small share in setting the "seam-rent" Macilente apart from the more fortunate in his environment. In II, 2, Brisk discourses to him at length on the virtues of rich apparel, and offers to take him to court provided he is suitably dressed. When Macilente, in new attire, finds himself in an apartment at court, he reflects on the sovereignty of clothes (III, 3, p. 108):

> I was admiring mine own outside here,
> To think what privilege and palm it bears
> Here in the court! be a man ne'er so vile,
> In wit, in judgment, manners, or what else;
> If he can purchase but a silken cover,
> He shall not only pass, but pass regarded:
> Whereas let him be poor and meanly clad,
> Though ne'er so richly parted, you shall have
> A fellow that knows nothing but his beef,
> Or how to rince his clammy guts in beer,

[1] Cf. *Poetaster*, IV, 1, p. 239, where Tucca characterizes Horace.

Will take him by the shoulders or the throat,
And kick him down the stairs. Such is the state
Of virtue in bad clothes!

The same theme is proposed for discussion by the interlocutor Spudeus in Stubbes's *Anatomy* (p. 39 in Furnivall's edition): "Gorgiouse attyre . . . maketh a man to be accepted and esteemed of in euery place; wheras otherwise they should be nothing lesse." Philoponus answers with a long disquisition on the reverence due to virtue, wisdom, etc., but not to attire, and often expresses Jonson's ideas; as,

Vnder a simple cote many tymes lyeth hid great wisdom & knowledg; & co*n*trarely, vnder braue attyre somtime is couered great ydiotacy and folly. . . .

For surely, for my part, I will rather worshippe & accept of a pore ma*n* (in his clowtes & pore raggs) hauing *the* gifts and orname*n*ts of the mind, than I will do him *that* roisteth & flaunteth daylie & howrely in his silks, veluets, satens, damasks, gold or siluer, what soeuer, without *the* induments of vertue, wherto only al reuerence is due (pp. 41, 42).

One of the many examples that Stubbes cites is of a certain philosopher, who, rejected at court when basely clad and reverently accepted in fine raiment, "kneled down, and ceased not to kisse his garme*n*ts," saying, "That whiche my vertue and knowledge could not doe, my Apparell hath brought to passe" (p. 47).[1] Thoroughly commonplace as are the ideas expressed by Stubbes, they show how Jonson is affected by the thought of contemporaries. Stubbes is a perfect storehouse for illustrating Jonson's satire on the dress of the age, as may be seen from Furnivall's notes. Whether Jonson actually utilized Stubbes or not, the prominence of the *Anatomy of Abuses* and its emphasis on evils in dress doubtless had their influence on the almost Puritanical spirit which Jonson shows toward dress.

In some respects, Macilente's immediate forerunner as an intriguer is to be found in Lemot of *An Humorous Day's Mirth.* Lemot is not characterized either as envious or as malcontent, but

[1]Dr. Furnivall points out no source for the incident, which is doubtless classic. In Kerton's *Mirror of Mans lyfe*, 1576 (translated from the Latin of Lotharius), among several short chapters dealing with dress, chapter 37 of the second book has the heading, "That more fauoure is shewed vnto a man for his apparell sake, than for his vertue," and here the story is told of the man who kissed his garments because they secured his admission to court.

in rounding up all the humour types of the play, laying traps to overthrow them, taking malicious delight in their embarrassment, and showing slight sympathy in his dealings with them, he performs exactly the function of Macilente. The chief difference lies in the fact that Lemot, after having all the humour-ridden characters in his power, lets them off without complete exposure. As in *Every Man out,* the foundation for the resolution of the plot in *An Humorous Day's Mirth* is laid in an arrangement to meet at an ordinary and make merry. Though the meeting becomes the means of grouping the characters and bringing confusion to a number at once, the details in the two plays differ widely. Lemot's plan to expose the Puritan Florilla, however, is like Macilente's scheme for curing Deliro's humour of dotage. Labervele, the jealous husband of Chapman's play, dotes upon Florilla, as Deliro does upon Fallace, and surrounds her with ceremonious attentions. Lemot invites the wife to meet him at an ordinary, and she, though a Puritan with great pretensions to sanctity, is readily led into making the assignation.[1] When she reaches the ordinary, Lemot secretly summons the husband, and she is threatened with exposure.[2] Macilente uses the feast at the Mitre to have Brisk arrested, and then carries the news to Fallace, who rushes to Brisk's rescue. Meanwhile Macilente brings the doting husband to see for himself the perfidy of his wife.

When Macilente has put all of the other characters out of their humours and is himself purged of the humour of envy, he appears again in Asper's mood, "though not his shape," as an epilogue. The same device is found in the old play of *Timon,* where Timon, after scourging all the sycophants from his presence, speaks the epilogue in a changed mood. Hart has pointed out the fact that *Timon* is closely related to *Every Man out* and the two succeeding plays of Jonson (*The Works of Ben Jonson,* Vol. I, pp. xliii ff.), and has cited a number of parallels to Jonson's work, though by no means all. His conclusion is that *Timon* preceded the humour plays, in

[1]Lemot wins Florilla by tricking her husband with a proposal to court her in his presence as a test of her constancy. A kindred motive Jonson uses in *The Devil is an Ass,* but he has made the incident conform rather closely to a story of the *Decameron* (III, 5) that may be the source also of Chapman's device.

[2]A device of the same sort is used to entangle two of the men at the ordinary and put them in a bad light with their wives, so that the motive is tripled. The men, however, are guiltless.

which case we must consider it among the most important of Jonson's sources. The matter is uncertain, but the parallels were worth pointing out if only to show the immediate influence of Jonson. The parallel between the close of the two plays is not suggested by Hart. The Quarto, which I quote, is nearer *Timon* than is the Folio.

Macilente	Timon
Why, here's a change: Now is my soule at peace,	I now am left alone: this rascall route
I am as empty of all Enuie now,	Hath left my side. What's this? I feele throughout
As they of merit to be enuied at,	A sodeine change: my fury doth abate,
My Humor (like a flame) no longer lasts	My hearte growes milde, and laies aside its hate.
Than it hath stuffe to feed it. . . .	Ile not affecte newe titles in my minde,
. . . .	Or yet bee call'd the hater of mankinde:
I am so farre from malicing their states,	Timon doffs Timon, and with bended knee
That I begin to pittie them. . . .	Thus craues a fauour,—if our comedie
. . . .	And merry scene deserue a plaudite
And now with *Aspers* tongue (though not his shape)	Let louing hands, loude sounding in the ayre,
. . . .	Cause Timon to the citty to repaire.[1]
. . . [we] entreat	
The happier spirits in this fairefild Globe,	
. . . .	
That with their bounteous *Hands* they would confirme	
This, as their pleasures *Pattent*.	

[1]In regard to the date of *Timon* Hart says: "Since the parallels extend from the Humour-plays to *Poetaster*, it [*Timon*] must have preceded them all; for if it was intended to mock Ben it would have to succeed them all, and it could not be devoid of allusions to the 'humours,' or to the *Satiromastix* battle." It seems indeed strange that a play which is so close to Jonson's work should not use humour. On the other hand, various dramatists took up Jonson's vein immediately, often with scarcely a mention of humour. Gull is likely to occur, but some followers of Jonson pay little attention to either. The borrowing often consisted not even in the humour point of view, but in material for satire on the foolish types of London. Dekker in *Patient Grissell*, Marston, the author of the Parnassus plays, and others seem to have imitated Jonson's plays almost immediately and yet to have been but slightly influenced by the word humour. The crudeness of *Timon* might argue for a date before Jonson, except for the fact that other plays which apparently follow Jonson's—*Sir Gyles Goosecappe*, for example—are almost as crude. Moreover, the author of the academic *Timon* was probably an amateur. Dyce put the play in 1600. If it was as late as this, it prob-

As near as the parasite in Carlo Buffone brings him to the rogue class, his function in the play places him with Macilente rather than with Shift. A glutton, whoremonger, coward, sycophant, and parasite, he is still stressed chiefly for his power of abuse and railing. Macilente has real courage and some respect for self. He is called a backbiter by one of his victims, but, in spite of his malice, he is not pictured as a liar, a hypocrite, or a sycophant. Detraction and secret malice are represented in Carlo, who is strictly the backbiter. As an abstraction he is called Mischief and Wickedness (II, 1, p. 82).[1] As a scourger, the *"Grand Scourge,*[2] or *Second Untruss of the time"* (II, 1, p. 86), he represents a third type of the satirical spirit abroad, the

> open-throated, black-mouthed cur,
> That bites at all, but eats on those that feed him (I, 1, p. 76).

He is a buffoon, a low jester, who confounds with similes, and his satire is of the basest sort, mere detraction, not at all to be compared with the noble rage of Asper or the curable envy of the poor scholar Macilente.[3] The mouth of Detraction must be sealed by folly itself. Carlo's office in the play thus associates him with

ably came after *Poetaster.* Cf. pp. 209 f. *infra* for further discussion of the date. Jonson could hardly have had any share in *Timon.* It does not suggest his style.

[1]So Anaides of *Cynthia's Revels,* who resembles Carlo closely, is twice called Mischief in IV, 1 (pp. 174 and 179). In III, 2 (p. 166) he is addressed as Detraction.

[2]The reference in "Grand Scourge" has frequently been taken as a hit at Marston. It may be, though I believe that Jonson has borrowed from Marston in this play. Even if the expression refers to Marston's *Scourge of Villainy,* it does not mean that Carlo is intended for Marston. "Grand Scourge," however, may have no reference to Marston's work in particular, for whip, scourge, and mastix were favorite words expressing the attitude of satire. Cf. Asper's "whip of steel," and "I will scourge these apes." Guilpin (*Skialetheia,* "Satyre Preludium") uses scourge and also Chester—the name of the man who was the original of Carlo—as synonyms for the spirit of satire. Nashe refers to a "ballet of vntrusse," apparently by Munday, in such a way as to indicate that it was scurrilous enough for the term untruss to be applied aptly to Carlo as a "prophane jester." Cf. *Works of Nashe,* Vol. V, p. 195; Vol. I, p. 159; and Vol. IV, p. 90. See also Hart, 10 *N. and Q.*, Vol. I, pp. 381-383. The title *Children of the Chapel Stript and Whipt,* 1569, combines the two ideas as Jonson does.

[3]Aristotle attempts a similar three-fold classification: "Righteous indignation, again, is a mean state between envy and malice. . . . A person who is righteously indignant is pained at the prosperity of the undeserving; but the envious person goes further and is pained at anybody's prosperity, and the malicious person is so far from being pained

Macilente, whom he understands, admires, and fears; and he becomes a second to Macilente in the intrigues of the play. Macilente, however, utilizes him chiefly to bring about his downfall.

Spenser in *The Faerie Queene* (V, xii) associates Envy with Detraction, who dwells near Envy. Detraction, however, is feminine, and not suggestive of Carlo. In *Wits Miserie,* Lodge has a number of characters that embody traits of Carlo, but none that shows a very close approach to his assemblage of qualities. Of Derision, for instance, it is said:

> Marry he will run ouer all his varietie of filthie faces, till he light on yours: beat ouer all the antique conceits he hath gathered, til he second your defect, and neuer leaue to deride you, till he fall drunke in a Tauerne while some grow sicke with laughing at him, or consult with Rash Iudgement how to delude others, that at the length hée proueth deformity himself (Hunterian Club, p. 10).

"Scandale and Detraction" is described as a skulking villain and malcontent.

> In beleife he is an Atheist . . . hating his countrie wherein hée was bred, his gratious Prince vnder whom he liueth, those graue counsailors vnder whom the state is directed, not for default either in gouernement, or policy, but of méere innated and corrupt villanie; and vaine desire of Innouation (p. 17).

This last quotation may be compared with a description of Carlo at the end of the induction giving him a characteristic of which we see nothing in the play itself: "He will prefer all countries before his native, and thinks he can never sufficiently, or with admiration enough, deliver his affectionate conceit of foreign atheistical policies."

In *The Castle of Perseverance* there is a character Detraccio, or Backbiter, who resembles Carlo in a number of points (ll. 651-702). He is a liar and a tutor in evil; he plots against duke and clown alike; he will "speke fayre be-forn, & fowle be-hynde." It

that he actually rejoices *at misfortunes*" (*Ethics*, trans. Welldon, pp. 52, 53). Aristotle's treatment could not have given Jonson more than the fundamental idea of his three-fold division of scourgers, but it is possible that Jonson had some other source developed from Aristotle. Welldon calls attention to the weakness of Aristotle's distinction between envy and malice (p. xxi). Jonson found much more definite distinctions in English literature. Cf. p. 172 *infra* for the filling in from Aristotle of the abstraction represented in Carlo.

is through him that the Seven Deadly Sins, including Envy, are introduced to Man. Cloaked Collusion of Skelton's *Magnificence,* who declares himself of one mind with Division, Dissension, and Derision, is another abstraction of the early drama that is related to Carlo. In lines 689 ff. he gives a character sketch of himself which corresponds in many respects to the characterization of Carlo as intriguer, backbiter, dissembler, and flatterer. In particular, Carlo is described as "one whose company is desired of all men, but beloved of none," and Cloaked Collusion says of himself:

> And though I be so odyous a geste,
> And euery man gladly my company wolde refuse,
> In faythe, yet am I occupyed with the best;
> Full fewe that can themselfe of me excuse.

Outside of the abstraction Derision, there are to be found distinct treatments of jesting alone as a folly which prepare for Carlo as a jester. In Aristotle's *Ethics* the Buffoon is described as follows (pp. 130, 131):

> Now they who exceed the proper limit in ridicule seem to be buffoons and vulgar people, as their heart is set upon exciting ridicule at any cost, and they aim rather at raising a laugh than at using decorous language and not giving pain to their butt. . . . There will be some kinds of jest then that he [the good jester] will not make, for mockery is a species of reviling, and there are some kinds of reviling which legislators prohibit; they ought perhaps to have prohibited certain kinds of jesting as well. . . . But the buffoon is the slave of his own sense of humour; he will spare neither himself nor anybody else, if he can raise a laugh, and he will use such language as no person of refinement would use or sometimes even listen to.

This classical idea of the distinction between gentlemanly and clownish wit is brought over into Renaissance literature in Wilson's *Arte of Rhetorique* (pp. 137-139). From the point of view of classic and Renaissance culture, scurrilous jesting was obnoxious as inconsistent with the highest ideal of gentlemanly refinement,—an ideal that was stressed in Italian courtesy books and, for England, in the works of Elyot, Ascham, Lyly, etc. Wilson emphasizes the difference "betwixt a common iester, and a pleasant wiseman." Of jesting at the expense of persons, the type of jesting by which Carlo transforms men into deformity, Wilson says:

For, he that exceedeth and telleth all: yea, more then is needfull, without all respect or consideration had: the same shalbe taken for a common iester, such as knowe not how to make an ende, when they once begin, being better acquainted with bible bable, then knowing the fruite of wisedomes lore.

Witty sayings constitute Wilson's second division of "pleasaunt behauiour." Of word wit he continues:

But euen as in reporting a tale, or counterfeiting a man, to much is euer naught: So scurrilitie or (to speake in olde plaine English) knauerie in iesting would not be vsed, where honestie is esteemed. Therfore, though there be some witte in a pretie deuised iest: yet we ought to take heede that we touche not those, whom we would be most loth to offende. And yet some had as leue lose their life, as not bestowe their conceiued iest, and oftentimes they haue as they desire.[1]

Carlo is described as a "public, scurrilous, and prophane jester; that . . . with absurd similes will transform any person into deformity" (p. 62); and Cordatus says of him in the induction, "He will sooner lose his soul than a jest, and profane even the most holy things, to excite laughter; no honourable or reverend personage whatsoever can come within the reach of his eye, but is turned into all manner of variety, by his adulterate similes" (p. 71). Wilson's warning that it is "meet to auoyd . . . alehouse iesting" gives force to Jonson's characterization of Carlo as a public jester, one who prostitutes his wit at every tavern and ordinary (I, 1, p. 76).[2]

It is not an accident that these passages from Wilson agree so well with Jonson's treatment of rude jesting. Criticism early took jesting into account. Cicero's *De Oratore* gave classic sanction for its study as a literary art, and for the Renaissance Castiglione in portraying the ideal gentleman takes pains to deal with the matter of wit. Wilson, we have seen, discusses jesting as a part of his theory of rhetoric in the first really influential English rhetoric. Again, Sir Thomas More's ready wit made no small part of the charm which his personality held for the Renaissance

[1]Wilson's classification of jests and his conception of the "common jester" were probably drawn from Cicero's *De Oratore*, Book II, chapters lvii ff. Cicero, however, does not seem so important for Jonson as does Aristotle or the Renaissance expression of Cicero's ideas in Wilson.

[2]Cf. p. 61 *supra* for some phrases of Harvey's characterization of Nashe that are parallel to Jonson's sketch of Carlo.

public, so that no life of More in that age was complete without its accounts of his happy jests.

In the passages that I have quoted on jesting one commonplace especially indicates conventionality. Aristotle's test of refinement in wit is that the buffoon "will spare neither himself nor anybody else, if he can raise a laugh." According to Wilson, "some had as leue lose their life, as not bestowe their conceiued iest." Cordatus says of Carlo that he "will sooner lose his soul than a jest," and Tucca in *Poetaster* (IV, 1, p. 239) says of Horace, "He will sooner lose his best friend than his least jest." It is a rather strange nemesis that the cultured Drummond, in summing up Jonson's character after the latter's visit to Scotland, should have applied to him the same touchstone that Jonson applied to Carlo, and should have found him wanting. Jonson, Drummond says,—almost in the words that Jonson puts in the mouth of Tucca as a bit of slander against himself in the rôle of Horace,—was "given rather to losse a friend than a jest." It is probable that Drummond had the passage of *Poetaster* in mind when he wrote.[1]

Carlo is one of Jonson's most interesting studies, because, although Jonson was naturally led to express in him as a humour type an abstract principle or trait, there is very little doubt that the concrete Carlo was drawn to life from a notorious London character, Charles Chester. He thus furnishes evidence that the crafty Jonson had the gift of embodying personal satire in his studies of types, and embodying it so skilfully that it renders the character more concrete but not a whit less typical. Aubrey in his *Brief Lives* declares, on the authority of Dr. John Pell, that Carlo Buffone is taken from Chester, and that "one time at a taverne Sir W. R. beates him and seales up his mouth (*i. e.* his upper and neather beard) with hard wax." Collier identified Chester with Charles the Fryer of Chester in Nashe's *Pierce Penilesse,* and Hart has gathered and quoted five other contemporary references to Chester as a jester—three from Harington's works and two from Guilpin's *Skialetheia*—besides a reference in the *Calendar of State Papers.*[2] The statement of Aubrey and the like-

[1]Jonson's passage was suggested by Horace; see p. 309 *infra.*

[2]*The Works of Ben Jonson,* Vol. I, pp. xxxvi ff. Small, *Stage-Quarrel,* pp. 35 ff., had already mentioned some of these references, and had stressed the connection of Carlo and Chester.

ness of Carlo's character to that of Chester as revealed by these allusions to him leave no doubt that Jonson portrays Chester in Carlo's railing and in the sealing of his mouth by Puntarvolo at the Mitre.[1]

Nashe's sketch (*Works,* Vol. I, pp. 190, 191) is the fullest and the most valuable for the "absurd similes" that Jonson puts in the mouth of Carlo:

> There be those that get their liuing al the yeere long, by nothing but rayling.
>
> Not farre from *Chester,* I knewe an odde foule mouthde knaue, called *Charles* the Fryer. . . . Noblemen he would liken to more vgly things than himself: some to After my hartie commendations, with a dash ouer the head: others, to guilded chines of beefe, or a shoomaker sweating, when he puls on a shoo: another to an old verse in *Cato, Ad consilium ne accesseris, antequam voceris*: another, to a Spanish Codpisse: another, that his face was not yet finisht, with such like innumerable absurd illusions: yea, what was he in the Court but he had a comparison in stead of a Capcase to put him in. Vpon a time, being chalenged at his owne weapon in a priuate Chamber, by a great personage (rayling, I meane), he so far outstript him in vilainous words, and ouerbandied him in bitter tearmes, that the name of sport could not perswade him patience, nor containe his furie in any degrees of ieast, but needs hee must wreake himselfe vppon him: neither would a common reuenge suffice him, his displeasure was so infinite . . . wherefore he caused his men to take him, and brickt him vp in a narrow chimney, that was *Neque maior neque minor corpore locato;* where he fed him for fifteene dayes with bread and water through a hole, letting him sleep standing if he would, for lye or sit he could not, and then he let him out to see if he could learne to rule his tongue any better.
>
> It is a disparagement to those that haue any true sparke of Gentilitie, to be noted of the whole world so to delight in detracting, that they should keepe a venemous toothd Cur, and feed him with the crums that fall from their table, to do nothing but bite euery one by the shins that passe by. If they will needes be merry, let them haue a foole and not a knaue to disport them, and seeke some other to bestow their almes on, than such an impudent begger.

Nashe gives this portrait as an example of "Wrath, a branch of Enuie," and his use of "rayling" and "detracting" connects the character with Detraction. In Carlo, as in the satire on Harvey's

[1]In the dedication to *Volpone* Jonson asks: "Where have I been particular? where personal? except to a mimic, cheater, bawd, or buffoon . . .?" This is an admission that personal satire enters into his work, and it was probably written with Carlo, for one, in mind.

vocabulary, Jonson seems to have been following Nashe's trail. Many of Nashe's phrases suggest Jonson's. Compare "get their liuing . . . by nothing but rayling" with Jonson's "His religion is railing" (p. 62). The Fryer is given to "absurd illusions" and has a comparison to put each man in; Carlo "with absurd similes will transform any person into deformity" (p. 62). Nashe calls the Fryer a "foule mouthde knaue" and rebukes those who "keepe a venemous toothd Cur, and feed him . . . to do nothing but bite euery one by the shins that passe by"; Macilente speaks of Carlo as a

> black-mouthed cur
> That bites at all, but eats on those that feed him (I, 1, p. 76).

The "great personage" who is roused to so violent a revenge on the Fryer is represented in the knight Sir Puntarvolo, who in the end cures Carlo's humour. The jests that are worked out in Jonson's play may also be compared with those of Nashe's sketch.[1] The Fryer's comparison of noblemen to "guilded chines of beefe" is like Carlo's comparison of Puntarvolo to "a shield[2] of brawn at Shrove-tide . . . or a dry pole of ling upon Easter-eve, that has furnished the table all Lent" (IV, 4, p. 116). The simile of the "Spanish Codpisse" is of a kind with Carlo's comparison of Puntarvolo's face to "a Dutch purse, with the mouth downward, his beard the tassels" (V, 4, p. 133). The Fryer's jest of the face that "was not yet finisht" is in intent like a score of Carlo's similes that transform men into deformity. Of Sogliardo Carlo says, "He looks like a musty bottle new wickered, his head's the cork" (I, 1, p. 76); of Cinedo, "He looks like . . . one of these motions in a great antique clock; he would shew well upon a haberdasher's stall, at a corner shop, rarely" (II, 1, p. 79); of Puntarvolo, "He looks like the sign of the George" (II, 1, p. 82). These passages may also be compared with part of two that Hart quotes as referring to Jonson's original for Carlo. Harington says parenthetically, "To use *Charles Chester's* jest, because you

[1]Hart calls attention to the relationship between Carlo and Nashe's sketch of Charles the Fryer, though he does not go into details. In 10 *N. and Q.*, Vol. I, p. 383, he also points out a remark of Mayne in *Jonsonus Virbius* which would indicate that Jonson had a personal reason for being hostile to Chester.

[2]The Quarto has "Chine."

are faced like *Platina;*" and Guilpin says of a woman who paints her face,

> Or would not Chester sweare her downe that shee
> Lookt . . .
> . . . like a new sherifes gate-posts, whose old faces
> Are furbisht over to smoothe time's disgraces?

Carlo's jests are much closer to those of Chester as given by Nashe, Harington, and Guilpin than is justified by their being merely of the same class, for while Jonson, who wished that "poets would leave to be promoters of other men's jests" (induction to *Cynthia's Revels*), does invent his own, it is interesting to note that the jests which he would not borrow still furnish close models for several specific types of jests that are repeated frequently in Carlo's mouth. To my mind, Jonson always seeks in literature the general principle, the fundamental idea, of a character, an episode, or even a jest, and strives to give it fresh clothing. In fact, his own notes to some of his work, *The Masque of Queens,* for instance, are a sufficient indication of his method of working. Nashe's portrait of Chester naturally had an influence on Jonson, for it had already classified Chester as representing a type of evil. Jonson was not likely to take a character entirely from life. In his practice, the character must stand for a certain evil, must be almost an abstraction, and the real poet drew characters only as true to life as might be consistent with their conformity to a type.

In characterizing Carlo as one that "will swill up more sack at a sitting than would make all the guard a posset" (p. 62), Jonson has given a special scene to his drinking. Carlo's manipulation of the cups is in the manner of a puppet-show, and probably illustrates Jonson's early interest in such performances. At the same time, the scene burlesques the conventions of drinking bouts. Setting two cups before him, Carlo goes through the ceremony of pledging healths as he drinks from first one cup and then the other (V, 4):

> *1 Cup.* Now, sir, here's to you; and I present you with so much of my love.
> *2 Cup.* I take it kindly from you, sir [*drinks,*] and will return you the like proportion.

Then the first cup proposes the health of the "honourable countess, and the sweet lady that sat by her," and the second cup responds,

"I do vail to it with reverence." After that health has been drunk and one to the "divine mistress" of the first cup, the second cup proposes: "And now, sir, here is a replenished bowl, which I will reciprocally turn upon you, to the health of the Count Frugale;" and they pledge it upon their knees. A quarrel arises, the second cup exclaiming, "Nay, do me right, sir," and "Mine was fuller," and the whole scene ends in the giving of the lie and a threatened stabbing.

Nashe in *Pierce Penilesse* says of excessive drinking (*Works,* Vol. 1, pp. 205-207):

> Now, he is no body that cannot drinke *super nagulum,* carouse the Hunters hoop, quaffe *vpsey freze crosse,* with healthes, gloues, mumpes, frolickes, and a thousand such dominiering inuentions. He is reputed a pesaunt and a boore that wil not take his licour profoundly. And you shall heare a Caualier of the first feather . . . stand vppon termes with, Gods wounds, you dishonour me sir, you do me the disgrace if you do not pledge me as much as I drunke to you: and, in the midst of his cups, stand vaunting his manhood . . . we haue generall rules and iniunctions, as good as printed precepts, or Statutes set downe by Acte of Parliament, that goe from drunkard to drunkard; as still to keepe your first man, not to leaue any flockes in the bottome of the cup, to knock the glasse on your thumbe when you haue done, etc.

In *Summer's Last Will and Testament,* again, there is a drinking scene (Vol. III, pp. 264-269, ll. 962 ff.) that illustrates many of the details in the passage from *Pierce Penilesse*:

> *Bacchus.* . . . *A vous, moũsieur Winter,* a frolick vpsy freese, crosse, ho, *super nagulũ.*
>
> *Winter.* . . . For this time you must pardon me perforce.
>
> *Bacchus.* What, giue me the disgrace?

Then Bacchus forces Summer to drink, on his knees, to the "health of Captaine *Rinocerotry,*" and insists that Summer shall "haue weight and measure" of wine. "Wee'le leaue no flocks behind vs, whatsoeuer wee doe,"[1] Bacchus declares as he departs.

[1]A drinking song that is repeated several times runs:

> Mounsieur Mingo for quaffing doth surpasse,
> In Cuppe, in Canne, or glasse.
> God Bacchus, doe mee right,
> And dubbe mee knight Domingo.

Cf. *II Henry IV*, V, 3; *Return from Parnassus,* Part I, l. 1469; *Pierce Penilesse, Works of Nashe,* Vol. 1, p. 169. Could the lost play of *Mingo* have dealt with drinking scenes?

After Bacchus leaves the scene with his merry crew, Summer reflects:

> What a beastly thing is it, to bottle vp ale in a ma*n*s belly, whe*n* a man must set his guts on a gallo*n* pot last, only to purchase the alehouse title of a *boone companion*? Carowse, pledge me and you dare: S'wounds, ile drinke with thee for all that euer thou art worth. It is eue*n* as 2. men should striue who should run furthest into the sea for a wager.

Collier has cited as illustrative of the passage just quoted from *Pierce Penilesse,* one from Riche's *Irish Hubbub* showing that "the institution in drinking of a Health, is full of ceremonie, and obserued by Tradition." Though Riche's work is later than Jonson's, it describes more exactly than Nashe does, the custom of drinking healths as Jonson put it on the stage:

> He that begins the Health, hath his prescribed orders: first vncouering his head, he takes a full cup in his hand, and setling his countenance with a graue aspect, he craues for audience: silence being once obtained, hee begins to breath out the name, peraduenture, of some Honorable Personage, . . . his Health is drunke to, and hee that pledgeth, must likewise of with his Cap, kisse his fingers, and bowing himselfe in signe of a reuerent acceptance; when the Leader sees his Follower thus prepared, he soupes vp his broath, turnes the bottome of the Cuppe vpward, and in ostentation of his dexteritie, giues the cup a phylip, to make it cry *Tynge.* And thus the first Scene is acted.
>
> The cup being newly replenished to the breadth of a haire, he that is the pledger must now begin his part, and thus it goes round throughout the whole company, . . . till the Health hath had the full passage: which is no sooner ended, but another begins againe, and he drinkes a Health, to his *Lady of little worth,* or peraduenture to his *light heel'd mistris* (Quoted from McKerrow's note, *Works of Nashe,* Vol. IV, p. 130).

A part of Carlo's function throughout the early part of the play is to instruct the gull Sogliardo in conduct. Carlo's advice is largely drawn from the *Familiar Colloquies* of Erasmus, as Whalley and Gifford have pointed out. Sogliardo is advised to live in the city; to provide fine clothes at any cost; to play at cards and dice; to talk of kindred and allies; to have forged letters from the great brought to him, and provide that those present shall know the contents while he pretends to be displeased; to keep richly clothed servants who shall steal for him; to render his creditors obsequious by not paying them; to secure a coat of arms; etc. All this is taken from "The False Knight," practically the whole of the colloquy being utilized by Jonson. In addition, Carlo advises Sogliardo to acquire peculiar oaths; at ordinaries to be melancholy; at plays to be humorous and sit on the stage and flout (all of this in I, 1); to pretend to austerity and pride, and yet play the sycophant and backbite; and to be impudent and affected at ordinaries, swearing and offering wagers (III, 1). Carlo also comments on the power of delicate diet to refine the wit, using city wives as an example. Almost all of these points are treated by the satirists of the time, and most of them are common. The oaths and melancholy appear in the gulls of *Every Man in* as well as in satire. Davies in Epigrams 3 and 28 satirizes the behavior of gallants on the stage; Nashe, Lodge, Davies, Guilpin, and others give sketches of the upstart who poses as scornful and of the flatterer who backbites. Many of the principles laid down by Carlo, which belong to his function as a scoffer and railer and represent his ironic satire, are made concrete in the action of the characters, and will be taken up later.

A second parasite in the play, though of an entirely different class from Carlo, is the "thread-bare shark" Shift, who haunts Paul's. Shift represents for *Every Man out* Jonson's interest in the coney-catcher. Like Brainworm, he plays the begging soldier, carries a sword, and boasts of his campaigns. He is more pretentious, however, affecting the standards of a gentleman, and, like Carlo, pressing into the company of would-be gallants. The name is an old one for rogues. *The Fraternitye of Vacabondes,* according to the title page, deals with "Cousoners and Shifters," and in *The Groundworke of Conny-catching* (1592), shifter is a cant term for one class of coney-catchers.[1] In the early drama, Shift appears as one of three rogues in *Common Conditions,* and Subtle Shift in *Sir Clyomon and Sir Clamydes.* There are also some early sketches in which characters are described as shifters, but, like many other sketches of their period, they lack that exactness of classification and that attention to particular details which distinguishes Renaissance character delineation in England, especially

[1]The story is told here (*Rogues and Vagabonds of Shakspere's Youth,* pp. 102, 103) of how a shifter ingratiated himself into a company of clothiers at an inn, and cozened them of the money for their reckoning. According to the author of *The Groundworke,* the jest is falsely attributed "to a man of excellent parts about London." As practically the same jest is attributed to Peele (*Jests of Peele, Shakespeare Jest-Books,* Vol. II, pp. 296, 297), we have here a pretty good indication that the *Jests* were in circulation early enough to influence Jonson's plays. Cf. p. 134 *supra.*

with the rise of satire. The shifter seems less fixed and developed than most of the early types taken up by Jonson. Certain more or less commonplace phases of Jonson's Shift are also illustrated in various sketches not connected with the name Shift, or Shifter.

Fulwell in *The Arte of Flatterie* has several sketches showing the general characteristics of the type, though they are perhaps closer to Carlo than to Shift. In the fifth dialogue it is said of Pierce Pickthanke that "to picke thankes and profit at all mennes handes hee can frame himselfe to feede all men's humours," a characteristic common to Carlo and Shift and all the fraternity of those who live by their wits, preying upon others. In another sketch, after describing Drunken Dickon as a "saucye and malaperte varlet, who useth very broad iesting," Fulwell continues: "And because hee noteth that wise men take sporte to see fooles in a rage, hee will counterfait himselfe to bee in a mad moode, when hee is nothing at all angry;—he is a common cosoner, and a subtle shifter." The counterfeit rage of Fulwell's character is worked out very fully by Jonson in III, 1, where Shift appears "expostulating with his rapier," and Carlo remarks, "Did you ever in your days observe better passion over a hilt?"[1] The suggestion that he sell the rapier immediately sends Shift off into another feigned passion. In this same chapter of *The Arte of Flatterie,* Pierce describes "a proper man"[2] in terms that often fit Shift:

> And now to thy properties, thy use is to counterfaite thy selfe, . . . and wilt not blush to place thyselfe in euery man's company, and taste of euery mans pot. And if thou perceiuest the company to bee delighted with thy ieastes, then art thou in thy ruffe, but if they be so wise as to mislike of thy saucines, then thou hast this subtile shift. . . . Also thou canst prate like a pardoner, and for thy facility in lying, thou art worthy to weare a whetstone in thy hat insteede of a brouch.[3]

The willingness to place oneself "in euery man's company, and

[1]Puntarvolo's rejoinder, "Except . . . that the fellow were nothing but vapour, I should think it impossible," is interesting for the use of the word vapour, which later, as in *Bartholomew Fair,* was often applied to similar performances of cozeners.

[2]On Shift's first appearance Sogliardo admiringly calls him "a proper man" (III, 1, p. 102). The expression is of course common enough in this sense. At the same time, there is a chance that Jonson was slyly playing upon the meaning of the words in rogues' cant, a use probably illustrated in this quotation from Fulwell.

[3]The quotations are from Corser's *Collectanea,* Part 6, pp. 389 ff.

taste of euery man's pot" is common to all of Shift's class. Shift has recourse to Paul's in order to make acquaintances, and, being without a groat, is rejoiced to have Sogliardo take him to the ordinary. "He is of that admirable and happy memory, that he will salute one for an old acquaintance that he never saw in his life before" (p. 64)—a commonplace trick of the coney-catcher. Shift also, like "the proper man," has the faculty of infinite gab, and besides the tales of his campaigns, which belong to him as "one that never was a soldier, yet lives upon lendings," he "usurps upon cheats, quarrels, and robberies, which he never did, only to get him a name" (p. 64). He is Jonson's early study of the boastful liar.

Suggestions of Shift come out in various sketches of *Wits Miserie* also:

> [Vainglory] appeareth in diuers shapes to men, applying himselfe to all natures and humors. . . .
>
> In Powls hée walketh like a gallant Courtier, where, if hée méet some rich chuffes worth the gulling, at euery word he speaketh, hée makes a mouse of an elephant, he telleth them of wonders done in *Spaine* by his ancestors: . . . if any worthy exploit, rare stratageme, plausible pollicie, hath euer past his hearing, hée maketh it his owne by an oath . . . where (poore asse as he is) were hée examined in his owne nature, his courage is boasting, his learning ignorance, his ability weaknesse, and his end beggery: yet is his smooth tongue a fit bait to catch Gudgeons; and such as saile by the wind of his good fortune, become Cameleons like ALCIBIADES, féeding on the vanity of his tongue with the foolish credulity of their eares (pp. 3, 4).

Though some of the omitted parts connect this sketch with Brisk or Amorphus rather than with Shift, the portion quoted describes Shift exactly. He is Cavalier Shift, Signior Whiffe, or Squire Apple-John to fit the occasion. In Paul's he appears as the cavalier, and after the manner of Lodge's sketch, succeeds in gulling Sogliardo by tales of his marvelous exploits. Another sketch of *Wits Miserie* showing traits of Shift is that of Adulation (p. 20):

> He can . . . court a Harlot for [his friend] . . . If he méet with a wealthy yong heire worth the clawing, Oh rare cries he, doe hée neuer so filthily. . . . This DAMOCLES amongst the retinue caries alwaies the Tabacco Pipe, . . . he hath an apt and pleasing discourse, were it not too often sauced with *Hiperboles* and lies: and in his

apparell he is courtly, for what foole would not be braue that may flourish with begging?[1]

Here are found Shift's function as bawd and as instructor in the art of taking tobacco. Under the character of Brocage Lodge again describes the haunter of Paul's who preys upon the foolish (p. 31), and again the treatment is suggestive of Shift. So Brawling Contention (p. 63) resembles Shift in a few details. Jonson's character was of course built upon the follies of contemporary life, but those same follies had already received literary treatment in sketches that exemplify Jonson's method of characterization.

In *The Returne of Pasquill,* Pasquill, who is humorously called Caualiero, sets up a bill upon London Stone (*Works of Nashe,* Vol. I, p. 101) which in its tone of whimsical burlesque might have been the forerunner of Shift's two bills (III, 1). Shift's first bill, however, more nearly resembles a bill that Slipper of *James IV,* himself something of a shifter,[2] sticks up (I, 2, ll. 453 ff.):

If any gentleman, spirituall or temperall, will entertaine out of his seruice a young stripling of the age of 30 yeares, that can sleep with the soundest, eate with the hungriest, work with the sickest, lye with the lowdest, face with the proudest, etc., that can wait in a gentlemans chamber when his maister is a myle of, keepe his stable when tis emptie, and his purse when tis full, and hath many qualities woorse then all these, let him write his name and goe his way, and attendance shall be giuen.

Shift's first bill reads (III, 1, p. 98):

If there be any lady or gentlewoman of good carriage that is desirous to entertain to her private uses a young, straight, and upright gentleman, of the age of five or six and twenty at the most; who can . . . hide his face with her fan, if need require; or sit in the cold at the stairfoot for her, as well as another gentleman: let her subscribe her name and place, and diligent respect shall be given.

Greene's burlesque turns on the vices of the would-be servant;

[1]This passage and one from *Wits Miserie* quoted later in connection with Amorphus are used by Prof. Penniman as illustrative of Jonson's method of characterization (introduction to *Satiromastix* and *Poetaster*).

[2]Cf. the discussion of shifters in ll. 756 ff. of *James IV.*

Jonson's on the vices of masters, though at the same time it is made to suggest the rascality of the servant.[1] The phrases that are most nearly parallel in the two bills doubtless give us merely the usual formula of the bills posted by those seeking service.

In the second bill Shift advertises for a gentleman who wishes "to know all the delicate sweet forms for the assumption" of tobacco, and other mysteries of smoking. Sogliardo comes under his tutorage, and in IV, 4, Carlo tells how Shift is training Sogliardo in "the patoun, the receipt reciprocal, and a number of other mysteries not yet extant." There are passages in Nashe's work which seem to indicate that certain ceremonies were growing up at this time in connection with smoking, similar perhaps in spirit to the drinking customs that Jonson burlesques in *Every Man out*. In *Haue with you to Saffron-walden,* Nashe says of Chute (*Works,* Vol. III, p. 107):

> For his Oratorship, it was such that I haue seene him *non plus* in giuing the charge at the creating | of a new Knight of *Tobacco;* though, to make amends since, he hath kneaded and daub'd vp a Commedie, called The transformation of the King of *Trinidadoes* two Daughters, Madame *Panachæa* and the Nymphe *Tobacco;* and, to approue his Heraldrie, scutchend out the honorable Armes of the smoakie Societie.

It is a pity that Chute's "Commedie," if it ever existed, is not available to throw some light on this passage and on Jonson's satire. Trinidado is the favorite tobacco of Bobadill.[2]

The function of Clove and Orange is merely to fill up the Paul's group and talk fustian.[3] Cordatus says of Clove (III, 1, p. 97): "He will sit you a whole afternoon sometimes in a bookseller's shop, reading the Greek, Italian, and Spanish, when he understands not a word of either; if he had the tongues to his suits, he were an excellent linguist." Lodge has a good deal of satire on this type of pretension. For instance, he says of Boasting (p. 9): "In the Stationers shop he sits dailie, Iibing and flearing ouer

[1]Collins refers to a scene of *Greene's News both from Heaven and Hell* as illustrating this custom of setting up bills, but he tells nothing of the nature of it. Cf. *The Plays and Poems of Greene*, Vol. II, p. 352.

[2]The Lieutenant Shift of Jonson's Epigram XII is only slightly similar to Shift.

[3]With the character sketches that Jonson gives of the two, compare the sketches of Daw and La-Foole in *The Silent Woman*, I, 1.

euery pamphlet with Ironicall ieasts; yet heare him but talke ten lines, and you may score vp twentie absurdities."[1] Hart (*Works of Ben Jonson,* p. xlv) traces the pair to Stilpo and Speusippus, "two lying philosophers" of *Timon,* who speak a nonsensical philosophical jargon. In *Timon* the two represent academic satire on philosophical terms and syllogisms. Clove and Orange may have been suggested by them, but, except in the association of the pair and in the fact that they speak nonsense, there is little likeness. Clove's speech is a hodge-podge, not close enough to any particular jargon to represent similar satire, though many philosophical terms do enter it. Gifford points out a parallel use of nonsense in Rabelais. Jonson, however, had a still better parallel near at hand in certain passages of Nashe's *Haue with you to Saffron-walden* (Vol. III, pp. 42 ff.), where Nashe represents Harvey's speech as made up of just such nonsense. Both men are satirizing the absurd vocabularies of the day, and several speeches put in Harvey's mouth have the movement and the conglomerate absurdity of Clove's fustian, though not the words. The particular words of Clove have been studied by Simpson and others, and traced in part to Marston's works. Orange expresses the opposite quality of foppery, paucity of vocabulary and the use of a single phrase for every occasion. A short scene in *All's Well* (II, 2) is given to satire on the use of Clove's pet phrase, "O Lord, sir," the clown maintaining that for the court it will serve as an answer to all questions. The same vacancy of mind is satirized by Guilpin in a long epigram (No. 68) on Caius, who says, "Oh rare" to everything.

So much evidence exists for the fact that the numerous follies and fads pilloried in the figure of Brisk represent current fashions of fashionable London that the study of analogous literary treatments may seem to be of little value in throwing light on the development of Jonson's satire. In the case of Jonson's rogues, we can feel more confident, for each Elizabethan treatise on rogues obviously borrows from those that precede it. To a less extent, the same thing must be true of the gallants also. In Jonson's work, Mathew is suggestive of Brisk and Brisk of Hedon. More nearly related, even, than Jonson's own characters are Brisk and

[1]Other passages on Boasting and his brother Vainglory, who precedes him, are strongly suggestive of Sir John Daw.

Gullio of *The Return from Parnassus,* Part I; and Emulo of *Patient Grissell* is akin to both. We must feel either that some individual was satirized excessively often; or that men were becoming surprisingly similar in an age in which "singularity" was cultivated; or that a certain type figure developed in literature around which were grouped a number of extreme fads that naturally varied very little at a given period. Undoubtedly the types grew up from observation of life, for the satire was probably directed against actual evils. Among the ultrafashionable gallants numbers of fads in dress, conduct, and speech must have prevailed generally as fashions prevail now, though in most cases we can feel that the satire imparted a defensible comic exaggeration, which was often too extreme to allow reality in character drawing. But the grouping of characteristics, the comic emphasis, the established devices for presenting follies, the names indicative of types and fundamental abstractions are the most obvious indications of literary conventions. A type figure based on life began in the old abstraction of Pride in the moralities. It continued in prose satire, where in the figures of the upstart and ape kindred follies were attacked by such men as Greene and Nashe. Later, particularly in verse satire, the figure became somewhat more specialized, and several types grew out of the old one. The gull is one of these special types. He is not very different from the upstart, but simply represents a narrower convention. The broader line of development was from the old abstraction of Pride to the pretentious gallant or the court dandy. Brisk shows conventions of both gull and courtier.

The fundamental gull[1] in Brisk is set forth by Macilente (IV, 1, p. 111):

> [Courtiers] he counterfeits,
> But sets no such a sightly carriage
> Upon their vanities, as they themselves;
> And therefore they despise him: for indeed
> He's like the zany to a tumbler,
> That tries tricks after him, to make men laugh.

[1]Brisk is called a gull in II, 1, p. 82, and in IV, 4, p. 118. Among the other terms applied to him, Catso (II, 1, p. 80) occurs as a character in Marston's *Antonio and Mellida,* and Nymphadoro (II, 1, p. 86) in *The Fawne.* Brisk is also called a "good empty puff" (II, 1, p. 82). Cf. the character Puff in *Jack Drum's Entertainment.* In *Cynthia's Revels* (III, 2, p. 167), Anaides is called a "strange arrogating puff."

As a gull, Brisk is nearer to Guilpin's type than to that of Davies. In some of the most general aspects of the town gull he continues the type seen in Mathew; that is, he is an ape and a pretended gallant, he is scorned of those whom he cultivates, he uses affected speech and distinctive oaths, and he serves as model for a country gull. Both borrow from Daniel. Brisk, however, is not a poet, though he "speaks good remnants" (p. 63). But Mathew and Brisk are set in different scales. Mathew is a fishmonger's son and impecunious; he aspires no higher than to appear as a suitor in the family of a wealthy merchant. Brisk has lands, which he consumes, and a merchant who furnishes him money whereby to change his costume constantly. He is a courtier and the "servant" of a court lady, so lofty a figure that the rich merchant's wife dotes upon him as an ideal. He is also a much more composite portrait than Mathew, with far more extensive follies. With Brisk it seems to me that the early and more exact meaning of gull as seen in Davies, Chapman, and Jonson is breaking down. Brisk follows, rather, a certain type of the upstart that shows the fundamental traits of the gull but carries to an extreme the excesses of the courtier.

The narrowing of the older and more general courtier type toward Brisk and, at the same time, the growing complexity in the specific details connected with the character can easily be traced in the literature of the time. The figure of Pride in Medwell's *Nature,* as I have pointed out above, is strongly suggestive of Brisk. Other old plays, also, began to fix the character of the courtier as a popular figure for satire. Skelton's *Magnificence* has in Courtly Abusion a good example of the type (ll. 829 ff.). Courtly Abusion introduces the fashions from France, follows the most extreme styles, and is a model for others. "A carlys sonne" is especially mentioned as one who in order to ape him will

> Spende all his hyre
> That men hym gyue,

until he is brought to ruin. Magnificence is charmed with Courtly Abusion's speech and manners (ll. 1537 ff.):

> He is not lyuynge your maners can amend;
> Mary, your speche is as pleasant as though it were pend,
> To here your comon, it is my hygh comforte,
> *Poynt deuyse,* all Pleasure is your porte.

In these and other characteristics Courtly Abusion is the forerunner of Brisk, but the courtier has not yet become the exaggerated type of folly that Jonson portrays.

The figure that embraces all the obnoxious qualities of the frivolous courtier and dandy began to be worked out in the last ten years of the sixteenth century with much greater concreteness and a far more telling comic effect. Among the most important of the various characters who represent the follies of the courtier is the upstart as characterized by both Greene and Nashe in 1592. With the upstart emerges a figure who sums up the follies of the gallant in one character and carries them all to extravagant lengths. In *A Quip for an Upstart Courtier,* Greene, dealing as he tells us, with *"the abuses that Pride had bred in* Englande" (*Works,* Vol. XI, p. 209), pictures in the person of Velvet-breeches "an vpstart come out of *Italy,* begot of Pride, nursed vp by selfe loue, & brought into this country by his companion Nufanglenesse" (p. 294). The concrete details of the treatment are almost as true to Brisk as is this general characterization. Nashe's best description of the upstart is given in *Pierce Penilesse* (*Works,* Vol. I, pp. 168, 169) under the general subject of pride. The portrait is a much more composite one than Greene's, and includes pretensions to ancestry, to individuality in fashions, to poetic gift, elegance of language, and experience in travel and in war. All these details of the upstart are found in Jonson but distributed to narrower types. Portions of the description have already been quoted as illustrative of Mathew and Bobadill. Brisk is aptly described in such expressions as, "Hee will bee humorous, forsoth, and haue a broode of fashions by himselfe," and "Hee will . . . . weare a feather of her rainbeaten fan for a fauor, like a forehorse." Compare Brisk's, "This feather grew in her sweet fan sometimes, though now it be my poor fortune to wear it" (II, 1, p. 88). In *The Terrors of the Night,* also, Nashe has a sketch of "filthie Italionat complement-mungers . . . who would faine be counted the Courts *Gloriosos,* and the refined iudges of wit" (Vol. I, p. 361). Just so much of the sketch applies to Brisk's boasts of popularity in the court and his praise of Saviolina's wit, but it probably fits better the courtiers of *Cynthia's Revels.*

In the satire directed against Harvey, Nashe holds Harvey up to scorn as an upstart and affected dandy, and the description often recalls Brisk. In *Haue with you to Saffron-walden* (*Works,* Vol. III, pp. 91, 92), there is an account of how a friend of Nashe's was received by Harvey:

> Two howres good by the clocke he attended his pleasure, whiles he . . . stood acting by the glasse all his gestures he was to vse all the day after, and currying & smudging and pranking himselfe vnmeasurably. *Post varios casus,* his case of tooth-pikes, his combe case, . . . run ouer, . . . downe he came, and after the *bazelos manus,* with amplifications and complements hee belaboured him till his eares tingled and his feet ak'd againe. Neuer was man so surfetted and ouer-gorged with English. . . . The Gentleman swore to mee that vpon his first apparition . . . he tooke him for an Vsher of a dancing Schoole.

Nashe also tells (p. 109) how Barnes, a consort of Harvey, "getting him a strange payre of *Babilonian* britches . . . went vp and downe Towne, and shewd himself in the Presence at Court, where he was generally laught out by the Noblemen and Ladies." Again, Nashe says of Harvey (Vol. III, p. 116; compare p. 138):

> But afterward, when his ambitious pride and vanitie vnmaskt it selfe so egregiously, both in his lookes, his gate, his gestures, and speaches, and hee would do nothing but crake and parret it in Print, in how manie Noble-mens fauours hee was, and blab euerie light speach they vttred to him in priuate, cockering & coying himselfe beyond imagination; then Sir *Philip Sidney* . . . began to looke askance on him, . . . though vtterly shake him off | hee could not, hee would so fawne & hang vpon him.

The spirit of these travesties is much like that with which Jonson treats Brisk. The comparison of Harvey to the usher of a dancing school seems especially happy for Brisk. Brisk, too, according to the prefatory character sketch, "practises by his glass how to salute," and his "neat case of pick-tooths" is one of the things that calls forth Fallace's admiration (IV, 1, p. 111). His inflated diction is illustrated at the beginning of IV, 6 (p. 122), where he falls into a rapt eulogy of court life. Jonson has also developed with considerable effectiveness the fact that Brisk "cares not what lady's favour he belies, or great man's familiarity" (p. 63). Brisk claims to be beloved of great lords (II, 1, p. 88) and graced by great ladies (II, 2, p. 94 and IV, 4, p. 118), whereas Macilente reports that the few court ladies who know him "deride and play upon his amorous humours" (IV, 1, p. 111).

Of the formal satirists, Donne does not give, so far as I know, any portrait that combines the various follies of the court gallant. In his first satire, however, he touches upon some of the absurdities of shallow men of fashion, and mentions the "brisk perfumed pert courtier." Hall in *Virgidemiarum* (Book IV, Satire IV) rebukes Brisk's type of follies under the figure of Gallio, who is given to dainty diet, uses perfumes, oils his locks, shields his chalked face with a plumed fan, and spends his time in gentlemanly diversions or in courting his "lovely dame." Davies, who is earlier than Hall, has developed a number of well defined types around which he groups certain characteristics. Besides the gull, he gives us in Epigram 22, *In Ciprum,* the picture of a gallant who, like Brisk, is "tierse and neate,"—compare Jonson's "neat, spruce, affecting courtier,"—follows the newest fashion with constant changes, takes tobacco, and "wastes more time in dressing then a wench."

In the satire of Marston and Guilpin the sketches of gallants and courtiers assume a still greater definiteness and approach nearer to Jonson's portrait. Marston, in the first satire of *Pygmalion's Image and Certain Satires,* gives a series of rapid sketches, nearly all of which have details fairly close to Brisk. One of them, which has often been pointed out for its likeness to Brisk, uses the word brisk, here Latinized to Briscus, as the name of the character. It seems worth while to quote at some length from this satire.

> Tell me, brown Ruscus, hast thou Gyges' ring,
> That thou presumest as if thou wert unseen?
> If not, why in thy wits half capreal
> Lett'st thou a superscribèd letter fall?
> And from thyself unto thyself dost send,
> And in the same thyself thyself commend?
> For shame! leave running to some satrapas,
> Leave glavering on him in the peopled press;
> Holding him on as he through Paul's doth walk,
> With nods and legs and odd superfluous talk;
> Making men think thee gracious in his sight,
> When he esteems thee but a parasite.
>
> . . . .
>
> Come, Briscus, by the soul of compliment,
> I'll not endure that with thine instrument
> (Thy gambo-viol placed betwixt thy thighs,
> Wherein the best part of thy courtship lies)
> Thou entertain the time, thy mistress by.

> Come, now let's hear thy mounting Mercury.
> What! mum? Give him his fiddle once again,
> Or he's more mute than a Pythagoran.
> But oh! the absolute Castilio,—
> He that can all the points of courtship show;
> He that can trot a courser, break a rush,
>
> . . . .
>
> Can set his face, and with his eye can speak,
> Can dally with his mistress' dangling feak,
> And wish that he were it, to kiss her eye
> And flare about her beauty's deity:—
> Tut! he is famous for his revelling,
> For fine set speeches, and for sonnetting;
> He scorns the viol and the scraping stick,
> And yet's but broker of another's wit.
>
> . . . .
>
> Yet I can bear with Curio's nimble feet,
> Saluting me with capers in the street,
> Although in open view and people's face,
> He fronts me with some spruce, neat, cinquepace.

The first sketch that I have quoted here is to illustrate the use of Erasmus's instructions to the False Knight before Jonson utilized the same thing in Carlo's advice to Sogliardo and in Brisk's pretence to familiarity with the great. In the next sketch, Brisk's courting with the viol is anticipated. In fact, the courting of Briscus is just that of Brisk, for the best part of Brisk's courtship lies in filling up with recourse to tobacco and viol the intervals wherein words fail him for all of his phrases learned by rote. Like Castilio, Brisk has his fast horse, who runs "with the very sound of the spur" (II, 1, p. 80). Castilio's wish that he were his mistress's curl to kiss her eye suggests Brisk's protestation to Macilente: "I have wished myself to be that instrument, I think, a thousand times, and not so few, by heaven . . . to be in use, I assure you" (III, 3, p. 109). A whole series of such lover's wishes is given in Satire VIII of Marston's *Scourge of Villainy* (ll. 118-137)—to be a mistress's busk, dog, monkey, flea, verdingal, fan, or necklace. Compare also Watson's *Hekatompathia,* No. 28, and Barnes's sixty-third sonnet. The "fine set speeches" of Castilio and his inability to be more than "broker of another's wit" are characteristic of Brisk as of the gallant in general. Brisk "speaks good remnants" according to the sketch that Jonson gives of him, and his fine speaking is pronounced "not extemporal" (IV,

6, p. 112). The few lines on Curio deal with a side of gallantry that appears also in Brisk as well as in Guilpin's satire on the gallant quoted below (pp. 193, 194).

In the second satire, again, Marston gives a picture of a courtesan dressed as a gallant of Brisk's type. The conventional adjectives that Jonson applies to Brisk—neat, spruce, etc.—appear here also:

> In faith, yon is a well-faced gentleman;
> See how he paceth like a Cyprian!
> Fair amber tresses of the fairest hair
> That ere were wavèd by our London air;
> Rich lacèd suit, all spruce, all neat, in truth.
> Ho, Lynceus! what's yonder brisk neat youth?
> . . . .
> Fair Briscus, I shall stand in doubt
> What sex thou art, since such hermaphrodites,
> Such Protean shadows so delude our sights.

The third satire contains three sketches. The first of them describes a "dapper, rare, complete, sweet nitty youth," similar to Brisk except that Brisk's lechery is not so openly stressed. The word fantastic, which is twice applied to Brisk (pp. 101 and 111), is used three times in describing this character.[1] The gallant is satirized chiefly for the elaborateness of his dress,—his ruff, his falling band, his crossed and recrossed lace, his hat with small crown, great brim, and band filled with feathers, his perfume, etc.[2] The wearing of feathers, Marston says, "is a sign of a fantastic still" (l. 26). The second sketch, which describes the "inamorato Lucian" in the throes of love, has no value for Brisk unless it be in the extravagant praise of a mistress (cf. *Every Man out,* II, 1, p. 88). Marston continues:

> When as thou hear'st me ask spruce Duceus
> From whence he comes; and he stranght answers us,
> From Lady Lilla; and is going straight

[1]The descriptive term fantastic, like the terms brisk or shift, seems to have stood for a fairly definite type. Nashe speaks of "Senior Fantasticos" (*Works,* Vol. III, p. 31). In *The Jests of Peele* (*Shakespeare Jest-Books,* Vol. II, p. 294) a gull, on account of dress, is called a "Fantasticke whose braine was made of nought but Corke and Spunge."

[2]His prayer (ll. 8, 9) that

> The fashion change not (lest he should despair
> Of ever hoarding up more fair gay clothes)

suggests Fungoso.

To the Countess of (———), for she doth wait
His coming, and will surely send her coach,
Unless he make the speedier approach:
Art not thou ready for to break thy spleen
At laughing at the fondness thou hast seen
In this vain-glorious fool, when thou dost know
He never durst unto these ladies show
His pippin face?

Brisk in II, 2 (p. 94) boasts: "There was a countess gave me her hand to kiss today, i' the presence: did me more good by that light than—and yesternight sent her coach twice to my lodging, to intreat me accompany her, and my sweet mistress, with some two or three nameless ladies more: O, I have been graced by them beyond all aim of affection." In the preceding scene, when Brisk mentions by name a number of lords who contend for his society when he is at court, Carlo remarks (p. 88): "There's ne'er a one of these but might lie a week on the rack, ere they could bring forth his name; and yet he pours them out as familiarly as if he had seen them stand by the fire in the presence, or ta'en tobacco with them over the stage, in the lords' room."

Satire VII of *The Scourge of Villainy* contains another picture of the "brisk," "spruce" gallant in "sumptuous clothes," but it is meagerly sketched. This later work, indeed, is of less interest for Jonson's types than are the satires included with *Pygmalion's Image.* Not only are the portraits in *The Scourge of Villainy* less minute, but Marston deals especially with all forms of lechery, a subject that Jonson is not given to treating. In the dedication to *Volpone* Jonson declares: "I have ever trembled to think toward the least profaneness; have loathed the use of such foul and unwashed bawdry, as is now made the food of the scene." The excessive crabbedness of Marston's newer style was also repellent to Jonson.

Guilpin's first picture of the type to which Brisk belongs is in Epigram 38 of *Skialetheia,* "To Licus":

He's a fine fellow who is neate and fine,
Whose locks are kem'd & neuer a tangled twine,
Who smels of Musk, Ciuet, and Pomander,
Who spends, and out-spends many a pounde a yeare,
Who piertly iets, can caper, daunce, and sing,
Play with his Mistris fingers, her hand wring,
Who companying with wenches nere is still:

> But either skips or mowes, or prates his fill,
> Who is at euery play, and euery night
> Sups with his *Ingles*, who can well recite
> Whatsoeuer rimes are gracious, etc.

In II, 1 (p. 82) Carlo says of Brisk, "He sleeps with a musk-cat every night, and walks all day hanged in pomander chains for penance; he has his skin tanned in civet," etc. Here the same perfumes are mentioned as in the epigram above. The capering and dancing of Guilpin's character is paralleled in Brisk's courtship of Saviolina (III, 3, p. 108), when he wishes for his vaulting horse in order to display his activity, and the page suggests that but for the lack of long stockings he might dance a galliard. In Epigram 14, also "To Licus," Guilpin repeats the satire on dancing, vaulting, and extreme dress. Epigram 53, "Of Cornelius," again describes in detail the dress of the ultrafashionable gallant, and elsewhere in the epigrams and satires of *Skialetheia* there are suggestions of Brisk. In Satire V, a picture is drawn of Don Fashion which might be taken for Brisk:

> But see, see,
> Heere comes *Don Fashion*, spruce formality,
> Neat as a Merchants ruffe, that's set in print,
> New halfe-penny, skip'd forth his Laundres mint;
> Oh braue! what, with a feather in his hat?
> He is a dauncer, you may see by that;
> Light heeles, light head, light feather well agree.
> Salute him, with th' embrace beneath the knee?
> I thinke twere better let him passe along,
> He will so dawbe vs with his oyly tongue,
> For thinking on some of his Mistresses,
> We shall be curried with the briske phrases,
> And prick-song termes he hath premeditate:
> Speake to him, woe to us, for we shall ha'te,
> Then farewell he.

With the first two lines quoted from the satire, compare the opening words of the character sketch of Brisk, "A neat, spruce, affecting courtier, one that wears clothes well, and in fashion." The "light head, light feather well agree" may be compared with Carlo's remark about Brisk, "His brains lighter than his feather already" (II, 1, p. 82). Brisk's premeditated speeches, his praise of his mistress, and his dancing have already been mentioned.

Immediately upon the description of Don Fashion there follows the picture of another type of the foolish, vainglorious courtier, but with humours in sharp contrast to those of Don Fashion:

> But soft, whom haue we heare?
> What braue Saint *George*, what mounted Caualiere?
> He is all court-like, Spanish in's attire.
> He hath the righte ducke, pray God he be no Frier:
> Thys is the Dictionary of complements,
> The Barbers mouth of new-scrapt eloquence,
> *Synomicke Tully* for varietie,
> And Madame Conceits gorgeous gallerie,
> The exact patterne which *Castilio*
> Tooke for's accomplish Courtier: but soft ho,
> What needs that bownd, or that curuet (good sir)
> There's some sweet Lady, and tis done to her,
> That she may see his Iennets nimble force:
> Why, would he haue her in loue with his horse?
> Or aymes he at popish merrit, to make
> Her in loue with him for his horses sake?

The juxtaposition of these two characters is not accidental. The one satirizes the newer and more degenerate type of the Italianate courtier; the other, the older, more formal type represented, as Guilpin indicates, in the ideal which Castiglione sets forth in *The Courtier.* The contrast undoubtedly emphasizes two phases of gallantry to be observed and easily distinguished every day in London, and the two types readily lent themselves to treatment in satire. The same contrast is seen in Brisk and Puntarvolo, and is continued, though less sharply, in Hedon and Amorphus of *Cynthia's Revels.*[1] In connection with Brisk, I have already discussed the two corresponding sketches in Marston's work—those of Briscus and Castilio. Here again the second type is connected with the author of the most famous of the Italian courtesy books. I quote the sketch in full, though parts of it have already been quoted as applicable to Brisk.

> But oh! the absolute Castilio,—
> He that can all the points of courtship show;
> He that can trot a courser, break a rush,
> And arm'd in proof, dare dure a straw's strong push;
> He, who on his glorious scutcheon

[1]Cf. the discussion of these types under *Cynthia's Revels*, pp. 264 f. and 272 f. *infra.* The pomp of the Puntarvolo type, however, is not so well developed in Amorphus.

Can quaintly show wit's new invention,
Advancing forth some thirsty Tantalus,
Or else the vulture on Prometheus,
With some short motto of a dozen lines;
He that can purpose it in dainty rhymes,
Can set his face, and with his eye can speak,
Can dally with his mistress' dangling feak,
And wish that he were it, to kiss her eye
And flare about her beauty's deity:—
Tut! he is famous for his revelling,
For fine set speeches, and for sonnetting;
He scorns the viol and the scraping stick,
And yet's but broker of another's wit.
Certes, if all things were well known and view'd,
He doth but champ that which another chew'd.
Come, come, Castilion, skim thy posset curd,
Show thy queer substance, worthless, most absurd.
Take ceremonious compliment from thee!
Alas! I see Castilio's beggary.

With the early part of this sketch compare Carlo's characterization of Puntarvolo (II, 1, p. 82): "He has a good riding face, and he can sit a great horse; he will taint a staff well at tilt . . . instead of a dragon, he will brandish against a tree, and break his sword as confidently upon the knotty bark, as the other did upon the scales of the beast." It is evident, however, that with Marston the line of demarkation between the two types is not so clear as with Guilpin or with Jonson in *Every Man out.*[1] Castilio has many of the characteristics of Brisk, whereas Guilpin's sketch of the Castilio type shows distinctly the formality and pompousness of Puntarvolo. In Puntarvolo, with his formality, his love of compliment, his stilted vocabulary and set speeches, and his practice of chivalric customs, we have just the follies that the Elizabethan inspired by the Italian ideal of rounded perfection

[1]Again in *Antonio and Mellida,* Marston's treatment of the character Castilio Balthazar indicates his failure to stress the formality of the type as Guilpin and Jonson do, for Castilio Balthazar shows many characteristics that ally him with Brisk. It is noticeable that Marston's machinery for satire in *Antonio and Mellida* is very similar to Jonson's in *Every Man out,* Feliche corresponding to Macilente in his attitude to the courtier and the gull. It is interesting, also, to find Marston at this early date apparently distinguishing between the courtier and the gull; although Castilio and Balurdo have very similar fashions and fads, Bullen is clearly right in calling the first a "spruce courtier" and the second a gull.

in a nobleman might be guilty of when the formal side of his culture meant more to him than the spirit underlying the ideal.[1]

Guilpin's sketch is closest to Jonson's character both in point of time and in scope of treatment, as I have indicated, and the two may bear a somewhat detailed comparison. For phrasing, the line—

What braue Saint *George*, what mounted Caualiere?

may be compared with the description of Puntarvolo in II, 1 (p. 82): "When he is mounted he looks like the sign of the George." By "all court-like, Spanish in's attire," Guilpin probably intends to indicate a stiffer, more formal dress than Don Fashion's. Jonson perhaps made the same distinction in Brisk and Puntarvolo. Brisk's dress at least allows him to be active. Puntarvolo is described by Carlo as stiff and formal (II, 1, p. 84): "Heart, can any man walk more upright than he does? Look, look; as if he went in a frame, or had a suit of wainscot on: and the dog watching him, lest he should leap out on't." Later, in answer to Macilente's question, "What's he there?" Carlo says, "Who, this in the starched beard? it's the dull, stiff knight Puntarvolo" (IV, 4, p. 116). Whether the statement in the prefatory character sketch of Puntarvolo that he "hath lived to see the revolution of time in most of his apparel" means that his dress is threadbare or that it is out of fashion is uncertain, but from the remainder of the characterization I should be inclined to the second interpretation. One of Carlo's "stabbing similes" is to the effect that Puntarvolo "looks like a shield of brawn at Shrove-tide, out of date," etc. (IV, 4). The lines of Guilpin's sketch,—

[1]Hart has worked out an elaborate identification of Puntarvolo with Raleigh (*Works of Ben Jonson*, pp. xl ff.), chiefly on account of the fact that Sir W[alter] R[aleigh] sealed up Chester's mouth. Earlier he identified the character with Harvey (9 *N. and Q.*, Vol. XII, p. 343). Some details of Puntarvolo would fit either. But Nashe's satire on the Italianate manners and dress of Harvey was doubtless based on a certain element of truth, and Nashe portrays Harvey as of the Brisk type. Harvey seems to have admired Castiglione's ideals highly, however (cf. *Works*, Vol. I, p. 245). On the other hand, Raleigh undoubtedly had the manners and ideals of the Italianate courtier of the "gorgeous" or pompous type. That there should be personal satire in Puntarvolo would not be at all inconsistent with Jonson's primary treatment of the character as a type, as we have seen in Carlo, but the type here certainly seems to dominate over the individual.

> Thys is the Dictionary of complements,
> The Barbers mouth of new-scrapt eloquence,
> *Synomicke Tully* for varietie,
> And Madame Conceits gorgeous gallerie,—

suggest parts of the character sketch of Puntarvolo: "A vain-glorious knight . . . wholly consecrated to singularity; the very Jacob's staff of compliment. . . . He deals upon . . . strange performances, resolving, in despite of public derision, to stick to his own particular fashion, phrase, and gesture." Guilpin's lines, however, are better illustrated by Puntarvolo's strange and whimsical devices in the play than by the wording of Jonson's sketch. "Complements," eloquence, variety, and conceits are all illustrated at Puntarvolo's first appearance, in II, 1. Approaching his own home, he goes through the elaborate ceremony of a medieval knight approaching a guarded castle, and has trained his household to engage with him in a well nigh endless rigmarole of complimentary queries and replies. His affected language in this scene completely eclipses Brisk's as "new-scrapt" and singular. Brisk, like Mathew and Bobadill, strives after elegance rather than singularity. Puntarvolo affects such expressions as "splendidious,"[1] "heavenly pulchritude," "organs to my optic sense," "debonair and luculent lady,"[2] and "decline as low as the basis of your altitude" (all in II, 1).[3] One of Puntarvolo's conceits, which is described by Carlo as erecting a "dial of compliment," is expressed in the following figure: "To the perfection of compliment (which is the dial of the thought, and guided by the sun of your beauties) are required these three specials; the gnomon, the puntilios, and the superficies: the superficies is that we call place; the puntilios, circumstance; and the gnomon, ceremony; in either of which, for a stranger to err, 'tis easy and facile" (II, 1, p. 83).[4] Every action

[1]This is one of the words used in Wilson's inkhorn letter, *Arte of Rhetorique*, p. 163. Cf. also *Cynthia's Revels*, V, 3, p. 200.

[2]Cf. "organons of sense" in *The Scourge of Villainy*, Satire VIII, l. 210, satirized in *Poetaster*, V, 1, p. 257. For "luculent" see Hart, *Works of Ben Jonson*, Vol. I, p. xlv.

[3]Cf. Hart, 9 *N. and Q.*, Vol. XII, p. 343, for the fact that some of Harvey's affected terms are used by Puntarvolo and Brisk.

[4]*The Diall of Princes* and the figurative use of dial in Shakespeare's works illustrate the basis in current speech for the conceit which Jonson makes Puntarvolo work into his discourse with such elaboration. There is a figurative use of "diall *Gnomon*" in *Histriomastix*, IV, l. 108. Jonson uses the same figure again in *Cynthia's Revels* (V, 2, p. 194; cf. II, 1, p. 160).

of the knight, as well, illustrates the phrase "Madame Conceits gorgeous gallerie," and we may add "of Gallant Inventions."

Puntarvolo's knightly procedure in approaching his home, and the indentures for his venture, part of which Gifford says furnishes a burlesque upon the oaths taken by the combatants of romance (Vol. I, p. 113, n. 2), obviously hark back to the chivalric romances. The same thing is true of the account that Brisk gives of his long battle with Signior Luculento (IV, 4), in which pieces of rich apparel are substituted for parts of armor that were slashed away in the long engagements of the romances.[1] I have happened upon nothing similar enough to Puntarvolo's entry or to Brisk's battle to be suggestive of Jonson, though doubtless good parallels for both are to be found. Such scenes may have existed in plays now lost. There is little doubt, however, that Jonson was satirizing living rather than dead follies. That like echoes of old knightly manners were found, at least in the pastimes of the courtiers of the day, is clear from such sources as the "Challenges to a Tourney" of the Lansdowne Manuscripts published in the *Collections* of the Malone Society (Vol. I, pp. 181 ff.). Conventions of various sorts from the days of chivalry and courtly love as continued or revived in the Renaissance are satirized rather exhaustively in *Cynthia's Revels.* In *Every Man out,* Jonson merely makes his first essays in the study of follies belonging to the court.

The part of Puntarvolo's indentures that parodies the old oath of combatants reads (IV, 4, p. 113):

> That, after the receipt of his money, he shall neither, in his own person, nor any other, either by direct or indirect means, as magic, witchcraft, or other such exotic arts, attempt, practise, or complot anything to the prejudice of me, my dog, or my cat: neither shall I use the help of any such sorceries or enchantments, as unctions to make our skins impenetrable, or to travel invisible by virtue of a powder, or a ring, or to hang any three-forked charm about my dog's neck, secretly conveyed into his collar . . . but that all be performed sincerely, without fraud or imposture.

Mr. Tennant in his edition of *The New Inn* (pp. lix, lx) quotes two forms of the combatant's oath in connection with the court of love material in his play. The one which he cites from Stow is as follows:

[1]Dekker's use of the same idea in *Patient Grissell* seems to me almost certainly copied from Jonson.

This hear, you justices, that I have this day neither eat, drunk, nor yet have upon me either bone, stone, ne glass, or any enchantment, sorcery or witchcraft, where through the power of the Word of God might be inleased or diminished, and the devil's power increased, and that my appeal is true, so help me God and his saints, and by this Book.

The second, which is from the *Black Book of the Admiralty,* is in part to the effect that the combatant neither has nor shall have "stone of vertue, ne herbe of vertue, ne charme, ne experiment, ne carocte, ne othir inchauntment by the, ne for thee, by the which thou trusteth the bettir to ovircome . . . thine adversarie."[1] For the remainder of the indentures the "Challenges to a Tourney" which I have just mentioned is of some interest. The challenger offers certain "Condicions and ordre," which concern the forfeit, the equipment, the mode of procedure, and the mode of decision between the combatants. Puntarvolo's indentures cover practically the same points.

Such a venture as is satirized in Puntarvolo's trip to Constantinople with his dog and his cat on the condition that he is to receive five for one if he and his animals return, seems to have been not unusual at the end of the sixteenth century. There is a well known passage in *The Terrors of the Night* (*Works,* Vol. I, p. 343) in which Nashe speaks of *"such poore fellowes as I, that cannot put out money to be paid againe when wee come from* Constantinople." In Epigram 42, *In Licum,* Davies mentions Venice instead of Constantinople:

Lycus, which lately is to Venice gone,
Shall if he doe returne, gaine three for one.

Saviolina is Jonson's first study in the type of court lady elaborated so fully in *Cynthia's Revels.* Two scenes are given to her,— one to Brisk's courtship and her affectation of wit, and the other to her overthrow. Elsewhere, however, she is constantly praised by Brisk, especially for her wit. One expression which he applies to her, "anatomy of wit" (III, 1, p. 98), at once suggests *Euphues.* In an earlier scene (I, 2, p. 88), Brisk says of her, "She does observe as pure a phrase, and use as choice figures in her ordinary conferences, as any be in the *Arcadia";* and Carlo adds, "Or rather

[1] I quote from Tennant in both cases. The example from Stow he cites from Neilson's *Trial by Combat.*

in Green's works, whence she may steal with more security." Euphuism and the variations on it for affected speech are thus satirized in Saviolina as well as in other characters of the play. Fungoso and Fallace use expressions from *Euphues,* and Brisk's speech often betrays the trick of Euphuism. Sufficient evidence exists that many gallants of the day still affected the jargon, and its use is satirized frequently. Macilente's remark that Saviolina's "jests are of the stamp March was fifteen years ago" again seems to connect her with the fashion of Lyly and his followers. In fact, whether she is true to life or not, Saviolina belongs to the type that Lyly loved to portray and that Greene and other followers of Lyly often treated; or, to be more exact, she is a burlesque on the type which these earlier writers treated seriously. Iffida of *Euphues,* as she is portrayed in the account which Fidus gives of his passion for her, is a good example of the type. She is proud and haughty to the obsequious lover, meets his advances with rebuffs, and has a quiver of sharp replies or perversions of his language to return to him. The lover, like Brisk, stands in awe before his mistress and pours out upon her grandiloquent compliments and addresses. It is chiefly Iffida's rare wit that is stressed, however, and some examples of it will best illustrate the point of Jonson's satire on Saviolina's antiquated jests. "Gentleman," says Iffida, "in arguing of wittes, you mistake mine, and call your owne into question" (*Works of Lyly,* Vol. II, p. 55). "O, Monsieur Brisk," Saviolina retorts, "be not so tyrannous to confine all wits within the compass of your own" (V, 2, p. 126). Iffida tells a number of anecdotes that illustrate wit in women. One of them turns upon a play on the words son and sun (p. 60). So Brisk is delighted with Saviolina's wit in playing upon for and 'fore (III, 3, p. 109). A second anecdote told by Iffida is of a woman's ready reply when a man tells her that he can not judge of her wit (p. 60): "No quoth she, I beleue you, for none ca*n* judge of wit, but they that haue it, why then quoth he, doest thou thinke me a foole, thought is free my Lord quoth she, I wil not take you at your word. He perceiuing al outward faults to be reco*m*penced with inward fauour, chose this virgin for his wife." There is not much choice between this and the witticism with which Saviolina meets Brisk's question as to whether she will take some tobacco (III, 3, p. 110):

Sav. O, peace, I pray you; I love not the breath of a woodcock's head.
Fast[idious Brisk]. Meaning my head, lady?
Sav. Not altogether so, sir; but, as it were fatal to their follies that think to grace themselves with taking tobacco, when they want better entertainment, you see your pipe bears the true form of a woodcock's head.
Fast. O admirable simile!

It is then that Macilente makes his remark about the age of Saviolina's jests.

In the second scene given to Saviolina, V, 2, she is put out of her humour by being deceived into believing that the clown Sogliardo is a gentleman. A device of the same kind, with a different result, occurs in the play *Sir Thomas More,* where More dresses his servant as himself in order to deceive Erasmus, and in *Friar Bacon and Friar Bungay,* where Ralph dressed as the Prince fails to deceive Bacon. Professor Bang, however, has pointed out (*Englische Studien,* Vol. 36, pp. 330, 331) in Hoby's translation of *The Courtier* (Tudor Translations, pp. 192, 193) what may well have been the actual source of this scene. Here a country fellow, well dressed, has been described to certain court ladies as a perfect courtier who is able to play the perfect countryman. The ladies are completely duped by the trick, amid the laughter of the onlookers, and are with difficulty persuaded of their mistake. In these details the trick is like that played upon Saviolina.

While I have compared Saviolina with Lyly's types, it must be remembered that wit as an element of courtliness was a part of the ideal of the age, and that *The Courtier* and other works of the kind gave prominence to the witty woman. But the courtly lady of Castiglione's work is very different from the affected type portrayed by Lyly. Castiglione, indeed, condemns affected speech while praising wit highly. There is little doubt, however, that Lyly's type is a development of the Italian, and probably as little doubt that the manners of English women were influenced by Italian courtesy books.[1]

The other humorists of *Every Man out*—Sordido, Sogliardo, Fungoso, Fallace, and Deliro—all belong to a family group. Of

[1]Prof. Raleigh in his introduction to *The Courtier* claims that the witty women of *The Courtier* influenced Shakespeare's witty women. Miss M. A. Scott has elaborated the idea in *Modern Language Publications,* Vol. XVI, pp. 475 ff.

these the most conventional figure is Sordido, the corn-hoarder. Allusions to the custom of hoarding corn are frequent from early times.[1] In *A Merry Knack to Know a Knave* (Hazlitt's *Dodsley,* Vol. VI, p. 561) one of the indictments brought against the farmer is that "he keeps corn in his barn, and suffers his brethren and neighbours to lie and want; and thereby makes the market so dear, that the poor can buy no corn." Stubbes deals with the same evil in the second part of *The Anatomy of Abuses* (New Shakspere Society, pp. 45, 46), commenting on the brutal selfishness of the corn-hoarder. In Greene's *Quip for an Upstart Courtier,* among the abuses of the grasping farmer, Cloth-breeches describes that of corn hoarding in terms which fit Sordido perfectly (*Works,* Vol. XI, p. 285):

> Besides the base chuffe if he sées a forward yeare, & that corne is like to be plenty, then he murmereth against God and swereth and protesteth he shall be vndoone: respecting more the filling of his owne coffers by a dearth then the profit of his country by a generall plenty. Beside sir may it please you when new corne comes into the market, who brings it in to relieue the state? Not your mastership, but the poore husbandman, that wants pence. For you kéepe it till the back end of the yeare, nay you haue your Garners which haue come of two or thrée yeares old, vpon hope still of a deare yeare, rather letting the weasels eate it, then the poore should haue it at any reasonable price.

The hard year of 1594, which is supposedly described in *Midsummer Night's Dream,* produced in England numbers of regraters, as they were called, and before the end of the century other hard years seem to have followed. So great did the abuse of regrating become that the Queen's Proclamation of November, 1596, insisted upon the execution of previous orders to the effect that "the Iustices of peace in euery quarter should stay all Ingrossers, Forestallers, and Regraters of Corne, and to direct all Owners and Farmers hauing Corne to furnish the Markets ratably and weekly with such quantities as vsually they had done before time, or reasonably might and ought to doe."[2] It will be remembered that in *Every Man out* (I, 1, pp. 77, 78) an order arrives from the justice charg-

[1]Cf. *Ship of Fools,* ed. Jamieson, Vol. II, pp. 167-169; and *Works of Nashe,* Vol. II, pp. 158 and 286.

[2]Quoted from Furnivall's introduction (p. xx) to *The Second Part of the Anatomy of Abuses* by Stubbes.

ing Sordido to market his grain, and that he immediately plans to hide it in the earth.[1]

Sordido is hoarding corn in expectation of a dear year because his almanac has prophesied almost continual bad weather. He reads aloud from the almanac on the stage, and exults over its prognostications. Satire on the prophecies of almanacs is as common as the rest of Jonson's treatment of Sordido. Stubbes in *The Second Part of the Anatomy of Abuses* (p. 66) rebukes directly what Jonson satirizes indirectly—the foretelling of seasons of plenty and dearth. "Therefore prognosticators are herein much to be blamed, for that they take vpon them to foreshew what things shall be plentie, and what scarce, what deere, what good cheape. When shal be faire weather, when foule, and the like," etc. The reading from an almanac on the stage is paralleled in one of the entertainments provided for Queen Elizabeth at Sudeley (printed in Bond's *Works of Lyly,* Vol. I, pp. 481 ff.). An almanac is called for, and Cutter produces one, saying: "I euer carrie it, to knowe the hye waies to euerie good towne, the faires, and the faire weather." Then Melibæus reads the prognostication for certain days, but chooses dates notable in Elizabeth's life or connected with her visit, thus turning the device to neat compliment of the Queen.[2]

The prophecies of Sordido's almanac fail, the crop promises to be abundant, and Sordido prepares to hang himself (III, 2). His declaration that all his wealth is hidden so that his children can not enjoy it belongs to the miser. It will be sufficient to instance the fact that Plautus in the prologue of *Aulularia,* which Jonson had already used, represents Euclio's grandfather as "of such an

[1]The scarcity of corn at this period naturally resulted in the production of some literature on the subject before Jonson's play. "Newes from Jack Begger under the Bushe, with the advise of Gregory Gaddesman his fellow begger touchinge the deare prizes of corne and hardnes of this present yere" was entered on the Stationers' Register Dec. 28, 1594. Cf. Alden, *Rise of Formal Satire*, p. 233, n. 3. In 1596, Deloney wrote a ballad in dialogue "Containing a Complaint of the great want and scarcitie of corn within this realm." Cf. Sievers, *Thomas Deloney*, etc., Palaestra, No. 36, pp. 2 and 3.

[2]The similarity between the prophecy "the twelfth the weather inclined to moisture" and Sordido's "29, inclining to rain" would indicate that both plays follow the phraseology of current almanacs. Indeed, it does not seem to me improbable that Jonson was burlesquing some actual almanac of the time. Cf. his use of Broughton's works in *The Alchemist* and of Harsnet's or Darrel's in *The Devil is an Ass.*

avaricious disposition, *that* he would never disclose it [his buried treasure] to his own son, and preferred rather to leave him in want than to show that treasure to *that* son" (Bohn Library). Sordido's attempt to hang himself is equally conventional. Small (*Stage-Quarrel,* p. 54) calls attention to number clxiv of the *Exempla* of Jacques de Vitry, where the story is told of one who hung himself because, on account of continued good harvests, the grain that he had collected did not rise in price. The most suggestive parallel for the scene in which Sordido attempts suicide has been pointed out by Professor Raleigh (introduction to *The Courtier,* p. lxxix) in a passage from Hoby's translation of *The Courtier* (Tudor Translations, p. 179).[1] The passage reads:

> And M. Augustin Bevazzano toulde, that a covetous manne whiche woulde not sell hys corne while it was at a highe price, whan he sawe afterwarde it had a great falle, for desperacion he hanged himself upon a beame in his chamber, and a servaunt of his hearing the noise, made speede, and seeing his maister hang, furthwith cut in sunder the rope and so saved him from death: afterwarde whan the covetous man came to himselfe, he woulde have had hys servaunt to have paide him for his halter that he had cut.

A detail indicating that Jonson took his version of the story from *The Courtier* is found in the fact that the peasant who saves Sordido is rebuked for cutting the rope instead of untying it.

The characterization of Fungoso is simple, though fairly effective. The son of the miserly farmer Sordido, he is put at the Inns of Court to study law and become a gentleman. He is infected, however, with a passion for dress, attempts to follow Brisk's fashions, and in consequence is put to extreme shifts, begging from his sister, pawning his clothes, going in debt to his tailor, and writing lying letters to his father. The number of satirical references in English literature to sons of peasants who aspire to gallantry and spend their stingy fathers' money in fast living is untold. Nashe has a brief sketch of the general type in *The Anatomie of Absurditie* (Vol. I, p. 35) and again in *Pierce Penilesse* (Vol. I, p. 160). Prodigal Zodon in the second satire of Middle-

[1]Prof. Bang in *Eng. Studien,* Vol. 36, p. 331, has later quoted the passage in connection with Sordido. Cf. also Miss M. A. Scott in *Mod. Lang. Publ.,* Vol. XVI, p. 488 f. Prof. Raleigh would trace to Castiglione all Elizabethan references to a farmer's hanging himself, but the parallel pointed out by Small shows a wider distribution of the anecdote.

ton's *Micro-Cynicon* spends in high living the patrimony left him by his father, Greedy Cron, who, like Sordido, "in a humour goes and hangs himself" on account of certain losses (Satire I). More suggestive of Fungoso is Hall's satire on the son of "driveling Lolio" (Book IV, Satire II). Lolio drudges and saves that his son may be a gentleman, while the son, who is at the Inns of Court, neglects law and spends everything on dress and gay living. The seeking of a coat of arms which is mentioned by Nashe and Hall is found with Jonson in Sogliardo. The word Fungoso is merely a translation into Italian of a name commonly given to the type. Nashe calls Harvey "a mushrumpe sprung vp in one night" (Vol. I, p. 323; cf. also Vol. III, p. 109), and in *Skialetheia,* Satire III, we have the lines,

> How like a *Musherom* art thou quickly growne,
> I knew thee when thou war'dst a thred-bare gowne.[1]

The special details in the treatment of Fungoso are in general fairly fresh, however. His heartbreaking efforts to keep pace with Brisk's suits furnish the most distinctive point in the characterization, and I recall no dramatic device of the sort except that already cited from Skelton's *Magnificence.* The scene in which Fungoso is surrounded by tradespeople who deliver his finery and are paid for it (IV, 5) is more commonplace. There is a scene in *Captain Stukeley* where Stukeley, who comes from the country and neglects law for gallantry, pays his furnishers (ll. 543 ff.). In *James IV* (IV, 3) the clown Slipper orders a fine outfit from tailor, shoemaker, and cutler, and pays them. The Epistle Dedicatory to Nashe's *Lenten Stuffe,* also, describes the scene in a gallant's chamber when he settles his accounts. In *Histriomastix,* again, (III, 1) the ladies and citizens' wives are waited on by

[1]In Jonson's work the term mushroom becomes almost a synonym for a gull. Of the two typical gulls in *Every Man out,* one is named Fungoso, and the other is called a puck-fist and is classed among

> these mushroom gentlemen,
> That shoot up in a night to place and worship (I, 1, p. 75).

In the expression "some idle Fungoso" (IV, 1, p. 175) which is applied to Asotus, the only typical gull in *Cynthia's Revels,* the word Fungoso merely means a mushroom, I take it, and involves no identification of Asotus with Fungoso. The gull Daw of *Silent Woman* is also called a mushroom, II, 2, p. 419. According to Gifford, Upton traces this last passage to Plautus, *Bacchides,* IV, 7, 23. Jonson again uses the term for an upstart in *Catiline,* II, 1.

tradespeople and order marvelous jewels and dresses. Jonson later opens *The Staple of News* with a scene in which Pennyboy Junior receives his various tradesmen and settles with them. In III, 2, Sordido reads a letter from Fungoso which is signed, "Yours, if his own" (repeated in *Cynthia's Revels,* V, 2, p. 194). The signature is evidently in mockery of a commonly affected close of euphuistic letters, and is appropriate to Fungoso, who reads the *Arcadia.* Koeppel in *Ben Jonson's Wirkung* (p. 67) traces the phrase to *Euphues,* but similar signatures are to be found scattered in Greene's works, in *A petite Pallace of Pettie his pleasure,* and in Gascoigne's *Adventures of Master F. I.* In *The Woman in the Moon* (V, 1, l. 145), "Yours, as his owne" occurs. When the party at the Mitre is broken up at the end of the play, Fungoso, though a guest, is held as a pawn for the score. His predicament suggests certain jests of Peele which involve leaving dupes as pawns for the reckoning at ordinaries (*Shakespeare Jest-Books,* Vol. II, pp. 293-297).[1]

Sogliardo embodies Jonson's sharpest satire on those who pretend to gentility merely by reason of wealth. Fungoso, for all his intellectual weakness, seems at least capable of appreciating the standards of the gallants whom he apes; but Sogliardo is always essentially the witless boor. In fact, he is another of the characters in whom Jonson enforces a fundamental principle so strongly that the character becomes a cross between a pure abstraction and a type. Sogliardo is almost a personification of ignorance. He is described as "an essential clown" (p. 63); "a tame rook," fit to be "a constable for . . wit," and "a transparent gull" (I, 1, p. 72); "one of those that fortune favours"—a favorite phrase for a fool (p. 75); "this hulk of ignorance" and "a shallow fool" with "no more brain than a butterfly, a mere stuft suit" (p. 76). His coat of arms is made to represent his ignorance chiefly. The variety of colors suggests the fool's motley, and the headless boar, or boor, is interpreted by Carlo as representing "a swine without a head, without brain, wit, anything indeed, ramping to gentility" (III, 1, p. 100). Still another analysis of Sogliardo as Ignorance is put in the mouth of Carlo in IV, 6 (p. 122): "He is a man of fair revenue, and his estate will bear the charge

[1]Cf. also *Groundworke of Conny-catching,* in *Rogues and Vagabonds of Shakspere's Youth,* pp. 102, 103.

well. Besides, for his other gifts of the mind, or so, why, they are as nature lent him them, pure, simple, without any artificial drug or mixture of these too threadbare beggarly qualities, learning and knowledge, and therefore the more accommodate and genuine." Apart from the broad types of fools, personifications of ignorance are common in the sixteenth century. Ignorance is a character in *The Four Elements, The Longer thou Livest,* and *Wyt and Science.* A good illustration of the situation from the opening scene of *Every Man out* where, on the first appearance of Sogliardo, the scholar Macilente exclaims (p. 72),

> 'Sblood, why should such a prick-eared hind as this
> Be rich, ha? a fool! such a transparent gull
> That may be seen through! wherefore should he have land,
> Houses, and lordships? O, I could eat my entrails,

is to be found in a passage of *Histriomastix* (Act III, ll. 310-313), where Envy, coming to reign after Pride, declares:

> Fat Ignorance, and rammish Barbarisme
> Shall spit and drivell in sweete Learnings face:
> Whilst he, half starv'd in Envie of their power,
> Shall eate his marrow, and him-selfe devoure.[1]

But Sogliardo, though almost an abstraction, is not so primitive or simple a type as Ignorance. He is the true gull, mixing with his clownish love of the hobby-horse and motions a serious determination to take tobacco like a gentleman. His stupidity, however, places him with the earlier type of gull like Stephen and Labesha. In the epigrams of Davies and Guilpin on the gull, the climax stresses his witlessness, which evidently sums up the type for both writers.

A number of points in the characterization of Sogliardo have already been mentioned, especially those that illustrate his aspirations as a gull. His independent tastes are for the hobby-horse (II, 1, p. 81) and for news, particularly of the puppet-shows of London (II, 1, p. 87). It is as a lover of the marvelous that he is captivated by the tales of Shift's exploits (IV, 4). In all these respects he represents the English clown. Davies in Epigram 43 satirizes the somewhat similar tastes of the country-bred Publius, who is more interested in the famous bears of Paris Garden than

[1]Cf. pp. 160-161 *supra.*

in his study of law. Sogliardo's insistence upon getting the news when he meets Sordido (II, 1, p. 87) is noteworthy as a first indication of Jonson's interest in a folly to which he later gave so much emphasis. There are many satirical references to newsmongers at the end of the sixteenth century, especially in Nashe's attack on the Martinists and the Harveys.[1] In *Sapho and Phao,* II, 3, Molus accosts Criticus with the question, "What newes?" as Sogliardo does Fungoso. Davies, again, in Epigram 40, *In Afram,* has an interesting sketch of the purveyor of news, which furnishes a forerunner of Sir Politick Would-be as a newsmonger. A still more striking portrait of the type is to be found, however, so early as Lodge's characterization of "Multiplication of words" in *Wits Miserie* (p. 85).

The coat of arms that Sogliardo procures (III, 1) in pursuance of Carlo's advice has already been spoken of as typical of Sogliardo's character. Such coats of arms are not uncommon in literature. The one suggested in "The False Knight" of Erasmus, from which Carlo drew his advice, in a measure represents the character of the Knight. In Bullein's *Dialogue against the Fever Pestilence* (E. E. T. S., p. 96), an appropriate coat of arms is given for Mendax, and in *The Three Ladies of London* (Hazlitt's *Dodsley,* Vol. VI, pp. 350, 351) the coat of arms of a thief is described. So the old *Timon* gives the absurd coat of arms of Gelasimus (I, 3).[2] In regard to a motto for Sogliardo's crest,

[1]Cf. Nashe, Vol. I, pp. 72, 82, 289, 298, 308, 365; Harvey, Vol. I, pp. 68 ff. and Vol. III, p. 18; *Tell-Trothes New-yeares Gift,* p. 3; Crowley, *One and Thirty Epigrams,* ll. 1113-1140, "Of Inuenters of Straunge Newes." Cf. also the following sixteenth century titles: *Sack-Full of Newes; Newes come from Hell of love unto all her welbeloved frendes,* by Copland; *Newes out of Powles Churchyarde,* by Hake; *Joyfull newes oute of the new founde worlde . . .* Englished by John Frampton; *Straunge Newes out of Calabria,* etc., by Doleta; *Strange Newes of the intercepting certaine Letters,* by Nashe; *Greene's News both from Heaven and Hell; Tarlton's News out of Purgatory; Newes from Jack Begger* (already cited); etc.

[2]Two boars form a part of the coat, along with three asses and three thistles. Doubtless the pun on boor is implied here as in Sogliardo's coat. The three thistles may denote fruitlessness; they remind one of the three thorns, or "spinas," of *Poetaster* (II, 1), though the resemblance is too uncertain to afford any conjecture as to whether Jonson borrowed from *Timon.* The possible combination of Jonson's two coats of arms in *Timon* is the chief indication I have been able to find, however slight, that the play may have come after Jonson's plays and combined details from them. One other indication is that the scene in *Timon* (I, 4) where Pseudocheus instructs Gelasimus how to woo successfully

Puntarvolo suggests (p. 100), "Let the word be, *Not without mustard.*" This probably goes back to Nashe. In *Pierce Penilesse* (Vol. I, p. 171), the story is told of a "Ruffion" who vowed to God that if he were delivered from a severe storm at sea, he would never again eat haberdine, but "readie to set foote a Land, cryed out: not without Mustard, good Lord, not without Mustard." Beyond a possible implication that Sogliardo was not to be taken without a sauce, there seems to be no especial point to Jonson's use of the phrase except that it introduced a bit of nonsense and recalled a jest that was probably popular.

Deliro and Fallace, the only other characters of any importance in the play, seem to have fewer conventional traits than is usual with Jonson. The motive of a husband's obsequiousness to a proud and peevish wife Jonson treated several times afterwards, and it became common enough in the drama. Perhaps the best forerunners of Deliro and Fallace are to be found in Lyly's *Woman in the Moon.* There is nothing in the half pastoral, half mythological figures of Lyly's play to associate them with the London citizen and his wife; but under the influence of the various planets Pandora falls into several moods in which she is strongly suggestive of Fallace, and the lovers are at times infatuated with her after the manner of Deliro.

Pandora's first mood is one of melancholy controlled by Saturn, who wills (I, 1, ll. 148, 149):

> She shalbe sick with passions of the hart,
> Selfwild, and toungtide, but full fraught with teares.

And Pandora says of herself (l. 174),

> I grudge and grieue, but know not well whereat.

Gunophilus, servant and lover, whose name, like Deliro's, expresses his infatuation, is the first to present himself, and he is met with railing. Next, the four shepherds put themselves at her service, only to be rebuffed in turn. Then Pandora falls to weeping, and the lovers sing "to sift that humor from her heart" (l. 221). Ac-

would more probably have been borrowed from Amorphus's instructions to Asotus in *Cynthia's Revels* than the reverse, for Jonson had, according to his habit, been developing the motive through several plays. Cf. *The Case is Altered*, IV, 3 and 4, and *Every Man out*, V, 1. The evidence, however, is too slight to enable us to determine which of the two plays influenced the other. See pp. 168 ff. *supra.*

cording to a stage direction, "she starteth vp and runs away at the end of the Song saying,"

> What songs? what pipes? & fidling haue we here?
> Will you not suffer me to take my rest?

whereupon one of the lovers in despair cries out (l. 227),

> What shal we do to vanquish her disease?

In the next mood, which is inspired by Jupiter, Pandora becomes proud and aspires to place, but her action is consistent with that of the preceding mood. To Jupiter she says (II, 1, ll. 73, 74),

> I tell thee *Iupiter*, *Pandoras* worth
> Is farre exceeding all your goddesses,

and to her lovers (l. 148),

> For wot ye well *Pandora* knowes her worth.

Mars inspires in her a still more vixenish mood, in which she strikes her lovers. One, however, Stesias, still dotes (II, 1, l. 230 ff.):

> But fondling as I am, why grieue I thus?
> Is not *Pandora* mistris of my life?
> Yes, yes, and euery act of hers is iust.
> Her hardest words are but a gentle winde.

In the succeeding moods she marries Stesias and then proves fickle, setting at naught her husband, who continues to adore her. Ultimately she is betrayed to him. At this point, however, all similarity between the two plays ends.

Quite dissimilar as Fallace is to Pandora on the whole, a surprising amount of what I have just cited from Lyly's play is paralleled in the part of Fallace and Deliro. In II, 2 (p. 91) Deliro protests to Macilente:

> I have such a wife!
> So passing fair; so passing-fair-unkind!
> But of such worth, and right to be unkind,
> Since no man can be worthy of her kindness.
> . . . .
> Ay, and she knows so well
> Her own deserts, that when I strive t' enjoy them,
> She weighs the things I do with what she merits;
> And, seeing my worth outweighed so in her graces,

> She is so solemn, so precise, so froward,
> That no observance I can do to her
> Can make her kind to me.

Deliro goes to the greatest pains to gratify her various whims, and finds, after all is done, that her humour has changed. In one scene (IV, 1, p. 111), he brings in musicians to play for her, saying, "O, begin, begin, some sprightly thing. . . . Heaven grant it please her." Fallace, however, cries out, "Hey—da! this is excellent! I'll lay my life this is my husband's dotage. . . . I know you do nothing but study how to anger me, sir." Shortly after, she peevishly leaves his presence, and shuts her door against him when he attempts to follow.[1]

As a prosperous London merchant, Deliro is a rather colorless figure. Independently of Fallace's attitude to her husband, however, she is interestingly characterized as a citizen's wife yearning for attention, especially for the notice of gallants. She desires to be in fashion and to have friends at court; she regards Brisk as the perfection of all that is charming, finally becoming desperately enamored of him; she quotes from *Euphues,* and in other ways shows her passion for fads of the fashionable (cf. IV, 1, pp. 110, 111 and V, 7, pp. 137, 138). There is a good deal of satire on citizens' wives who live in luxury and strive after the fashions of the courtly, but I do not recall elsewhere just such satire on the longing of these women for gallant lovers.

Through Cordatus in the induction, Jonson has described *Every Man out* as "strange, and of a particular kind by itself, somewhat like *Vetus Comœdia.*" The phrase *Vetus Comœdia* would naturally be interpreted at once as referring to classic comedy, and the context seems to support this interpretation. I am tantalized, however, by the question whether the reference may not, after all, have been to the older forms of English drama. Nashe in *The Returne of Pasquill* twice uses the term in connection with old English plays (Vol. I, pp. 92 and 100), and Drummond reports

[1]One unimportant point in the treatment of Deliro and Fallace was probably suggested by Chaucer's *Merchant's Tale* and such stories as *Greenes Vision,* where the husband is persuaded that he saw his wife on a lover's knee only in a dream or delirium. When Deliro unexpectedly finds his wife at the Counter with Brisk, Macilente says (V, 7, p. 138): "Nay, why do you not dote now, signior? methinks you should say it were some enchantment, *deceptio visus,* or so, ha! If you could persuade yourself it were a dream now, 'twere excellent."

Jonson himself as saying that "according to *Comedia Vetus,* in England the Divell . . . caried away the Vice." At any rate, there is little in the structure, the type of incident, or the method of characterization to connect *Every Man out* with classic comedy. The characters, though undoubtedly finished from life, follow types from English literature, and the allegorical tone of the play which results from the emphasis on a mastering humour associates *Every Man out* with the morality.

CHAPTER VIII

CYNTHIA'S REVELS

The allegorical tendency shown in *Every Man out* reaches its fullest expression for Jonson's early period in *Cynthia's Revels.*[1] The plot of *Cynthia's Revels* as given in the induction is a pure allegory, the characters bearing allegorical names and the relations existing among them having an allegorical significance, so that the reversion of the humour types to the older abstractions is here almost complete. In spite, however, of the fundamental abstraction in the characters and the comic exaggeration, the play impresses us as perhaps giving a more searching picture of one segment of London life than any of Jonson's earlier comedies. The ordinary gallants of *Every Man in* give way in *Every Man out* to types that belong to a higher social plane, one near that of the court; in *Cynthia's Revels* Jonson has laid his scene entirely in the court itself, even studies of the rogue class being omitted except among the pages. The characters thus represent fewer walks of life, but the study of social trivialities within the narrower sphere is exhaustive, let us hope.

The induction of *Cynthia's Revels,* unlike the body of the play, is more dramatic than that of *Every Man out.* The parts of Asper and Grex are omitted here, and with them the effort to set the tone of the play through a presenter, and the attempt to explain the author's art. As a substitute Jonson has been careful to give an analysis of the plot of *Cynthia's Revels* so as to stress the allegory. A device similar to that in the most dramatic part of the induction to *Every Man out*—the appearance of Carlo and the debate about the prologue—forms the foundation of the induction to *Cynthia's Revels.* In the later play the induction thus has fewer elements and is more unified as well as more dramatic. The mimicry of audience and playwright that Jonson indulges in

[1]Acted in 1600 according to the Folio, doubtless after the lease of Blackfriars to Henry Evans on September 2, 1600. That *Cynthia's Revels* was performed late in the year is indicated by Jonson's reference in the induction to the fact that "the *umbræ* or ghosts of some three or four plays departed a dozen years since, have been seen walking on your stage here." Apparently the house opened in the fall with the production of old plays before *Cynthia's Revels* and other new plays were secured.

through the children is more appropriate than the expository and indignant manner of Asper. While this new induction, especially as it repeats themes of *Every Man out,* seems to be merely a development of earlier devices for inductions, it nevertheless has fewer connections than the preceding play with the common devices of playwrights who used the induction before Jonson. The two fundamental elements, the appearance of certain actors and the use of the debate, had not before been combined in the induction so far as I know. *The Downfall of Robert Earl of Huntington* uses the appearance of actors beforehand, who discuss their parts and thus pique the curiosity of the audience by suggesting the nature of the play,[1] but the purpose here, as in most of the early inductions, is to set the tone of the piece.[2] The device of a contest in the induction was also for the most part merely a more dramatic way than the old prologue, chorus, or other such device furnished of introducing the commanding genius or dominant tone of the play. But Nashe had used the spectator in the induction for the expression of criticism, and the contest type of induction also became in *A Warning for Fair Women* a notable means of allowing the author to give direct expression to his critical views in regard to the drama. Jonson utilized the induction almost purely for such criticism after *Every Man out,* and even in *Every Man out* the function of the induction is largely critical. A further step toward Jonson's induction in *Cynthia's Revels* is found in the induction of *The True Tragedy of Richard III,* where Truth and Poetry enter upon a discussion that serves not so much to set the tone of the play as to furnish the ground for introducing what the author wishes to tell the audience in regard to the occasion or plot. That at least the critical tendencies if not the devices of these earlier inductions had attracted Jonson is shown by the fact that the prologue of *Every Man in* and in part the induction of *Every Man out* echo the critical material of earlier inductions.[3]

The material in the induction of *Cynthia's Revels* is comparatively fresh, largely because it is not general but consists in great

[1]This discussion of parts in Munday's play is more like the induction of Marston's *Antonio and Mellida.*

[2]Cf. pp. 146-148 *supra* for a discussion of various early inductions.

[3]Cf. pp. 142, 143, and 146-148 *supra.*

part of such direct and specific attacks on the follies of spectators and playwrights as perhaps no other dramatist dared to utter. Following the quarrel of the children over the speaking of the prologue, comes the plot of the play. Next one of the children mocks the gallants who sit upon the stage smoking and flouting actors. In *Every Man out* Jonson three times refers to those who sit on or over the stage, with hits at such abuses as smoking, gay dressing, and mocking of actors (Induction, p. 68; I, 1, p. 73; II, 1, p. 88). In *Cynthia's Revels* the satire is more fully elaborated. The satirists had already begun to attack these abuses before Jonson took them up, Davies in Epigrams 3 and 28 and Guilpin in Epigram 53 of *Skialetheia*. Hall also seems to have an allusion to the custom and to absurd critics in a passage in which he satirizes the abuses of tragedy, though the tone is entirely unlike Jonson's (*Virgidemiarum,* I, 3). Earlier the part of Will Summer in *Summer's Last Will and Testament* had given Nashe's indirect satire on the custom of flouting actors, and Summer's criticism of Nashe's prologue as "scuruy" illustrates Jonson's point in the induction of *Cynthia's Revels* that "one miscalls all by the name of fustian, that his grounded capacity cannot aspire to." Jonson next attacks playwrights for obscenity, for borrowing their jests, and for boasting of rapidity of work. The charge of immodesty and obscenity in plays was common among those who attacked the drama. Whetstone in the dedication of *Promos and Cassandra,* for example, criticises the lasciviousness of Italian, French, and Spanish plays. The attack on old jests was also becoming frequent. It occurs in *A Warning for Fair Women* (ll. 33, 34), where Tragedy speaks of Comedy's having

> Some odd ends of old jests scrap'd up together,
> To tickle shallow unjudicial ears;

and in *Histriomastix* (III, ll. 206, 207), where Chrisoganus scores those who

> load the stage with stuff
> Rakt from the rotten imbers of stall jests.

With these lines compare Jonson's: "Besides, they could wish your poets would leave to be promoters of other men's jests, and to way-lay all the stale apothegms, or old books, they can hear of, in print or otherwise, to farce their scenes withal." Jonson's criticism of the Children of the Chapel for presenting old plays echoes a passage on the Children of Paul's from *Jack Drum's Entertainment* (V, ll. 111-114), cited by Gifford:

> I, and they had good Plaies. But they produce
> Such mustie fopperies of antiquitie,
> And doe not sute the humorous ages backs,
> With clothes in fashion.

Finally, Jonson attacks under five classes injudicious critics among the auditors: the one whose only claim to wit lies in his clothes, the one who pronounces the old Hieronimo the only "judiciously penned play in Europe," etc. Much of this is repeated from *Every Man in* and *Every Man out,* and part of it goes back to Nashe.[1] Marston, also, in the section introducing *The Scourge of Villainy* sketches briefly the different types who dare pass judgment on his work.

The general plot of *Cynthia's Revels* is composed of a large number of diverse elements, although far more attention is given to character analysis than to incident, so that the play is even more devoid of movement than is *Every Man out.* In the prologue Jonson claims originality for the work:

> In this alone, his Muse her sweetness hath,
> She shuns the print of any beaten path;
> And proves new ways to come to learned ears.

There is something appropriate in the expression "learned ears" in connection with a play that probably suggested to the well read many diverse types of literature. Indeed, the passage was perhaps not intended to mean that Jonson used no literary material but rather that, in the combination of elements and in the tone of the whole, the work was new. It may be, also, that Jonson was influenced by a growing convention of claiming originality on the part of those who are not always original. Sidney declares in Sonnet 74,

> I am no pick-purse of another's wit.

Drayton, in the opening of his sequence *Idea* (1594), makes the same claim, repeating Sidney's line. Nashe in *Strange Newes* (*Works of Nashe,* Vol. I, p. 319) boasts of the vein of his "owne

[1]Cf. p. 127 *supra.*

begetting" which "cals no man father in England but my selfe." And yet all of these men would have considered skilful adaptation not borrowing but merely the imitation that is the mark of the well trained writer.

In *Cynthia's Revels* there are four fairly distinct lines of treatment. First, there is the pastime of courtship with the fancies that had grown up around it, an element representing in the main Jonson's adaptation of court of love conventions to current fashions in courtly love. It accounts for much of the framework and for a certain amount of the mythological and allegorical interest in the play. Second, a still larger part of the mythological element in *Cynthia's Revels* is probably to be explained by the influence of the mythological play, which became so prominent in the hands of Lyly during the latter part of the sixteenth century. Third, there is the motive of the conflict between virtues and vices, which furnishes the most important part of the allegory, and out of which grows the grouping and the balancing of the characters, though Jonson's interest in humours also seems to have affected the grouping. Naturally certain conventions of the morality plays are utilized for handling dramatically the conflict between good and evil. Jonson in addition has made the vices and virtues of *Cynthia's Revels* in part Aristotelian. Fourth, there are individual studies in which the abstractions are made vital by details from contemporary fads and fashions that are appropriate to the folly studied and emphasize the primary inclination, or humour. In adapting these phases of the play to each other, Jonson would naturally modify practically everything that he has borrowed. Moreover, he has enriched the main elements of his work by minor borrowings here and there, the most important of which are the mock tournament, or duello, as a form of entertainment, the allegory of money as distributed by Fortune to fools, and especially certain conventions of older plays, such as the Diana-versus-Cupid intrigue. An attempt will be made to follow in order the four chief lines of study and to suggest wherever it is most convenient the minor elements that enter into this complex drama.

There are distinct traces in *Cynthia's Revels* of court of love conventions. Indeed, to my mind, they form the basis of the play. In them is perhaps to be seen the extension of the popular court of love ideas into the general literature and the pastimes of the

Renaissance, and perhaps, also, some of the kinship is to be attributed to accident. On the other hand, from the time when Jonson studied the knightly procedure of Puntarvolo, an interest in medieval conventions of chivalry apparently grew upon him, and gradually this interest became centered in the court of love as an excellent device for satirizing women. Certainly throughout Jonson's work groups of women with social pretensions are treated under the form of organizations by means of which contemporary social follies are satirized. In *The Silent Woman* the Ladies Collegiates[1] with their President (I, 1, p. 406), their pretence to wit (III, 2, p. 432), their instructions to Epicœne in regard to what she shall demand of her husband as her privilege (IV, 2), their rules in amatory pursuits (IV, 2), and the accounts given Morose of the customs, claims, and privileges of women (II, 1)—here become vices—seem to indicate the court of love machinery carried into the social life of women. Again in *The Devil is an Ass,* when Wittipol dressed as a Spanish lady comes to Lady Tailbush, supposedly from her friends at court (IV, 1, p. 253), in honor of her projects for an improved fucus in the service of her sex, the plan to hold a sitting of the "academy" or "school" (III, 1, p. 248; III, 3, p. 250; IV, 1, p. 256), of which the Spanish lady, described as a "mistress of behaviour" (II, 3, p. 239), is called "lady-president"; the elaborate discussion of perfumes and fucuses; Lady Eitherside's interest in the customs of love and her scorn of being loved only by her husband; and finally the opinions expressed as to proper conduct in woman's gallantry and the proper messengers in love affairs (IV, 1) represent more clearly Jonson's satire on women's vices through the burlesque of court of love conventions.

Jonson's still more extensive use of the varied machinery traditionally connected with the academies and courts of love is to

[1]The term college is used in English for the group of women at the court of love as early at least as Lydgate's *Reson and Sensuallyte.* Venus says to the poet in regard to his admittance into the Garden of Deduit (ll. 2691 ff.):

> For thou shalt han a priuelege
> For to be of my college,
> Amonge folkys amerouse.

De Arte Honeste Amandi of Andreas Capellanus (*ca.* 1200) has the fiction of a "dominarum collegia" dwelling with Cupid.

be found later in *The New Inn.*[1] In this play the court of love is formally organized with Prudence as "queen-regent" and "sovereign of love" and "of the day's sport" (I, 1, p. 348; II, 2, p. 355; II, 2, p. 365; etc.). Frances is called before the court on charge of heresy in love; Lovel as appellant tells the "infidel" what love is; the refractory lady follows the usual formula of repenting, and suggests the possible penance of a pilgrimage to Love's image to say penitential verses "out of Chaucer's Troilus and Cressid" or of making offering at the shrine of Venus; and finally the Queen commands the culprit to forfeit a kiss (III, 2). Though the trial before the court of love is usually described as legal, Jonson in *The New Inn* has made it conform more closely to the trial by combat before the ecclesiastical court, and the oaths taken by Lovel are parodies of the combatant's oaths, as Gifford and Tennant point out.[2] Indeed, the whole trial in *The New Inn,* with the talk of heresy, penances, etc., echoes the ecclesiastical, and is merely an extension of the many court of love parodies of ritualistic ceremonies. Moreover, Lovel's description of his passions and pains in love (I, 1) and the elaborate analysis of love that he makes before the court (III, 2) have many points suggestive of the rules of love as given in court of love poems, though Lovel's analysis often follows the tradition not of Ovid but of Plato.[3] The later argument before the "sovereign of Love" (IV, 3, pp. 373 ff.) on Valour is more like the discussion of set themes engaged in by groups of the courtly in their pastimes. Finally, in V, 1 (p. 380), Frances promises that, if her love speeds, she will use her fortunes reverently and religiously, and adds:

> Love and his mother,
> I'll build them several churches, shrines, and altars,
> And over head I'll have, in the glass windows,
> The story of this day be painted, round,
> For the poor laity of love to read:
> I'll make myself their book, nay, their example,
> To bid them take occasion by the forelock,
> And play no after-games of love hereafter.

[1]Cf. Prof. Fletcher's discussion in *Journal of Comparative Literature,* 1903, pp. 131-135, and Mr. Tennant's introduction to his edition of *The New Inn,* pp. lvi-lxii.

[2]Cf. pp. 199 f. *supra* for Jonson's preceding use of these oaths.

[3]Cf. pp. xliv-xlix of Tennant's introduction to *The New Inn.*

There can be no question that Frances is here describing the usual temple or palace of Love in the court of love poems, one of the commonest features of which was the symbolic paintings. In *The Court of Love* (ll. 229 ff.),

> The temple shoon with windows all of glas,
> Bright as the day, with many a fair image;

and there are depicted the stories of Dido and Aeneas, of Arcite and Anelida, and of many who suffered martyrdom for love.[1]

That social groups organized primarily for the discussion of love existed in essence if not with the formality indicated in Jonson's satire, is not to be doubted. Castiglione's *Courtier,* Gascoigne's *Adventures of Master F. I.,* Lyly's *Euphues,* Greene's *Tritameron of Love, Euphues, his Censure to Philautus,* and *Mourning Garment,* Lodge's *Margarite of America,* and various other works written between 1580 and 1600 show groups of the courtly at social gatherings discussing phases of love and of character, and often organizing with a presiding officer for the purpose.[2]

[1]Prof. Fletcher in *The Journal of Comparative Literature,* 1903, pp. 120 ff., has shown that under Charles I Platonic love became the fad of the courtly and that *The New Inn* is one of the early works which voices the new passion. It is an interesting fact that in this play, along with conceptions antagonistic to the court of love tradition, Jonson has used the court of love setting in its clearest form. Prof. Fletcher also points out the fact that the attitude of James I to women was scornful while that of Charles I was romantic, and that as a result the idealization of women under the cult of Platonic love gained prominence in the reign of Charles. In this connection it may be worth noting that, whereas in *The Silent Woman* and *The Devil is an Ass,* written during the reign of James, the groups of women organized for social power are used for the bitterest satire on the vices of the sex, *The New Inn,* early in the reign of Charles, comes as near as Jonson could come to idealizing love,—and that through the conventional organization which even before Elizabeth died had been used in *Cynthia's Revels* for satire. It is true that under Elizabeth an idealization of love through the application of Platonic ideas is met with in Spenser and Sidney. Cf. Prof. Fletcher's article, "Did Astrophel Love Stella?" *Mod. Phil.,* Vol. V, pp. 253 ff. But by the time of *Cynthia's Revels* such an ideal had probably degenerated into a popular fad which had become the property of the vicious. If the honor paid to the Virgin Queen had much to do with the vogue of the cult of chivalric love, doubtless the flippancy of the Queen aided in making the cult merely a sham.

[2]Cf. Bond's *Works of Lyly,* Vol. II, pp. 162 ff. and 522. See also Vol. I, p. 412 for a challenge at a tilt in which it is maintained that "Loue is worse than hate." A question of love casuistry, "whether riches were better than loue," formed the theme of an entertainment in the time of Henry VIII, in which "two persones plaied a dialog" and "six knightes fought a fair battail." See Brotanek, *Die engl. Maskenspiele,* p. 86.

It is hardly to be questioned, also, that gallants in England affected these debates in their gatherings as they did many other conventions of medieval love and gallantry. There is scarcely a phase of Renaissance love poetry influenced by the Italian and French that is not steeped in the spirit of the medieval court of love conceptions, and, if this poetry itself can not be taken as evidence on the point, the satires and such plays as *Cynthia's Revels* leave little doubt that the manners and fads connected with the court of love were often followed in actual life.

For the beginning of Jonson's interest in the machinery of the court of love we must go back to *Cynthia's Revels*. Here are suggested practically all the court of love elements that appear in the later plays, and even more; but they are mingled with so many other phases of allegory and are touched so vaguely that one is in perpetual doubt as to their origin. *Cynthia's Revels* indicates an extensive knowledge of the more general literary conventions of the court of love, though I can point out no single work preceding the play which might have furnished Jonson his material. So far as I know, certain English poems, or French poems translated into English, serve best to illustrate the court of love elements in *Cynthia's Revels*. Thus *The Romaunt of the Rose,* published in Chaucer's works, and *Les Échecs Amoureux,* a part of which makes up Lydgate's *Reson and Sensuallyte,* reveal the treatment of court of love ideas with the addition of new motives and machinery in the interest of allegory; and they deal with the conventions much in the free way of Jonson. These two poems with *The Court of Love* and other pseudo-Chaucerian pieces would furnish a sufficient basis for much of Jonson's allegory. It is not probable that Jonson knew Lydgate's poem, as it had not been published in 1600, but much of the pseudo-Chaucerian literature was of course familiar to him through Thynne's Stow's, or Speght's edition of Chaucer. Indeed, it is probable enough that Speght's edition in 1598, with its large number of court of love poems, influenced *Cynthia's Revels* directly.

In attempting to point out the kinship between Jonson's play and court of love conventions, I have chosen to instance, on account of their cumulative value, many very slight or questionable parallels as well as some important ones. At the outset I should like to express my indebtedness to Professor Neilson's *Origins and*

Sources of the Court of Love. For the material outside of the works that are readily accessible to the English student, I have been forced to rely entirely on the analyses which he gives of the court of love poems.

Cynthia's Revels opens with the coming of Cupid to practice in disguise in Diana's court, a motive that I shall mention later. He meets Mercury, who has been sent on an errand quite in keeping with the spirit of the court of love—to allow Echo to express her passion for Narcissus. To Mercury Cupid explains the occasion with the words: "Diana, in regard of some black and envious slanders hourly breathed against her, for her divine justice on Acteon . . . hath here in the vale of Gargaphie, proclaimed a solemn revels . . . in which time it shall be lawful for all sorts of ingenious persons to visit her palace, to court her nymphs, to exercise all variety of generous and noble pastimes." In addition, Diana is to justify herself. The Acteon charge, however, plays no real part in the plot, and the court is in complete possession of the amorous gallants and nymphs until Diana's appearance in the last act.

Since *Cynthia's Revels* is a compliment to Elizabeth, the court is that of Diana, and Jonson has had to modify the situation so as to allow the court of love group to enter. The association of Diana with the court of love as in *Cynthia's Revels* is not unusual, however. Naturally, in certain of the poems that bring out the contrast between love and cold chastity, the court of Diana and that of Venus or Cupid both appear. The contrast of course is inevitable. Thus in Douglas's *Palice of Honour,* the poet—who first sees Acteon torn by the hounds, suggestive enough of the charges against Diana mentioned at the opening of *Cynthia's Revels*—views the court of Diana and next of Venus as they pass to the Palace of Honor. In Lydgate's *Reson and Sensuallyte* and in its source, *Les Échecs Amoureux,* Diana appeals to the poet against Venus and her court, but the poet proceeds, notwithstanding, to the "Garden of Deduit." The temples of both Diana and Venus are described in Chaucer's *Knightes Tale,* as in Boccaccio. Again in *The Flower and the Leaf,* Diana leads the virtuous court, and the followers of Flora represent types of idleness and folly, a contrast of groups which we find in *Cynthia's Revels.* Very naturally the tendency to exalt chastity in the figure of Diana, even in literature utilizing the court of love machinery, became more striking during the reign of the Virgin Queen.[1]

In the opening scene, covering the first act, the setting is appropriate for the court of love. The place is a grove containing the fountain of Narcissus, or Self-Love. The dream setting that is so popular in connection with the court of love is always described elaborately as a garden with trees, birds, fountains, streams, etc. In *Le Roman de la Rose* the court is set in a meadow with trees and fountains, and the Fountain of Love, fatal to Narcissus, is described in detail, the story of Narcissus and Echo being rehearsed also. Guillaume de Lorris has explained the power of this fountain to make all who look in it fall in love as fully as Jonson in *Cynthia's Revels* has described its power to make all who drink of it dote upon themselves. In a number of other poems, the fountain is associated with the court of love, as Narcissus often is.[2] Of the poems that I know, the one most suggestive of conventionality in Jonson's handling of the fountain is Lydgate's *Reson and Sensuallyte*. In warning the poet against the Garden of Deduit, Diana tells of the poisonous fountains (ll. 3804 ff.). Some of them are "ful of sorwe and dool" to him who drinks of them, and others cause one who looks in to be ravished with his own image (ll. 3825-3846). She especially speaks of Narcissus as a victim of the enchanted wells, and later a long description is given of the well of Narcissus and of its marvels (ll. 5659-5790). The description is favorable in point of view, the water being praised for its clearness, its pleasing taste, and its incomparable sweetness of odor (ll. 5735 ff.). So Amorphus first and the other gallants later praise the water of the Fountain of Self-Love (*Cynthia's Revels,* I, 1, p. 153 and IV, 1, p. 181).

At the end of the first scene, the traveler Amorphus appears at the well, drinks of its water, falls even more inordinately in love with himself, and then passes on to the court, where later his praise of the well puts the other courtiers into a fever of impatience till

[1]Cf. Neilson, *Origins and Sources of the Court of Love,* p. 266.

[2]Cf. *Le Dit de la Fontaine Amoureuse;* Deschamp's *Le Lay du Desert d'Amours; L'Hospital d'Amours.* Cf. also Prof. Neilson's index under Narcissus. In 1572 a play called *Narcissus* was acted before Elizabeth. Cf. Feuillerat, *Documents relating to the Office of the Revels in the Time of Queen Elizabeth,* p. 145. Possibly some details that afterward filtered into *Cynthia's Revels* met here. The academic *Narcissus* of 1601-2 has a number of conventional details in common with *Cynthia's Revels.*

they also drink of its water. In the second act, which opens at the court, Hedon and Anaides enter devising compliments and oaths for the presence of their mistresses, an exercise which at least contains a hint of the lover's duty to study means of honoring and complimenting his lady. Later in this scene somewhat closer parallels begin. Amorphus leads Asotus into the court, telling him that he is "now within the regard of the presence," and begins to instruct him, among other things, how he must practice the face of the courtier elementary, "one but newly entered, or as it were in the alphabet, or *ut-re-mi-fa-sol-la* of courtship." Later the four court nymphs appear: Moria, the guardian of the nymphs, whose life has been given to court gallantry and pretence to wit; Argurion, "of a most wandering and giddy disposition," who will "run from gallant to gallant"; Philautia, proud and self-centered; and Phantaste, fickle and wavering. In another scene (IV, 1), the nymphs' interest in love comes out. Moria's great wish is to know all secret scandal; Philautia's, to have sovereignty over many lovers; and Phantaste's, to be all kinds of creatures and prove all kinds of suitors.[1] Act III discovers Amorphus consoling Asotus for his first failure in courtship and warning him that audacity is needed. After further instructions (III, 1 and 3), Amorphus brings Asotus into the presence of the ladies, and bids him woo Argurion (IV, 1). Asotus addresses himself to her immediately. Meanwhile Cupid has shot his arrows into Argurion's breast, and she becomes enamored of him, promising to reward him on condition that he be "faithful and kind" to her. Then follow certain courtly games, and at the end Hedon sings of the kiss and Amorphus of his mistress's glove.

The details cited from these four acts are all dimly suggestive of court of love poetry. Amorphus's office as guide and instructor of the newly introduced lover is usually held by a woman, though in *Die Minneburg* men have the function. In *The Court of Love,* the lover at his entrance is met by Philobone, the Queen's chamberer. A part of Philobone's instruction is that it is "hot

[1]In some respects Philautia and Phantaste are repeated in Frances, the central figure of the court of love in *The New Inn.* Of her it is said that she "hath an ambitious disposition to be esteemed the mistress of many servants, but love none" (Argument, p. 337), and that she is "phantastical: thinks nothing a felicity but to have a multitude of servants, and be called mistress by them" (Characterism, p. 339). Frances, however, is not sensual but Platonic.

corage" which "spedeth" in the affairs of the court. The lover's first wooing is a failure, but later Rosial relents, charging him to keep the statutes. In *The Romaunt of the Rose,* L'Amant, entering the garden, is invited by Courtesy to join the revelers, among whom is the God of Love, though not in disguise; and Love shoots L'Amant with his arrows (ll. 1714 ff.). The various allegorical characters are described as in *Cynthia's Revels* and *The Court of Love.* The poem, however, passes into a long account of contest unlike the simple story of one failure followed by quick acceptance of the recruit which we find in *Cynthia's Revels.* In *Reson and Sensuallyte,* the Garden of Deduit is especially described as a place where games are played, and the lover's pursuit of his mistress takes the form of a game of chess. Other slight general parallels to court of love poetry might be given, but to note any of them is worth while only on account of the additional indication of kinship that they furnish.

The four nymphs with their veiled sensuality and their hinted organization suggestive of later colleges are unlike anything in the poems just cited. A number of court of love poems show such elements, however. The *Romaricimontis Concilium,* in which an assembly of ladies is held for the discussion of love, suggests this group.[1] "The doorkeeper was that Sibilia who had been a soldier of Venus from her tender years, and had without reluctance done whatever Love commanded," a description that fits Moria admirably. The name Sibilia itself seems appropriate to a woman, like Moria, of somewhat advanced years. Moria's function as "guardian," however, is nearer that of a presiding officer, and in this respect she corresponds to the *cardinalis domina* of this poem. In reply to the *cardinalis domina,* who had been sent by the God of Love "to inquire into the lives of those who were present," "Elisabet de Granges rose and stated that they served Love as well as they could. 'Nothing that he wishes displeases us, and if we neglect anything, it is unwittingly. Thus we choose to keep no regular bond with any man, nor do we know any unless he be of our order.' "[2] The utterances of Philautia and Phantaste suggest ideals akin to those of Elisabet. The rest of the poem, with its

[1]Here and elsewhere I quote from Prof. Neilson's analyses of the poems.

[2]From much of the court of love literature one would gather that the rules of fidelity applied to lover rather than to mistress.

debate on clerks and knights as lovers, does not concern us except in the parody of the ritual to be mentioned later.

The long fifth act of *Cynthia's Revels* introduces the most complicated elements of Jonson's allegory, and especially the mock duello of the second scene shows interesting traces of court of love conventions. The Quarto *of Cynthia's Revels,* published in 1601, lacks a large part of this last act, so that much of the material most valuable for our purpose cannot with certainty be ascribed to the period of Jonson's work with which we are concerned. I have disregarded this fact, however, for I believe that the longer form was the original form, or at least was earlier than *Poetaster.* In the section omitted from the Quarto occurs the mock duello with the challenge at the four weapons of courtly ceremony; only here do Mistress Downfall and her husband appear; and here the hostility of the courtiers to Crites is treated most fully. This omitted section has apparently the bitterest personal satire, also, and the most daring attacks on the pastimes of the court. It is not inherently probable, I think, that this part was written after *Poetaster,* for Mistress Downfall furnishes a first study for the character of Chloe, and the efforts of the pseudo-gallants and poetasters to disgrace Crites foreshadow the hostility to Horace. *Satiromastix* (ll. 1654 f.) also contains a possible hint that the omitted portion of *Cynthia's Revels* had appeared on the stage before Dekker's play was written. Tucca, in bullying Horace's parasite, Asinius Bubo, asks him if he will fight, and calling forward his own boy,—who apparently has a number of weapons, as he entered "laden with swords and bucklers,"—says to Asinius, "I challenge thee thou slender Gentleman, at foure sundrie weapons." This may be merely a bit of absurdity, but the whole scene is a burlesque on Jonson, and in this point we may have a hit at Jonson's "four choice and principal weapons" of courtship.[1]

The scene of *Cynthia's Revels* in which the duello occurs (V, 2) opens with Amorphus still instructing his novice Asotus preparatory to making him "master in the noble and subtile science of courtship" (IV, 1, p. 182). Amorphus instructs him in the three ways of giving the dor by wearing of colors, and in such "im-

[1]But cf. *Mod. Lang. Publ.*, Vol. XIII (1898), p. 111, for a challenge at ten weapons given by George Silver and narrated in his *Paradoxes of Defence,* 1599.

brocatas in courtship" as the bitter bob in wit. During the discussion of colors Amorphus lays down for the guidance of Asotus the general principle that "it is the part of every obsequious servant, to be sure to have daily about him copy and variety of colours, to be presently answerable to any hourly or half-hourly change in his mistress's revolution." Then master and novice pass on to the assembly where the duello occurs. It will be noticed that the duello is organized in many respects as a court of love, though numerous other conventions that enter in obscure the relation. Morphides acts as doorkeeper, or porter. A citizen and his wife press for entry, and the wife, Mistress Downfall, is admitted, but the citizen is told, "Husbands are not allowed here, in truth" (V, 2, p. 186). Amorphus, grandmaster of the ceremony, then distributes gloves as "properly accommodate to the nuptials of my scholar's haviour to the lady Courtship"; the challenge of Asotus is read, with the announcement of the weapons and the prizes; and Moria, who is later succeeded by Philautia and Phantaste, is throned in state as "lady sentinel." After a slight delay, Crites enters introducing Mercury, disguised as a Frenchman, to answer the challenge. Amorphus himself engages the monsieur at the four chosen weapons of courtly grace. At the end of each contest, the judges, Hedon and Anaides, give their decision, and the "lady sentinel" announces the prize. In preparation for the third bout, a tailor, a barber, a perfumer, etc. are introduced,—and of course one receives a beating,—and the contestants bedeck themselves elaborately on the stage as a burlesque on the array of the fashionable gallant. In connection with the perfume, Mercury significantly quotes,

> May it ascend, like solemn sacrifice,
> Into the nostrils of the Queen of Love!

During the closing trial at courtship, Amorphus by changing colors with the change of mistress attempts to give Mercury the dor, but, as Mercury is playing without colors, Amorphus himself is disgraced. Finally Crites and Anaides engage in one test, and Anaides is flouted.

The whole description in this scene is filled with technical terms that belong to the art of the duello, as Gifford points out, so that the most obvious parody is of course that of the duel. The procedure, however, is a dramatization of the rules of courtship, taking the form apparently of a burlesque on contemporary customs of gallants. A possible source for such a combination in satire will be taken up later.[1] The connection of the duello with the court of love is not conventional so much as natural, and for Jonson the substitution of a form of trial by combat for the ordinary trial of lovers before the court of love meant no more, perhaps, than the association of kindred things. Closely related always to court of love allegory is romance, with its chivalric exaltation of women and with its tiltings, tourneys, and various forms of combat. In *The Flower and the Leaf,* there is jousting between the knights of Diana. In *Le Roman de la Rose,* romance has entered into the allegory, and battle after battle is described in terms of chivalry as symbolic of courtship. In Thibaut's *Roman de la Poire* (Neilson, pp. 56, 57), after an arming suggestive of the elaborate dressing and perfuming of Amorphus and Mercury, there is a tournament between the traitors and those loyal to love. The last two poems, however, represent the combat as a conflict between love and other forces rather than as a trial of skill in courtship. Such also are the battles in Dunbar's *Golden Targe,* Huon de Mery's *Tornoiement d'Antéchrist,* etc. But in *Florance et Blancheflor* (Neilson, pp. 36, 37) the knight-versus-clerk debate is settled by a combat between two champions, the nightingale and the parrot.

With the trouvère *jeu parti* of the *puys d'amour* in Northern France we have a much closer approach in form to the duel scene of *Cynthia's Revels.* Professor Neilson describes such a contest in part as follows (p. 246):

> After mass and the singing of sacred music, the crowd entered a hall. On an elevation sat the president, the judges, and other important persons. Hymns to the Virgin, love songs, and finally *jeux partis* were presented to the audience; the subjects of these last being the passion of love and the duties of marriage. One poet gave the challenge, another took it up, and sometimes three, rarely four, engaged in the contest, the challenger naming a judge. Sometimes each side named a judge, and rarely there were three. These gave the decisions, the crowd merely looking on; and crowns of flowers or of silver were awarded to the winners, who gained thus the privileges of (1) being called "Sire," etc.

We have in *Cynthia's Revels* the presiding officer and the judges,

[1]Cf. pp. 233, 234 *infra.*

the awarding of prizes, etc., and Asotus challenges in order to win the rank of "master." It may be that such courtly procedure as that of the *jeux partis* was carried into the fashionable duello. Undoubtedly the love conventions of the Middle Ages influenced customs and literature in the Renaissance far more penetratingly than we can ever determine.

Much of the duel scene in *Cynthia's Revels* is suggestive of the rules for behavior in love. The resemblances here, however, are perhaps no more striking than in the earlier scenes of this play or in Brisk's courtship of Saviolina. We can hardly with confidence say more than that in the worship of woman growing out of chivalry, an elaboration of dress and manners as suitable for winning her favor became customary in the Renaissance and was often emphasized by gallants with an affectation that reminds us of rules of love in the Middle Ages. The statement of Amorphus that the lover must "be presently answerable to any hourly or half-hourly change in his mistress's revolution" gives the fundamental law of a lover's devotion to his mistress in court of love poetry. In *The Court of Love* there are such expressions as

> Thou mayst no wyse hit taken to disdayn,
> To put thee humbly at her ordinaunce (ll. 374 f.),

and

> Give her sovereintee,
> Her appetyt folow in all degree (ll. 433 f.).

Similar expressions occur in Ovid and in most of the medieval writers on love. The "scholar's haviour" is of course the important thing. In *The Court of Love,* again, the eleventh statute demands that the lover know signs with eye and finger, soft smiles, low coughs, and sighs—conventions of flirtation which are emphasized in the prizes of *Cynthia's Revels.* The eighteenth statute of the same poem urges that the lover

> Be jolif, fresh, and fete, with thinges newe,
> Courtly with maner, this is all thy due,
> Gentill of port, and loving clenlinesse (ll. 473 ff.).

Le Roman de la Rose is more explicit, mentioning good dress, merriment, riding, pursuit of arms, singing, dancing, playing musical instruments, making "songes and complayntes," bestowing gifts, etc. (ll. 2254 ff. of the Chaucerian translation), so that we have here authority for all the devices in the courtship of Brisk and of the gallants in *Cynthia's Revels.* But the Italian courtesy books, which probably influenced Elizabethan customs far more than did the laws of chivalry, give much the same rules of gallantry. Castiglione, for example, mentions practically all the points of *Le Roman de la Rose,* and a great many more, though he is careful to condemn excesses and affectation.[1] It is sufficiently obvious, however, that Jonson needed only to go to life to get the whole foundation for this part of his satire.

In the weapons and the prizes of the duello we have a type of symbolism popular in a number of court of love poems. The four allegorical weapons of *Cynthia's Revels*—the Bare Accost, the Better Regard, the Solemn Address, and the Perfect Close—as parodies of modes of behavior in courtship recall the personified graces of manner in the court of love of *Le Roman de la Rose,* found frequently elsewhere in court of love poetry. They are especially suggestive of Bel Acueil, Dous Regart, Dous Parler, etc. The prizes in *Cynthia's Revels* are "two wall-eyes in a face forced," "a face favorably simpering, with a fan waving," "two lips wagging, and never a wise word," "a wring by the hand, with a banquet in a corner." Besides, members of the court make wagers of a "Discretion." Like symbolism is found, according to Mr. Neilson's analyses, in the *Chastel d'Amors,* where proverbs serve as arrows, evasions as bucklers, etc., and less extensively in *Li Fablel dou Dieu d'Amours,* where "ditches were of sighs, the water was lovers' tears," and youths in the palace played at chess with kisses for prizes. In Jean de Condé's *La Messe des Oisiaus,* also, there is an account of a banquet at the court of Venus, which is clearly of the same genre as the prizes in *Cynthia's Revels.* It is described in part by Professor Neilson as follows (p. 68): "The courses consisted of glances, smiles, and the like. . . . There was an *entremets* of sighs and complaints. . . . Next came roasted *ramprones* with sauce of jealousy, and prayers with sauce of tears. Then were given to the ladies vessels filled with fair replies and sweet favors. . . . Then the servants brought in a course to appease the fever of love,—embrace and kisses," etc. A very similar banquet occurs in *Li Dis de la Fontaine d'Amours.*

[1]But *The Courtier* itself, it will be remembered, is cast in the form of one of the set discussions associated with the court of love customs.

A few other details from this duello scene that are possibly related to the court of love may be mentioned. The statement to the citizen that husbands are not allowed at the assembly is obviously sufficiently true to the spirit of all medieval rules of love, and the fact that Downfall belongs to the citizen class makes his exclusion all the more appropriate, as villains were commonly denied entrance to the court of love.[1] The old debate of clerk versus knight that Professor Neilson calls attention to as occurring so frequently in the early love poetry, also finds an echo, perhaps, in Jonson's play, where Crites, the scholar, aided by Mercury, the god of wit, is set in opposition to courtiers, or knights, who attempt to disgrace him. The conflict between the two ideals is perennial. It is seen in various Italian courtesy books, in *Sapho and Phao* (I, 2 and 3), and between scholar and soldier on the one hand and courtier on the other in *The Coblers Prophesie.* The use of color, again, is stressed in court of love poetry, but colors in medieval times are too general in their significance to have any especial meaning for the idea of giving the dor by change of colors.[2] This part of Jonson's scene scarcely does more, perhaps, than point out the elaboration and emphasis given to such trifles among the courtly in the closing years of the sixteenth century.

To the classic conception of Eros and Anteros is due the masking of Cupid as Anteros before Diana in V, 3. The contrast takes a different form in the court of love poems but one rather kindred in spirit. In *Le Roman de la Rose* Cupid has two types of arrows in his quiver, one favorable and one unfavorable to true love. It is a familiar conception, as Professor Neilson points out (p. 54). A similar treatment is that of the exchange of arrows between Love and Death and Cupid's amazement at the result of his shafts.[3] Out of such conceptions doubtless springs the motive in *Cynthia's Revels* of Cupid's inability to wound with arrows of love those who have drunk of the Fountain of Self-Love

[1]Cf. *The Romaunt of the Rose*, ll. 1998 ff. and Neilson, pp. 24 and 36.

[2]In *Love's Labour's Lost* (V, 2) the ladies, masked, change favors, so that each of the lovers, also disguised, courts the wrong lady and is put to shame.

[3]Cf. Barnfield's *Affectionate Shepherd.* Neilson (pp. 261, 262) traces the idea to Lemaire des Belges.

and his chagrin at his failure.[1] Mercury twits him by saying that it was ominous for him to assume the name of Anteros, since the properties of his arrows were apparently changed to suit the character he personated. In *Le Roman de la Rose* one of the arrows unfavorable to love is named Orgueil, or Pride.

Finally, *Cynthia's Revels* closes with a palinode that is an adaptation of the English ritual. Such parodies were usual, of course, but the parody of all religious rites was especially associated with the praise of love and the worship of Venus in the court of love poetry—for example, the matins in *The Court of Love.* Jonson's palinode does not deal with love, however, and the immediate suggestion for it perhaps did not come from court of love poetry.

In regard to the challenge which Amorphus reads in V, 2, Gifford comments: "This *bill* is a parody on one of the licences formerly granted by *masters* of defence to their pupils, when they were supposed to be properly qualified for taking either of their three degrees in the fencing-school, viz., a *master's,* a *provost's,* or a *scholar's:* indeed, the whole of this scene is a burlesque imitation of these public trials of skill in the 'noble science of defence' " (p. 186). Toward the close of the sixteenth century several famous works on fencing were translated into English, especially Grassi's *True Arte of Defence;* and Saviolo's *Practise* appeared in 1595. The seven modes of giving the lie in *As You Like It* (V, 4) are usually connected with Saviolo's work. This scene in Shakespeare's play, with its parody of the procedure of fencing and its mockery of technical terms, as in the Retort Courteous, the Countercheck Quarrelsome, etc., is a forerunner of Jonson's scene.[2] *The Old Law,* again, in III, 2, makes use of the duello for satire on rivalry in the gallantries of courtship, and on account of the probability that the play in some form was acted in 1599 and hence the possibility that this scene preceded *Cynthia's Revels,* I shall point out some likenesses. Lysander, the old husband in *The Old Law,* jealous of his wife's courtly young lovers,

[1]Cf. p. 242 *infra* for his inability to wound Crites and Arete.

[2]Miss Marietta Neff of the University of Chicago, in a paper written at my suggestion on the court of love influence on *Cynthia's Revels,* first called my attention to this. It is noted by Fleay, *Biog. Chron. Eng. Drama,* Vol. I, p. 365. Miss Neff pointed out, also, some of the parallels between Jonson's play and court of love poetry. I make this general acknowledgment, for at this time it is impossible for me to tell just what details I may owe to her.

engages masters for dancing, riding, and fencing, and devotes his time to the acquirement of gallant accomplishments. While he is at practice with the dancing-master, his rivals appear, and Lysander challenges them,

> Bring forth the weapons, we shall find you play;
>
> . . . .
>
> And these the weapons, drinking, fencing, dancing.

Lysander plays the three gallants in turn, they choosing their weapons, and overthrows each. The drinking suggests the drinking bout of *Every Man out,* and the dancing is nearest to the duello of *Cynthia's Revels* in the display of accomplishments. In these bouts at drinking and dancing, as in *Cynthia's Revels,* duelling terms are used for the whole procedure, and those who stand by comment on the antagonists much as the courtiers of *Cynthia's Revels* do. There are naturally a number of unimportant verbal resemblances between the two scenes, but a few parallels are more significant. For example, when Amorphus is given the dor at the end, Anaides exclaims, "Heart of my blood, Amorphus, what have you done? stuck a disgrace upon us all, and at your last weapon. . . . D—n me, if he have not eternally undone himself in court, and discountenanced us" (pp. 193 f.). In *The Old Law,* also, the scene concludes with the heaviest disgrace of the series. When Lysander proffers Simonides the final glass in the drinking bout, saying "Here's long-sword, your last weapon," and Simonides is forced to beg off, the First Courtier says, "Why, how now, Sim? bear up, thou shamest us all, else," and the Second Courtier cries, "Out! the disgrace of drinkers!"[1]

Akin to the court of love influence on Jonson's play is that of the mythological comedy which became popular in the last quarter of the sixteenth century, and which undoubtedly furnished a strong impulse toward Jonson's use of allegory and mythology in *Cynthia's Revels.* The presence of gods interfering in the affairs of men is a part of the court of love machinery that probably in-

[1]In *The Masque of Flowers,* 1614, there is a double antimasque in the form of a duel between Silenus and Kawasha, "tried at two weapons, at song and at dance," Silenus maintaining that "wine is more worthy than tobacco." Cf. Evans, *English Masques,* pp. 100 ff. Here we meet Jonson's duello in a classic form, the contest in song. Similar in spirit, of course, was the pastoral contest in song. In *Midas* (IV, 1), a play that is akin to *Cynthia's Revels* in a number of features, there is a contest between Pan and Apollo in singing love songs.

fluenced Jonson, but the convention is even more conspicuous in this group of mythological plays. The type of play doubtless arose in part from the popularity of pageant and masque, for in both, mythological figures early became prominent and readily assumed symbolic significance through their appropriateness to a special occasion. A second important element in such pageantry was the interest in cults of love. Typical instances of how the game of love became the central theme of disguisings and pageants long before the romantic drama of love developed may be given. Thus, as early as 1501, in the "disguisings" in celebration of the marriage of Prince Arthur, Hope and Desire appear "as Ambassadors from Knights of the Mount of Love" unto certain ladies enclosed in a castle, and are repulsed; the knights themselves appear and win the ladies by assaulting the castle; and the eight ladies dance, four in Spanish and four in English garb.[1] The friendly group of English and Spanish ladies here furnishes an interesting contrast to the hostile groups of English and Spanish knights balanced in *The Three Lords and Three Ladies of London* towards the end of the century. Again, in a tournament held at the coronation of Henry VIII, there are knights of Pallas serving the king, who are challenged by knights of Diana "come to feats of armes, for the love of ladies."[2] In 1527, a masque of eight boys led by Cupid and Plutus, and eight maidens, or goddesses, with Mercury as presenter, was shown before the king.[3] The presence of Cupid and Mercury, the latter as messenger of Jupiter and presenter of the masque, reveals the conventionality of Jonson's mythological machinery in the masques of *Cynthia's Revels*. Indeed, Mercury, Venus, Cupid, Diana, and Pallas, so frequently met in court of love poems, are met in many sixteenth century masques as conventional figures symbolizing conceptions of the cult of love.[4] Towards the middle of Elizabeth's reign apparently,

[1]See Collier, *English Dramatic Poetry*, Vol. I, pp. 58 ff. Brotanek, *Die englischen Maskenspiele*, pp. 26 ff. and 325 f., points out a number of parallels in sixteenth century entertainments, and traces the extension of the idea of the siege.

[2]See Traill, *Social England*, Vol. III, p. 157.

[3]The masque is described by Einstein, *The Italian Renaissance in England*, pp. 77, 78. Prof. Einstein draws his account from Brewer's *Henry VIII*.

[4]Cf. Collier, *English Dramatic Poetry*, Vol. I, pp. 70, 183, etc.; Brotanek, *Die englischen Maskenspiele*, pp. 49 ff.; Feuillerat, *Documents relating to the Office of the Revels* (see index); etc.

when playwrights were seeking far and wide something fresh for their hybrid plays, and were willing to combine any elements, as we see in *Cambises,* the plays written for the court naturally began to make use of whatever features were popular with the courtiers. Thus mythological figures, flattery of the Queen or great nobles, as in the masque, and themes of pastoral love or of the more formal courtly love, naturally turning often toward conventions of courts of love, with which classic characters were already associated, were readily combined to form the mythological comedy.

The real prominence of the mythological comedy is due to Lyly. Indeed, the indications of an interest in this type of play before Lyly are slight. The *Narcissus* of 1572 already mentioned has a title that would suggest a mythological play dealing primarily, perhaps, with the fashionable cults of idealized love.[1] But there could scarcely have been many plays of the type before 1580. Apparently the plays that had the vogue at this period were drawn from the classics, from the heroic romance, or, according to Gosson, from the French and the Italian novel and play. But the titles that have come down to us from this time, as well as the few surviving plays, indicate that even the drama dealing with classic themes was not mythological or symbolic, though doubtless it was usually romantic.

Two plays, *The Arraignment of Paris* and *The Rare Triumphs of Love and Fortune,* seem to be independent of Lyly if not earlier. They both represent discord among the gods, naturally a favorite theme of the mythological plays on account of the influence of classic epics, and each play also has the trial form, a device used in *Cynthia's Revels. The Arraignment of Paris* may be earlier than any of Lyly's mythological comedies.[2] At any rate, it lacks the satiric element that belongs to most of the later mythological plays. The symbolic use of mythological characters in order to flatter Elizabeth—though here, as in Gascoigne's masque at Kenilworth, she is not Diana but the favorite of Diana;

[1]The thunder and lightning and the hunting of the fox, however,—the only details given in the accounts of the play (Feuillerat, *Documents relating to the Office of the Revels in the Time of Queen Elizabeth,* pp. 141, 142),—do not suggest the type of play that we are dealing with.

[2]According to the latest authorities, Professors Bond and Feuillerat, only *Sapho and Phao* among Lyly's mythological comedies could be as early as *The Arraignment of Paris,* and of all Lyly's plays this seems to me least like Peele's.

the presence of Mercury as a messenger; the suggestion of echo in the song of Thestylis with its "shepherds' echo" (III, 2); the numerous songs, pageants, and other masque-like elements; the Lucianic quarrels of the goddesses (II, 1); and the hint of conflicting ideals in love, all mark the vague kinship between Peele's play and *Cynthia's Revels* as a type of court drama. *The Arraignment of Paris* is closer still to Lyly's plays than to *Cynthia's Revels* on account of the presence of pastoral elements.

In *The Rare Triumphs,* where love is the primary theme, the interest in classic and pastoral themes is not so evident. To all appearances this play has neither symbolic flattery nor strongly marked allegory, but it is still interesting because of its rather independent use of mythological elements in a somewhat conventional form. The play combines a romantic love story with astrological motives and a contest of the gods, a combination not unlike that of Lyly's *Woman in the Moon.* In *The Rare Triumphs,* as a result of the dispute among the gods, Mercury is dispatched to bring "the ghosts of them that Love and Fortune slew." Though these shades appear only in dumb-show, the function of Mercury here is the same as in *Cynthia's Revels,* where he summons Echo to earth to lament her fate and utter her love. At the end of *The Rare Triumphs* Mercury is sent as an agent to effect the union of the lovers. But the presence of Mercury in both plays of course has little significance. Jonson in the induction to *Cynthia's Revels* comments on the popularity of Mercury as a stage figure. "Take any of our play-books without a Cupid or a Mercury in it," says the Third Child, "and burn it for an heretic in poetry."

The plays of Lyly and the mythological plays that follow him make use of allegory for a study of manners, and so they become of vital importance for Jonson. Personally Lyly must have been inclined to this type of play through his interest in the classics, through his position as a writer for the court and, consequently, his attention to pageantry and symbolism, and finally through a bent toward a combination of courtly elegance with didacticism and satire as shown in *Euphues.* For most of his plays Lyly uses mythological characters with an allegorical meaning. In *Sapho and Phao,* Cupid, Venus, and Vulcan appear; in *Gallathea,* Cupid, Venus, Diana, and Neptune; in *Endimion,* Cynthia and deities of second rank; in *Midas,* Apollo, Pan, and Bacchus; in *The Woman in the Moon,* Mercury, Venus, Cupid, etc.; and in *Love's Metamorphosis,* Cupid and Ceres. Comment has already been made on *The Woman in the Moon* as embodying studies in character inclination which prepare for the humour types.[1] But in all these plays there is a tendency to the portrayal of character under a single abstraction, of which the name is often significant. This is especially true of Lyly's women. Thus in his plays the mythological machinery is used as a setting for a subtle study in manners, and in spite of their romantic threads and their masque-like features, his comedies show a strong satirical vein. It is this combination of mythological elements with satire on manners that is the notable characteristic of *Cynthia's Revels.*

The grouping of Lyly's characters, also, suggests *Cynthia's Revels* strongly. The studies of detached individuals in *Every Man out* are replaced in *Cynthia's Revels* by studies of fairly compact groups—a group of gallants bound together by their social aims, tastes, and customs, and a similar group of women who are complements of each other as representatives of follies. Men had been grouped in Jonson's earlier plays, though less harmoniously, but *Cynthia's Revels* gives us his first satire on sets of fashionable women. The suggestion for such grouping Jonson may have owed to Lyly. Lyly's plays lack the satire on gallants and their frivolities that Jonson develops in his earlier comedies; the great part of Lyly's satire is directed against women. In his delineation of women with cultivated manners but with strong individual inclinations to fickleness, scorn, whimsicality, pride in wit, in fact, all the qualities appropriate to women who give their attention to the flirtations of courtly love, Lyly's plays stand fairly isolated in the drama before *Cynthia's Revels.* His effective device of setting women in contrast through the attention of each to some particular fancy or inclination, while at the same time they remain united in aim and in the worship of their common fashions and frivolities, shows just the art of Jonson's play. The influence of the medieval imagination thus continues in the two men. Distinctions among the varied abstractions that make up well unified groups in the allegory of the Middle Ages are clear enough,

[1]Cf. pp. 73, 74 *supra.* In some respects, also, Pandora under the influence of Luna corresponds to Phantaste, and under the influence of Jupiter to Philautia.

whether these groups are the Seven Deadly Sins, the Daughters of God, personifications with such names as Bel Acueil in court of love poetry, or the virtues of Spenser's *Faerie Queene.*

The ladies and gallants of Cynthia's court in *Endimion, ca.* 1586, are not so consistently grouped in their entries and their dialogues as are those of *Cynthia's Revels.* In *Endimion* the most obvious division is into pairs of men or women as associates or friends, the familiar device of the romantic play. There are, however, five men connected with the court, and a group of five women balanced against them. The scornful Semele, in particular, is suggestive of the scorn that springs from self-love in Philautia. Tellus, with her passion and her crafty vengeance, and the waiting women, Scintilla and Favilla, with their jealousy and their sharpness of tongue, are more in the vein of Jonson's general satire on women. The men of *Endimion* show little kinship to those of Jonson's play except in the relation of lover to mistress as fixed by court of love ideals. Eumenides is obsequious and flattering in the presence of his lady, Semele, and suffers with true lover-like humility from her pert wit and affected scorn. Endimion is naturally full of despair in his love for the divine Cynthia. The exalted love of Endimion for Cynthia is akin in spirit to the noble devotion of Crites to Arete, and contrasts with the more sensual or artificial passion of the other characters in the two plays. Possibly the allegory of both Lyly and Jonson involves the distinction between the spiritualizing power of true chivalric love and the decay of that love among its unworthy followers.[1] But perhaps the most interesting link between *Endimion* and *Cynthia's Revels* is the flattery of the Queen through the allegory connected with Cynthia. Of course such flattery of Elizabeth is frequent enough in the period, but Lyly's method of treatment is closest to Jonson's. Both plays contain obvious allusions to the isolation of the Maiden Queen in rank, wisdom, virtue, etc., and in both Cynthia appears at the end as a judge and righter of wrongs. The chief distinction is that Jonson's Cynthia is more the queen than the goddess, while in Lyly's Cynthia the attributes

[1]Mr. Long in *Mod. Lang. Publ.*, March, 1909, pp. 164 ff., develops practically this idea. Bond, *Works of Lyly,* Vol. III, pp. 83 and 103, notes the possibility of such allegory but slights it.

of the moon goddess prevail. In both plays, also, a magical fountain appears as part of the machinery.[1]

The pastoral and silvan groups of *Midas, Gallathea, Love's Metamorphosis,* and *The Woman in the Moon,* we may disregard; only the courtly groups are significant for Jonson's plays. In *Midas* the three courtiers who are contrasted as humour types are grouped as councillors of Midas. They do not, however, like the gallants of *Cynthia's Revels,* represent different types of fashionable follies; their bents are for gold, for war, and for love. The court women are more suggestive of the women of *Cynthia's Revels.* Sophronia in name and in character is akin to the virtuous Arete. She stands for the higher ideals of the true court life, though she does not hold aloof from the unworthy members of the court as Arete does. There is a group of four shallow court ladies: Suavia, whose chief interest is love; Amerulla, fond of stories, and accused of being bitter and spiteful; Camilla, given to dancing; and Cælia, who loves singing. In the variety of their inclinations, in the common bent of all except Cælia toward courtship, and in their frank self-analysis, the group is suggestive of the four court nymphs in *Cynthia's Revels.* The scene (III, 3) given to the pastimes of the women, story telling and discussion of love, is much in the manner of *Cynthia's Revels.* In I, 2, Cælia's page gives a humorous account of his mistress with special satire on her dress and ornaments, and the discussion here between the pages of a man and a woman recalls that in *Cynthia's Revels* between Mercury and Cupid, one serving a gallant and the other a lady, though Lyly's treatment is more burlesque. The meeting of Pipenetta and the two pages is slightly suggestive of the association of the pages Morus and Prosaites in *Cynthia's Revels* with Gelaia, who is disguised as a page.

The whole spirit of the court in *Midas* is revealed in the strictures of Martius, lover of war, on Eristus, a devotee of courtship and gallantry, and on Mellacrites, a lover of money (II, 1, ll. 57 ff.):

[1]Mr. Long's interpretation of the allegory in *Endimion* would perhaps make the play more closely akin to *Cynthia's Revels* than I have indicated. The characters, according to his interpretation of their allegorical significance as vices and virtues, would in several cases correspond to those of Jonson's play.

That greedines of *Mellacrites*, whose heart-stringes are made of *Plutus* purse-stringes, hath made *Mydas* a lumpe of earth, that should be a god on earth; and thy effeminate minde *Eristus*, whose eyes are stitcht on *Cœlias* face, and thoughts gyude to her beautie, hath bredde in all the court such a tender wantonnes, that nothing is thoght of but loue, a passion proceeding of beastly lust, and coloured with a courtlie name of loue. . . . Captaines . . . must account it more honorable, in the court to be a cowarde, so rich and amorus, than in a campe to be valiant, if poore and maimed. He is more fauoured that pricks his finger with his mistres needle, then hee that breakes his launce on his enemies face: and he that hath his mouth full of fair words, than he that hath his bodie ful of deep scarres. If one be olde, & haue siluer haires on his beard, so he haue golden ruddocks in his bagges, he must be wise and honourable. If young and haue curled locks on his head, amarous glaunces with his eyes, smooth speeches in his mouth, euerie Ladies lap shalbe his pillow, euery Ladies face his glasse, euery Ladies eare a sheath for his flatteries. . . . Hee is the man, that being let bloud caries his arme in a scarfe of his mistres fauour, not he that beares his legge on a stilt for his Countries safetie.

Sophronia, while admitting the charges of Martius, rebukes his passion for war, and expresses her own ideals thus (II, 1, ll. 104 ff.):

Let Phrygia be an example of chastitie, not luste; liberalitie, not couetousnes; valor, not tyrannie. I wish not your bodies banisht, but your mindes, that my father and your king may be our honor, and the worlds wonder. And thou, *Cœlia*, and all you Ladies, learn this of *Sophronia*, that beautie in a minute is both a blossome and a blast: Loue, a worme which seeming to liue in the eye, dies in the hart. You be all yong, and faire, endeuor all to be wise & vertuous.

In *Cynthia's Revels* (III, 2) Crites gives an analysis of the types that haunt the court, while Arete urges patience on the ground that Cynthia will sweep her court clean of all the follies that prevail. There are few resemblances of detail between the situations in the two plays, but the general contrast between the two ideals of courtly life is similar. The wise Sophronia, the types of frivolous women, the courtiers with their varied humours, the pages, the light jests and pastimes, the keen interest in courtship, the countercurrent of seriousness, and the classic deities determining the course of the action, furnish a combination of characters and motives akin to that of *Cynthia's Revels.*

In *Sapho and Phao* there is another grouping of characters and another combination of motives showing a vague kinship to

Cynthia's Revels. The gods controlling human affairs; the pages; the contrast between scholar and courtier, with its dim foreshadowing of that between Crites and the gallants of Jonson's plays; courtly love as the central interest; the rules that Sybilla, instructress in love, gives Phao for winning the love of women; the presence of Cupid armed with arrows that inspire love and some that inspire disdain; and the group of six court ladies, with their discussions of love and coquetry, their self-analysis, and their affectation, pride, and flippancy, all belong to the conventions of the narrower group of mythological comedies which includes *Cynthia's Revels.*

The last of Lyly's plays to be considered is *Gallathea,* which shows a different sort of resemblance to *Cynthia's Revels.* In *Gallathea* Cupid comes to the court of Diana in disguise to practice on her nymphs, and finally is discovered, rebuked, and punished. In *Cynthia's Revels* Cupid's invasion of Diana's court is treated similarly except that instead of being punished the presumptuous god is banished. Spenser takes up this motive in *The Faerie Queene* (Bk. III, Canto vi), but does not carry it to the same conclusion. When Cupid has been released in *Gallathea,* Venus says, "*Diana* cannot forbid him to wounde," and Diana replies, "Yes, chastitie is not within the leuell of his bowe" (V, 3, ll. 79, 80). In *Cynthia's Revels,* Cupid, having failed to wound those who have drunk of the Fountain of Self-Love, tries the virtue of his arrows on Crites, and again fails. Mercury explains to the incredulous Cupid, "Arete's favour makes any one shot-proof against thee, Cupid" (V, 3, p. 201). The idea here is very suggestive of the immunity of the virtuous in *The Faithful Shepherdess* and *Comus.*

Outside of Lyly's work there are a few plays with mythological elements that continue the study of manners in an allegorical framework. Such are *The Coblers Prophesie, Summer's Last Will and Testament, Histriomastix,* and *Old Fortunatus.* All four of these are more or less satirical, and represent the conflict of vice and virtue. Besides the general theme and plan, each one shows in some details a slight similarity to *Cynthia's Revels. Summer's Last Will and Testament* and *Histriomastix* need not be taken up here; a few minor resemblances between these plays and *Cynthia's Revels* are discussed later in other connections. *Old*

Fortunatus shows the following vague resemblances to Jonson's play, besides the fact that both open with an echo scene. The conflict between vice and virtue which underlies *Cynthia's Revels* is in Dekker's play added to the Fortunatus legend. At the end of IV, 1, indeed, Dekker's personified virtue is several times addressed as Arete, and like Jonson's Arete she is called divine.[1] Both are scorned and neglected. The allegory embodied in Fortunatus of an undeserving man's being endowed by Fortune with wealth appears with Jonson in Argurion's love of Asotus. Asotus's distribution of jewels and trinkets among the gallants of the court (IV, 1) is paralleled in *Old Fortunatus* by Andelocia's gifts of jewels and money at the court of England (III, 1). In fact, there are a few details of *Cynthia's Revels* in which Jonson seems to be glancing directly at the Fortunatus story. When Amorphus and Asotus exchange hats (I, 1), Amorphus tells how his hat, which Asotus regards ruefully because of its dilapidation, was secured in Russia and has marvelous magical powers. The wishing hat of Fortunatus, which is described as an insignificant looking "coarse felt hat" (II, 1, p. 319 and II, 2, p. 331), has been stolen out of Babylon.[2] In connection with these details certain general resemblances in character types may be mentioned. Fortunatus is the traveler who delights to visit strange lands, as Amorphus is the pretended traveler, praising travel and boasting of incredible experiences. The two characters are quite dissimilar, however. Agripyne represents the type of court lady that we find in Philautia and Phantaste. She is interested in discussions of love like those of the academies (III, 1) and is scornful and pitiless toward her lovers. In III, 1 (p. 340) she characterizes the typical court lover much as Jonson does in *Cynthia's Revels.* Agripyne says of women (pp. 340 f.): "Our glory is to hear men sigh whilst we smile, to kill them with a frown, to strike them dead with a sharp eye, to make you this day wear a feather, and tomorrow a sick nightcap. Oh, why this is rare, there's a certain deity in this, when a lady by the magic of her looks, can change a man into twenty shapes." Philautia wishes for "a little more command and

[1]Cf. *Cynthia's Revels,* III, 2, p. 169, and *Old Fortunatus,* pp. 313, 360 f. The page references for Dekker's play are to the volume of Dekker in the Mermaid Series.

[2]In the older form of the Fortunatus story, waters with magical power, suggestive of the fountain of Narcissus, play a part.

sovereignty . . . as if there were no other heaven but in my smile, nor other hell but in my frown." Phantaste would affect no lovers, except that she might "take pride in tormenting the poor wretches," but she wishes to "prove all manner of suitors, of all humours, and of all complexions" (IV, 1, p. 173).

The Coblers Prophesie, already mentioned in connection with *The Case is Altered* as important in the development of the stage cobbler, has a few parallels to *Cynthia's Revels.* At the opening of *The Coblers Prophesie* Mercury, on an errand from Jove, meets Ceres, as he encounters Cupid in *Cynthia's Revels.* To Ceres he explains that a synod of the gods has been called to consider the evils that prevail in Bœotia, for Venus, or Lust, is followed by all, Mars himself has become a reveler, and Cynthia bewails her isolation in virtue. The play then proceeds to picture conditions in Bœotia, presenting certain vicious types in contrast with virtuous types. The treatment of neglected virtue centers around the neglect of war, and thus the soldier is the principal type of virtue. The scholar is secondary, but also neglected. Opposed to the soldier and the scholar is the courtier type. The "little God" Contempt (I, 2, l. 216), or Olygoros as the scholar calls him, taking the name Content, holds sway over the characters who represent evil. This supremacy of Contempt is similar in spirit to the prevalence of self-love in the evil court group of *Cynthia's Revels* as a result of drinking of the Fountain of Self-Love. Besides the court of the Duke in *The Coblers Prophesie,* there is an especial establishment of Venus, which is entered by the "dore of Dalliance" (III, 1, l. 41) and where there is a group of attendants, Follie, Nicenes, Newfangle, Dalliance, and Iealozie (III, 3), similar in conception to Moria, Phantaste, Hedon, etc. of *Cynthia's Revels.* The court of Venus in *The Coblers Prophesie* is nearer to the court of love than is the group of Jonson's play, but the spirit that prevails in the court of Venus is that of the evil court in *Cynthia's Revels.* "Wiliness, wrong and wantonnes" are "at libertie" (III, 3, ll. 65 f.). Mars is as trim as a morris dancer, and Venus devotes herself to dress, diet, wantonness, fancifulness, etc. In the reform of the Duke's court, a priest offers a prayer (V, 4) pledging the whole court to entertain humility, obedience, love, and chastity in the place of pride, presumption, contempt, and lust. The four virtues opposed to the four vices suggest the balance of four virtues against four vices that is fundamental throughout *Cynthia's Revels.* There is in *The Coblers Prophesie*, also, an echo scene (II, 1) in which the cobbler pursues Echo as Amorphus does in *Cynthia's Revels.*

The kinship of this whole group of mythological plays including *Cynthia's Revels* does not seem to be accidental, but apparently shows a recognition on the part of the dramatists of certain rules and limitations, themes and characters, as appropriate to the type. Perhaps if we had the bulk of the dramatic work produced in the last quarter of the sixteenth century, the plays of this type would shade into each other with less perceptible differences, and the evolution would be more obvious. The plays that have been taken up also show a development of literary devices—medieval allegory of courtship, court of love conventions, mythological machinery, etc.—which led to a more and more successful satire on the special forms of social evils dealt with. These plays emphasize, moreover, the fact that, in a period when not all the resources of dramatic satire had yet been realized, dramatists, even masters like Jonson, fell back upon the art, the technique, the framework that had already proved successful.

The meeting of Mercury and Cupid, though it has been compared with the opening of some of the mythological plays, is drawn from Lucian, as Gifford points out. Its chief function is to allow Cupid and Mercury to engage in a wit combat over each other's failings and vices.[1] The device of echo, which occurs in a number of the mythological plays, is of course general. It is found in *The Old Wives' Tale* (ll. 482 ff.); *The Wounds of Civil War* (Hazlitt's *Dodsley,* Vol. VII, p. 148); *The Maid's Metamorphosis* (IV, 1); the second day's entertainment at Kenilworth (*Poems of Gascoigne,* Vol. II, pp. 96 ff.); *The Entertainment at Elvetham,* 1591 (*Works of Lyly,* ed. Bond, Vol. I, pp. 441 ff.); Barnfield's *Cynthia. With Certaine Sonnets,* Sonnet 13; Watson's *Hekatompathia,* 25, and *Tears of Fancie,* 29; Breton's "A Report Song," in *England's Helicon* (p. 243); and "Philisides and Echo" in

[1]One passage in this dialogue between the two gods had already been used by Marston in a Lucianic satire of *Pygmalion's Image and Certain Satires.* Cupid says to Mercury in *Cynthia's Revels* (I, 1), "Venus, at the same time, but stooped to embrace you, and, to speak by metaphor, you borrowed a girdle of hers, as you did Jove's sceptre," etc. Cf. Marston, Satire V, ll. 23-28.

Book II of Sidney's *Arcadia.*[1] Jonson's use of echo in *Cynthia's Revels* has no connection with the play. It seems to be a masque-like element introduced on account of the great popularity of echo songs and scenes at the period. Indeed, he satirizes his own device as the particular fad of the puppet-show. When Amorphus pursues Echo, Mercury remark (I, 1), "I guessed it should be some travelling motion pursued Echo so."

In dealing with the affected graces and accomplishments, the pastimes and fads, of the courtly, Jonson has naturally utilized the allegorical machinery that harmonized with the traditions and customs of fashionable life; but, while the framework of *Cynthia's Revels* and the representation of the court are drawn from courtly literature, Jonson has turned to philosophical ideas for the broad moral and social phases of his treatment, and the heart of his play—the grouping of characters and the conflict between vice and virtue—presents a study of manners organized not for the surface fancy of poetry but as a formal treatment of ethical and social qualities. Undoubtedly his grouping and pairing of vices and virtues is based on accepted systems in ethical treatises, though the narrowing of his field to court life, his conception of humours as influencing the individual, and his attempt to satirize concrete follies of his own day, would serve to modify any system.

The ultimate source of Jonson's ethical ideas must have been Aristotle. Indeed, to a certain extent Jonson was probably influenced directly by the *Nicomachean Ethics.* The kinship appears most clearly in the two masques of *Cynthia's Revels,* where the vices of the court are disguised as virtues, the basis of Jonson's treatment being the Aristotelian conception of vice as the excess of what in the mean state is a virtue. In the long sketch of Crites, also, (II, 1) there is decided emphasis on the Aristotelian mean in various phases of the character, in humours, courage, manners, etc. To another conception of Aristotle Jonson may have been indebted for the general basis of his division into groups. In the two masques the four court nymphs are grouped as the "four

[1]Erasmus also employed the device in his *Colloquies.* For further use of echo cf. Ward, *Hist. Eng. Dram. Lit.*, Vol. I, p. 417; Greg, *Pastoral Poetry*, etc., pp. 199, 343, and 344, n. 1. In *Mod. Lang. Publ.*, Vol. X, p. 269, there is reference to an echo song in *Courtlie Controversie of Cupid's Cautels.* The use of echo was very frequent in the early part of the seventeenth century also.

cardinal virtues, upon which the whole frame of the court doth move," and the four gallants as the "four cardinal properties, without which the body of compliment moveth not" (V, 3, p. 199), the one representing abstract qualities of character and the other the qualities as exhibited in action. As these virtues and properties are simply the mean of the vices represented in the nymphs and courtiers of the play, this division suggests that the same distinction was intended in the allegory of the general plot. In only one case, however, do Jonson's male and female characters exactly correspond. Phronesis, Prudence, one of Cynthia's nymphs, stands for the abstract quality, while Phronimus, mentioned as belonging to Cynthia's court (III, 2, p. 167), is the man prudent in action.[1] Though Aristotle makes no attempt to distinguish by name the moral states from the corresponding activities, he shows an obvious tendency to look at vices and virtues from the dual point of view of character and activity. Jonson's basis of division is suggested in the following passages of the *Ethics,* for example:

There remains what I may call the practical life of the rational part *of Man's being.* But the rational part is twofold. . . . The practical life too may be conceived of in two ways, *viz., either as a moral state, or as a moral activity*: but we must understand by it the life of activity, as this seems to be the truer form of the conception (*Ethics,* Bk. I, Chap. 6, Welldon's translation, pp. 15, 16).

In a word moral states are the results of activities corresponding to the moral states themselves. It is our duty therefore to give a certain character to the activities, as the moral states depend upon the differences of the activities (II, 1, p. 36).

If then the virtues are neither emotions nor faculties, it remains that they must be moral states (II, 4, p. 44).

For it would seem that the moral purpose is most closely related to virtue, and is a better criterion of character than actions themselves are (III, 4, p. 65).

Again, as the good may be either an activity or a moral state, etc. (VII, 13, p. 236).

As in the case of the virtues it is sometimes a moral state, and at other times an activity, which entitles people to be described as good, so is it also in the case of friendship or love (VIII, 6, p. 255).

[1]The nomenclature here hints at a reason for Jonson's distribution of parts to women as well as men, aside from the need of both sexes in his treatment of courtly love and follies. The Greek names for abstractions are feminine, and this fact may have suggested the groups of women contrasted with groups of men in *Cynthia's Revels.*

In the individual abstractions of *Cynthia's Revels,* the suggestions of Aristotle are to be found in the similarity of conception rather than in the use of Aristotelian names. Jonson's characters, though abstractions, are based on living types, and fresh names in preference to the well known terms of philosophy would appeal to him as indicating the individuality of the character. Thus, while Jonson's vices are clearly the excess of qualities that appear as virtues in the masques, the only exact correspondence between his characters and Aristotle's ethical qualities is found in Asotus, the Prodigal, who masques as the liberal man. In the *Ethics* (II, 7), prodigality, Asotia, is treated as the excess of liberality. Hedon, whose name Jonson translates by Voluptuous, bears as a virtue the name Eupathes, and the description of Eupathes (quoted p. 252 *infra*) may be compared with what Aristotle says of bodily pleasure (VII, 14, p. 241): "Now bodily goods admit of excess, and vice consists in pursuing the excess, not in pursuing the necessary pleasures; for everybody finds a certain satisfaction in rich meats or wines or the pleasures of love, but not always the proper satisfaction." Anaides, the Shameless, corresponds to shamelessness, one of the excesses treated by Aristotle, though in the *Ethics* the mean is modesty, not good audacity as in Jonson's masque. As a jester Anaides continues Carlo, who has already been discussed in connection with Aristotle's treatment of buffoonery as excess in the use of wit (p. 172 *supra*). Again, the treatment of Philautia, or Self-Love, who takes the *alias* Storgé, translated by Jonson "Allowable Self-Love," shows the same distinction that Aristotle makes between self-love in the usual sense and that proper love for self which issues in the worthy pursuit of honor, etc. (IX, 8, pp. 299 ff.). Finally, as the rounded man, judicious and devoted to virtue, Crites is the broad abstraction representing activity that corresponds to Arete, Virtue, the most general moral state. In him are combined all virtues, and his lack of excess in all phases of normal life is stressed. The probable influence of Aristotle's "highminded man" on the character of Crites will be taken up later.

The ethical ideas of Aristotle, however, had early made their way into the general literature of the English Renaissance,[1] and there were probably many reworkings of Aristotelian vices and vir-

[1]Cf. p. 28 *supra*.

tues which might have contributed to Jonson's allegory. Undoubtedly the native drama had a large share in determining the dramatic form that his abstractions take on. Indeed, many of Jonson's Aristotelian ideas as well as much of his art were probably derived from the morality, to which he would naturally turn in presenting dramatically the essential conflict between opposite ethical qualities. Two divergent types of the morality showing the influence of Aristotelian conceptions, Skelton's *Magnificence* and Wilson's *Three Lords and Three Ladies of London,* may be chosen as illustrating the kinship between the morality and *Cynthia's Revels.* It seems to me altogether probable that Jonson knew both of these plays, though I would make no claim for them as actual sources of *Cynthia's Revels.* His use of Skeltonic meter in his masques has already been mentioned, and *The Fortunate Isles* introduces Skogan and Skelton as characters, Skelton repeating lines from his own *Elynour Rummyng.* The general interest in Skelton in Jonson's time is evidenced by *The Downfall of Robert Earl of Huntington,* in which he is represented as taking the rôle of Friar Tuck, and by the play of *Scogan and Skelton,* which appeared shortly after *Cynthia's Revels.*

Magnificence undoubtedly sets forth contemporary manners at the English court, as Jonson's play does, though first consideration is given to the allegory. Skelton's morality depicts groups of courtiers representing allegorically certain evils and complementing each other ethically, who are arrayed against the principles of good, and through disguise effect entrance into the court and become powerful before they are overthrown. In this we have the general plan of *Cynthia's Revels.* Measure is the chief virtuous character of *Magnificence,* corresponding closely to Crites. The very name Measure implies the fundamental principle of Aristotle's *Ethics,* while other names that are applied to the character—Prudence, Continence, Judicial Rigor—indicate the comprehensive scope of the conception. Crites and Measure are thus both ideals of conduct and accomplishment set in contrast with evils and virtues of narrower scope. Both are naturally antagonized by the vices of the court. In *Magnificence* the courtiers plot against Measure (ll. 543 ff.) and by "a praty slyght" have him dismissed from the court (ll. 940 ff.). It is only at the end of the play that he returns to power.[1] The courtiers of *Cynthia's Revels* show the same hostility to Crites, and plot to disgrace him. He is also poor, and is unrecognized in the reign of follies except by Arete, Virtue; but with the coming of Cynthia he finds himself in royal favor. Though Crites has impressed most of Jonson's critics as chiefly echoing a personal quarrel, there is clearly an allegorical idea underlying the treatment which is similar to the conception of Measure in *Magnificence.*

The correspondence between *Cynthia's Revels* and *Magnificence* is much clearer in the evil types, where the grouping and the interrelations in the two plays are very similar. Four courtiers appear in *Magnificence* who represent conduct: Counterfeit Countenance, Cloaked Collusion, Crafty Conveyance, and Courtly Abusion; and two vices or fools who represent principles, Fancy and Folly. Jonson's four courtiers are Amorphus, or the Deformed, that is, one "made out of the mixture of shreds of forms"; Hedon, or the Voluptuous; Anaides, the Impudent or Shameless; and Asotus, or the Prodigal. These courtiers of *Cynthia's Revels* are paired with four court women: Moria, or Folly; Phantaste, Light Wittiness or Foolish Fancy; Philautia, or Self-Love; and Argurion, or Money. Jonson's explanation of the two masques (pp. 246 f. *supra*) makes clear enough the basis of his division of allegorical figures into male and female, the one representing conduct in life, the other, abstract quality guiding life. In Skelton's scheme for allegory women do not appear at all, and to my mind Jonson's evident difficulty in finding female types to balance against the male but emphasizes the kinship of his groups to Skelton's. Moria and Phantaste correspond in name to Skelton's Folly and Fancy, and Philautia, or Self-Love, a familiar abstraction with Lyly and his contemporaries, makes a good third. Argurion, however, is not so suitable. The personification of money is very usual in the moralities, but it does not fit into a scheme of moral principles. When Jonson grouped the women in the masque to be acted before Cynthia, Argurion was replaced by Gelaia, Laughter or Buffoonery, the daughter of Moria, a combination which is still imperfect, however.

[1]Even if Jonson derived his conception directly from Skelton, some variation of treatment was necessary at this point on account of his effort to flatter Elizabeth. Skelton's king Magnificence could go astray and drive Measure from the court, but Cynthia must be ideal throughout. The evil types thus appear in *Cynthia's Revels* only while the Queen is absent, and at her appearance reform is effected.

Another interesting link between the handling of characters in the two plays consists in the disguise of the follies as virtues. In order to deceive Magnificence and gain a foothold in the court, the gallants of Skelton's play assume the following false names: Counterfeit Countenance becomes Good Demeanance; Cloaked Collusion, Sober Sadness; Crafty Conveyance, Sure Surveyance; and Courtly Abusion, Lusty Pleasure. Fancy and Folly appear as Largess and Conceit. After ruining Magnificence, the false counsellors flee and leave him to repentance. In *Cynthia's Revels* the courtiers and court ladies appear before Cynthia in a masque under the names of the virtues corresponding to the follies which they represent—Self-Love as Allowable Self-Love, Prodigality as Liberality, etc. As soon as they are unmasked, Cynthia recognizes them as follies, rates them sharply, and banishes them from the court.

This disguise of vices as virtues which is found in both *Magnificence* and *Cynthia's Revels* is, however, an established convention of the conflict type of morality. In *Nature* the vices change their names in order to put themselves in a more favorable light. The device, which apparently became increasingly popular in the late moralities, is elaborately employed in *Respublica,* Lindesay's *Ane Satyre of Three Estates, Albion Knight,* Wager's *The Longer thou Livest,* and Wilson's *Three Lords and Three Ladies of London.* It is even found, also, in the romantic comedy *Sir Clyomon and Sir Clamydes,* where Subtle Shift passes as Knowledge. The use of the name Content by Contempt in *The Coblers Prophesie* has already been mentioned.

Beyond these general resemblances between *Magnificence* and *Cynthia's Revels,* the separate characters in the two plays show some correspondences, though it is evident that Jonson has made different equations and has developed the characterization to fit his own scheme. Thus in Skelton's group of four courtiers, Counterfeit Countenance, who appears first, like a herald of the other evils, suggests Amorphus, the first to appear in *Cynthia's Revels* and in some respects the leader of his group. The treatment of Amorphus as the counterfeit traveler, at least, associates him with Skelton's character. In assuming the disguise of a virtue, Amorphus takes the name Eucosmos, which Jonson translates by "neat and elegant." Decorous and orderly are common meanings of the word. Counterfeit Countenance takes the kindred name Good Demeanance. Attention to dress and speech Skelton treats in the figure of Courtly Abusion, who represents the elegance of Hedon. Hedon is a continuation of Brisk in *Every Man out,* and the similarity of Brisk to Courtly Abusion has already been mentioned (pp. 187 f. *supra*). The *aliases* of Courtly Abusion and Hedon indicate their kinship still better. Courtly Abusion takes the name Lusty Pleasure. Hedon, whose name could easily be translated by Pleasure, appears in the masque as Eupathes, and Jonson's description of Eupathes makes his identity with gay or Lusty Pleasure very convincing. "Eupathes . . . entertains his mind with an harmless, but not incurious variety: all the objects of his senses are sumptuous, himself a gallant, that, without excess, can make use of superfluity, go richly in embroideries, jewels, and what not, without vanity, and fare delicately without gluttony" (V, 3, p. 199). In name Skelton's third gallant, Cloaked Collusion (ll. 689 ff.), does not suggest Anaides of *Cynthia's Revels,* but the two are somewhat akin in character. Cloaked Collusion is hypocritical and dissentious, delighting in discord (ll. 700 ff.). Carlo Buffone of *Every Man out,* who is continued in Anaides, is closer to Cloaked Collusion (p. 172 *supra*) than is Anaides, except that position at court and pretensions to gallantry place Anaides in the same social class with Skelton's courtier. In some respects all three are characterized as Detraction.[1] Relations between the other characters of the two plays are vaguer and more confused. The *alias* of Fancy in *Magnificence* is Largess, or Liberality; that of Asotus in *Cynthia's Revels* is Eucolos, or the liberal man. Fancy, however, is to be associated with Phantaste, not only in name but in caprice, waywardness, whimsicality of character. Phantaste's *alias,* Euphantaste, or "well-conceited Wittiness," is closest to Conceit, the *alias* of Skelton's Folly. The conception of folly is represented in *Cynthia's Revels* by Moria and her kinsman Morus, the fool.

The resemblances that have been noted between *Magnificence* and *Cynthia's Revels* by no means make them similar, of course. The striking kinship between the two plays lies in their similar modification of ethical conceptions derived ultimately from Aris-

[1]Anaides is twice called Mischief, a name associated with Cloaked Collusion (l. 702), and once Detraction, when he has been planning a means of injuring Crites secretly (III, 2, p. 166; IV, 1, pp. 174 and 179).

totle, and in the similar grouping. The special feature of Jonson's treatment, the grouping of qualities of character in one class and of qualities of conduct in another, is found in *Magnificence,* but is far less obvious than in *Cynthia's Revels* and is apparently not consciously aimed at. In both plays, also, the gallants show traces of the Seven Deadly Sins diverging from the moral idea toward the social. Thus Cloaked Collusion and Anaides are influenced by the conceptions of Detraction and Derision, developments from Envy; and Courtly Abusion and Hedon are must like such a figure of Pride as is found in *Nature,* where Pride has become a gallant.

The Three Lords and Three Ladies of London is more interesting than the ordinary morality as a preparation for *Cynthia's Revels* because of its nearer approach to the portrayal of courtly pastime and pageantry, which were especially associated with the game of love, and because of the elaborate symmetry and balance maintained throughout the play in the system of grouping. The care with which both Wilson and Jonson balance their characters—lords or courtiers, ladies, pages, etc.—is no doubt partly the result of the attention paid in the two plays to love as the primary pursuit of the courtier, for each gallant must pursue a lady and be followed by a page. The ethical idea that vice consists in the excess of what is permissible gives the clue to much of the nomenclature in the contrasted groups of *The Three Lords and Three Ladies of London* also. In general, however, Wilson has gathered a heterogeneous mass of characters, perhaps drawing from any source and inventing at will so long as the various groups of three figures balance against each other. This is much Jonson's system except that he groups his characters in four. But on the whole Wilson's characters are not so suggestive of Jonson's as are those in *Magnificence.*

The opening of Wilson's play, in which the three Lords of London hang up their shields and challenge all comers in defence of their love for the three Ladies of London, may be compared with the duello scene in *Cynthia's Revels,* where Asotus formally challenges to a trial in courtship. The use of chivalric conventions in both cases would account for some vague resemblances. But it is in the masques presented by the courtiers and court ladies of *Cynthia's Revels* that we have the most striking resemblances to the plot of *The Three Lords and Three Ladies.* In *Cynthia's Revels* the four ladies representing excess in inclination of character appear in a masque as the moderate motives for action, and the four courtiers representing excess in phases of courtly compliment appear in a second masque as the virtuous and commendable means. Each character is distinguished by a certain color in costume and by a device and a motto which are symbolic of the virtue represented. The pages Cupid and Mercury act as presenters and explain elaborately the significance of each figure. A similar chivalric feature is found twice in *The Three Lords and Three Ladies.* At the opening of the play, the three Lords of London, appropriately attired, enter with their shields borne by pages, who interpret the devices and mottoes as symbols of the virtues represented in the lords. Later the three Lords of London encounter the three Lords of Spain, each bearing a shield with a device and motto and followed by a page bearing a "pendant" on which are a different device and motto. The whole Spanish group is composed of vices who take the names of the corresponding virtues. After Fealty, the herald of the three London Lords, acting as presenter, has repeated the interpretation of their character and array, Shealty, the herald of the opposing group, explains the colors, devices, and mottoes of the Spanish lords and pages so as to interpret their character. Thus with the appearance of the Lords of Spain we have a type of pageantry very similar to that in the masques of *Cynthia's Revels.*

In both *Cynthia's Revels* and *The Three Lords and Three Ladies* the courtiers represent types of action, external aspects of character. In Jonson's play the ladies come near to representing the humours or character inclinations of the courtiers. Amorphus leans to Phantaste, or court wit; Hedon to Philautia, or Self-Love; and Anaides to Moria, or Folly; and Asotus pursues Money. In Wilson's play it is the pages who represent the inclination moving the courtiers. Wit waits on Policy, Wealth on Pomp, and Will on Pleasure. The ladies of Wilson's play and the pages of Jonson's, whom we might then expect to find corresponding after a fashion, are inconsistently treated. Wilson pairs Policy with Love, Pomp with Lucre,—who duplicates the allegory found in the page Wealth,—and Pleasure with Conscience. No single idea would indicate the relation between lords and ladies unless it be that the ladies furnish the necessary saving quality that prevents the type of action represented in the lords from being evil. The plan here, as in *Cynthia's Revels,* is disturbed chiefly by the presence of Money in the allegory. The ideal type found in Crites, so far as it occurs at all in Wilson's play, is portrayed negatively in the figure of Nemo, who is treated throughout as supreme in authority, with power to judge and punish. In him Wilson has embodied the popular conception of vice as so prevalent that there is no one to check it and no one to reward virtue.

Naturally in plays setting forth so elaborate a scheme of allegory a number of similar abstractions occur, but there is no striking similarity in the treatment. The explanations which the pages and heralds in the one play and Cupid and Mercury in the other give of the significance underlying the figures of the London Lords and of Jonson's masquers are alike in method and are occasionally of similar tenor. A good example is found in the account of Pleasure given by his page Will (Hazlitt's *Dodsley,* Vol. VI, p. 384) and in Mercury's description of Eupathes (Hedon, the Voluptuous) in *Cynthia's Revels* (V, 3, p. 199). "And my lord," says Will, "is not Pleasure sprung of Voluptuousness, but of such honourable and kind conceit as heaven and humanity well brooks and allows: Pleasure pleasing, not pernicious." Mercury says of Eupathes: "All the objects of his senses are sumptuous, himself a gallant, that, without excess, can make use of superfluity, go richly in embroideries, jewels, and what not, without vanity, and fare delicately without gluttony." Obviously, however, the value of Wilson's play for Jonson lies not so much in its individual characters as in its pictures of courtly love and pageantry and in the symmetry and formality of its groups.

The following tables show at a glance the plan of grouping in the two plays. Of course a few of the *dramatis personae* in each case, the citizen and wife and certain officials, for example, fall outside of the groups. *The Three Lords and Three Ladies with* its exact and mechanical balancing lends itself admirably to tabulation. Jonson's play is more difficult. Two of his pages are not allegorical figures but the gods Mercury and Cupid, who must be disposed of while in disguise at Cynthia's court; and Argurion is omitted from the masque of women, being replaced by Gelaia, mistress and page of Anaides.

Three Lords and Three Ladies of London

Lords of London	Policy	Pomp	Pleasure
Their pages	Wit	Wealth	Will
Lords of Spain	Ambition	Pride	Tyranny
Their pages	Treachery	Shame	Terror
Aliases of Lords of Spain	Honour	Spanish Majesty	Government
Aliases of their pages	Action	Modesty	Regard
Ladies of London	Love	Lucre	Conscience
Stones upon which they are seated	Charity	Care	Remorse
Sages	Pure Zeal	Honest Industry	Sincerity
Lords of Lincoln	Delight	Desire	Devotion
Gallants	Fraud	Usury	Dissimulation[1]
Gallants disguised as virtues	Skill	Usury	Fair Semblance
Followers of the gallants	Falsehood		Double-Dealing

[1]Four gallants are continued from *The Three Ladies of London*, but when the gallants in disguise attach themselves to the three lords, Simony is omitted from the grouping.

Cynthia's Revels

Courtiers	Amorphus "Deformed"	Hedon Voluptuous	Anaides Shameless	Asotus Prodigal
Aliases of courtiers in the masque	Eucosmos "Neat and elegant"; seemly	Eupathes Luxurious	Eutolmos Properly audacious	Eucolos Liberal
Pages of courtiers	Cos Whetstone	[Mercury]	Gelaia Laughter	{ Prosaites, the beggar { Morus, the fool
Nymphs	Phantaste "Light wittiness"	Philautia Self-love	Moria Folly	Argurion Money
Aliases of nymphs in the masque	Euphantaste "Well-conceited wittiness"	Storgé "Allowable Self-love"	Apheleia Simplicity	Aglaia [Gelaia] "Pleasant conversation"
Men of Cynthia's court	Crites Judge; critic	[1]Chrestus Useful	[1]Euthus Frank	[1]Phronimus Prudent
Women of Cynthia's court	Arete Virtue	Timé Honor	Thauma Wonder	Phronesis Prudence

[1]Merely mentioned as belonging to the group (III, 2, p. 167).

This system of grouping by fours Jonson seems also to have carried into his character sketch of Crites (II, 1, pp. 161, 162). Crites is described on the basis of the four humours as "neither too fantastically melancholy, too slowly phlegmatic, too lightly sanguine, or too rashly choleric." He is of "a most ingenuous and sweet spirit, a sharp and seasoned wit, a straight judgment and a strong mind." Whatever determined Jonson's choice of four for his first group, the extension of the number to other groups and elements in the play would seem natural enough to an Elizabethan audience. Four, moreover, was perhaps a favorite number. Four court vices appear in *Magnificence.* Fours are frequent with Lyly, and they are the basis of the grouping in *Love's Labour's Lost,* a study of courtly love. In Harington's preface to *Orlando Furioso* there is described a "London Comedie," "the play of the Cards, in which it is showed how foure Parasiticall knaues robbe the foure principall vocations of the Realme, *videl.* the vocation of Souldiers, Schollers, Marchants, and Husbandmen" (Smith, *Eliz. Crit. Essays,* Vol. II, p. 210). Greene's *Royal Exchange* (translated from the Italian in part) and Breton's *Figure of Foure* are works made up of bits of lore and wise saws, in each of which four things are grouped. There were also four humours, four elements, etc.

In passing on to a study of the separate characters in *Cynthia's Revels* it is difficult to avoid repeating something of what has been said in regard to *Every Man out,* for Jonson's habit of returning to previous motives and types is easily traceable in *Cynthia's Revels;* not only does the influence of formal satire which is so marked in *Every Man out* persist, but many of the characters in the later play have marked prototypes in the earlier. First of all, the scholar who appears casually in *Every Man in* and as satirist and intriguer in *Every Man out* becomes in *Cynthia's Revels* the ideal social and courtly type and is set in opposition to the forces of folly and ignorance. Hedon is a variation on Brisk, Amorphus on Puntarvolo, and Anaides on Carlo. Asotus is in some respects a recombination of Sogliardo and Fungoso, but is far removed from the early type seen in Stephen. The father of Asotus, Philargyrus, who is only mentioned, corresponds to Sordido. In place of one court lady in *Every Man out,* a whole group fairly close akin to her is substituted, but Philautia is nearest to Saviolina. Phantaste carries on to some extent the whimsicalities of Fallace. Deliro and Fallace are dimly echoed in the citizen and wife of *Cynthia's Revels,* but in Mistress Downfall a new character is evolving which appears more fully elaborated in Chloe of *Poetaster.* In discussing the characters of *Cynthia's Revels,* I shall attempt to deal only with new characteristics of the recurring types, new devices for dramatizing the satirical material, and such details of plot as are connected with only one or two characters and thus have not been treated in the discussion of the general plot.

The strong hostility of certain characters to Crites, while allegorical in its significance, almost certainly reflects the hostility of others toward Jonson, especially as these characters are chiefly literary pretenders who attack the literary merit of Crites; and the strongly individualized portraits of some of the pretenders and the concreteness of the attack offer additional evidence that Jonson had contemporary litterateurs in mind. That at least Hedon and Anaides were taken by contemporaries as personal attacks is shown by a well known passage from *Satiromastix* (ll. 420 ff.). It is quite clear, I think, however, that Crites, though at times the mouthpiece of Jonson, is a type figure, and that the other characters represent fundamentally typical humours. The types that offended, indeed, carry on previous studies, and any personal satire involved is added to the abstractions, as in the case of Carlo Buffone. It seems to me that even Demetrius and Crispinus of *Poetaster* are types in which is embodied a certain amount of personal satire. Consequently, in studying the growth of Jonson's humour types, I have felt justified in disregarding the element of personal satire in *Cynthia's Revels* and have again dealt with the characters as literary types.

The function of Crites, like that of Macilente, sets him in opposition to the characters who represent social follies of the day, but the two are pretty distinct on the whole in methods and in character. In the body of *Every Man out* Macilente seldom speaks except as the envious man, though envy gives him a chance for satire. He is also the arch intriguer delighting to bring the humour characters into disgrace. The attitude of Crites to the foolish social types is supposedly that of indifferent contempt arising from his own rounded character. In a number of places, however, Jonson has spoiled the sublime indifference of his Crites by allowing him not only to assist in making the foolish courtiers ridiculous but also to express too strongly Jonson's own personal hostility to poetasters; and thus Crites echoes the personal indignation of Asper. In the main, however, the satire of Crites is calmer and more judicial. The most interesting bit of Crites' moralizing on manners forms a complete satire at the end of III, 2. It is a description of eight kindred types of foolish or vicious courtiers, and ends with a short sketch of a group of court women with their infinite small talk. The whole is exactly in the manner of contemporary satires—a series of epigrammatic character sketches describing a procession of characters who are in the main variations on one type and are often hardly to be distinguished except by some particular folly or fad of the day. Such groups are to be found in Donne's satires; in Guilpin's *Skialetheia,* satires III, IV, and V; and in Marston's *Pygmalion's Image and Certain Satires,* satires I, II, and III. All of these satires I have drawn upon to illustrate the treatment of the gallants in *Every Man out,* and they could equally well be used for many of the characters in *Cynthia's Revels* as well as for the sketches which Jonson puts in the mouth of Crites. Indeed, in this miniature satire Jonson seems to be describing several of his own types. The correspondence, however, is probably due to the fact that the sketches, like the characters of the plays, conform to certain narrow types that were evolving in the satire of the period and becoming conventional.

In spite of the fact that Crites is at times the mouthpiece of the author, it must be borne in mind that for Jonson he represents the ideal—a thing of which every Renaissance humanist and educator dreamed.[1] Castiglione's *Courtier* is of course the most notable example, though there was considerable variation in the treatment of the supreme type. Jonson himself has presented his ideal in different lights. Asper in *Every Man out* is the ideal satirist in contrast with Macilente and Carlo, while Horace and Virgil are the ideal satirist and poet in contrast not only with the poetaster but also with the more dilettante type of real poet. In Crites we have Jonson's most rounded study of the ideal. The treatment, however, is not altogether consistent. A satirical bent

[1]Mr. Woodward, *Education during the Renaissance,* especially chapters XII and XIII, has emphasized very effectively the attention paid by Renaissance writers to the development of this ideal. I have already pointed out the fact that the elder Knowell in *Every Man in* echoes many of the educational ideals of the Renaissance.

is justifiable in a character hostile to vice; but in spite of the fact that Jonson has embodied in Crites the medieval ideal of the clerk as contrasted with the knight or courtier, and, in opposition to the ideal of birth and wealth, from which pride and scorn might be expected to spring, has made him of humble origin and moderate means, Crites has all the pride of the knight and the self-sufficiency and scorn that easily attend high rank. It is not strange, however, that the personal point of view entered into Jonson's portrayal of Crites as into other Renaissance treatments of the ideal.

The possible influence of Aristotle's portrait of "the highminded man" on Jonson's treatment of Crites has already been suggested. Aristotle conceives the highminded man as lofty in station and highly regarded, but aside from this difference practically every element of Jonson's ideal type is to be found in Aristotle's. Especially is this true of the very qualities that have been regarded as identifying Crites with Jonson. Of his ideal type Aristotle says (IV, 7 and 8, pp. 113-118):

> It would seem too that the highminded man possesses such greatness as belongs to every virtue. It would be wholly inconsistent with the character of the highminded man to run away in hot haste, or to commit a crime . . . While the highminded man, then, as has been said, is principally concerned with honours, he will, at the same time, take a moderate view of wealth, political power, and good or ill fortune of all kinds, however it may occur. He will not be excessively elated by good, or excessively depressed by ill fortune . . . The highminded man is justified in his contempt for others, as he forms a true estimate of them, but ordinary people have no such justification. Again, the highminded man is not fond of encountering small dangers, nor is he fond of encountering dangers at all. . . . But he is ready to encounter great dangers, and in the hour of danger is reckless of his life. . . . He will, of course, be open in his hatreds and his friendships, as secrecy is an indication of fear. He will care for reality more than reputation, he will be open in word and deed, as his superciliousness will lead him to speak his mind boldly. . . . He will not be a gossip, he will not talk much about himself or about anybody else; for he does not care to be praised himself or to get other people censured. . . . He is the kind of person who would rather possess what is noble, although it does not bring in profit, than what is profitable but not noble, as such a preference argues self-sufficiency.

In II, 1 (pp. 161, 162) Mercury gives the following sketch of Crites:

A creature of a most perfect and divine temper: one in whom the humours and elements are peaceably met, without emulation of precedency; he is neither too fantastically melancholy, too slowly phlegmatic, too lightly sanguine, or too rashly choleric; but in all so composed and ordered, as it is clear Nature went about some full work, she did more than make a man when she made him. His discourse is like his behaviour, uncommon, but not unpleasing; he is prodigal of neither. He strives rather to be that which men call judicious, than to be thought so; and is so truly learned, that he affects not to shew it. He will think and speak his thoughts both freely; but as distant from depraving another man's merit, as proclaiming his own. For his valour, 'tis such that he dares as little to offer an injury as receive one. In sum, he hath a most ingenuous and sweet spirit, a sharp and seasoned wit, a straight judgment and a strong mind. Fortune could never break him, nor make him less. He counts it his pleasure to despise pleasures, and is more delighted with good deeds than goods. It is a competency to him that he can be virtuous. He doth neither covet nor fear; he hath too much reason to do either; and that commends all things to him.

The great resemblance between the character of Crites and what we know of Jonson's own mode of behavior in relation to his enemies is thus found largely in the details which reflect Aristotle's ideal. It is not at all improbable that Jonson's arrogance, frank egoism, and uncompromising attitude to those he scorned appealed to him as in keeping with the standard of conduct that Aristotle sets for the highminded man. Unfortunately there was too strong a tendency in Jonson's nature to insolence and egoism, but in the light of his unselfish devotion to what he conceived as the highest literary standards and of his faithfulness, in the face of poverty, to a type of work that was slow, painstaking, and probably less remunerative than he was capable of, it is pleasant to think that even his most repellent characteristics may have been partly the result of an honest effort not to set too base a value upon his gifts and his calling. This is the attitude that marks his famous defence of his blunt claim that *Cynthia's Revels* is good. The passage, which occurs in the prologue to *Poetaster,* suggests Aristotle's highminded man and mentions the mean:

Here now, put case our author should, once more,
Swear that his play were good; he doth implore,
You would not argue him of arrogance:
Howe'er that common spawn of ignorance,
Our fry of writers, may beslime his fame,
And give his action that adulterate name.

Such full-blown vanity he more doth loathe,
Than base dejection: there's a mean 'twixt both,
Which with a constant firmness he pursues,
As one that knows the strength of his own Muse.
And this he hopes all free souls will allow:
Others that take it with a rugged brow,
Their modes he rather pities than envies:
His mind it is above their injuries.

In connection with Jonson's supposed identity with Crites, it is interesting to read Castiglione's defence against the charge that he portrays himself in his ideal type, the courtier (*Courtier,* Tudor Translations, Epistle of the Author, p. 23):

Some again say that my meaning was to facion my self, perswading my self that all suche qualities as I appoint to the Courtier are in me. Unto these men I will not cleane deny that I have attempted all that my mynde is the Courtier shoulde have knowleage in. And I thinke who so hath not the knowleage of the thinges intreated upon in this booke, how learned so ever he be, he can full il write them.

There is also in the first book of *The Courtier* (pp. 50, 51) a discussion of self-praise that probably expresses perfectly Jonson's attitude to himself and his work.

He that is of skill, whan he seeth that he is not knowen for his woorkes of the ignoraunte, hath a disdeigne that his connynge should lye buried, and needes muste he open it one waie, least he should bee defrauded of the estimation that belongeth to it, whiche is the true rewarde of vertuous travailes. Therefore among the auncient writers he that muche excelleth doeth sildome forbeare praisyng hymself. They in deede are not to be borne withall that havyng no skill in theym, wyll prayse themselves: but we wyll not take our Courtyer to be suche a one.

Then the COUNT: Yf you have well understoode (quoth he) I blamed the praysynge of a mans selfe impudently and withoute respecte. And surelye (as you saye) a man ought not to conceyve an yll oppinion of a skilfull man that praiseth hymselfe dyscretely, but rather take it for a more certaine witnes, then yf it came out of an other mans mouth.

For the character of Crites as the rounded man there are one or two parallels in the earlier drama. For example, the character sketch of Crites quoted above (p. 262) opens with a sentence that has often been compared with Antony's tribute to Brutus in *Julius Caesar* (V, 5):

His life was gentle; and the elements
So mix'd in him, that Nature might stand up
And say to the world, *This was a man!*

Of the four men opposed to Crites, Amorphus is apparently the leader. In the plot of the play Asotus is closely associated with him as an understudy, while Hedon and Anaides usually appear together. Amorphus continues Puntarvolo in a number of respects, both represeuting extravagance and formality in speech and behavior. The following are some of the suggestive parallels between the two characters:

Puntarvolo	Amorphus
"A vainglorious knight." "So palpably affected to his own praise . . . that he commends himself" (p. 62).	Praises himself extravagantly at first appearance (I, 1, p. 152). Is first to drink of the Fountain of Self-Love. "He is his own promoter in every place" (II, 1, p. 161).
"Wholly consecrated to singularity." Sticks "to his own particular fashion, phrase, and gesture" (p. 62).	Claims that his behavior is not cheap or customary, his accent and phrase not vulgar, his garments not trite (I, 1, p. 152).
"Jacob's staff of compliment" (p. 62).	"The very mint of compliment" (II, 1, p. 161).
A pompous speaker (II, 1).	"Cannot speak out of a dictionary method" (IV, 1, p. 175).
Speaks French and Italian (II, 1, p. 84).	Speaks Italian and Spanish (I, 1, p. 154).
"A sir that hath lived to see the revolution of time in most of his apparel" (p. 62).	"No great shifter; once a year his apparel is ready to revolt" (II, 1, p. 161).
"Looks like the sign of the George" (II, 1, p. 82). Looks "as if he . . . had a suit of wainscot on" (II, 1, p. 84).	"Looks like a Venetian trumpeter . . . in the gallery yonder" (IV, 1, p. 171).
Has his beard starched (IV, 4, p. 116).	"His beard is an Aristarchus" (II, 1, p. 161).
"He deals upon returns" (p. 62).	"Has made the sixth return upon venture" (I, 1, 152).
The gull Fungoso is his godchild (II, 1, p. 85).	The gull Asotus is his protégé.

But in spite of their common characteristics Amorphus differs considerably from Puntarvolo. Though both make ventures upon returns, Amorphus as a traveler is primarily the boaster, the liar. He is evidently poor, as his intelligence is made to pay for his travels (I, 1, p. 155), and the wife of the ordinary gives him his diet for his talk. He is an arbiter of quarrels but a coward (II, 1,

p. 161), whereas Puntarvolo is dangerous. Altogether he is a far less dignified and honorable figure than Puntarvolo. His skill in "compliment" lies in the use not of antiquated chivalric customs like Puntarvolo's but of an exaggerated type of up-to-date courtship, no doubt something like the actual courtship of the Italianate lovers in Elizabeth's court. The sketch of Castilio in the first satire of *Pygmalion's Image and Certain Satires,* which has already been quoted in connection with Puntarvolo, is perhaps still more appropriate to Amorphus in some details. Amorphus is preeminently the one who "can all the points of courtship show." He is, indeed, the instructor of the neophyte Asotus in lovers' arts and is grandmaster in the duello of courtship.

The most interesting new phase in the characterization of Amorphus is his lying in regard to his travels. A kindred treatment is often seen in the braggart soldier. Bobadill, who like Amorphus is a master of the duello, a coward, and poor, has tales to tell not only of his exploits in war but of marvelous experiences with tobacco in strange countries. Amorphus owes nothing to the boastful soldier, however; his lying is of another type. One of his clearest forerunners is Mendax of Bullein's *Dialogue against the Fever Pestilence* (pp. 94 ff.). Mendax, who resembles Amorphus in being poor and dressing oddly, sharpens his knife on a whetstone when he is summoned to eat with Civis. Amorphus, it will be remembered, is followed by a page Cos, the whetstone. Mendax also has his accomplishments; he can play the zittern and dance. His boasts are of his ancestry and of his marvelous adventures with strange beasts and strange men, in lands of fabulous wealth, etc., while Amorphus has been incredibly honored by potentates wherever he has gone and "sued to, by all ladies and beauties" (IV, 1, p. 178). Mendax, however, tells a tale of a marvelous beer that he drank in his travels which matches Amorphus's remark about metheglin, a kind of Greek wine that he once came upon while roaming the earth, the very kind usually drunk by Demosthenes, in fact.

In *Wits Miserie,* which satirizes, indeed, practically every folly that the satirists and the satiric dramatists handle, there are a number of scattered passages suggesting Amorphus. Vainglory (pp. 3-5), in the "coat of Singularity," boasts of his travels, of honors paid him by foreign princes, and especially of gifts in the way of articles of dress. His hat, he claims, was bestowed upon him by Henry II of France.[1] "All that hée hath of you beléeue him," Lodge says, "are but gifts in reward of his vertue." Vainglory also pretends to learning and to musical skill. "Hée will prooue RAMUS to be a deeper Philosopher than ARISTOTLE, and presume to read the *Mathematiques* to the studious . . . vrge him in *Musike,* he will sweare to it, that he is *A per se* in it, where hée is skillesse in Proportion, ignorant in Discord," etc. So Amorphus arrogantly lays claim to a knowledge of the niceties of verse and music (IV, 1, pp. 178, 179). Again, Boasting of *Wits Miserie* (p. 10), who makes pretensions to literary gifts, declares, "PERSEUS is a foole in his stile, & an obscure Poet." Lucian, Amorphus pronounces absurd. "I will believe mine own travels before all the Lucians of Europe" (I, 1, p. 153). Lying (p. 35) is described by Lodge as "a sonne of MAMMONS that hath of long time ben a trauailer." His tales are more like those of Mendax than those of Amorphus, being accounts of strange sights in foreign countries. Another of Lodge's characters is "Superfluous Inuention or Nouel-monger or Fashions," who invents new sauces and banquets and absurd fashions (p. 13). Asotus of *Cynthia's Revels* "doth learn to make strange sauces, to eat anchovies, maccaroni, bovoli, fagioli, and caviare, because he [Amorphus] loves them" (II, 1, p. 161). Amorphus's garments, too, are not trite (I, 1, p. 152). In comparing himself with Crites, Amorphus asks (IV, 1, p. 181), "Have not I invention afore him? learning to better that invention above him? and infanted with pleasant travel—" Finally, in the sketch of Derision, part of which I have quoted in discussing Carlo (p. 171 *supra*), there is an expression that is interesting in connection with the meaning of Amorphus, deformed—"At the length hée prooueth deformity himself" (p. 10).[2]

Among the verse satirists, Guilpin in *Skialetheia,* Satire I, has a sketch of the boasting traveler who can tell of the remotest cranny of this world and has discovered some half dozen other worlds. With him Guilpin associates the antiquary, who displays souvenirs of various famous personages, including Cupid and Charlemagne. So the hat which Amorphus gives Asotus is said to have accompanied Ulysses on his travels (I, 1, p. 155). Hall in

[1]Cf. the hat of Amorphus, I, 1, p. 155.

[2]Cf. Penniman, *War of the Theatres,* p. 94, n. 2, for theories in regard to the "one Deformed" of *Much Ado.*

Virgidemiarum, IV, 6, satirizes the "sweet-sauc'd lies of some false traveller" who has read the "whet-stone leasings of old Mandeville," and mentions the same kind of marvels that Bullein and Lodge mention.

One of the remarkable boasts of Amorphus is that he has been "fortunate in the amours of three hundred forty and five ladies, all nobly, if not princely descended" (I, 1, p. 152) and that he "never yet sojourned or rested in that place or part of the world, where some high-born, admirable, fair feature died not for my love" (IV, 1, p. 178). Nashe in *Haue with you to Saffron-walden* (*Works,* III, p. 111) accuses Harvey of breeding *"an opinion in the world, that he is such a great man in Ladies and Gentlewomens bookes that they are readie to run out of their wits for him, as in the Turkes* Alchoron *it is written that 250. Ladies hanged themselues for the loue of* Mahomet."[1]

Asotus, [2] the protégé of Amorphus, is in some respects a development out of Fungoso in *Every Man out.* Both are upstarts and gulls, and both show the youth, fine dress, and eagerness to follow the fashion which belong to the type. Too much has been made of the similarity, however, by those who would identify Asotus and Fungoso with Lodge—Fleay, Penniman, and Hart. Asotus is rather distinct. Fungoso's chief claim to distinction lies in his effort to copy Brisk's suits, and that is made amusing largely through the pitiful shifts to which he is put in order to get the necessary money. But Asotus is a figure of lavishness. Moreover, he is not a follower afar of the elegant Hedon, as Fungoso is of Brisk, but associates himself with Amorphus, who corresponds to Puntarvolo. Again, a prominent feature in the characterization of Asotus is his careful training as an amorist and his acceptance at court by Argurion, to which nothing in the treatment of Fungoso corresponds. In his inheritance of wealth and his training at the hands of Amorphus Asotus corresponds to the wealthy

[1]In *II Henry IV,* III, 1, where Justice Shallow is characterized as a braggart, it is said of him that he "came ever in the rearward of the fashion." In *Cynthia's Revels,* IV, 1, pp. 171 f., Philautía declares that Amorphus "speaks to the tune of a country lady, that comes ever in the rearward or train of a fashion."

[2]The full name of Asotus is Acolastus-Polypragmon-Asotus (V, 2, p. 186). "Busie Polypragmon" is mentioned in the sixth satire of Guilpin's *Skialetheia.* Gnapheus's famous Latin play on the Prodigal is called *Acolastus;* Macropedius's, *Asotus.*

Sogliardo trained by Shift in the gallant accomplishments of taking tobacco, and swearing and swaggering at taverns, but the instruction which Asotus receives is in such courtly accomplishments as making set speeches. Thus, though a gull and a mere ape as Sogliardo and Fungoso are, Asotus is a far more brilliant figure.

The characterization of Asotus is largely subordinated to that of his sponsor Amorphus, and it is chiefly the association between the two that links Asotus with other literary treatments. Satire on the infatuation between gallants at first sight, their praise of each other's dress, their exchange of gifts, etc., which we have in the meeting between Amorphus and Asotus (I, 1), is not uncommon. Chapman in *An Humorous Day's Mirth* satirizes frivolous talk among gallants, especially the praise of each other's form and fashion (p. 35). In *Histriomastix,* during the reign of Pride, Vainglory, Hypocrisy, and Contempt, four abstractions symbolic of luxuriousness and excess in social life, and not unlike the four gallants of *Cynthia's Revels,* Mavortius and Philarchus comment on each other's apparel, Philarchus's hat being pronounced of better block than that of Mavortius (III, ll. 123-132). In Act IV of the same play (ll. 169-173), one of the players praises his ingle's hilt and has it bestowed upon him. An elaborate dramatization of the ingling of foolish gallants introduces Amorphus and Asotus to us in *Cynthia's Revels.* Amorphus praises various articles of Asotus's apparel, especially his beaver, which is exceedingly fine, and accepts the hat as a gift, proffering in exchange his own, which is decidedly dilapidated.

A striking parallel to the relationship between Amorphus and Asotus in *Cynthia's Revels* is to be found in the friendship of Pseudocheus and Gelasimus in *Timon.* Hart (*Works of Ben Jonson,* Vol. I, p. xliv) has called attention to a kinship between the two plays and has pointed out some details. The relationship possibly deserves further study, for, if *Timon* is the earlier, as Hart believes,[1] Jonson certainly followed the play very closely. The characterization of Gelasimus and Asotus is much the same. Both are citizen's heirs, wealthy, and just beginning to taste with extravagance the experiences of gallantry. Asotus is the son of Phil-

[1]Cf. pp. 168 ff. and 209 f. *supra* for some discussion of the relative dates.

argyrus and becomes the accepted lover of Argurion, while the same allegory is carried out in *Timon* by the love of Gelasimus for the daughter of Philargurus.[1] The personal appearance of Gelasimus also tallies with that of Asotus. The beard of Gelasimus is undeveloped; he has small, gentleman-like ankles; ladies wish for features like his (I, 3); and Pseudocheus calls him "a spruce, neate youth" (I, 4).[2] Asotus's beard, according to Mercury, "is not yet extant" (II, 1, p. 161); Amorphus pronounces his new acquaintance "a pretty formal young gallant" (I, 1, p. 153); and Argurion speaks of him as "a most delicate youth; a sweet face, a straight body, a well proportioned leg and foot, a white hand, a tender voice" (IV, 1, p. 172). In the early part of each play the gull leagues himself with the boasting traveler, and the two situations are handled alike. In *Timon* Gelasimus, entering with his page Pædio, is joined by Pseudocheus, the returning traveler, whose absurd exaggeration and inordinate vainglory suggest the boaster of Latin comedy. Pseudocheus boasts of his travels in remote lands and of the honors conferred upon him by foreign potentates, and he brings home souvenirs of his travels. His chief concern, like that of Amorphus, however, is not to rouse wonder but to glorify himself. In *Cynthia's Revels* Asotus enters with Crites, who like the page of Gelasimus comments satirically as the scene progresses. The boasting of Amorphus is more rational than that of Pseudocheus, but not a whit less vainglorious. The following passages, which describe the meeting between the pair in each play, will indicate the relation.

[1]The allegorical use of this name is apparently rather frequent. According to Warton, Skelton's *Nigramansir* had a character called Philargyria. A work entitled *Philargyrie of greate Britayne*, 1551, is mentioned by Dyce in *The Works of Skelton*, Vol. I, p. cxxix.

[2]The page tells Gelasimus in regard to virgins' opinion of him,

> This the like eyes, that the like nose desires;
> This your cheekes, and that your leggs.

Compare Crites' satire on ladies' talk about gallants (III, 2, p. 168):

> Where you shall hear one talk of this man's eye,
> Another of his lip, a third, his nose,
> A fourth commend his leg, a fifth, his foot,
> A sixth, his hand, and every one a limb.

Cf. also Dowsecer in *An Humorous Day's Mirth*, p. 33.

Cynthia's Revels, I, 1

Amo. Ha! a pretty formal young gallant, in good sooth . . . Hark you, Crites, you may say to him what I am, if you please.

. . . .

Aso. Crites, . . . pray you make this gentleman and I friends. . . . In good faith he's a most excellent rare man, I warrant him. . . . And withal, you may tell him what my father was, and how well he left me, and that I am his heir. . . . O gods! I'd give all the world, if I had it, for abundance of such acquaintance.

. . . .

Amo. Since I trod on this side the Alps, I was not so frozen in my invention. Let me see. . . . Feign to have seen him in Venice or Padua! or some face near his in similitude! . . . or . . . come to some special ornament about himself, as his rapier, or some other of his accoutrements? I have it: thanks, gracious Minerva!

Aso. Would I had but once spoke to him, and then—He comes to me!

. . . .

Amo. I think I shall affect you, sir. . . .

Aso. O lord, sir! I would there were anything in me, sir, that might appear worthy the least worthiness of your worth. . . .

Amo. . . . Good faith, this hat hath possest mine eye exceedingly; 'tis so pretty and fantastic: what! is it a beaver?

. . . .

Aso. Sir, it is all at your service.

. . . .

Amo. I take your love, gentle Asotus; but let me win you to receive this, in exchange—

. . . .

Timon, I, 4

Gel. Shall I speake to him, Pædio? he seemes
A man of greate accompt, that hath oreveiu'd
Soe many countreyes: what shall I saye first?
Shall I salute him after our manner?

Pseud. A spruce, neate youth: what, yf I affront him?

Gel. Good gods, how earnestlie doe I desire
His ffellowshipp! was I e're soe shamefac't?
What yf I send and gyue to him my cloake?

Pseud. What shall I saye? I saw his face at Thebes
Or Sicilie?

Gel. Ile send it. Pædio,
Gyue him this cloake: salute him in my name;
H'st, thou may'st tell him, yf thou wilt, how rich
My ffather was.

. . . .

Pseud. Tell him I will salute him.

Pæd. The strainger, sir, desires to salute you.

Gel. That's my desire: I will meete him.

Pseud. I will affront him.

Gel. I wish admittance of societie.

. . . .

Pseud. I thee admitt, thou needst not be ashamed;

. . . .

Gel. Lord, what a potent friend haue I obteyned!—

. . . .

Pseud. This ring he [the king of the Antipodes] gaue me.

Gel. Prythee, lett me se it.

Amo. Sir, shall I say to you for that hat? . . . It is a relic I could not so easily have departed with, but as the hieroglyphic of my affection . . . and was given me by a great man in Russia, as an especial prized present. . . .

Aso. By Jove, I will not depart withal, whosoever would give me a million.

Wilt thou that wee exchainge, my Pylades?

Pseud. I am a man; Ile not denye my ffreind.—
By Joue, my ringe is made of brasse, not gould. [*Aside.*

Gel. O happie me, that weares the kings owne ringe
Of th' Antipodes!

Pseud. Soe I blesse my ffriends.

In both plays the traveler immediately takes the citizen's heir in charge and begins to train him in the art of love making. The first lesson that Amorphus gives Asotus is a study of the various kinds of faces, the merchant's, the courtier's, etc. (II, 1, p. 160). Gelasimus is a master of assumed gravity in countenance before he meets Pseudocheus (I, 3).[1] The instruction of Pseudocheus as to how to approach a mistress is of a kind with that of Amorphus but cruder and less elaborate. Pseudocheus recommends merriment, dancing, and pricksong. In *Timon,* after some preliminary instruction master and pupil present themselves at the home of Callimela (II, 1). The final injunction of Pseudocheus is, "It is a synn to blush: be impudent"; and Gelasimus replies, "I blush! I scorne to blush." Once in the presence of his beloved, Gelasimus pours out the mixture of pricksong and lover's jargon which Pseudocheus has taught him; but, as the conversation proceeds, he has to be prompted again and again, and each time he repeats word for word the phrases of his tutor. So under the direction of Amorphus (III, 1 and 3) Asotus practices how to conduct himself in the presence of a mistress, learning by rote the set speeches suggested by Amorphus, and later repeating them for the benefit of the ladies. A part of his exercise consists of dancing and singing (III, 3, p. 170). According to Amorphus, one advantage of his protégé's novitiate at court is that it will teach him

[1]The practiced faces of gallants are several times satirized by Guilpin. In Epigram 30 of *Skialetheia* he says:

> *Chrysogonus* each morning by his glasse,
> Teacheth a wrincled action to his face.

In Satire V, he speaks of one who "wries his face" and of a troop who look

> As if their very countenaunces would sweare,
> The Spanyard should conclude a peace for feare.

"to be careless and impudent" (III, 1, p. 165), and Asotus so far profits by his opportunities that he is soon bestowing on Anaides a ruby ring, with an inscription of his own device, "*Let this blush for me*" (IV, 1, p. 182). In *Timon* the relationship between the pair leads finally to the complete gulling of the "cittie heyre." In *Cynthia's Revels* Amorphus continues to tutor Asotus seriously in the conduct of courtship, and the whole treatment is greatly expanded.[1]

An earlier example of the association between this pair is to be found in *The Defence of Conny-catching* (*Works of Greene,* Vol. XI, pp. 72 ff.), where the braggart traveler is treated as a type of coney-catcher. Dressed in extravagant foreign fashion, he haunts the resorts of gallants with his eye open for "nouvices." He has a "superficiall insight into certain phrases of euerie language"—compare Amorphus's "choice remnant of Spanish or Italian" (I, 1, p. 154)—and speaks glowingly of foreign countries and especially of the advantages of travel. The interest here centers in his scheme for gulling the novice, and the account is thus very much nearer to the treatment of the traveler in *Timon* than in *Cynthia's Revels.* Indeed, this sketch of the pretended traveler in *The Defence of Conny-catching* may well have served as the source for the dénouement of the plot of *Timon* so far as Pseudocheus and Gelasimus are concerned.[2]

Jonson's third courtier, Hedon, is complementary to Amorphus, the two representing two aspects of the courtier which are often in contrast. It will be remembered that in discussing Brisk and Puntarvolo, the forerunners of Hedon and Amorphus in *Every Man out,* I attempted to show that the same line of cleavage was recognized in other literary treatments of social types, especially in the satire of Guilpin and Marston, but that the characteristics of the two types were not always distinct. Marston's sketch of Castilio, which shows best the confusion of the types, contains some lines

[1]The relationship between these two plays is exceedingly tantalizing. Compare, for example, the speech of Gelasimus (III, 3) when Callimela casts him off, with the soliloquy of Amorphus (I, 1) when Echo flies from him. With totally dissimilar wording the passages are still evidently akin.

[2]Prof. Penniman (*War of the Theatres,* p. 89) notes the fact that Asotus (V, 2, p. 190) quotes from Davies, Epigram 29. This is interesting here only as another indication of the extensive use which Jonson seems to have made of the epigrams of Davies.

that fit Hedon better than they do any of the other characters to whom the sketch has been applied:

> Tut! he is famous for his revelling,
> For fine set speeches, and for sonnetting;
> He scorns the viol and the scraping stick.

Amorphus and Hedon blend chiefly in their absorption in the game of love, though Amorphus centers his attention largely on the machinery of courtship. It is clear, however, that Hedon belongs first of all to the type represented in Brisk, the gallant who is elegant and dapper and who follows the conventions of courtship. The type is constantly satirized, and the character sketches given above as illustrative of Brisk often fit Hedon also. The two are alike in their love of elegant dress and rich perfume, in having almost reached the end of their money and their credit as a result of high living, in their constant attention to courtship, particularly in the effort to win the admiration of ladies by their activity, and finally in their affectation of euphuistic address, neat or witty conceits, etc.[1] But these correspondences are in the main general, and the specific fads of Hedon even in dress and pastimes differ from those of Brisk. The difference is largely one of social class, for in spite of his access to court, Brisk is only a mimic courtier, and the world in which he really shines is that of the citizen. Indeed, Jonson has represented the characters of *Cynthia's Revels* on the whole as of a higher social grade than those of the preceding play, with natural reserve, assurance, pride, etc.

Nashe, whose picture of the upstart has been discussed above (pp. 188 f.) for its bearing upon the literary treatment of the Brisk-Hedon type, gives in the Epistle Dedicatory to *Lenten Stuffe* (*Works of Nashe,* Vol. III, pp. 148, 149) a character sketch that tallies surprisingly with the sketch which Mercury gives of Hedon (I, 1, pp. 157, 158). It is the more interesting because in a number of points it corresponds to the characterization of Hedon and yet will not fit the figure of Brisk. Nashe says:

> *To any other carpetmunger or primerose knight of Primero bring I a dedication, and the dice ouer night haue not befriended him, hee sleepes fiue dayes and fiue nights to new skin his beautie, and will not bee knowne hee is awakt till his men vppon their owne bondes . . . haue tooke*

[1]For Hedon cf. especially the character sketch II, 1, pp. 157, 158.

vp commodities or fresh droppings of the minte for him: and then; what then? he payes for the ten dozen of balles hee left vppon the score at the tennis court; hee sendes for his Barber to depure, decurtate, and spunge him, whome hauing not paide a twelmonth before, he now raines downe eight quarter angels into his hande, to make his liberalitie seeme greater. . . . The chamber is not ridde of the smell of his feet, but the greasie shoomaker . . . enters . . . and after shewes his tally. By S. Loy, *that drawes deepe, and by that time his Tobacco marchant is made euen with, and hee hath dinde at a tauerne, and slept his vnder-meale at a bawdy house, his purse is on the heild and only fortie shillings hee hath behinde, to trie his fortune with at the cardes in the presence; which if it prosper, | the court cannot containe him, but to* London *againe he will, to reuell it, and haue two playes in one night, inuite all the Poets and Musitions to his chamber the next morning; where, against theyr comming, a whole heape of money shall bee bespread vppon the boord, and all his trunkes opened to shewe his rich sutes; but the deuill a whit hee bestowes on them, saue bottle ale and Tobacco; and desires a generall meeting.*

Compare with this the sketch of Hedon:

Himself is a rhymer, and that's thought better than a poet. He is not lightly within to his mercer, no, though he come when he takes physic, which is commonly after his play. He beats a tailor very well, but a stocking-seller admirably: and so consequently any one he owes money to, that dares not resist him. He never makes general invitement, but against the publishing of a new suit; marry, then you shall have more drawn to his lodging, than come to the launching of some three ships; especially if he be furnished with supplies for the retiring of his old wardrobe from pawn: if not, he does hire a stock of apparel, and some forty or fifty pound in gold, for that forenoon, to shew. He . . . sometimes ventures so far upon the virtue of his pomander, that he dares tell . . . how many shirts he has sweat at tennis that week; but wisely conceals so many dozen of balls he is on the score.

In the characterization of Hedon, a great deal of attention is given to the elegant accomplishments which make him a leading figure in the court circle. He devises set speeches showing wit of the euphuistic type; invents pretty oaths, wishes, prophecies, and posies for rings (II, 1, pp. 158, 159); and composes both the "ditty, and the note" to a song on a kiss given him by his lady (IV, 1, pp. 177, 178). Crites ridicules him for the conceits in his love poetry (V, 2, p. 194). In other words, he is the typical courtly lover. Amorphus, too, in rivalry of Hedon, sings a song on the glove of one of his victims. Of the many satiric references to the frivolous subjects of current love poetry, it will suffice to quote one from Nashe, who says in *Lenten Stuffe* (*Works,* Vol. III, p. 176): "The wantonner sort of them [oaten pipers] sing descant on their mistris gloue, her ring, her fanne, her looking glasse, her pantofle, and on the same iurie I might impannell *Iohannes Secundus,* with his booke of the | two hundred kinde of kisses." The poet-lover's hackneyed comparisons in praise of beauty are satirized by Jonson in Mercury's trial at the "Solemn Address" (V, 2, pp. 192, 193) and in Crites' burlesque of Hedon (V, 2, p. 194). Fleay (*Biographical Chronicle of the English Drama,* Vol. I, p. 97) cites Sonnet 19 of Daniel's *Delia* for its similarity to Hedon's figures. The basis of the compliment which Crites ascribes to Hedon—that a mistress's "beauty is all composed of theft"—may be unusual, but the figures which make up the lover's rhapsodies of both Crites and Mercury are usual enough, practically all of them occurring, for example, within pages 82 to 89 of *England's Helicon* according to Bullen's edition of 1899. In *Love's Labour's Lost* (IV, 3) the King satirizes the effusions of lovers who protest of their ladies

> One's hairs were gold, crystal the other's eyes.

The use of the names Ambition and Honor by Hedon and Philautia probably represents another convention of courtship. In *Every Man out* Sogliardo and Shift call each other Countenance and Resolution. Such names, however, doubtless belong to courtly love as in *Cynthia's Revels,* rather than to ingling, as in *Every Man out.* In Gascoigne's *Adventures of Master F. I.* Ferdinando and Frances give each other the names Trust and Hope, and play upon them as Hedon and Philautia play upon Ambition and Honor in *Cynthia's Revels.* The games at which Hedon is clever are often mentioned in the period. Lodge in *Wits Miserie* (p. 47) says of Fornication, "Put him to a sonnet, Du Portes cannot equall him; . . . at Riddles, he is good; at Purposes, better; but at Tales he hath no equall." Here we have the chief accomplishments of the courtly lover. Purposes as a game is mentioned as early as *The Courtier* (p. 33). The line,

> He that can purpose it in dainty rhymes,

in Marston's sketch of the "absolute Castilio" seems to refer to the same game. In one of his early works Gascoigne says (*Poems,*

Vol. I, pp. 47, 48): "The Aucthor knowing that after supper they should passe the tyme in propounding of Ryddles and making of purposes, contriued all this conceipt in a Riddle." Then follow two riddles. "An excellent dreame of ladies, and their riddles" is given in the *Cambridge History of English Literature* (Vol. IV, p. 135) as the title of a poem by Breton which appears in *The Phoenix Nest.* When Philautia suggests riddles or purposes as a pastime in *Cynthia's Revels,* Phantaste is in favor of prophecies because the others are stale (IV, 1, p. 175). Apparently new games are chosen, and these I have not found mentioned elsewhere.

According to Mercury, Anaides "has two essential parts of the courtier, pride and ignorance; marry, the rest come somewhat after the ordinary gallant" (II, 1, p. 159). The character is a complex one. Anaides is first of all a near kinsman of Carlo Buffone. Both are impudent jesters, railers, detractors, sycophants, and haunters of ordinaries; both are given to drinking and swearing and to lewdness.[1] The two characters are very distinct, nevertheless. Carlo, of whom it is expressly said that he "comes not at court" (IV, 6, p. 123), is a mere "feast-hound" following the great, who feed and tolerate him, whereas Anaides is a courtier and "a man of fair living" (IV, 1, p. 174). The chief difference between the two to my mind is that in passing on to Anaides Jonson has shifted his emphasis. Anaides is a jester and railer, but in the action of the play he is important chiefly in his relation to Crites and Hedon as literary men. Indeed, nearly all his participation in the plot may be taken as literary allegory. He is a type of the vulgar, the untrained, scorning scholarship and refinement. He associates himself with Hedon, the rhymer, the popular and artificial love poet, and leads in the hostility against Crites, the scholar and genuine literary man. He has thus formed a new literary alliance, for Carlo, though he fears Macilente, yet seeks to ally himself with him. There is also the same difference between Carlo and Anaides that we find between Asper and Crites. Asper and Carlo represent merely two phases of satire, but the treatment of Crites and Anaides is much broader in its literary significance.

[1]Cf. *Every Man out*, prefatory character sketch of Carlo, p. 62; induction, p. 71; and I, 1, p. 76: *Cynthia's Revels*, II, 1, p. 159; III, 2, pp. 165-167; IV, 1, pp. 172, 174, and 179; and V. 2, pp. 187-189. Small, *Stage-Quarrel*, p. 34, has tabulated most of the important correspondences.

Anaides is not the buffoon with respect to his satiric vein alone, but as a literary man in general, and especially as a critic. Anaides "speaks all that comes in his cheeks"; will absurdly censure any thing; and "does naturally admire his wit that wears gold lace or tissue" (II, 1, p. 159). He has put Crites down a thousand times, he says, though he has talked to him only twice and Crites has laughed at him for not being able to construe an author quoted by Anaides himself (IV, 1, p. 181).

Anaides continues so many of the characteristics of Carlo that the study of Carlo as a buffoon and a type of detraction will serve for many phases of the character of Anaides. The new phase in the treatment of the type, the great elaboration of literary jealousy, is well illustrated by the satirists. Professor Penniman has noted the fact that the charges of Anaides against Crites as well as those of Demetrius against Horace echo Lodge's study of literary jealousy.[1] In fact, Anaides, like Carlo, is a figure much in the style of Lodge, and several passages from *Wits Miserie* besides those quoted in connection with Carlo are interesting in connection with Anaides. After telling how Adulation praises whatever his lord writes, Lodge continues (pp. 20, 21): "Of al things he cannot abide a scholer, and his chiefest delight is to kéepe downe a Poet, as MANTUAN testifieth in these verses . . . There is in Princes and great mens courts (saith he) a rude, enuious, and rusticke troupe of men, ieasters, flatterers, bauds, soothers, adulterers, plaiers, and scoffers, who hating all vertue find a thousand inuentions to driue Poets thence." Here we have the enemy of the scholar and poet described in terms that Jonson uses for Anaides. It is almost exactly the same character in the same situation. The words "hating all vertue," translated from Mantuan, apparently become the basis of a later sketch, in which Lodge analyzes more narrowly literary jealousy (pp. 55 ff.):

> [Hate-Vertue] is a foule lubber, his tongue tipt with lying . . . he is full of infamy & slander, insomuch as if he ease not his stomach in detracting somwhat or some man before noontide, he fals into a feuer that holds him while supper time: he is alwaies deuising of Epigrams or scoffes. . . .

[1] *Poetaster and Satiromastix*, Belles-Lettres Series, introduction. The passage from Lodge on Hate-Vertue (*Wits Miserie*, pp. 55 ff.) is also quoted by Laing in his edition of Lodge's *Defence of Poetry*, etc., Shakespeare Society, 1853, pp. xliv, xlv, for its references to various writers.

The mischiefe is that by graue demeanure, and newes bearing, hée hath got some credite with the greater sort, and manie fooles there bée that because hée can pen prettilie, hold it Gospell what euer hée writes or speakes: his custome is to preferre a foole to credite, to despight a wise man, and no Poet liues by him that hath not a flout of him. Let him spie a man of wit in a Tauerne, he is an arrant dronckard . . . Let a scholler write, Tush (saith he) I like not these common fellowes: let him write well, he hath stollen it out of some note booke: let him translate, Tut, it is not of his owne: let him be named for preferment, he is insufficient, because poore.

Then follows an appeal to the great English writers to put aside all petty animosities and stand together for the honor of their calling. The decision of Anaides to claim that the work of Crites is stolen, the scorn of Hedon and Anaides that Crites is chosen to write the masque for Cynthia, and the contempt of the pair for the poverty of Crites are anticipated by Lodge in this sketch.[1] A few other details from *Wits Miserie* illustrate phases of Anaides. Blasphemy, who haunts ordinaries and "accounts it an impeach of his honour if any outsweare him" (p. 65), represents the profanity of Anaides, who will "blaspheme in his shirt," and whose oaths "at one supper would maintain a town of garrison in good swearing a twelve-month" (II, 1, p. 159). Again, "IMMODERATE and DISORDINATE IOY . . . incorporate in the bodie of a ieaster" with his intemperate laughter (p. 84) suggests the jester Anaides with his page Gelaia, or uncouth laughter.

The pages, except Mercury and Cupid, are little more than names that help to characterize their masters. Morus had already been used as a name in Wager's *The Longer thou Livest.* Prosaites sings a beggar's song (II, 1, p. 164), the greater part of which is omitted in the Folio. The omitted portion contains a doggerel list of humble trades and rogues' callings which suggests such works as *The Fraternitye of Vacabondes* and the accompanying *Quartern of Knaves.* Nearer still to Jonson's list is that given in *Cocke Lorelles bote* of the various classes of people who throng after Cock Lorel. In Wager's play, also, (ll. 1704-1723) there is a series of doggerel rhymes forming an alphabet of rogues. Lydgate's *Assembly of Gods* (ll. 666 ff.) has a list not altogether dis-

[1]The literary quarrels and jealousies of the age and the sharp satire on pretenders are too common to follow out. Nashe has a good deal to say of literary jealousy, but his treatment is usually personal rather than general like Lodge's.

similar to Jonson's.[1] Cos, who follows the traveler, has several times been spoken of as a symbol of lying. The symbolic use of the whetstone in connection with a liar is frequent in literature of the time. Small (*Stage-Quarrel,* p. 50, n. 2) instances several examples. Gelaia is one of the most piquant figures in the play, but I know of no similar treatment in literature. Her slight resemblance to Pipenetta of Lyly's *Midas* has already been mentioned (p. 240 *supra*).

In regard to the four women of *Cynthia's Revels* I can add very little to what I have already said of them in the study of Jonson's allegory and of the groups in the mythological plays. Moria, the guardian, is apparently of middle age. She is garrulous, devoted to scandalous gossip, and prurient. The attention which Anaides pays her is of course allegorical. A passage dealing with her gossip and love of prying (IV, 1, p. 173) is in some points much like Donne's description of a courtier's interests (Satire I). Certain traces of Moria as a type are to be found in the court of love poetry (p. 226 *supra*), but she shows most clearly perhaps a continuation of the medieval treatment of old women. Certainly old women in the Middle Ages and the Renaissance were not likely to be portrayed with sympathy. The ugliness of age was taken as symbolic of an evil nature, and an old woman was conceived as malignant or vicious, a conception illustrated in witchcraft. In the drama the nurse is the usual type, as in *Romeo and Juliet,* the old *Timon,* and *Wily Beguiled.* The nurse's garrulity, raciness of speech, and sensuality recur in Moria, and both show traces of the procuress of the novella. On the whole, however, Moria is a loftier figure than the vulgar types with which Jonson's treatment allies her. She is most distinct, perhaps, in her perversion of diction. Cupid (II, 1, p. 162) likens her to "one of your ignorant poetasters of the time, who, when they have got acquainted with a strange word, never rest till they have wrung it in, though it loosen the whole fabric of their sense." She is thus a forerunner of the *précieuses.*

Argurion is so purely an allegorical figure that she is scarcely to be considered in any other light. Gifford long ago pointed out (II, 1, p. 162) the kinship of the character to the Plutus of Aris-

[1]Cf. also Triggs's notes in the E. E. T. S. edition.

tophanes with the blending of literal and metaphorical meanings in the characterization. Barnfield's portrait of Lady Pecunia also indicates the conventionality of Jonson's treatment. Lady Pecunia and Argurion are both loved and quickly neglected by young men, though constant love alone will win their faith.

One immediately recognizes, on the other hand, that Philautia and Phantaste, abstractions as they are, represent pretty well contemporary ladies of fashion and position. Hints of them have already been pointed out in court of love poetry, in Lyly's plays, in *Old Fortunatus,* etc. Their manners and pastimes fill the stories and love poetry of the Renaissance. Philautia and Phantaste represent two types of courtliness in women,—Philautia, the hauteur, pride, and exclusiveness of birth and position; Phantaste, the fickleness, sportiveness, restless ingenuity, and fancy of idleness and fashion. It is useless to point out the conventionality of hauteur in the woman of Renaissance story. The court of love convention that humbled the lover in the presence of his lady emphasized this quality of haughtiness in the delineation of the court lady. The name Philautia is met frequently. Philautus in *Euphues,* though a man, is of the same type, and earlier still the name is given to a character in Gascoigne's *Glass of Government.* In *James IV* (ll. 1239 f.) there occurs the expression, "Such as giue themselues to *Philautia* as you do." Lodge's *Catharos. Diogenes in his Singularitie* contains two or three passages in which the term *philautia* is used. In one (Hunterian Club, p. 5) the idea is personified: "*Damocles* lately acquainted with *Philautia* in speaking hir faire spendeth hir much." In the second (p. 49) "the sinne of Philautia, that is to say selfe-loue" is discussed as the source of many evils, and the discussion suggests Jonson's conception of the Fountain of Self-Love. So Nashe in *Pierce Penilesse* (*Works,* Vol. I, p. 220) mentions in his list of humours the "hatefull sinne of selfe-loue, which is so common amongst vs." Fenton, also, (*Tragicall Discourses,* Vol. II, p. 214) speaks of "the generall evill whiche the Grecians cal *Philautia.*" Thus the conception and the Greek name for it were commonplaces in English literature before Jonson's play.[1] Phantaste represents

[1]Cf. also Watson, *Poems,* ed. Arber, p. 7; Greene, *Quip for an Upstart Courtier, Works,* ed. Grosart, Vol. XI, p. 294; Stubbes, *Anatomy of Abuses,* ed. Furnivall, p. 29; Harington, Preface to *Orlando Furioso* (Smith, *Eliz. Crit. Essays,* Vol. II, p. 218).

not only fancy and fickleness but light court wit in women. The questions asked in the old discussions of love often turned on the qualities of women, and one of the favorite qualities for discussion was wit. I have already several times referred to the prominence given to light wittiness in the delineation of the Renaissance woman of the higher social type.

The early part of Act IV is given to the characterization of the four nymphs as a group. In the Folio, all but Argurion tell at length their supreme desires in a way that serves for self-characterization, but in the original form the scene was entirely one of small talk about lovers and dress. Phantaste proposes to run the gallants over, and then short sketches of them are given by the group of nymphs. This readily recalls the dramatic device of *The Merchant of Venice* (I, 2) where Portia characterizes her suitors. A similar device occurs in the *Two Gentlemen of Verona* (I, 2). In *Love's Labour's Lost,* also, (II, 1) the three ladies attending the Princess characterize briefly the three lords who have caught their fancy.

Though Jonson's portrayal of the court women in *Cynthia's Revels* associates them most clearly with the court of love tradition, the undercurrent in the portraiture connects the treatment with the satirists. Nashe in *Pierce Penilesse* (Vol. I, p. 216) makes a veiled attack on the prevalence of sensuality among court ladies. Among them, he says, there "be many falling starres, and but one true *Diana.*" A more pessimistic picture is given earlier by Lyly in *Euphues* (*Works,* ed. Bond, Vol. I, pp. 319 f.), and here, as in *Cynthia's Revels* and in the quotation from Nashe, the contrast between the queen and the women of her court is made. The passage reads:

The Empresse keepeth hir estate royall and hir maydens will not leese an ynch of their honour, shee endeauoureth to settle downe good lawes and they to breake them, shee warneth them of excesse and they studye to exceede, she sayth that decent attire is good thoughe it be not costly, and they sweare vnlesse it bee deere it is not comely. She is heere accompted a slut that commeth not in hir silkes, and shee that hath not euerye fashion, hath no mans fauour. They that be most wanton are reputed most wise, and they that be the idlest liuers are deemed the finest louers. There is great quarrelling for beautie, but no question of honestie. . . .

The Empresse gyueth ensample of vertue, and the Ladyes haue no leasure to followe hir . . . yet this I must adde that some there bee whiche for their vertue deserue prayse, but they are onely commended for theire beautie, for this thincke courtiers, that to be honest is a certeine kinde of countrey modestie, but to bee amiable the courtly curtesie.

Cynthia's Revels closes with a palinode that gives a pretty complete list of the follies Jonson is attacking and shows how his program corresponds with that of Nashe and other satirists.[1] Amorphus and Phantaste in turn name follies and vices in groups,—affected humours, fantastic humours, swaggering humours, etc.,—and the response is, "Good Mercury defend us." This use of the litany has already been mentioned in connection with the court of love elements in the play. The parody suggests the song at the close of *Summer's Last Will and Testament* with its refrain, "From winter, plague, & pestilence, good Lord, deliuer vs." Earlier in the same play there is a song with the refrain, "Lord, haue mercy on vs." A similar use of the litany is found later in Jonson's *Gipsies Metamorphosed.* A passage in Satire II of Guilpin's *Skialetheia* may be quoted as showing the conventionality of Jonson's lists also. Guilpin says:

Not that I weigh the tributary due,
Of cap and courtship complements, and new
Antike salutes, I care not for th' embrace,
The Spanish shrug, kiss'd-hand nor cheuerell face,
God saue you sir, good sir, and such like phrases,
Pronounc'd with lisping, and affected graces.

The foolish courtiers and nymphs in *Cynthia's Revels* pray Mercury to defend them from "Spanish shrugs, French faces, smirks, irpes, and all affected humours," and from "waving fans, coy glances, glicks, cringes, and all such simpering humours."

If my conclusions in regard to *Cynthia's Revels* are correct, the play is the most important of Jonson's early comedies as an indication of the fundamental nature of his work. The strong tendency shown toward abstractions even in the type characters that must have been drawn from life and that had been treated in Jonson's preceding plays with slightly different significance indicates the student of philosophies and systems, the follower of books rather than the observer of life. Some of the conventions that Jonson apparently borrows from the court of love could hardly

[1]Cf. p. 67 *supra.*

have been drawn from life, and much of the play that is actually true to the manners of the time is probably likewise indebted to literary treatments. At least the dramatic handling of the material owes much to specific English writers who had already treated the follies and fashions of the age. The whole play illustrates a technical handling of details, a building of systems and correspondences, a vesting of abstractions with the likeness of men and women, which is artificial, and while presenting the illusion of life, yet does not show the creative imagination of an original genius.

CHAPTER IX

POETASTER

The last comedy of Jonson's formative period, and also the least significant as an indication of his intimate acquaintance with English literature, is *Poetaster*. Indeed, the play is usually considered triumphant evidence of his perfect classicism, the English element being rather generally discounted, for, presumably as a matter of defence, Jonson seems to have taken the greatest care to clothe all his satire in classic garb. That he consciously entertained such an idea is clear from his representation of Envy as falling into despair upon finding that the scene of the play is laid at Rome. In fact, with *Poetaster* Jonson entered a period in which he borrowed the greater part of his material from classic sources, as in *Sejanus, Volpone,* and even *The Silent Woman* despite its English tone; and it is only with *The Alchemist* and *Bartholomew Fair* that a preponderant interest in English literature reasserts itself.

A discussion of *Poetaster* from the point of view of English influence will of necessity be somewhat brief. First of all, much of the material of the play, being classic, has only a slight connection with the humour types, which in their inception and development were so strongly impregnated with English tradition. Second, the proportion of obvious personal satire in the part of the play recognized as English is so large that personal portraiture has undoubtedly had its effect upon the characterization of the types continued from Jonson's earlier plays. Finally, so much study has been devoted to *Poetaster,* especially in connection with the stage quarrel, that there is little one can hope to add even in the way of English parallels to the play.

The classic sources for *Poetaster* have been studied by a number of scholars. They are best indicated, perhaps, in Small's *Stage-Quarrel* (pp. 25-27) and in Mallory's edition of the play (Yale Studies in English, pp. xxx ff.). Mr. Mallory, who is the latest editor of the play, has discussed the subject of sources most fully and systematically, and, as his edition is easily accessible and is much more convenient for the purpose than Gifford's, in view of its line numbering, I shall merely refer the reader to his discussion. It will be seen, upon estimate, that considerably less than half the play has so far been connected with classic material. This statement, however, hardly represents the truth of the matter; for there is much in the treatment of the characters and in the details invented by Jonson that accords with Roman history or with the tradition in regard to the characters handled, and from his rich knowledge of Roman life Jonson has undoubtedly added a great deal that cannot be traced to direct sources. Moreover, the classic setting and the classic figures weaken decidedly the emphasis on the study of English manners and types even in the many incidents and scenes which are more suggestive of English than of classic sources; and the result is a tendency to break down the rigidity of the narrower humour idea. Indeed, Jonson's later satire and character study are in general less restricted in point of view than during this early period. The most interesting phase of Jonson's classicism in *Poetaster* is seen in his blending of English and classic elements. The absorption is not a complete success, it must be said, for one constantly feels a certain discord as he becomes aware of allusions to London life and characters or of bitter attacks on contemporary playwrights and actors. There are also a number of lapses into savage wrath that are out of keeping with the urbanity of Horace, whom Jonson has chosen as his model in a presumably calm and judicial handling of his enemies. But, allowing for all this, we still acknowledge that he has done a masterly piece of work in making some of his English types harmonize with the classic figures from whom they take their names.

In the more English portion of *Poetaster,* notwithstanding the classic atmosphere, there are many indications of the alignment of the play with the other comedies of Jonson's early period. Albius, Chloe, Tucca, and Histrio owe practically nothing to classic material, and a decided English flavor pervades the treatment of Crispinus and Demetrius, and of Horace as the representative of Jonson. A number of the types in *Poetaster* have been carried on from preceding plays, and especially in Chloe and Tucca Jonson has given us fresh studies in humour that show a marked advance over his preceding studies of very similar types. One of the most interesting advances in his program of character study lies in his satire on the typical professional man, the soldier, the lawyer, the player. The satire in *Poetaster* on bombastic style, also, shows a continuation of preceding tendencies. Closely related to this phase of the play is the rather elaborate expression of Jonson's theories of poetry, which are largely classic but are often influenced by English tradition. With this general view of the English elements in *Poetaster,* we may pass on to a brief consideration of some English conventions embodied in the play and of a few characters that are continued from Jonson's earlier comedies.

Jonson's strong tendency to use the induction of his plays for the double purpose of expounding his ideas and defending himself is continued in *Poetaster,* though here the induction is not much more elaborate than a prologue. In connection with *Every Man out* and *Cynthia's Revels,* I have already tried to show the relation of the induction as Jonson used it to the inductions of earlier plays (pp. 146 ff. and 214 ff. *supra*). The introduction of Envy as a hostile force, her failure to find anything in the play suited to her purpose of stirring up hostility, her final departure, and the prologue's defence of the author's confidence, carry on the critical aim of most of the older inductions, to defend the play against opposing standards and modes. But the conflict between modes and types of the drama, or between ideals and standards of audience and dramatist, which was suggested in a broad, dignified or humorous fashion by many of the older prologues and inductions, is not felt in this induction of *Poetaster* so much as is a sort of personal animosity between author and audience or critics. Envy is, of course, an appropriate figure for this hostile attitude which the author is attempting to forestall. She naturally sets the tone of the attack on Horace, or Jonson, and the answer of the prologue shows the supposedly calmer mood of Jonson's defence.

Jonson's use of Envy arises out of a convention that culminated in the school of satirists—that of defying envy or detraction. But, before the convention became closely associated with satire, it began to fix itself in the general literature of the time. With the writers of the sixteenth century, envy often meant no more than spite, ill will, or hostility; and, with a public to whom the conception of the Seven Deadly Sins had descended as a part of man's moral legacy, envy and detraction were doubtless felt as rather real and vivid motives of action. The feeling that an author had to defend himself against malicious slander or misinterpretation was largely, perhaps, an outgrowth of the many pamphleteering wars of the century, in which religious, political, or critical disagreement led to an exchange of billingsgate and an obscuring of argument in personalities. Every writer felt that some critic was likely to attack him purely from personal malice or envy; and it became conventional to forestall these attacks by declaring in a dedication that they would come. In the Epistle Dedicatory of Vicary's *Anatomie of the Bodie of Man* (E. E. T. S., p. 6) the envy that pursues even physicians is mentioned. Stafford, in his *Examination,* addressing Elizabeth, complains that envy and reprehension are usual. Dickenson (*Arisbas,* ed. Grosart, pp. 76, 77) declares that ignorance and envy are hostile to poetry, as Jonson in *Poetaster* calls his detractors and those envious of him the "spawn of ignorance." Reference to envy is made also in some prefatory lines of the play of *Virtuous Octavia;* and *Grim, the Collier of Croyden* opens with the shade of Dunstan declaring that envy, hostile to the virtuous, has brought him back to earth. Casual references to the envy that writers must accept as their portion are too numerous to catalogue. This contemporary feeling that no merit exempted a writer from attack, or rather that merit was certain to call forth the attack, finds expression in Lodge's notable sketch of Hate-Vertue, a form of Envy (*Wits Miserie,* pp. 55-57). "Doubtles," Lodge declares, "it will be as infamous a thing shortly, to present any book whatsoeuer learned to any MAECENAS in England, as it is to be headsman in any frée citie in Germanie."

However true this remark may be to conditions in England at the end of the sixteenth century, with the quarrels between authors and the hostilities of critics, the attitude became a highly fashionable pose. Men added to their works addresses to Envy, hurling defiance or assuming resolute indifference. P[roctor's] *Triumph of Trueth,* (Collier, *Illustrations of Old English Literature*) ends with "An Inuectiue against Enuie." With the satirists an address to Envy or Detraction is usual, as I have said.[1] Lodge explains the title of one of his works by saying, "I entitle my booke *A fig for Momus,* not in contempt of the learned, for I honor them . . . but in despight of the detractor, who hauing no learning to iudge, wanteth no libertie to reproue." So at the close of *Skiale-*

[1]Cf. p. 155 *supra* for a discussion of this convention in connection with the part of Asper.

theia Guilpin cries, "A *Fico* for the *Criticke* Spleene." Hall introduces his *Virgidemiarum* with a "Defiance to Envy" in verse. Marston's *Scourge of Villainy* opens with a poetic address in disdain of envy entitled "*To* Detraction *I present my* Poesy." *Micro-Cynicon,* also, greets its readers with a verse "Defiance to Envy." The introduction of Envy in *Poetaster* and the author's scorn for her are thus in accord with contemporary modes of satire. So much Jonson borrowed, but the compact and vivid picture of Envy and the powerful denunciation in Jonson's induction are unlike anything that had gone before. There is a new note of strength here.

For Jonson's concrete representation of the personified Envy on the stage, the figure of Envy in the induction and epilogue of *Mucedorus* is suggestive. In the older play, the contest between Envy and Comedy has no bearing on a personal quarrel between playwright and public, for Envy is represented merely as the opponent of whatever pleases—of comedy in this case. Like Revenge in *The Spanish Tragedy* or Megæra in *Gismond of Salern,* he is a spirit propitious to tragedy. He enters smeared with blood, and through spite threatens to turn the events to bloodshed and disaster.[1] The snakes clinging around Envy in Jonson's play are a conventional accompaniment of the abstraction.[2] Spenser's two pictures of Envy in *The Faerie Queene* (I, iv, 30 ff. and V, xii, 29 ff.) are made vivid in the same manner. The male Envy

did chaw
Between his cankred teeth a venemous tode,
That all the poison ran about his chaw;
. . . .
And in his bosome secretly there lay
An hatefull Snake, . . .
. . . .

[1]In the Quarto of *Mucedorus* published in 1610 a new ending of the epilogue is found, and in this the plan outlined by Envy for bringing Comedy into disrepute connects with the plot of *Poetaster* in two points. The lean cannibal of a poet battened on malice, who is to be whetted on to write a comedy full of abuse, is twin brother to the jester Demetrius, who by reason of his malice and his "overflowing rank" wit is employed to write a comedy abusing Horace; and Envy as informer, except for his service as trencher, suggests the part of Æsop in *Poetaster*.

[2]The kindred Megæra of *Gismond of Salern* (Brandl, *Quellen des weltlichen Dramas in England,* p. 569) is represented on the stage accompanied by snakes.

> And eke the verse of famous Poets witt
> He does backbite, and spightfull poison spues
> From leprous mouth on all that ever writt.

Jonson's Envy entreats:

> Here, take my snakes among you, come and eat,
> And while the squeezed juice flows in your black jaws,
> Help me to damn the author. Spit it forth
> Upon his lines, and shew your rusty teeth
> At every word, or accent.

The function of the prologue is to defend Jonson's frank assertion that *Cynthia's Revels* is good, and to justify confident but reasonable self-praise. In connection with the character of Crites I have already had occasion to refer to the tone of this prologue in *Poetaster,* and to cite what Aristotle and Castiglione say in defence of self-praise (pp. 261 ff. *supra*) ; Jonson may have been influenced by these two writers. The idea, however, was common in literature. Jonson repeats it in Virgil's defence of Horace (V, 1, p. 258).

The plot of *Poetaster* gives very little indication of Jonson's English bent. There is more action, perhaps, than in the two preceding plays, but most of the incidents are drawn from classic literature. Some of the classic incidents and devices in the play had already been adapted by the skilful Latinists who had learned the principles of Renaissance imitation, and Jonson may have been influenced in some cases by the effectiveness of these adaptations. But, even in such cases, he has made his treatment conform closely to the classic model. Indeed, neither incidents of this type nor the few that are more independent of classic influence deserve elaborate discussion. Accordingly, the plot will be disregarded, and incidents of the play will be taken up in connection with the character for which they are most significant.

On the basis of classic influence the characters of *Poetaster* fall roughly into three classes. First, there are the purely classic figures like Augustus, Mæcenas, and Virgil, who, though only dimly characterized, are of value in giving a setting and tone of classic dignity to the play. Second, by far the largest group in *Poetaster* consists of historical Roman characters who have become Elizabethan in part by virtue either of their manners or of their identification with the individuals engaged in the stage quarrel. Many of these characters are so slightly handled as types that we may dismiss them. Such are Gallus and Propertius, who show some characteristics of the Elizabethan gallant as portrayed in *Cynthia's Revels.* On the other hand, Ovid and his father, with an admixture of classic details, represent more clearly aspects of London life. Finally, there are pure Elizabethan types, like Chloe, who merely bear classic names. These classes of course shade into each other. For our discussion a more convenient division of the characters is on the basis of their relation to the plot. Acts I, II, and most of IV depict a group of dilettante poets and women of fashion, with the social underlings who gather about them. Part of Act III is given to some satire on players which really stands outside of the action of the play. Much of Act III and all of V is concerned with the intrigue against Horace. The chief connecting link between the parts of the play is Tucca, who is present in almost all the important scenes from beginning to end.

Ovid as a gallant is an important figure in the play, because, through his conflict with his father and his love for Julia, he sets the tone of the piece at the very opening and introduces the group of worldlings who are so prominent in the play. His relation to Julia suggests some aspects of gallantry as treated in *Cynthia's Revels*, but the classic element that enters into the treatment of the two characters and into the events connected with them—as in the banquet, which is drawn from Homer—is so pervasive that a discussion of conventionality in the intrigue is scarcely safe. Ovid's farewell to Julia after his banishment and her imprisonment (IV, 6) has been compared with a similar farewell between the lovers in *Romeo and Juliet* (III, 5). The effort of Ovid Senior to force his son from the pursuit of poetry to the more profitable pursuit of law repeats a motive found in *Every Man in,* where the elder Knowell rebukes his son's absorption in "idle poetry." It has been conjectured that both plays reflect the stepfather's disapproval of Jonson's tastes. There may well have been some one in Jonson's circle who felt this opposition to poetry, for it was a heritage from medieval asceticism handed down by the Puritan and the more serious Englishman in general. The characterization of Ovid as unconsciously reciting law in verse has a parallel in *Haue with you to Saffron-walden,* where Harvey is reported as planning to turn the law into English hexameters (*Works of Nashe,* Vol. III, p. 86). The attack on lawyers, the bitterest passages of which were omitted from the Quarto, probably, like the Apologetical Dialogue, at command, is mainly incidental to Ovid Senior's preference for law over poetry. Satire on the profession of law is abundant in the sixteenth century, as in Stubbes's *Anatomy of Abuses* (pp. 117, 118), Hake's *Newes out of Powles Churchyarde,* Donne's *Satires* (II), Hall's *Virgidemiarum* (II, 3), Marston's *Scourge of Villainy* (Satire VII, ll. 81 ff.), *James* IV (l. 2032), etc.; but the usual attack turned upon dishonesty and unscrupulousness,[1] whereas Jonson stresses chiefly the ignorance, stupidity, and impudence of the lawyer. In *Lenten Stuffe,* there is a severe arraignment of "learned counsaile" (*Works,* Vol. III, pp. 214-216), who, Nashe says, "being compounded of nothing but vociferation and clamour, rage & fly out they care not howe against a mans life, his person, his parentage, twoo houres before they come to the poynt." After further satire on the way in which lawyers obscure issues in words, Nashe declares: "Latinelesse dolts, saturnine heauy headed blunderers, my inuectiue hath relation to, such as count al Artes puppet-playes, and pretty rattles to please children, in comparison of their confused barbarous lawe, which if it were set downe in any christian language but the Getan tongue, it would neuer grieue a man to studie it." Interestingly Nashe concludes the matter with a statement that Ovid and Ariosto could not be persuaded by their parents to pursue the study of law.

The gallants and ladies associated with Ovid are of slight value for this study. In Albius and Chloe, however, whose house is used as a rendezvous, we have another entertaining study of the citizen and wife. Albius is completely subordinated to Chloe, and their relations suggest immediately Deliro and Fallace of *Every Man out.* There is the same subserviency on the part of the husband and scorn on the part of the wife, whose desires are centered on the courtly. Chloe's pride in her servant Crispinus, the sheerest pretender as a poet and courtier, recalls Fallace's admiration for the gilded Brisk. Both husbands accept the petulant contempt of the wives as a mark of their helpmeets' superiority. Albius, however, is not only dotard but slavey, and is the willing tool of his wife in her vulgar social ambitions. The citizen and

[1]Jonson's phrase "chevril conscience" in connection with law is used in the same way by the author of *Histriomastix* (V, l. 29), as Mr. Mallory points out: "The cheverell conscience of corrupted law."

wife of *Cynthia's Revels,* briefly as they are introduced, furnish the germ for much of the treatment of Albius and Chloe. Mistress Downfall, delighted and unabashed, makes her way into the court and evidently accepts the effacement of her husband as a matter of course. Weak compliance in a husband and social ambition and unscrupulousness in a wife, accompanied by excessive vulgarity, engaged Jonson's attention in Lady Politick Would-be and Mistress Otter of his next two comedies, *Volpone* and *The Silent Woman.* But the especially interesting feature of the similar studies in the three plays closing Jonson's early period of comedy is the satire on the city types that were pressing into the social life of the courtly, probably an echo of the social upheaval in England.

In spite of all the contemporary satire on women's control of their husbands and on their craze for fine dress and luxurious life, I have not found in previous literary treatments any adequate preparation for Jonson's types with their definiteness and realism. The dramatic projection of the figure was apparently slow in coming. In a short paragraph of *Pierce Penilesse* (*Works,* Vol. I, p. 173) Nashe succeeds in presenting very concretely the proud "Mistris Minx, a Marchants wife," but the figure is not just that of the city wife with ambitions for a gallant servant. Chloe's choice of marriage with a citizen on the ground that citizens make the most tractable and lavish husbands, adds another to the already long list of parallels between Jonson's work and the old *Timon,* a play which has so far proved perplexing in its relation to Jonson's early comedies. Chloe in one of her tirades to her husband declares (II, 1, p. 217): "I was a gentlewoman born, I; I lost all my friends to be a citizen's wife, because I heard, indeed, they kept their wives as fine as ladies; and that we might rule our husbands like ladies, and do what we listed; do you think I would have married you else?" Later in the same scene, when Chloe is mortified by the bearing of Albius in the presence of the court ladies, Cytheris assures her, "They all think you politic and witty; wise women choose not husbands for the eye, merit, or birth, but wealth and sovereignty." In *Timon* Callimela, being urged to marry the citizen's heir Gelasimus for his wealth, replies (II, 1):

I'le subject my neck
To noe mans yoake. Is this a cittizen?
Phil. A wealthy one.
Cal. I shall the better rule:
The wyfes of cittizens doe beare the sway,
Whose very hands their husbands may not touch
Without a bended knee, and thinck themselves
Happie yf they obteyne but so much grace,
Within theire armes to beare from place to place
Their wyues fyne litle pretty foysting hounds;
They doe adore theire wyues; what ere they say,
They doe extoll; what ere they doe, they prayse,
Though they cornute them. Such a man gyue me![1]

Though Callimela and Chloe by no means have corresponding parts in the two plays, Callimela, self-centered, unscrupulous, and vulgar in her sharp replies, is not unlike Jonson's city wife. In *Jack Drum's Entertainment,* again, (Act I, ll. 263 ff.) a girl is advised that it is better for her to marry a rich fool in order to spend his money, enjoy other lovers, and have her own way, than to marry a wise man and be curbed.

A word in passing seems necessary in regard to the literary significance of this frivolous group, with its amours ranging from the poet Ovid and the Emperor's daughter to the poetaster Crispinus and the citizen's wife. Such a group doubtless represents well enough social conditions in England, and it would be useless

[1]This parallel is pointed out by Mr. Mallory in his edition of *Poetaster*, p. 159. Mr. Mallory, indeed, is in advance of Hart in recognizing the kinship between *Timon* and *Poetaster.* Fleay, however, (*Biog. Chron. Eng. Drama*, Vol. I, p. 369) had already noted the use of asses' ears to symbolize the folly of Lupus in Jonson's play and of Gelasimus in *Timon* (V, 3). There are a number of other parallels between the two plays. Hart, *Works of Ben Jonson*, Vol. I, p. xliv, compares the song which Horace is composing as he enters in III, 1, with a typical Elizabethan drinking song in *Timon* (I, 2). Hermogenes is introduced as a singer in *Timon,* but refuses to sing before the people on the ground that he is a noble (III, 5). Hermogenes appears in *Poetaster*, also, and cannot be induced to sing until his professional jealousy is aroused (II, 1). It may be mentioned, too, that Blatte, the nurse in *Timon*, enumerates among her former lovers Albius and Demetrius (II, 1). The hostility of the servant Luscus to the flattering Tucca who attempts to prey upon Ovid Senior, and the side remarks of Luscus on the Captain's rascality (I, 1) suggest the open hostility of Laches to the sycophants who prey upon Timon (I, 1, and I, 5). Again, Timon twice releases debtors from their creditors (I, 2 and II, 4), as Tucca secures the release of Crispinus at the moment of his arrest (III, 1). Finally, Crispinus's application of the terms "paranomasie, or agnomination" to the figure he has just used (III, 1, p. 224) offers a slight parallel to Demeas's application of the rhetorical names for figures in *Timon*, II, 5; III, 1; etc.

to attempt distinguishing in Jonson's treatment of flirtations, flippant chatter, interest in love poetry, etc. what may be due to English influence and what may have been drawn from classic love poetry as a background. The group not only continues Jonson's study of the courtly, with their fashions and their frivolities, but to my mind it has its significance for what Jonson believed to be the effect of fashionable standards on the work of the literary man. Even gifted poets who like Ovid and Tibullus give themselves up to the banalities of courtship and love poetry, frittering away time in such entertainments as the banquet of the gods and neglecting the wisdom which it is the essential purpose of poetry to teach, are justly doomed to meet finally their condemnation at the hands of the imperial figure who represents not only the best civil, social, and intellectual traditions of a people but also the truest patronage of poetry. But it is not alone the courtly, with their Roman or their English-Italian stimulus to erotic poetry, who are drawn into the stream. The citizen's wife, catching the fever, longs for a poet, and Crispinus arises in answer to her desire. The influence of the erotic poets thus produces in the end the detestable Poetaster. Nashe expresses exactly Jonson's critical attitude to the trivialities of Ovid's disciples in poetry when he declares in *The Anatomie of Absurditie* (*Works,* Vol. I, p. 10):

> When as lust is the tractate of so many leaues, and loue passions the lauish dispence of so much paper, I must needes sende such idle wits to shrift to the vicar of S. Fooles . . . Might *Ouids* exile admonish such Idlebies to betake them to a new trade, the Presse should be farre better employed, Histories of antiquitie not half so much belyed, Minerals, stones, and herbes, should not haue such cogged natures and names ascribed to them without cause, Englishmen shoulde not be halfe so much Italinated as they are, finallie, loue would obtaine the name of lust, and vice no longer maske vnder the visard of vertue.

With the ambition of Crispinus to be a poet and his determination to win recognition from Horace, the center of interest shifts from Ovid and his associates. Tucca has already been spoken of as the chief connecting link between the parts of the plot. He is conspicuous in one meeting of the gallants at the home of Albius, and in the banquet of the gods; he is the medium for the satire on players; he is the patron of the Poetaster, and eggs on Crispinus and Demetrius in the conspiracy which proves their undoing. The name Tucca is found in the works of Horace. The character, however, is strikingly fresh and original, and is the most thoroughly English of the figures in *Poetaster.* Guilpin had already dealt with a Captain Tucca in the "Satyre Preludium" of *Skialetheia,* as Small has pointed out (*Stage-Quarrel,* p. 26):

A third that falls more roundly to his worke,
Meaning to moue her were she Iewe or Turke,
Writes perfect *Cat and fidle,* wantonly,
Tickling her thoughts with masking bawdry:
Which read to Captaine *Tucca,* he doth sweare,
And scratch, and sweare, and scratch to heare
His owne discourse discours'd: and *by the Lord*
It's passing good: oh good! at euery word
When his Cock-sparrow thoughts to itch begin,
He with a shrug swearest *a most sweet sinne.*

Guilpin's sketch may have suggested the name Tucca to Jonson as suitable for his lascivious captain, who was to approve the poetry of Crispinus and emphasize the vulgarity of Chloe and the courtly group.[1] Dekker, in the address "To the World" prefixed to *Satiromastix,* apparently identifies Tucca with a Captain Hannam. Dekker, however, was defending himself against the charge that in adopting Jonson's character he showed barrenness of invention, and he makes this statement as evidence that his use of Tucca was as original as Jonson's. No satisfactory conclusion as to how much truth lies in Dekker's claim seems possible, but it is not probable, I think, that Tucca has much of Captain Hannam in him. Men of the type—braggarts, cowards, irrepressible meddlers, and buoyant blackguards—were perhaps not uncommon figures in the age, but Jonson at most only gave his character touches from life, for the type was well known in the drama before Tucca was created, and nearly every trait that distinguishes the character can be accounted for as conventional. The Jonsonian Tucca carries on lines of treatment found in Juniper, Simon Eyre, Falstaff, and Bobadill; in fact, he continues the traditions of a group of characters to the development of which Jonson himself contributed much.

Tucca is an interesting variation on the usual type of braggart soldier, however. In his association with gallants, in his pretence to bravery, and in the exposure which quickly overtakes him, he

[1]The name Tucca is met a number of times in the Latin epigrams of Campion.

carries on conventions already seen in Bobadill; but these aspects of the character have less to do with our final impression of Tucca than the mental and moral traits that distinguish him. He is keen in mentality, aggressively interested in whatever comes to hand, irrepressibly zealous in affairs not his own, and calculating in his effrontery. Penniless, an inferior socially, a coward, and a lecher, he is yet active enough mentally to win his way in a forbidding world, and meet all the needs of his nature. It is his ceaseless scheming, his grasping of every opportunity, his use of every man he meets for his own purpose, that marks Tucca's effort to gain for himself prominence. The most conspicuous aspect of his impudence lies in the rushing torrent of his talk, his bold skipping from one idea to another. It is by this rush of words and ideas and by his air of patronage that Tucca sweeps inferior men along and overwhelms them. Juniper's attitude to his fellow servants suggests this phase of Tucca, but the Captain is not a word-monger, a poser in speech. Instead of Juniper's words for mere sound, Tucca's abundance of high-sounding proper names and slang epithets, often obscene in suggestion, practically always has a definite bearing. The active mind and the irrepressible zest of life that often make rapid talkers and ready leaders of men we find represented in Simon Eyre of *The Shoemaker's Holiday,* Murley of *Sir John Oldcastle,* and the Host of *The Merry Wives of Windsor,* but their vigorous and picturesque speech is characteristic of Elizabethan portrayals of the bourgeois leader. Simon Eyre and the Host of *The Merry Wives of Windsor* are suggestive of Tucca not so much in the vigor of their speech as in their fondness for proper names. Eyre and Tucca are also both given to a bluff but kindly use of opprobrious terms for women.

Falstaff, in spite of his greater complexity, is more interesting for Tucca than are the citizen types just mentioned, not because both are soldiers who have enrolled ragged companies (III, 1, p. 231), but because they are akin in mind and morals. They have the same lechery, the same restless mentality prostituted to the worst uses, the same power to turn all threatened reverses to profit by their effrontery, and the same pompous and fatherly dignity made ludicrous by their utter selfishness and moral degeneracy. They have also something of the same gift of language. The Chief Justice rebukes Falstaff by saying (*II Henry IV,* II, 1), "It is not a confident brow, nor the throng of words that come with such more than impudent sauciness from you, can thrust me from a level consideration." Of course, Falstaff's wit combats with the Prince, his love of theatrical poses, and his versatility in general render it difficult to compare him with Tucca, but, on the whole, it seems to me that in mental and moral contradictions they belong to the same type.

One of the offices of Tucca is to serve as the means by which Jonson's satire on players and playwrights is bound to the action of *Poetaster*. Some of the most interesting passages in the play are to be found in Tucca's picture of stage abuses. That Jonson's characterization of Histrio and certain actors associated with him is a fierce bit of satire on some contemporary company I have no doubt. Jonson, indeed, admits in the Apologetical Dialogue that he has attacked some players, though he denies the other charges. An identification of the individuals is of little interest for our purpose, however. The scene between Tucca and Histrio (part of III, 1) sets forth the misfortunes and the vices of the worst class of actors, and the Puritan's objections to the stage are turned specifically against Histrio. The actor is prompt with his assurance that the plays of his company are generously spiced with ribaldry, and that "all the sinners in the suburbs come and applaud our action daily" (p. 232). Indirectly, also, Jonson makes even more serious charges against the players for their unscrupulousness in business dealing, their licentiousness, etc. (p. 234). Lack of wit and love of rant in the commonplace actor are touched upon by Tucca in his sportive abuse of Histrio (p. 231), but the rodomontade of the pages develops very fully Jonson's satire on the rant of players and the bombast of their playwrights. The naive, inartistic, and excessively explanatory treatment of classic themes was especially burlesqued by Shakespeare and others in the early period of satire on stage evils, and, following this burlesque of weak classicism, a more extensive and formidable satire was developed against rant. The great advance made by Kyd and Marlowe in the effectiveness with which human emotions and passions were portrayed was accompanied by an excess of effort that often resulted in much "sound and fury." The weakness of certain passages in *The Spanish Tragedy* and *Tamburlaine* was quickly recognized, and mockery of them became stereotyped. The passages which Jonson puts in the mouths of Tucca's pages as typical fustian have been studied by various students, and a number of them have been traced back to their sources.[1] Several are taken from *The Spanish Tragedy* and *The Battle of Alcazar,* one from *The Blind Beggar of Alexandria,* one from *Antonio and Mellida,* etc. Some of the rant, also, is parallel to that of Pistol in *II Henry IV* and *The Merry Wives of Windsor;* and it is an interesting fact that Pistol is a follower of Falstaff as the actor-pages of *Poetaster* are in the service of Tucca.

A favorite method of introducing into the drama the conventional satire on lack of art in plays and players was to represent on the stage a company of actors who are worse than novices. The device is found in *Midsummer Night's Dream* and *Love's Labour's Lost,* and, in a more elaborate form, in *Histriomastix.* This last play, which is so perplexing in its relation to Jonson, demands a closer study. In the first place, *Histriomastix* represents satire on a company of professional players and their poet Posthaste, while Chrisoganus, the nobler type of poet, who is commonly identified with Jonson, is set at naught by the players. The similarity of this to Jonson's satire on stage matters and to his portrayal of the poet Horace is obvious. What is supposedly Marston's portrait of Jonson in Chrisoganus agrees strikingly with Jonson's portrait of himself in Horace. In *Histriomastix* (II, ll. 63 ff.) the retort made to Chrisoganus—

> How you translating-scholler? you can make
> A stabbing *Satir*, or an *Epigram*,
> And thinke you carry just *Ramnusia's* whippe,
> To lash the patient—

gives us the principal charges brought against Horace (IV, 1, p. 239 and V, 1, pp. 255, 257). Further, Chrisoganus's condemnation of popular taste (III, ll. 189 ff. and IV, ll. 132 ff.)[2] advances the same points in regard to the commonplace poet's appeal to ignorance, the baseness of his ideals, his lack of originality, etc. that are the grounds for Horace's condemnation of poetasters. Besides these general resemblances, a number of minor parallels have been suggested by Fleay (*Biog. Chron. Eng. Drama,* Vol. I, p. 368). The actors in *Histriomastix* are called "politician

[1]The fullest and latest discussion of the sources will be found in the notes to Mallory's edition.

[2]This last passage has already been cited, p. 165, for its similarity to a speech of Macilente.

players" (I, ll. 128 and 146), and of their poet it is said that he should be employed in matters of state (II, l. 130). In *Poetaster,* the player Æsop is called "your politician" (III, 1, p. 234 and V, 1, p. 253), while both Æsop and Histrio meddle in political affairs as informers. Again, Gulch, one of the picturesque epithets which Tucca applies to Histrio (III, 1, p. 231), is the name of one of the players in *Histriomastix.* One line from *Histriomastix* in regard to the players (II, l. 251),

> Besides we that travel, with pumps full of gravell,

is practically repeated by Tucca (III, 1, p. 231). In the matter of burlesque on plays, the subplay of "Troilus and Cressida" in *Histriomastix* follows the older vein of parody on classic themes, but the rehearsal scene in Act IV shows that the repertory included also "huffing parts."

The rather striking resemblance between *Histriomastix* and *Poetaster* is not easy of interpretation. Jonson may merely have been strongly under the influence of a play with which he had every reason to be familiar. It may be, however, that he was consciously connecting the two plays, and that he wished to present in Horace of *Poetaster* his own version of the Chrisoganus who had apparently given him offence. On the other hand, both treatments of the poetaster and commonplace players in contrast with the scholarly and serious poet, who is driven to write satires on the abuses that spring up in an age of plenty, may be in large part independent reflections of the attention paid in contemporary literature to the ideal of the poet and to a critical creed which commended certain definite things in literature and condemned others just as definite.

In connection with Jonson's treatment of the players, a word may be said in regard to his attack on informers. The unscrupulous attempt of Histrio to make something serious of even Ovid's pastimes, and the information of Æsop in regard to the treasonableness of Horace's poetry, though reflecting one phase of the Roman life that Jonson was depicting, are not altogether due to classic influence. Elizabethan references to the abuses of the informer are common. Cloth-breeches in Greene's *Quip for an Upstart Courtier*, for example, (*Works,* ed. Grosart, Vol. XI, p. 257) inveighs against the informer, whose bag contains "a hundred & od writtes," chiefly for people of whom he knows nothing except that they are wealthy enough to pay for immunity from disturbance. In particular, there is much evidence that literary men, especially playwrights, not infrequently suffered at the hands of those who were overzealous in discovering treasonable or seditious matter. There occurs a passage in *Lenten Stuffe* (*Works of Nashe,* Vol. III, pp. 213-218) which seems worth quoting in part in connection with the satire on informers in *Poetaster* and especially with Lupus's interpretation of the emblem begun by Horace (V, 1, p. 253):

For if but carelesly betwixt sleeping and waking I write I knowe not what against plebeian Publicans and sinners . . . and leaue some termes in suspence that my post-haste want of argent will not giue mee elbowe roome enough to explane or examine as I would, out steps me an infant squib of the Innes of Court . . . and he, to approue hymselfe an extrauagant statesman, catcheth hold of a rush, and absolutely concludeth, it is meant of the Emperour of Ruscia, and that it will vtterly marre the traffike into that country if all the Pamphlets bee not called in and suppressed, wherein that libelling word is mentioned. An other, if but a head or a tayle of any beast he boasts of in his crest or his scutcheon be reckoned vp by chaunce in a volume where a man hath iust occasion to reckon vp all beasts in armory, he strait engageth hymselfe . . . to thresh downe the hayry roofe of that brayne that so seditiously mutined against hym, etc.

Nashe then passes on to "a number of Gods fooles, that for their wealth might be deep wise men" (p. 214):

These, I say, out of some discourses of mine, which were a mingle mangle cum purre, and I knew not what to make of my selfe, haue fisht out such a deepe politique state meaning as if I had al the secrets of court or commonwealth at my fingers endes. Talke I of a beare, O, it is such a man that emblazons him in his armes, or of a woolfe, a fox, or a camelion, any lording whom they do not affect it is meant by. The great potentate, stirred vppe with those peruerse applications, not looking into the text it selfe, but the ridiculous comment, or if hee lookes into it, followes no other more charitable comment then that, straite thunders out his displeasure, & showres downe the whole tempest of his indignation vpon me, etc.

The satire on lawyers already referred to (p. 291 *supra*) follows. Then Nashe tells a tale of how the herring wooed the proud Lady Turbut, and concludes (p. 218):

O, for a Legion of mice-eyed decipherers and calculaters vppon characters, now to augurate what I meane by this: the diuell, if it stood vpon his saluation, cannot do it, much lesse petty diuels and cruell Rhadamants vppon earth . . . men that haue no meanes to purchase credit with theyr Prince, but by putting him still in feare, and beating into his opinion that they are the onely preseruers of his life, in sitting vp night and day in sifting out treasons, whe*n* they are the most traytours themselues, to his life, health, and quiet, in continual commacerating him with dread and terror, when but to gette a pension, or bring him in theyr debt, next to God, for vpholding his vital breath, it is neither so, nor so, but some foole, some drunken man, some madde man in an intoxicate humour hath vttered hee knewe not what, and they, beeing starued for intelligence or want of employment, take hold of it with tooth and nayle, and in spite of all the wayters, will violently breake into the kings chamber, and awake him at midnight to reueale it.

Nashe's complaint that his talk of a bear, a wolf, a fox, or a chameleon is perversely applied is a specific reference to his allegory in *Pierce Penilesse* (*Works,* Vol. I, pp. 221 ff.), the riddle of which Gabriel Harvey had professed to read. In *Poetaster* the tribune Lupus, thrusting himself into the presence of Caesar, plays the part of interpreter. After declaring that Caesar is represented in the figure of an eagle in Horace's device, Lupus finds that the bird is not an eagle but a vulture.

Lup. A vulture! Ay, now, 'tis a vulture. O abominable! monstrous! monstrous! Has not your vulture a beak? has it not legs, and talons, and wings, and feathers?

. . . .

Hor. A vulture and a wolf—

Lup. A wolf! good: that's I; I am the wolf: my name's Lupus; I am meant by the wolf. On, on; a vulture and a wolf.

Hor. Preying upon the carcass of an ass—

Lup. An ass! good still: that's I too; I am the ass. You mean me by an ass.[1]

The frequent emphasis on the vice of the "decipherer" and the informer which is found in the works of both Nashe and Jonson,[2] and particularly the similarity of certain phases of *Poetaster* to the satire on informers and lawyers in *Lenten Stuffe* may be of some significance. *Lenten Stuffe,* Nashe tells us, grew out of his exile in consequence of the uproar following the production of *The Isle of Dogs* in 1597, so that his attitude to the mischief maker who could ferret some dark meaning out of any

[1]This particular trick, however, of making an asinine character call himself an ass is frequent in the drama. Cf. *Much Ado*, IV, 2.

[2]Cf. p. 154 *supra* and the dedication to *Volpone.*

matter is perhaps natural. If the treatment of Lupus and Æsop in *Poetaster* has any meaning for Jonson personally, as I think probable, we may have here another echo of the trouble over *The Isle of Dogs.* The evidence seems to me pretty convincing[1] that Jonson was the player-poet who was imprisoned in the fall of 1597 for completing *The Isle of Dogs* begun by Nashe, and that Jonson was referring to his part in this play when he declared in his famous letter to the Earl of Salisbury at the time of his trouble over *Eastward Hoe:* "I protest to your honour, and call God to testimony, (since my first error, which, yet, is punished in me more with my shame than it was then with my bondage,) I have so attempered my style, that I have given no cause to any good man of grief; and if to any ill, by touching at any general vice, it hath always been with a regard and sparing of particular persons." The admissions which Jonson makes to Salisbury hardly apply to any of his acknowledged work. Though he had trouble about *Poetaster* and told Drummond that he was "called before the Councell for his Sejanus, and accused both of poperie and treason," there is no suggestion that he was imprisoned in either case, and so far from confessing a fault or feeling shame for the plays that have come down to us, Jonson strictly maintained his innocence of intentional offence. If it was indeed Jonson who carried on the work on *The Isle of Dogs* which Nashe had begun, the bitterness of both men toward those who were ready to turn any literary work into an allegory of contemporary politics must have arisen in part from a common source.

It will be noticed that in the case of both Ovid's banquet and Horace's poetry, it is a player who carries the information to the meddling magistrate in *Poetaster,* and the possible implication is that Jonson had come in contact with spies among players and had suffered from the chicanery and sensation to which rival playhouses resorted in order to injure popular writers. If so, the experience may again be connected with *The Isle of Dogs.* There is, at any rate, a passage in *Satiromastix* (ll. 1523 ff.) which refers to *The Isle of Dogs* and at least intimates that Jonson's satirical plays were an outgrowth of his failure as an actor and of his difficulties with player-folk. "And when," says Tucca in part, "the

[1]Cf. Chambers, *Mod. Lang. Rev.*, Vol. IV, pp. 410 f. and 511; and McKerrow, *Works of Nashe*, Vol. V, pp. 29-31.

Stagerites banisht thee into the Ile of Dogs, thou turn'dst Bandog (villanous Guy) & euer since bitest," etc. Indeed, it does not seem to me improbable that *The Isle of Dogs* is responsible for the beginning of the hostilities which finally had their outcome in the stage quarrel. Jonson's reference in the Apologetical Dialogue to having been provoked on every stage for three years would point to lampooning that grew out of his disgrace in connection with *The Isle of Dogs* late in 1597 as a beginning more nearly than to the appearance of the revised *Histriomastix* probably in 1599. Jonson told Drummond, it will be remembered, that the beginning of his quarrels with Marston was Marston's representing him on the stage. While the representation of Jonson as Chrisoganus is friendly, and while the satire on the players who cannot appreciate the gifts and the standards of Chrisoganus is apparently Marston's attack on Jonson's enemies, Jonson would naturally resent being represented on the stage, even in a favorable way, if *Histriomastix* portrayed in burlesque the war that arose from the unfortunate affair of *The Isle of Dogs,* for which even in 1605 he expressed shame. Thus Jonson, when he came to attack Marston as Crispinus, may intentionally have made the satire more biting by representing him (III, 1, p. 234) as the ideal poet for a troop of players of just the type that Marston had burlesqued. The whole matter, however, is highly problematical, and after all turns aside from the purpose of this study.

The most significant satire in connection with the plot against Horace centers, of course, around Horace, Crispinus, and Demetrius. These three unquestionably represent in part Jonson, Marston, and Dekker. How personal the sketches are, we have no way of determining with any real certainty. In the Apologetical Dialogue Jonson declares that it is his practice to "spare the persons and to speak the vices," but to accept Jonson's satire in *Poetaster* as having "neither tooth nor gall" would undoubtedly be a mistake. On the other hand, it would be a greater mistake to judge him by our standards or by the verdict of his enemies. He was at least, I believe, unselfishly devoted to his art; and the principles of that art made personal portraiture altogether secondary to symbolism. Even in *Poetaster,* I regard Jonson's figures as less individuals than types with personal touches added from time to time. This view of Jonson's method gains force from a comparison of *Poetaster* with *Satiromastix,* where the satire is beyond any question primarily aimed at the peculiarities of the man Jonson. Dekker, indeed, in his address to the World by way of preface to *Satiromastix,* tries to meet the criticism *"that in vntrussing* Horace, I *did onely whip his fortunes, and condition of life, where the more noble* Reprehension *had bin of his mindes* Deformitie." But Dekker, unlike Jonson, scarcely dared to plead literary standards as the basis of his attack.

Outside of the arguments I have tried to bring forward in proof of the fact that in his portrayal of character Jonson was primarily a follower of Renaissance standards and ideals, the best proof that there is a large amount of conventionality in the treatment of Crispinus and Demetrius would be to show that in the similar pair of *Every Man out* and *Cynthia's Revels* there is no satire on Marston and Dekker. Though I am fully convinced, for my part, that no character of *Every Man out* represents either Marston or Dekker and that the satire on the two in *Cynthia's Revels* is incidental and decidedly secondary to the treatment of type figures, it is impossible to speak with certainty. Dekker, at any rate, (*Satiromastix,* ll. 420 ff.) saw fit to consider himself and Marston attacked in Anaides and Hedon, and even the planning of *Satiromastix* may have been in reply to *Cynthia's Revels.* It seems fairly probable, also, that in *What You Will* Marston replied to *Cynthia's Revels* before *Poetaster* and *Satiromastix* appeared on the stage (Small, *Stage-Quarrel,* pp. 101-107). But the problem of how far personal satire on Marston and Dekker determined the characterization of Hedon and Anaides is one that I cannot attack fully enough for my own purposes, and I shall have to content myself with pointing out what appears to me most conventional in the figures of Horace, Crispinus, and Demetrius and in their relation to each other, and what suggests most strongly the treatment of types.

Disregarding, then, the personal significance of these three characters, we can say with the utmost confidence that they represent literary types and that in their motives and ideals, their attitude and utterances, Jonson has embodied his critical judgments, correct or incorrect. Though many of the conventional elements in the treatment of the three as literary types Jonson derived directly from Horace, there is an English influence discernible. Some details of this literary characterization, again, may also have been decidedly personal; for the treatment turns upon the classification of poets, and, as skilful portraiture would be more likely to sting than unrecognizable perversion, Jonson probably put Marston and Dekker where it was understood that they belonged. There is nevertheless a certain amount of literary symbolism involved in the relations of the trio. The hostility against Horace has its root in literary jealousy. Both Crispinus and Demetrius are declared envious and are accused of calumny and detraction. But Crispinus represents envy, I think, rather than detraction, and in slandering Horace merely follows Demetrius. His real folly is word-mongery. The same relation exists between Hedon and Anaides in *Cynthia's Revels.* Hedon is envious but not skilful in forging slander, and it is the inventive genius of Anaides that checks Hedon's plan for a direct attack on Crites and points out the way to wound him by the charge of plagiarism (III, 2). Crites and Horace also have the same attitude of indifference and superiority to the pair. The literary allegory is the same in the two plays, and, on this side at least, the personal hits are probably the same.

When Demetrius is characterized separately, it is as the base jester whose vein is envious detraction (III, 1, p. 235 and V, 1, p. 258). His malice, his gift for slander, and his "overflowing rank wit" commend him for the office of abusing Horace. He is of the company of those who will bite

> And gnaw their absent friends, not cure their fame;
> Catch at the loosest laughters, and affect
> To be thought jesters; such as can devise
> Things never seen, or heard, t'impair men's names,
> And gratify their credulous adversaries;
> Will carry tales, do basest offices, etc.

While much of this passage is taken from one of Horace's satires (Book I, Sat. IV), Jonson probably adopted it because Renaissance thought in England had adopted the ideas. The Renaissance condemnation of the jester as discussed above (pp. 172 ff.) in connection with Carlo shows clearly the conventionality in the contemptuous verdict that Horace and his fellows pass upon Demetrius. Jonson treats the general type in Carlo, Anaides, and Demetrius. A base use of gifts of the mind is the foundation for the satire in all three cases, but the emphasis varies. Carlo is a social jester of a scurrilous and insulting type; he is a buffoon and a sycophant, putting his wit to unworthy uses for his food. In Anaides jesting is only slightly treated; his perversion of wit takes the form of vulgar railing. Demetrius is merely a hireling poet who envies a better poet and is base enough to employ his wit in slandering him. The association of detraction with rude jesting, as in Carlo, is inevitable, and in the character of Demetrius detraction has been developed at the expense of purer jesting. The malice of Demetrius toward Horace as a literary man carries on, in a more concrete form, the spirit typified in Envy of the induction,[1] and the discussion of literary enmities in that connection (pp. 286 ff. *supra*) illustrates the prevalence of the vice satirized in Demetrius and the conventional recognition of just such hostilities among literary men.

Envy is the ground for the enmity of Crispinus[2] toward Horace, and the immediate occasion for his spite is the fact that Horace refuses him fellowship. But the real attack on Crispinus in the play is not for envy or detraction. He is the unworthy courtly poet, perverted in literary purposes. The satire on him in connection with the group of worldlings in *Poetaster* has already been indicated—his admiration for the shallowest of citizen wives and his pursuit of poetry in order to please a silly mistress. Not even in *Cynthia's Revels* has Jonson rendered the "courtly maker" so contemptible. Though Hedon, like Crispinus, is the conventional lover, except for his envy of Crites and his association with Anaides, the character suggests Crispinus only as Anaides suggests Demetrius[3]—in a thoroughly conventional rôle. On the other hand, in some traits that do not appear in the elegant courtier Hedon, Crispinus reverts to Jonson's earlier treatments of the

[1]Demetrius is especially close to Hate-Vertue of Lodge's *Wits Miserie*.

[2]His full name is Rufus Laberius Crispinus. The name Crispinus is used in Juvenal's first satire for a pampered, effeminate gallant, and while this character is rather dissimilar to Jonson's Crispinus, the use of the name in Juvenal for a gallant and in Horace for a shallow poet gives classic precedent for both phases of the characterization in *Poetaster*. Penniman, *War of the Theatres*, p. 110, has pointed out the fact that the name Laberius was associated with affected diction.

[3]In opposition to the view that Hedon represents Marston in the sense that Crispinus does, it is interesting to note that while the exquisite Hedon resents the fact that Crites is allowed in the presence poorly clad (III, 2, p. 166), Crispinus, whose shabbiness is several times hinted, is eager for the recognition of Horace.

gull. His facility in rhyming, his plagiarism, his eagerness to be received among the great, his veneer of fashionableness, and his real poverty associate him with Mathew. The absurd coat of arms of which he boasts recalls Sogliardo.

In his encounter with Horace (III, 1), Crispinus characterizes himself as a literary man. He claims to be a scholar, a Stoic, a poet newly turned to the art, a satirist in Horace's vein, and a student of architecture. For the benefit of Horace, he sings a song of his mistress's cap, applying to a figure in it rhetorical terms of great pomposity. "Lewd solecisms, and worded trash," Horace calls his discourse.[1] Later (III, 1, p. 231) Tucca recommends Crispinus to Histrio as one who "pens high, lofty, in a new stalking vein" for the stage. In the variety of these accomplishments there is doubtless a personal hit at the restless genius of Marston, who was not content with efforts in one line. But the real satire on Crispinus as a litterateur is focused on word-mongery. If according to Jonson's critical standards anything was more to be condemned than frivolous poetry, it was the stilted, affected, and crabbed vocabularies of the day. When Crispinus is tried for calumny, a poem by him filled with affected and pompous terms is produced. On the strength of it, a purge is administered, Crispinus vomiting up the characteristic Marstonian vocabulary. The device is drawn from Lucian's *Lexiphanes,* but already attention has been called (p. 44 *supra*) to similar dramatizations in connection with the Martinist controversy, which may have gained Jonson's attention and suggested the possibilities in the use of this stage device.[2] It was also pointed out at the same time that the idea of the vomit of inflated diction had been used by Nashe with reference to Harvey. When sentence is finally passed on Demetrius and Crispinus, Demetrius, apparently considered hopeless, is condemned to wear the fool's coat and cap. Crispinus, how-

[1]This dialogue between Crispinus and Horace, in which Crispinus pours forth praise of his own gifts, and Horace struggles vainly to escape, is based on the Latin Horace, Bk. I, Satire IX, the same order of incidents being followed by the two writers. Already in Deliro's futile attempts to escape Brisk (*Ev. M. out,* II, 2, p. 95) Jonson had suggested the theme. Donne in Satire IV imitates this scene from Horace, adapting the bore's talk very skilfully to suggest such phases of London follies as newsmongery and the boastfulness of travelers. In *Wyt and Science,* the fiend Tediousness overcomes Wit, but the symbolism is different from that of *Poetaster.*

[2]In *All for Money,* out of a vomit certain evils are born on the stage.

ever, is recognized as merely perverted, and a strict literary diet is prescribed. Virgil charges him in part (V, 1, p. 261):

> You must not hunt for wild outlandish terms,
> To stuff out a peculiar dialect;
> But let your matter run before your words.
> And if at any time you chance to meet
> Some Gallo-Belgic phrase, you shall not straight
> Rack your poor verse to give it entertainment,
> But let it pass; and do not think yourself
> Much damnified, if you do leave it out,
> When nor your understanding, nor the sense
> Could well receive it. This fair abstinence,
> In time, will render you more sound and clear.

The treatment of Crispinus as poetaster and word-monger represents the culmination of the satire on perverted taste and diction which Jonson had been developing for several years. Every type of uncouth diction he had already attacked in Juniper, Puntarvolo, Brisk, Amorphus, and others. In *The Case is Altered* (I, 1, p. 520) Valentine says of Juniper's phrases, "O how pitifully are these words forced! as though they were pumpt out on's belly." In the Quarto of *Every Man in,* when Clement at the conclusion is passing judgment on Mathew and Bobadill,—a situation suggestive in some details of the condemnation of Crispinus and Tucca,—the justice says (ll. 2925 f.) in connection with degenerate taste in poetry, "But she must haue store of *Ellebore,*[1] giuen her to purge these grosse obstructions." In *Cynthia's Revels,* again, there is a passage (II, 1, p. 162) applied to Moria which sounds as if it were taken from Virgil's charge to Crispinus: "She is like one of your ignorant poetasters of the time, who, when they have got acquainted with a strange word, never rest till they have wrung it in, though it loosen the whole fabric of their sense." Thus, while the treatment of Crispinus is an attack specifically on Marston and the Marstonian vocabulary, it expresses on Jonson's part a rage against perverted diction in general which had been waxing at least since the time of *The Case is Altered.*

In Horace, the literary program of *Every Man out* and

[1]The pills which are administered to Crispinus are "mixt with the whitest kind of hellebore."

Cynthia's Revels is repeated. He is the type of satirist whom Jonson was ready to defend. It can hardly be said that the author boldly portrays Horace-Jonson as the ideal, though the implication is unquestionable. As I have already urged, the portraits of Asper and Crites seem to me less personal than that of Horace—not intended primarily for Jonson himself. The similarity of Horace to Asper-Macilente and Crites lies chiefly in the similar charges brought against the three as satirists, and the discussion in the preceding chapters of these characters from *Every Man out* and *Cynthia's Revels* serves to indicate how far Jonson in treating Horace was glancing at Renaissance and classic ideals of character. One of the chief charges brought against Horace is that of railing (V, 1, p. 255). Indeed, under cover of the character of Horace Jonson seems to have felt it necessary to meet the very charges which had been made against Demetrius in the degrading classification of him as a jester. The same satire of the Latin Horace (Book I, Satire IV) from which is drawn the chief passage condemning Demetrius for malice, slander, and the vices of the jester (V, 1, p. 258) furnished Tucca's characterization of Horace (IV, 1, p. 239):

> A sharp thorny-toothed satirical rascal, fly him; he carries hay in his horn; he will sooner lose his best friend than his least jest. What he once drops upon paper against a man, lives eternally to upbraid him in the mouth of every slave, tankard-bearer, or water-man; not a bawd, or a boy that comes from the bakehouse, but shall point at him: 'tis all dog and scorpion; he carries poison in his teeth, and a sting in his tail.

The similarity of this to Drummond's judgment on Jonson, which has already been quoted (p. 174), suggests that there was a measure of truth in Tucca's condemnation. Dekker in *Satiromastix* strikes very effectively at the sharpness of Horace's vein when Sir Vaughan administers to him the oath (ll. 2637 ff.):

> In brieflynes, when you Sup in Tauernes, amongst your betters, you shall sweare not to dippe your Manners in too much sawce, nor at Table to fling Epigrams, Embleames, or Play-speeches about you (lyke Haylestones) to keepe you out of the terrible daunger of the Shot, vpon payne to sit at the vpper ende of the Table, a'th left hand of Carlo Buffon.

The charges which Jonson's Tucca makes against Horace are much the same as those which Carlo and Anaides make against Macilente and Crites,[1] and were doubtless intended to show the wholesome fear in which the base hold the satirist's whip.

But Jonson is careful that Horace shall be viewed through other eyes than those of his victims. Virgil, the supreme poet, gives the picture of the true satirist, and distinguishes between the two standards in satire (V, 1, p. 254):

> 'Tis not the wholesome sharp morality,
> Or modest anger of a satiric spirit,
> That hurts or wounds the body of the state;
> But the sinister application
> Of the malicious, ignorant, and base
> Interpreter; who will distort, and strain
> The general scope and purpose of an author
> To his particular and private spleen.

It is Virgil, again, who defends Horace against the further charge of self-love and arrogance (V, 1, p. 258). The ground of the defence is that perfect merit and high ideals are inconsistent with humility and justify self-praise. This view is strongly expressed in the prologue of *Poetaster,* and connects readily with classic and Renaissance theory.[2]

An interesting part of the critical material in *Poetaster* is that dealing with the treatment of Virgil as the ideal poet (V, 1, pp. 249 ff.). All that represents for Jonson the spirit of humanism, the newly arising art, and especially purity of diction, is made to meet in the characterization of Virgil. Not only is he set in contrast with Crispinus, the shallow dandy who affects poets and poetry, but he is even placed on an eminence above Horace, who is hampered by being the object of envy and malice. The characterization, I take it, is that of the Latin poet, but modified to accord with Renaissance ideals as interpreted by Jonson; and the character, in my opinion, is not to be identified with any of Jonson's contemporaries, assuredly not with Shakespeare. At the time when *Poetaster* was written, Jonson's adherence to a rather

[1]Cf. *Ev. M. out*, I, 1, p. 76 and IV, 4, p. 115, and *Cynthia's Revels*, III, 2, p. 166. The verdict of Demetrius on Horace (IV, 1, p. 239), "He is a mere sponge; nothing but Humours and observation; he goes up and down sucking from every society, and when he comes home squeezes himself dry again," recalls Carlo's remark (V, 4, p. 130), "Now is that lean, bald-rib Macilente, that salt villain, plotting some mischievous device, and lies a soaking in their frothy humours like a dry crust, till he has drunk 'em all up."

[2]Cf. pp. 261 ff. *supra* for illustrative passages from Aristotle and Castiglione.

formal classic art and his tendency to follow models and principles were perhaps stronger than at any other period of his life; and Shakespeare's art was certainly not of a type to arouse Jonson's ardor. If Jonson did have any contemporary in mind, it was Chapman, I should say. The two men differ in many of their theories, but Jonson must have recognized Chapman as the most notable and influential exponent of a scholarly and classical art. In the introduction to his edition of *Poetaster* (pp. lxxxix ff.) Mr. Mallory has given an excellent argument against the identity of Virgil with Shakespeare, but to my mind he underestimates the respect that Jonson probably felt for Chapman in spite of their divergences.[1]

There is a vast amount of critical material scattered throughout *Poetaster* and distributed to many characters. Some of the most eloquent passages in the play exalt true poetry. In I, 1 (p. 215), Ovid praises "sacred Poesy" and contrasts with the "jaded wits" of hirelings the "high raptures of a happy muse." In V, 1 (p. 248), Caesar pays tribute to poetry that is "true-born, and nursed with all the sciences." Soon after comes the magnificent characterization of Virgil as a poet—his art, his reflection of life, his creation of beauty. These lyric passages belong with the fine lines in the Quarto of *Every Man in* (ll. 2889 ff.) in which Jonson exalts poetry nourished with "sacred inuention" and "sweete philosophie" and clothed in the "maiestie of arte." In these passages Jonson has repeated and varied a simple text with great feeling and great freshness. Especially has he stressed with ardent zeal the sacredness of the poet's calling.[2] Throughout *Poetaster* there is also fierce emphasis on the need of learning in a poet. Horace (V, 1, p. 249) makes ignorance the soil in which envy and detraction take root in the poet's mind. The deep reproach which ignorance carried with it in the eyes of the humanist is illustrated in the early humanist allegories *Four Elements* and *Wyt and Science,* where Ignorance is the fool.[3] Among the Renaissance writers who decry ignorance in the poet and the resulting baseness

[1]Cf. pp. 312-314 *infra* for the similarity of their critical utterances.

[2]For various English expressions of poetic ideals, especially in regard to the high moral mission of poetry, see Smith's *Eliz. Crit. Essays,* Vol. I, pp. xxi ff. Cf. also *Works of Nashe,* Vol. 1, pp. 25 f. In *Timber* Jonson has given a fuller discussion of poetic principles than in *Poetaster,* but it is more largely from a critical than from a moral point of view.

[3]See also p. 208 *supra.*

of ideals, Nashe is conspicuous, especially in *The Anatomie of Absurditie.* There is in *Poetaster,* also, a representation of true poetry as unappreciated except by the elect, but the idea is not so prominent with Jonson as with other Renaissance writers, for example with Nashe in the opening of *Pierce Penilesse* and Lodge in Eclogue III of *A Fig for Momus,* which is a melancholy complaint of the failure of true poetry through the scorn of the ignorant, the greed of the great, and the decline of patronage. Epistle V of *A Fig for Momus,* again, with its picture of the lofty aims of the true poet and the base use of gifts in the poetaster, echoes the spirit of Jonson's play.

> Alas for them that by scurrilitie,
> Would purchase fame and immortalitie:
> But know this friend, true excellence depends,
> On numbers aim'd to good, and happie ends:
> What els hath wanton poetrie enioy'd
> But this? *Alas thy wit was ill imploy'd.*
> What reason mou'd the golden *Augustine,*
> To name our poetrie, vaine errors wine?
> . . . .
> Nought but the misimployment of our guifts,
> Ordain'd for arts, but spent in shameles shifts,
> . . . .
> So poetrie restrained in errors bounds,
> With poisoned words, & sinful sweetnes wounds,
> But clothing vertue, and adorning it,
> Wit shines in vertue, vertue shines in wit:
> True science suted in well couched rimes,
> Is nourished for fame in after times.

Not only for idea but for the recurrence of several words the last two lines may be compared with Caesar's tribute to poetry (V, 1, p. 248):

> If she be
> True-born, and nursed with all the sciences,
> She can so mould Rome, and her monuments,
> Within the liquid marble of her lines,
> That they shall stand fresh and miraculous,
> Even when they mix with innovating dust.

The community of critical ideas between Jonson and his contemporaries may be illustrated by the utterances of Chapman. Parallels between the early work of the two men—in the treatment of the gulls and the humour types, for example—are numerous enough to suggest very similar tastes and ideals, and, as I think, an indebtedness on Jonson's part. In some very fundamental points of the author's attitude to his art, also, Chapman almost seems to have been Jonson's mentor. The conception of poetry as elevated by labor and studious learning to a degree of nobility or sacredness and placed above the reach of the vulgar mind, is expressed by Chapman in his addresses to Roydon prefixed to *The Shadow of Night* and *Ovid's Banquet of Sense* and in the poetic epistle to Harriots appended to *Achilles' Shield.* It was just this attitude on Jonson's part which brought about his continual conflict with the populace and popular writers. In the preface to *Ovid's Banquet of Sense* Chapman declares, "The profane multitude I hate, and only consecrate my strange poems to those searching spirits, whom learning hath made noble, and nobility sacred." Among Jonson's many avowals that his appeal is only to the elect, it will be sufficient to point out a passage near the end of the Quarto of *Every Man out,* in which occur the lines—

> The Cates that you haue tasted were not season'd
> For euery vulgar Pallat,[1] but prepar'd
> To banket pure and apprehensiue eares.

Though actual parallels between the critical expressions of the two men would be difficult to point out, a comparison of the close of Chapman's epistle introducing *The Shadow of Night* with a passage near the close of the Apologetical Dialogue will illustrate the relation. Chapman, after declaring that the "high-deserving virtues" of certain noblemen may cause him "hereafter strike that fire out of darkness, which the brightest Day shall envy for beauty," concludes with the expression, "Preferring thy allowance in this poor and strange trifle, to the passport of a whole City of others, I rest as resolute as Seneca, satisfying myself if but a few, if one, or if none like it." In the Apologetical Dialogue Jonson declares his intention of turning to tragedy,

> Where, if I prove the pleasure but of one,
> So he judicious be, he shall be alone
> A theatre unto me. Once I'll say
> To strike the ear of time in those fresh strains,
> As shall, beside the cunning of their ground,
> Give cause to some of wonder, some despite,
> And more despair, to imitate their sound.

[1]Chapman uses the expression "vulgar palates" near the end of the epistle to Harriots.

Finally, the tenet that lies back of Jonson's attack on Crispinus and other word-mongers is succinctly expressed in Chapman's verdict, "Obscurity in affection of words and indigested conceits, is pedantical and childish" (Epistle prefixed to *Ovid's Banquet of Sense*).

In a great number of minute points in which Jonson's defence of his art echoes the Renaissance treatment of narrow and specific problems, *Poetaster* is most closely allied with the work of Nashe, who is akin to Jonson in genius and experience. This community of experience between Jonson and Nashe—and a number of other Renaissance writers, indeed—may account for many of the detailed parallels between them in the defence of their work, though no little of the similarity must be due to the Renaissance practice of recognizing a formula for everything. I shall merely cite one passage from Nashe as illustrative of the relation between his work and Jonson's. In *Pierce Penilesse* (*Works,* Vol. I, p. 154), after crying out against "this moralizing age, wherein euery one seeks to shew himselfe a Polititian by mis-interpreting," Nashe protests:

> The Antiquaries are offended without cause, thinking I goe about to detract from that excellent profession, when (God is my witnesse) I reuerence it as much as any of them all, and had no manner of allusion to them that stumble at it. I hope they wil giue me leaue to think there be fooles of that Art as well as of al other; but to say I vtterly condemne it as an vnfruitfull studie or seeme to despise the excellent qualified partes of it, is a most false and iniurious surmise. There is nothing that if a man list he may not wrest or peruert.

The use of "politician" here may be compared with Jonson's use of the politician player as one who finds some damning significance in the most innocent affair. The antiquaries of *Pierce Penilesse* correspond to the professions of law and arms which Jonson attempts to conciliate in the Apologetical Dialogue. Of law and the ministers of the law, Jonson says, in phraseology similar to Nashe's, "I reverence both"; and of soldiers, "I love your great profession." Both writers pay a tribute to the worth of the offended professions.[1] Reference has already been made (p. 154 *supra*) to Jonson's complaint in *Every Man out* (II, 2, p. 96) against those who come to the theatre "only to pervert and

[1]Nashe, *Works*, Vol. III, p. 215, also pays a tribute to lawyers, some of whom he attacks in the manner of Jonson.

poison the sense of what they hear." Compare Nashe's, "There is nothing that if a man list he may not wrest or peruert."[1] Finally, immediately following this quotation from *Pierce Penilesse* Nashe holds over misinterpreters the threat that his satire has power to make them smart, as Jonson in the Apologetical Dialogue boasts of his ability to

> write Iambics,
> Should make the desperate lashers hang themselves.

These are very minor points indeed, but such correspondences are rather telling when they increase to large numbers.

The literary life of Elizabethan England as Jonson lived it can never be reconstructed with entire truth; for it is a difficult thing at best to revivify the genius of a past age even in regard to letters. Much of the literature of the time is lost, and much of what remains I have not been able to compass for this study. Still there are many traces of Jonson's sympathy with the English literature which came to his hand, and those cited are, I hope, representative enough and full enough to indicate the temper of the man. If I have interpreted them truly, we have not always seen Jonson from the right point of view. The powerful influence of his classical training and sympathies is clear, and on it the greatness of his literary art depends. But in two respects we need to regard Jonson's work in a new light. First, a sufficient number of parallels have been traced here to suggest that Jonson is rarely altogether original in ideas. In the petty details expressing an attitude to audiences which I have instanced as repeating Nashe and other writers, I may seem to be overstressing Jonson's accord with contemporary literature; but there is so much of just such minor parallelism to be found in his work that one inevitably comes to regard him as almost absolutely dependent upon tradition and precedent, upon the conservative attitude of his fellows. Wherever he looks, a precedent, a rule, a well defined attitude attracts him and seems sane and judicial. Second, the most interesting phase of Jonson's English prejudice is seen in the moral symbolism that underlies his treatment of characters and even of incidents; his vein is only more artistic and subtle but not less purposeful than that of allegory. This bent in Jonson is evident in his choice of material from English literature, where the moral

[1]Cf. also *Works*, Vol. I, p. 260, and Vol. III, p. 235.

and the symbolic are so tenacious. The unusual originality of the man considering his age lies in his creation of classic form to suit his ideas, in the fresh combination of all the details that he uses, and in his mastery of dramatic construction and rhetorical excellence. Herein consists the supreme power out of which grew his influence.

INDEX